W9-APX-358

A TO Z OF
AMERICAN
INDIAN
WOMEN

REVISED EDITION

A TO Z OF WOMEN

A TO Z OF
AMERICAN
INDIAN
WOMEN

REVISED EDITION

LIZ SONNEBORN

Facts On File
An imprint of Infobase Publishing

A to Z of American Indian Women, Revised Edition

Copyright © 2007, 1998 by Liz Sonneborn
Maps © 2007 by Infobase Publishing

Facts On File, Inc.
An imprint of Infobase Publishing
132 West 31st Street
New York, NY 10001

ISBN-10: 0-8160-6694-9
ISBN-13: 978-0-8160-6694-0

Library of Congress Cataloging-in-Publication Data

Sonneborn, Liz.
  A to Z of American Indian women / Liz Sonneborn. — Rev. ed.
     p. cm. — (A to Z of American women)
  Rev. ed. of: A to Z of Native American women. c1998.
  Includes bibliographical references and index.
  ISBN 978-0-8160-6694-0 (alk. paper)
  1. Indian women—North America—Biography. 2. Indian women—North America—History. 3. Indian women—North America—Social life and customs. I. Sonneborn, Liz. A to Z of Native American women. II. Title.

  E98.W8S65 2007
  920.72089′97—dc22   2007008162

Facts On File books are available at special discounts when purchased in bulk quantities for businesses, associations, institutions, or sales promotions. Please call our Special Sales Department in New York at (212) 967-8800 or (800) 322-8755.

You can find Facts On File on the World Wide Web at http://www.factsonfile.com

Text design by Joan M. McEvoy and Cathy Rincon
Cover design by Salvatore Luongo

Printed in the United States of America

VB Hermitage 10 9 8 7 6 5 4 3 2 1

This book is printed on acid-free paper.

NOTES ON PHOTOS

Many of the illustrations and photographs used in this book are old, historical images. The quality of the prints is not always up to modern standards, as in some cases the originals are damaged. The content of the illustrations, however, made their inclusion important despite problems in reproduction.

CONTENTS

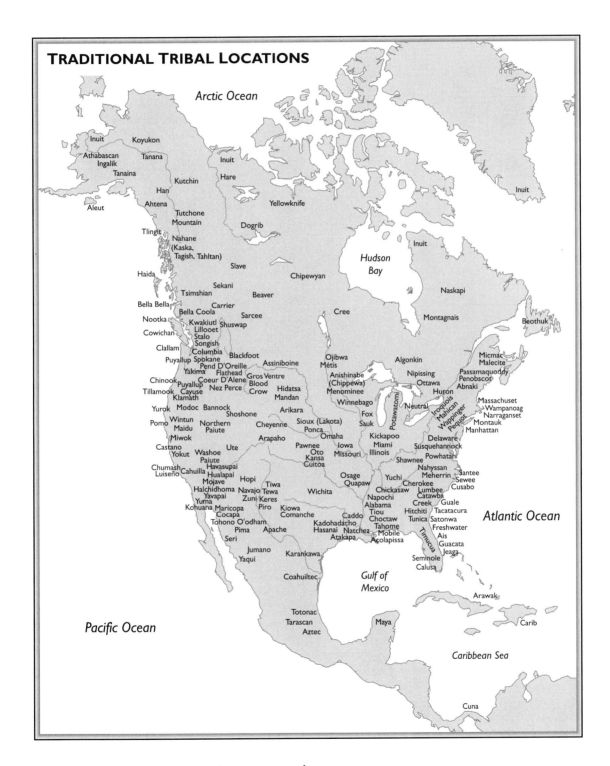

TRADITIONAL TRIBAL LOCATIONS

Arctic Ocean

Inuit
Koyukon
Athabascan
Ingalik
Tanana
Tanaina
Inuit
Kutchin
Hare
Han
Ahtena
Yellowknife
Tutchone
Mountain
Dogrib
Aleut
Tlingit
Nahane
(Kaska,
Tagish, Tahltan)
Slave
Haida
Chipewyan
Sekani
Tsimshian
Beaver
Bella Bella
Carrier
Cree
Nootka
Bella Coola
Sarcee
Cowichan
Kwakiutl
Lillooet
Shuswap
Clallam
Stalo
Songish
Columbia
Blackfoot
Puyallup
Spokane
Assiniboine
Ojibwa
Métis
Algonkin
Nipissing
Yakima
Pend D'Oreille
Flathead
Gros Ventre
Anishinabe
(Chippewa)
Ottawa
Chinook
Coeur D'Alene
Blood
Menominee
Huron
Tillamook
Cayuse
Nez Perce
Crow
Hidatsa
Mandan
Neutral
Klamath
Winnebago
Yurok
Modoc
Bannock
Arikara
Fox
Sauk
Pomo
Wintun
Northern
Cheyenne
Sioux (Lakota)
Maidu
Paiute
Ponca
Miwok
Arapaho
Omaha
Kickapoo
Delaware
Castano
Ute
Pawnee
Iowa
Miami
Susquehannock
Yokut
Washoe
Oto
Missouri
Illinois
Powhatan
Paiute
Kansa
Shawnee
Chumash
Havasupai
Cuitoa
Nahyssan
Luiseño
Cahuilla
Hualapai
Osage
Yuchi
Meherrin
Mojave
Hopi
Quapaw
Cherokee
Halchidhoma
Navajo
Tiwa
Tewa
Wichita
Chickasaw
Lumbee
Yavapai
Zuni
Keres
Napochi
Catawba
Yuma
Piro
Alabama
Creek
Guale
Kohuana
Maricopa
Kiowa
Tiou
Hitchiti
Cocapa
Comanche
Caddo
Choctaw
Tunica
Tohono O'odham
Kadohadacho
Tahome
Pima
Apache
Hasanai
Natchez
Mobile
Seri
Atakapa
Acolapissa
Jumano
Karankawa
Yaqui
Coahuiltec
Totonac
Tarascan
Aztec
Maya

Hudson
Bay
Inuit
Naskapi
Montagnais
Beothuk
Micmac
Malecite
Passamaquoddy
Penobscot
Abnaki
Massachuset
Wampanoag
Narraganset
Mahican
Wappinger
Pequot
Montauk
Manhattan
Potawatomi
Iroquois
Santee
Sewee
Cusabo
Tacatacura
Satonwa
Freshwater
Ais
Guacata
Jeaga
Timucua
Seminole
Calusa
Arawak
Carib
Cuna

Atlantic Ocean

Pacific Ocean

Gulf of
Mexico

Caribbean Sea

INTRODUCTION

Lakota Sioux girls at puberty look for guidance from White Buffalo Calf Woman, who gave their people the pipe and made them great buffalo hunters. The Iroquois pause before each meal to give thanks to the Three Sisters, who ensure the tribes' survival with the gifts of corn, beans, and squash. The Navajo revere the powerful Changing Woman, who, by imaging the Navajo's world, helped to bring it into being.

Through the telling and retelling of these ancient stories and many others, Native Americans have long celebrated the varied roles and contributions of women in their societies. As mothers, Indian women have given life. As workers, they have farmed fields, built houses, and performed other labor crucial to their tribes' well-being. As caregivers and teachers, they have instructed young tribespeople in how to live properly and productively. And as storytellers, they have created new worlds beyond the realm of sight and touch.

The oral traditions of Native Americans provide a major source of information about Native American women of the past. But because most Indian languages traditionally did not have a written form, before the mid-19th century, the only written records of Indians and Indian life were those left by early European and American settlers and explorers. All too often, these chroniclers—most of whom were white males—denigrated the status of Indian women. They admired the hard work that Indian women performed on behalf of their families, but instead of seeing this labor as a source of pride and self-worth, these historians generally concluded that Indian women were virtually the slaves of their husbands. These writers failed to understand that both Indian men and women labored, though at different tasks, and that in most tribes their work was valued equally. These accounts of Indian life were likewise colored by the assumptions about women that the writers had learned from their own cultures. Accustomed to seeing women as subordinate to men, they took for granted that Indians shared their beliefs about the inferiority of women. This misogyny also led many chroniclers to dismiss the subject of Indian women as unworthy of detailed discussion in their writings. If Indian women appeared at all in these records, they are depicted as an anonymous group, with little regard for the ideas thoughts, or feelings of individual women.

As a consequence, the names of very few Indian women appear in the historical records from the early years of Indian-white contact. Those who do are exceptional figures—usually women whom whites deemed worthy of mention because they could be depicted, often inaccurately, as supporters of the non-Indian conquest of North America. The first Indian woman to be portrayed as a helpmate to whites was Pocahontas. Beginning in the early seventeenth century, a myth grew around the young daughter of Powhatan, an Indian leader who controlled the region in which the English established the settlement of Jamestown in 1607. The girl was depicted as a beautiful Indian "princess" who proved her love and loyalty to the English by begging Powhatan to spare the life of Jamestown leader Captain John Smith. The Pocahontas myth also held that she saved the Jamestown colonists by offering them food and supplies. Although Pocahontas undoubtedly did show great generosity toward the English settlers in her father's land, this popular account of Pocahontas's life strategically omits known facts that reflect poorly on the residents of Jamestown—for instance, that the colonists rewarded her kindness by kidnapping her and that they later paraded her before London's elite in an effort to raise money for Jamestown. The sanitized version of the Pocahontas story served an important purpose for the white settlers. By implying that "noble" Indians like Pocahontas recognized the superiority of non-Indian culture and consequently wanted Europeans to overrun their lands, it allowed whites to rationalize their illegal and immoral seizure of Indian lands. Stories that arose around other mythic Indian women—including Sacagawea, Kateri Tekakwitha, and Milly Francis—followed aspects of the Pocahontas prototype by presenting these women as primarily sympathetic to the goals and desires of whites. If these women had had the opportunity to tell their stories, their versions would likely be very different from those recorded and retold by non-Indians.

Whites' romanticizing of selected heroines, however, does not diminish the very real significance many Indian women had in the early years of Indian-white relations. In addition to Pocahontas, figures such as Nancy Ward and Winema made courageous efforts to prevent open warfare between their people and white newcomers to their lands. Women involved in the fur trade, such as Natawista and Thanadelthur, also were instrumental in, at least temporarily, establishing a relatively peaceful coexistence. Some Indian women—including Molly Brant and Mary Musgrove—learned to deal

shrewdly with whites with an eye as much toward personal gain as toward interracial harmony.

Despite the best efforts of Indian women and men to protect themselves and their homes, white settlers had overtaken much of their territory by the mid-19th century. Decimated by non-Indian diseases and overwhelmed by the intruders' firepower, many Indian populations were forced by settlers and the U.S. government to vacate their ancestral homeland or to remain confined to only a small portion of it. The theft of Indian lands was a devastating blow to Indian societies and economies. Particularly in the case of Plains Indians, whose cultures were structured around buffalo hunting, loss of tribal territory made it impossible for Indian groups to practice many aspects of their traditional ways of life. Equally threatening to Indian traditions was the introduction of white customs, beliefs, and goods. Some elements of white culture were welcomed by Indians, but many more were foisted on them by the U.S. government, which by the late 19th century had adopted a policy of compelling Indian groups to give up their native customs and take on in their place the ways of whites.

One effect that this assimilation campaign initially had on Indian women was a devaluation of the clothing, dishes, pots, storage containers, and other necessary goods they had traditionally crafted for their families. Although these items were made to be used, they were also carefully created and decorated. A woman who could shape a beautiful pot or weave an intricate basket was highly respected by her tribespeople. The status of the craftswoman, however, was eroded as white traders introduced Indians to cotton cloth, metal pans, and other manufactured objects. Over time, these goods replaced the items Indian women had painstakingly made by hand. As fewer women practiced these crafts, the knowledge of how to make a Pueblo pot or a Pomo basket was in danger of being lost.

But starting in the late 19th century many traditional Indian crafts were revived, ironically in part because of the efforts of white businessmen. They recognized that non-Indians were willing to pay high prices for the works of Indian craftswomen. Impoverished by their loss of land, women such as the Hopi potter Nampeyo and the Washoe basket maker Louisa Keyser were eager for the opportunity to earn an income for their families. Both of these masters combined traditional techniques with forms and motifs of their own invention, thereby elevating their chosen craft into an art form and making themselves famous among art collectors worldwide. Although they and other pioneering craftswomen were sometimes exploited by their white patrons, their work helped to bring much-needed funds to their people. Their success also inspired Indian women of following generations—including Tonita Peña, Pablita Velarde, and Angel DeCora—to become artists working in non-Indian media of paint on canvas and pencil on paper.

Aside from art collectors, anthropologists took an interest in the lives of Indian women during the late 19th and early 20th centuries. As assimilation threatened native customs, these scholars rushed to visit Native American communities to study their cultures and societies. Their interpretations sometimes displayed an ignorance of or lack of sensitivity to their subjects, but their writings provide one of the most comprehensive records of how Indians coped with the pressures brought on by contact with whites.

In addition to studying tribes, some anthropologists took down the life histories of their informants. Most subjects of these anthropological autobiographies were male warriors and leaders from Plains tribes, who had emerged as romantic figures in the popular fiction of white Americans. However, a few anthropologists sought out the stories of women, among them Pretty-Shield of the Crows, Waheenee of the Hidatsas, and Maria Chona of the Tohono O'odhams. Unlike the sometimes bombastic accounts of Plains Indian men, these stories quietly detail the trials and triumphs of everyday life and the network of personal relationships Indian women traditionally had relied upon for their survival. They also reveal

the remarkable resiliency many Native American women displayed as they developed ways of integrating new customs into their lives while fighting to retain their people's ancient values and traditions.

During the assimilation era, other Indian women began to compile their own autobiographies. Many of these authors were graduates of Indian boarding schools established by the federal government. The curricula of these schools were designed to teach Indian children to live like whites. Attending school sometimes hundreds or even thousands of miles from home, many students were traumatized by the verbal and physical abuse of their teachers as they tried to force their charges into the mainstream. But those students who survived the experience usually emerged from the institutions with a command of spoken and written English, which at least gave them the power to record their stories in their own words for future generations. Earlier anthropological life histories were generally compiled with the help of a translator, so the risk of misunderstanding or mistranslation was high. But later autobiographies—both those written by the subject and those told to a trusted friend who then transcribed and edited the material—provide a more trustworthy record of the subjects' lives (or at least of the way in which the subjects wished to present themselves). Beginning with the publication of Sarah Winnemucca's *Life among the Piutes* (1883)—the first book written in English by a Native American woman—written autobiographies became an important new source of information about Indian women. Notable examples of the genre include *Mountain Wolf Woman* (1961), Polingaysi Qoyawayma's *No Turning Back* (1964), Helen Sekaquaptewa's *Me and Mine* (1969), Maria Campbell's *Halfbreed* (1973), and Anna Moore Shaw's *A Pima Past* (1974).

Non-Indian education also afforded Indian women the language skills and social tools they needed to take a public role in the growing movement to reform federal Indian policy. By the late 19th century U.S. policies toward Indians had deeply impoverished most tribes, particularly those confined to reservations in the West. A group of elite white liberals—sometimes called "friends of the Indians"—hoped to improve the lot of Indians by pressing for sweeping changes in the government's treatment of tribal groups. Despite their noble intentions, these reformers sometimes exploited the very people they proposed to help. Wa Wa Chaw and Zintkala Nuni, for instance, were taken from their Indian families as infants and adopted by white reformers, who later pushed their reluctant children into the limelight to elevate their own status in the reform movement. But other Indian women benefited from their association with non-Indian reformers. The education of Susan La Flesche, the first Indian woman physician, was financed by wealthy reformers. Her older sister, Suzette, who advocated radical policy reforms, was given the opportunity to air her theories by lecturing to high-placed and influential "friends."

By the early years of the 20th century, a small group of Indian intellectuals emerged from the reform movement with its own agenda. Rather than assimilating into non-Indian society as their schooling had trained them to do, these educated Indians were determined to fight for the rights of Indian people without the aid of non-Indian advocates. Indian women, such as Gertrude Simmons Bonnin and Ruth Muskrat Bronson, rose to prominence in this movement, which became known as Pan-Indianism because it encouraged Indians of many different tribes to work together to solve their common problems. Through national multitribal associations such as the Society of American Indians and the National Congress of American Indians, these activists sought to help Indians free themselves of control by the federal government so they could better determine their own destinies.

These women's promotion of self-determination contributed to the passage of the Indian Reorganization Act (1934). Among its many provisions, this act of Congress allowed Indian tribes whose traditional governments had been disbanded by the United States to create new tribal governments according to a set of guidelines. Traditional native

systems of governing had generally been fairly egalitarian. Even in tribal groups in which women were not permitted to hold leadership positions, they still wielded a fair amount of political influence behind the scenes. However, in these new tribal governments, which were modeled after American governing bodies, Indian women discovered that they had to fight to be heard. To their alarm, they also found that many of their male constituents had internalized from non-Indian society the belief that women were not capable leaders. Nevertheless, through hard work and persistence, a number of women eventually broke through these sexist barriers and won seats on their tribal councils. During the past several decades, trailblazers such as Wilma Mankiller, Betty Mae Jumper, Ramona Bennett, and Annie Dodge Wauneka have earned high positions within their tribal governments, which they have used to push for improvements in their people's education, housing, and health care.

Beginning in the early 20th century, Indian women such as Minnie Kellogg and Alice Mae Jemison have also been at the forefront of the battle for more radical reforms. From this tradition blossomed the Indian rights movement, or Red Power movement, of the early 1970s. Many female activists were members of the movement's central organization, the American Indian Movement (AIM), which initialed the takeover of Alcatraz, the Trail of Broken Treaties, and the occupation of Wounded Knee. Among the leading activists in AIM during this era were Mary Brave Bird, who in *Lakota Woman* (1990) wrote a stirring account of her involvement in the Wounded Knee protest, and Anna Mae Aquash, whose death highlighted the great risks the AIM activists took to promote their cause.

Also beginning in the 1970s, Indian women took center stage in a renaissance of Native American literature. Before this period, several Native women, such as Emily Pauline Johnson and Mourning Dove, had experimented with writing poetry and prose. But following the publication of N. Scott Momaday's Pulitzer Prize–winning *House Made of Dawn* (1968), many more were inspired to take up these non-Indian forms of expression as vehicles for exploring what it means to be an Indian in the late 20th century. By the late 1980s, Louise Erdrich, Leslie Moramon Silko, Linda Hogan, and Joy Harjo had emerged as leaders of this literary movement.

The past several decades have also seen a revitalization of Native American arts. Helen Hardin, Jaune Quick-to-See Smith, Nora Naranjo-Morse, and Roxanne Swentzell have been recognized as masters of painting and sculpture, while other artists have concentrated on modernizing older Indian art forms. Kenojuak and Pitseolak, for instance, have borrowed design motifs found on traditional Inuit clothing for their drawings and prints. Similarly melding old and new, Ramona Sakiestewa has reproduced forgotten weaving techniques of her Pueblo ancestors to create abstract tapestries. In addition to their contributions to the visual arts, Indian women such as singer Buffy Sainte-Marie, actress Tantoo Cardinal, and filmmaker Alanis Obomsawin have employed their creativity to help their audiences look beyond stereotypes toward a more multifaceted view of Indianness.

The birth of Native American studies programs in universities and colleges has offered contemporary Indian women still another forum through which they can explore and preserve their cultural heritage. Ethnomusicologist Charlotte Heth and linguist Ofelia Zepeda have worked to revive the music, dance, and languages of Indian peoples, whereas literary scholar Paula Gunn Allen and anthropologist Beatrice Medicine have concentrated on creating a more detailed and less culturally biased picture of Native American women than white male scholars have provided in the past. To share this ongoing reexamination of Indian history and society, many Indian women, such as Janine Pease and Ruth Roessel, have also pursued distinguished careers as educators. Although these scholars and teachers work from a classroom instead of a hogan, tipi, or earthlodge, they are embracing the traditional duty of Native American women to be cultural preservationists, ensuring their survival as

a people by keeping alive the memories of those who came before them.

Increased access to higher education has had a dramatic effect not only on the lives of American Indian women but also on their tribes. A 2003 study found that 60 percent of all bachelor's degrees granted to Indians were earned by women. Many of these educated women have taken jobs with their tribes, helping to manage funds and administer programs. The phenomenon is especially important among tribes with substantial income from the gambling industry, because they rely on educated professionals to oversee complex business and financial dealings. Work in these areas has often translated into careers in tribal politics. In just the 25-year period between 1981 and 2006, the number of tribes headed by a woman has almost doubled. Many of these women—including Vivian Juan-Saunders of the Tohono O'odham Nation in Arizona and Cecelia Fire Thunder of the Pine Ridge Reservation in South Dakota—are the first female leaders of their people in modern times. Programs for social services, child welfare, and education have grown substantially as more and more Indian women have entered tribal government. Although many live untraditional lives, in a new way, they have taken on the traditional Indian women's role as caretakers for their people.

The myriad roles Indian women have played throughout the past 500 years are reflected in the great diversity of the stories contained in this book. Ranging from Pocahontas (b. circa 1596) to Hopi soldier Lori Piestewa (b. 1979), the subjects are mothers and wives, politicians and diplomats, warriors and peacemakers, scholars and educators, healers and spiritual leaders, writers and artists. Despite this broad spectrum, the one hundred biographies here are far from a comprehensive list of Native American women of note. Chosen to represent a variety of tribes, regions, chronological periods, and fields, the subjects selected are but a cross-section of the many Native American women who have influenced both Indian and non-Indian society. The stories of hundreds of other historically important Indian women can be found in the works listed in the bibliography of selected sources at the end of the book. For more information on a woman who is profiled, consult the brief list of recommended reading that concludes the biography.

Many of the women included in this book knew or associated with one another. To help the reader trace these relationships, references to a profiled subject that appear in the text of another biography are set in small caps. Following the biographies are lists of subjects arranged by area of activity, year of birth, and tribe as well as a comprehensive index. These tools may also be helpful in drawing from the individual biographies a larger picture of the lives of Indian women, their history, and their future.

A

Allen, Elsie

(1899–1990)   *Pomo basketmaker, educator*

Elsie Allen defied tribal tradition in order to share great works of Pomo Indian basketry with art lovers from around the world. She was born on September 22, 1899, in a hop field near Santa Rosa, California. Elsie was reared by her grandmother in the Pomo village of Cloverdale. Following her father's death and her mother's remarriage, she moved into her mother's household in Hopland village.

Traditionally, the Pomo had been hunters and gatherers who occupied the region just north of San Francisco. As whites moved into their territory, they were compelled to give up much of their land as well as their time-honored means of making a livelihood. Like most other Pomo in the early 20th century, Elsie's parents worked as wage laborers on farms owned by non-Indians. By the time Elsie was 10, she too began working the fields to help her family.

She had a respite from this difficult labor when she was sent to an Indian boarding school in Covelo, California, nearly 80 miles away from her home. But the experience was bitter for Elsie. Homesickness, unsympathetic teachers, and unfamiliarity with the

English language drove the girl back to her village in less than a year. She was much more comfortable attending a local day school, where during her early teen years she became proficient in English.

At 18, Elsie moved to San Francisco to escape farm work. She found jobs as a housekeeper and hospital worker but returned home after marrying a Pomo man named Arthur Allen in 1919. The couple had four children.

While raising a family and working in the fields, Elsie Allen was active in several Pomo women's clubs. These organizations sought to improve the social and economic conditions of Pomo communities. In addition to organizing fund-raisers and helping to establish scholarships for Pomo students, Allen was involved in a lawsuit that succeeded in desegregating non-Indian–owned businesses that would not allow Pomo and whites to sit together.

Allen was also a dedicated defender of Pomo tradition—a role that placed her in a difficult situation when her mother, Annie Burke, fell ill. On her deathbed, Burke begged her daughter not to observe Pomo custom by burying her with the baskets she had made. Like many Pomo women of her generation, as a girl Burke had learned to weave willows

Elsie Allen wears strings of clamshell beads, circa 1970.
(Mendocino County Museum, #72-29-5)

people, she also began teaching the art to Indians and non-Indians at the Mendocino Art Center. To further disseminate information about the Pomo art, Allen also wrote *Pomo Basketmaking* (1972), which through detailed text and pictures describes the tribe's traditional basket making techniques.

As Allen headed into her seventies, both Pomos and non-Indians applauded her efforts to preserve Pomo culture and nicknamed her "the Pomo Sage." From 1979 to 1981, she served as an adviser to a research study on Pomo culture and history conducted by Sonoma State University. She was also asked to contribute her knowledge of plants native to the Pomo homeland when the U.S. Army Corps of Engineers made plans to build a dam in the area. Allen's counsel helped organize an effort to replant endangered species that the dam project may otherwise have destroyed.

Elsie Allen died in 1990, but she left behind a lifetime of good works. Her most tangible legacy is the Elsie Allen Collection. On long-term loan to the Mendocino County Museum, the collection includes 131 baskets made by Allen and her friends and relatives. In keeping with Allen's determination to pass ancient knowledge along to future generations, detailed records about the crafting of individual baskets and stories about the basketmakers have been preserved with the works themselves.

Further Reading/Resources

Abel-Vidor, Suzanne, Dot Brovarney, and Susan Billy. *Remember Your Relations: The Elsie Allen Baskets, Family and Friends.* Berkeley, Calif.: Heyday Books, 1996.
Allen, Elsie. *Pomo Basketmaking: A Supreme Art for the Weaver.* Healdsburg, Calif.: Naturegraph Publishers, 1972.
Ludwig, David, producer. *Pomo Basketweavers: A Tribute to Three Elders.* Rohnert Park, Calif.: Creative Light Productions. Videotape, 59 min., 1994.

Allen, Paula Gunn
(1939–) *Laguna Pueblo educator, poet, novelist*

Considered one of the United States's most important Indian intellectuals, Paula Gunn Allen has

and other wild plant materials into beautiful and intricate baskets. Burke wanted Allen to save and preserve the baskets she had made throughout her life. Allen's mother also asked her daughter to show them to non-Indians as proof that the Pomo people were not "dumb," as some local whites maintained.

Although torn, Allen decided to abide by her mother's wishes. Relatives and friends were appalled by her defiance of tradition, but over time, she became only more convinced that she had been right. Allen feared that the art of Pomo basketry would be lost if the tribe did not share their work and methods with others.

Although she had been taught basket making as a youth, Allen did not start crafting her own baskets until she was 62. To the shock of many tribes-

brought attention and respect to the growing field of Native American literature. Her scholarly writings, including the seminal feminist study *The Sacred Hoop* (1986), have also explored the roles of women in Indian societies from a Native perspective.

Born in Albuquerque, New Mexico, in 1939, Allen was reared in Cubero, a small rural village located between the reservations of the Laguna Pueblo and the Acoma Pueblo. Alluding to her mixed ancestry, she has described herself as a "multicultural event." Her mother was of Laguna, Sioux, and Scottish descent, and her father's parents were Lebanese.

Despite the many cultural influences on her upbringing, Allen explained in a 1987 autobiographical essay, "I always knew I was Indian." She was raised primarily by her mother and maternal grandmother, from whom she learned firsthand of the revered position of women in traditional Laguna society. As Allen has said, "I grew up with the notion that women are strong. I didn't know that I was supposed to be silly and weak." She maintains that she was unaware of the second-class status of women among non-Indians until she became involved in the Women's Movement of the late 1960s and early 1970s.

Another great influence on her youth was books. Paula devoured "the Hardy Boys and the Bobbsey Twins and *Anne of Green Gables* and Shakespeare, whatever there was to read." As a teenager she became more discriminating. Her favorite author was Gertrude Stein, whose work she imitated in her earliest writing. Stein's experiments with stream-of-consciousness narratives later inspired Allen to use the technique in her novel *The Woman Who Owned the Shadows* (1983).

After attending a local day school, Allen was sent to a Catholic boarding school in Albuquerque, from which she graduated in 1957. She was raised as a Catholic and considers Catholicism to be "terribly important to me." However, she has also been highly critical of the church, particularly its historic role in the colonization of Indian nations.

Allen began her college career at the University of New Mexico. She aspired to write fiction and essays, but became interested in poetry after she came upon poet Robert Creeley's *For Love*. After reading the collection, she discovered that Creeley was teaching a poetry-writing course at the university. To meet Creeley, she enrolled in the class and found that she enjoyed writing poems. Allen eventually transferred to the University of Oregon, where she received a bachelor's degree in English (1966) and a master's of fine arts in creative writing (1968).

While in Oregon, Allen so missed Laguna that she began to feel depressed and alienated—a malady identified as "land-sickness" in Kiowa author N. Scott Momaday's *House Made of Dawn* (1968). The first novel by a Native American to win the Pulitzer Prize, *Dawn* was an enormous critical success and inspired many young Indians to write. Allen was struck by the nonlineal structure of the novel, which duplicated Indian storytelling styles, and by the confusions of Abel, its part-Indian, part-white protagonist. In a 1987 interview, she explained the great impact *Dawn* had on her: "Abel [had] the same sickness that I had—or something like it—but Momaday had enough control over that sickness to write a book about it. That said to me, 'You're okay.' . . . [I]f that line hadn't been thrown in my direction, I wouldn't be here now."

After receiving her master's degree, Allen married. She and her husband had three children before they divorced. Allen then returned to school at the University of New Mexico. She had hoped to study Native American literature, but the dean maintained literature by Indians did not exist. Allen instead majored in American studies and was awarded her doctorate in 1975. She has subsequently held teaching posts at several universities, including San Francisco State University, the University of New Mexico, and the University of California, Berkeley. Before her retirement in 1999, Allen spent 13 years on the faculty of the Department of English at the University of California, Los Angeles.

While Allen was completing her Ph.D., she published her first book of poems, *The Blind Lion*

(1974). She has since written seven more poetry collections and one novel. In an effort to introduce mainstream readers to Native American literatures, she has also edited several anthologies for a popular audience, including *Spider Woman's Granddaughters: Traditional Tales and Contemporary Writing by Native American Women* (1989), which was given the American Book Award in 1990.

Perhaps Allen is even better known for her scholarly writings and collections. In 1983, she edited *Studies in American Indian Literature: Critical Essays and Course Designs,* a landmark resource for teachers and students of Native American studies. The book has helped guide the study of Native American literature by insisting that the works be examined and evaluated from an Indian perspective rather than by the standards and expectations of European and American society. Three years later, Allen published another greatly influential work, *The Sacred Hoop: Recovering the Feminine in American Indian Traditions* (1986). In this collection of 17 essays, she examines woman-centered tribal traditions and uncovers the feminine aspects of Indians' cultural and literary history that non-Indians have ignored or suppressed. In one pivotal essay, Allen explains that lesbians were treated with great respect in many Indian cultures; this piece and much of her subsequent work has been dedicated to increasing tolerance for gays and lesbians in Indian communities. She has also continued her investigation into the cultural influence of Native American women in *Grandmothers of the Light* (1991), a collection of stories, and in *Women in American Indian Myth* (1994). More recently, Allen has challenged the earliest non-Indian myths about Native American women in her biography *Pocahontas: Medicine Woman, Spy, Entrepreneur, Diplomat* (2003).

Through her scholarly work, Paula Gunn Allen has both saved older Native American literature from obscurity and championed new writers and their works. In her eyes, the preservation of Indian literature is vital to the continuance of Indian peoples. This literature, she once explained, "tells us who we are; it tells us what our history is; it tells us what we look like; and it tells us of the significance of our lives within the human community."

Further Reading

Allen, Paula Gunn. "The Autobiography of a Confluence." In *I Tell You Now: Autobiographical Essays by Native American Writers,* edited by Brian Swann and Arnold Krupat, 142–154. Lincoln: University of Nebraska Press, 1987.

———. *Pocahontas: Medicine Woman, Spy, Entrepreneur, Diplomat.* San Francisco, Calif.: HarperSanFrancisco, 2003.

———. *The Sacred Hoop: Recovering the Feminine in American Indian Traditions.* Boston: Beacon Press, 1986.

———. *Skins and Bones.* San Francisco, Calif.: West End Press, 1988.

———. *Spider Woman's Granddaughters: Traditional Tales and Contemporary Writing by Native American Women.* Boston: Beacon Press, 1989.

———, ed. *Studies in American Indian Literature: Critical Essays and Course Designs.* New York: Modern Language Association, 1983.

———. *The Woman Who Owned the Shadows.* San Francisco, Calif.: Spinster's Ink, 1983.

Coltelli, Laura. "Paula Gunn Allen." In *Winged Words: American Indian Writers Speak,* 11–39. Lincoln: University of Nebraska Press, 1990.

Bruchac, Joseph. "I Climb the Mesas in My Dreams." In *Survival This Way: Interviews with American Indian Poets,* 1–21. Tucson: University of Arizona Press, 1987.

Hanson, Elizabeth J. *Paula Gunn Allen.* Boise, Idaho: Boise State University, 1990.

Alvord, Lori Arviso (Janette Lorraine Cupp)
(1958–)   *Navajo physician*

The first Navajo (Dineh) woman to become a surgeon, Lori Arviso Alvord is an advocate for the melding of Western medicine with traditional American Indian methods of healing.

Born Janette Lorraine Cupp in 1958 in Tacoma, Washington, she was raised in the small town of Crownpoint, New Mexico, on the Navajo Indian Reservation. Her mother was a white woman who married her Navajo father when she was 15. In the Cupp home, English was spoken and observing Navajo customs was discouraged.

Growing up, Lori's greatest influence was her paternal grandmother, Grace Cupp, who told her stories about the Navajo and their history. As she later explained, "From [my grandmother's] example [I] learned that to be Navajos was to be part of the *Diné* [Navajo] nation as well as the larger Native American culture, proud and strong."

Lori Cupp made good grades in high school and planned to go to college. At first, she assumed she would go to a school close to home. But on a whim, she decided to apply to Dartmouth College in Hanover, New Hampshire. Very few American Indian students then attended elite eastern schools. But Dartmouth, with a growing Native American studies program, had about 50—enough to convince Cupp that she could feel comfortable there.

Accepted by Dartmouth, Cupp found adjusting to the school more difficult than she had hoped. She disliked the cold weather and found the terrain, full of hills and trees, claustrophobic after growing up in the desert Southwest. Cupp also often felt uncomfortable around her non-Indian classmates. She was put off by their aggressive competitiveness—considered an undesirable trait in Navajo culture.

After graduating with honors in 1979, Cupp returned to the Southwest. She took a job in Albuquerque as a laboratory assistant at the University of New Mexico. Impressed by Cupp's work, her boss suggested she go to medical school. At first Cupp dismissed the idea. She later recalled thinking, "A Navajo woman physician. I couldn't remember ever hearing of one in my entire life. . . . *I don't have what it takes,* I thought." But after taking a few science classes and doing well in them, she changed her mind. Cupp quit her job and headed off to study medicine at Stanford University in Palo Alto, California. While there, Cupp fell in love with surgery, a demanding discipline that attracted relatively few woman and far fewer American Indian students.

Completing her residency in 1991, Cupp landed her dream job—working at the Indian Health Service's hospital in Gallup, New Mexico. There, she had an opportunity to give back to her tribe, since most of her patients were Navajo. But treating Navajo patients turned out to be difficult. Because of the cultural importance of privacy, Navajo often balked at the personal questions she asked when taking medical histories. Her patients also were often wary of mainstream medical treatments and distrustful of her explanations of disease. For instance, one young female cancer patient was hesitant to get treatment. She did not want others to know she was ill, fearing she would be shunned by friends and family, since many traditional Navajo believed cancer was contagious.

Cupp began to adapt her practice to suit her patients' needs. After surgery, for example, she let them take home any body parts she removed. This eased her patients' fears that the body parts might fall into the hands of witches who could use them to cause the patients harm. Cupp also encouraged people to seek out the care of *hataalii,* Navajo medicine men. *Hataalii* believe illness occurs when the body is out of balance. This balance can only be restored through their songs and rituals. As Cupp observed, the mental comfort the *hataalii* provided greatly improved her patients' chances for a good surgical outcome.

In 1994, Cupp married Jon Alvord and changed her name to Lori Arviso Alvord. (To honor her grandmother, she took her grandmother's maiden name as her middle name.) The couple have two children—son Kodiak and daughter Katie.

The family left Gallup after Alvord was asked to join the faculty of Dartmouth Medical School. There, she serves as associate dean of student and minority affairs and assistant professor of surgery and psychiatry. In her teaching and lectures, Alvord has continued to promote the lessons she learned while practicing medicine among the Navajo. In her 1999 autobiography, *The Scalpel and the Silver Bear,* she explained her approach: "Healing is not only a one-to-one relationship, it is multi-dimensional. At the basis of Navajo philosophies of healing is a concept of called 'Walking in Beauty.' It is a way of living a balanced and harmonious life, in touch with all components of one's world. This is a path to better health and healing and life."

Further Reading

Alvord, Lori Arviso, and Elizabeth Cohen Van Pelt. *The Scalpel and the Silver Bear: The First Navajo Woman Surgeon Combines Western Medicine and Traditional Healing.* New York: Bantam Books, 1999.

Krol, Debra Utacia. "Healing Hands: Dr. Lori Arviso Alvord." *Native Peoples,* November/December 2003, pp. 68–69.

Anderson, Owanah

(1926–)   *Choctaw activist*

Through her involvement in a wide variety of organizations and government committees, Owanah Anderson has worked to bring the needs and concerns of Native American women to the attention of policy makers. A member of the Choctaw tribe, Anderson was born in Choctaw County, Oklahoma, in 1926. She attended school in the town of Boswell and was elected valedictorian of her graduating high school class. Her grades helped win her a scholarship to the University of Oklahoma, where she studied journalism.

In the late 1970s, Anderson became an advocate for the rights of Native Americans and women. After serving as a cochairperson of the Texas delegation to the 1977 Houston Women's Conference, she joined the Committee on Rights and Responsibilities of Women formed by the Department of Health, Education, and Welfare. Working with this committee between 1977 and 1980, Anderson drew attention to problems with Indian health care and educational opportunities. From 1978 to 1981, she also served on the Advisory Committee on Women organized by President Jimmy Carter.

With the support of the Department of Education, Anderson founded the Ohoyo Resource Center in 1979. (*Ohoyo* is the Choctaw word for "woman.") The center was devoted to improving employment and educational opportunities for Indian women. In addition to sponsoring conferences and leadership training, the center produced *Ohoyo One Thousand* (1982). This publication, edited by Anderson, features brief biographical profiles of more than a thousand Native American women from 231 tribes who have excelled in the fields of art, business, communication, education, health care, law, sciences, and social work. Intended to create a network through which these successful women could help Indian youths, *Ohoyo One Thousand* remains the only directory of its kind. As director of the Ohoyo Resource Center, Anderson also edited *Words of Today's American Indian Women: Ohoyo Makachi,* a collection of speeches presented at a women's conference in Tahlequah, Oklahoma, in 1981.

After the center closed in 1983, Anderson moved to New York City and became the chairperson of the National Committee on Indian Affairs of the Episcopal Church. In this position, she oversaw a budget of $1.5 million used to fund Episcopal missions in Native American communities. Anderson also authored *Jamestown Commitment* (1988), a history of the church's missionary activities in the early years of interaction between Europeans and Indians. In 1997, Anderson published an updated and expanded edition of her book titled *400 Years: Anglican/Episcopal Mission among American Indians.* The next year, Anderson retired from her post with the Episcopal Church.

Continuing her work as a rights advocate, Anderson has served on the board of directors of the Association for American Indian Affairs and acted as a project director for the National Women's Development Program. Among the many honors she has received are the 1981 Anna Roe Howard Award from the Harvard Graduate School of Education and a 1989 honorary doctorate from Seabury-Western Theological Seminary in Evanston, Illinois.

Further Reading

Anderson, Owanah. *400 Years: Anglican/Episcopal Mission among American Indians.* Cincinnati, Ohio: Forward Movement Publications, 1997.

———, ed. *Ohoyo One Thousand: A Resource Guide of American Indian/Alaska Native Women.* Wichita Falls, Tex.: Ohoyo Resource Center, 1982.

Clay, Catherine A. "Owanah Anderson." In *Notable Native Americans,* edited by Sharon J. Malinowski, 13–14. Detroit: Gale Research, 1995.

Aquash, Anna Mae (Anna Mae Pictou)
(1945–1975)   *Micmac activist, educator*

During her lifetime, Anna Mae Aquash was a dedicated activist, determined to lead and inspire others in the fight for Indian rights. Upon her death, however, she sadly became a symbol—a martyr of one of the most bitter and bloody periods in the history of recent relations between Indians and the U.S. government.

On March 27, 1945, Anna Mae Pictou was born into poverty in a small Micmac Indian village near the town of Shubenacadie in Nova Scotia, Canada. Her mother, Mary Ellen Pictou, had left school after the third grade and had to rely on welfare payments to feed and clothe Anna and her two older sisters. Her father, Francis Thomas Levi, abandoned the family shortly before Anna's birth.

When Anna was four, her mother married Noel Sapier. The son of a Micmac leader, Sapier moved the family to a nearby Micmac reserve (the Canadian term for a reservation). There Anna lived in a house with no heat, water, or electricity and subsisted largely on the wild turnips and potatoes harvested by her family. Although Anna's stepfather was unable to improve his daughters' financial lot, he provided them with other resources that Anna would treasure for the rest of her life. He taught the girls to value discipline and, most important, instructed them about the traditional ways of their people.

Following Sapier's death from cancer in 1956, Anna's family returned to their old village. For the first time, she also began to attend an off-reserve school, where Indian students were in the minority. Her non-Indian classmates taunted her with racial slurs, and amidst this hostile environment her grades fell. Her problems mounted when she arrived home from school one afternoon in 1961 and discovered that her mother had run off with her boyfriend, leaving her children to fend for themselves. Anna moved in with her oldest sister, who had already left home and started a family. Anna also then gave up on her education. She dropped out and took wage work harvesting pota-

toes and berries, one of the few jobs open to Micmacs on the reserve.

Looking for a better life and a little adventure, Anna Mae Pictou at 16 impulsively moved to Boston with a friend, Jake Maloney. The two set up house together and helped each other adjust to life in a big city. Pictou found work in a factory and gave birth to two daughters, Denise and Deborah. After Deborah's birth, the couple married and began dividing their time between Boston and a Micmac reserve where Maloney's relatives lived. Pictou wanted her daughters to spend time among the Micmacs and to learn about tribal culture firsthand as she had as a girl.

In Boston, Pictou began to volunteer her time at the Boston Indian Council, an organization that provided support and services to Indians living in the city. Like Pictou, many young Indians in the 1960s left their impoverished reservation communities for the possibility of a brighter future in the nearest urban area. Some of these new city dwellers had difficulty coping, especially when they were unable to find jobs or in desperation fell victim to drug and alcohol abuse. Pictou counseled these troubled youths and, when possible, placed them in jobs or treatment programs.

When Pictou's marriage began to falter, she decided to move with her children to Bar Harbor, Maine. There her volunteer experience landed her a job with TRIBES (Teaching and Research in Bicultural Education School project). This program provided Indian dropouts with a second chance at an education. Remembering her own bitter experiences in a non-Indian school, Pictou helped develop a curriculum that aimed to instill confidence and cultural pride in the students by teaching them about Indian traditions and history.

In 1972, Pictou returned to Boston and enrolled in a program at Wheelock College. While taking classes, she worked at a day-care center in an African-American neighborhood. Impressed by her commitment to both her classroom and community work, Brandeis University offered her a full scholarship. Although, as a ninth-grade dropout, she was flattered by the offer, she declined out of fear that she could not attend school full time and also adequately support and care for her daughters.

Despite her responsibilities, Pictou found the time to become involved in the growing Indian rights movement. Largely composed of young urban Indians inspired by the African-American civil rights movement of the early 1960s, this movement advocated a renewed respect for Indian traditions and sought to make the U.S. government live up to the treaty promises it had made to Indians throughout the country. Pictou's increasing interest in activism was shared by her boyfriend Nogeeshik Aquash, a Chippewa artist from Ontario, Canada. Together, the couple traveled to Washington, D.C., in 1972 to participate in the Trail of Broken Treaties, a protest march that brought hundreds of angry young Indians to the capital. The demonstration drew national attention to their grievances with the federal government.

An even more dramatic protest took place early the next year on the Sioux's Pine Ridge Indian Reservation in South Dakota. The reservation's tribal chairman, Dick Wilson, had been accused of corruption and of ordering violent attacks on his political opponents, many of whom were elders dedicated to keeping old traditions alive. These traditionalists asked for help from the American Indian Movement (AIM), the most prominent organization in the Indian rights movement. AIM's young leaders staged an armed takeover of Wounded Knee, a site on the reservation of great symbolic importance. In 1890, Wounded Knee had witnessed the slaughter of more than 300 Sioux men, women, and children at the hands of U.S. soldiers.

When Pictou and Aquash heard of the Wounded Knee occupation, they rushed to Pine Ridge, South Dakota, to join the protest. By the time they arrived, the site was swarming with FBI agents, who were blocking all routes into the area. They hoped to force the demonstrators out by cutting off their access to supplies. To help the protesters, Pictou and Aquash spent days hiking through the hills and evading agents armed with rifles before they were able to sneak into the Indian camp with

food and medicines. The couple stayed at Wounded Knee for a month. While there, Pictou assisted fellow activist MARY BRAVE BIRD as she gave birth. In the protesters' camp, she also married Aquash. The bride wore blue jeans, but otherwise the ceremony adhered to Sioux traditions. For Anna Mae Aquash, the Wounded Knee wedding was a public declaration of her commitment to the fight for Indian rights.

The Aquashes escaped from the camp and returned to Boston after several weeks, but the occupation continued. In the end, AIM surrendered after 71 days. Although the protest had little immediate effect on the United States's Indian policy, AIM had won a clear moral victory. Through the publicity surrounding the event, the organization and its leaders succeeded in eliciting substantial public sympathy for their cause. This support for AIM outraged the FBI, which felt humiliated by the standoff. Its agents set about punishing as many of the Wounded Knee protesters as possible; eventually more than five hundred arrests were made. The FBI possibly reasoned that if AIM's leaders were tied up in litigation, the organization would fall apart.

After Wounded Knee, Anna Mae Aquash became a passionate and valuable member of the AIM leadership. She helped organize demonstrations at several reservations and worked at AIM headquarters in a number of cities. Aquash was particularly proud of her work at AIM's "survival school" in St. Paul, Minnesota. The organization's survival schools sought to raise a new generation of Indian leaders. Aquash spearheaded an effort to educate students at the St. Paul school in researching and writing history. Recognizing that most Indian history was written by non-Indians, she worked with a local historian to develop a program to teach young Indians to use sophisticated research methods so that they could tell their peoples' stories in their own words.

In spring 1975, AIM sent Aquash back to Pine Ridge. The conditions on the reservation had worsened. Chairman Dick Wilson's police force allegedly had become even more violent. During the first six months of that year, the reservation saw 18 murders and 67 serious attacks. Most of the perpetrators were never arrested.

Aquash was put in charge of eliciting support for AIM among the women at Pine Ridge, who often were put off by the brash, aggressive style of AIM's largely male leadership. Urging these women to join AIM's battles, Aquash told them about the personal sacrifices she had made in the fight for Indian rights. She gained their sympathy by explaining that in part because of her long absences from home, she and Nogeeshik Aquash had separated. Even more traumatic for her, she rarely saw her daughters because of her work. Without her consent, her ex-husband and his second wife had adopted the girls following Aquash's involvement in Wounded Knee.

On June 26, 1975, the tensions between the FBI and AIM exploded when two FBI agents were shot and killed near the town of Oglala, South Dakota. Determined to find the killers, hundreds of FBI agents descended on Pine Ridge. Suddenly, the reservation was filled with men in full military gear as helicopters rumbled overhead. Aquash had been in Cedar Rapids, Iowa, on the day of the shootings. When she returned to Pine Ridge, she kept a low profile, successfully hiding from the FBI for months. She was convinced that the FBI intended to punish her for her participation in Wounded Knee and was frightened by what agents might do to her in the paranoid atmosphere of the reservation. Aquash was also growing afraid of some of her old friends in AIM. Rumors had been circulating that she was secretly working for the FBI. She feared that if the more violent members of AIM came to believe what was said about her, she would become a target for them as well.

In September, the FBI raided a Pine Ridge home where Aquash was living. She was arrested on a weapons charge but released on bail. Afraid for her life, she chose to flee South Dakota rather than stand trial. Several months later, she was discovered in Oregon and arrested. As the police prepared to return her to the Pine Ridge authorities, she told a reporter of her terror: "If they take me back to South Dakota, I'll be murdered." Before the trial was held, she was again granted bail and again took the opportunity to run from the law. Where she went at that point is unknown. For months, she did not contact her friends or family. Their concern about her turned to panic when no one received their customary call from Aquash on Christmas.

On February 24, 1976, the huddled corpse of a young woman was found by a Pine Ridge rancher on his property. The badly decomposed body was examined by a doctor employed by the Bureau of Indian Affairs (BIA)—the agency of the U.S. government that oversees its dealings with Indian tribes. He ruled that the woman had died of exposure and on the order of the BIA had her immediately buried in an unmarked grave. Before the burial, however, the hands of the corpse were cut off and shipped to FBI headquarters in Washington, D.C. There, through the fingerprints, the body was identified as that of Anna Mae Aquash. Her grieving family demanded a second autopsy, which revealed that she had died not of exposure but of a bullet shot point-blank at the base of her skull. Her body was then reburied with traditional Sioux rites as the AIM flag—an American flag hung upside down—waved overhead. As a gesture of rage against the government's handling of the body, her relatives used axes to hack up the coffin in which the BIA had buried Aquash and then set the pieces on fire.

Who killed Anna Mae Aquash? The question sparked a fevered debate for nearly 30 years. Many Indians—including most AIM members—accused the FBI. To them, the inaccurate first autopsy and quick burial suggest a cover-up. Some have even speculated that her hands were cut off to hide evidence of her identity. For its part, the FBI maintained that a member of AIM was responsible.

The mystery surrounding Aquash's death was finally answered in 2004. On February 6, a federal jury in Rapid City, South Dakota, convicted former AIM member Arlo Looking Cloud of the crime. During the four-day trial, several AIM members testified that the organization, suspicious that Aquash was telling its secrets to the authorities, found her in Denver and forcibly took her back to Pine Ridge, where she was executed. Looking Cloud claimed that he had witnessed her murder but had no prior knowledge that she was going to be killed. Prosecutors continue to seek the extradition from Canada of John Graham, another suspect in Aquash's death.

In June 2004, the body of Anna Mae Aquash was moved to Nova Scotia, Canada. At her family's request, her remains were reburied at the Indian Brook First Nation after a traditional funeral ceremony.

Further Reading/Resources

Brand, Joanna. *The Life and Death of Anna Mae Aquash.* Toronto: James Lorimer, 1978.

Chobanian, Arthur, producer. *Incident at Oglala.* Van Nuys, Calif.: Live Home Video. VHS, 90 min., 1991.

Davey, Monica. "Member of Indian Movement Is Found Guilty in 1975 Killing." *New York Times,* 7 February 2004.

Martin, Kent, producer. "The Spirit of Annie Mae." Montreal: National Film Board of Canada. Videotape, 73 min., 2002.

Matthiessen, Peter. *In the Spirit of Crazy Horse.* New York: Viking, 1983.

Mihesuah, Devon A. "Anna Mae Pictou-Aquash: An American Activist." In *Sifters: Native American Women's Lives,* edited by Theda Perdue, 204–223. New York: Oxford University Press, 2001.

Weir, David, and Lowell Bergman. "The Killing of Anna Mae Aquash." *Rolling Stone,* 7 April 1977, pp. 51–55.

Armstrong, Jeannette
(1948–) *Okanagan novelist, educator*

The grand-niece of the novelist MOURNING DOVE, Jeannette Armstrong was the first Native woman to publish a novel in Canada. A member of the Penticton Band of the Okanagan, she was born in 1948 on the Okanagan Reserve near Penticton, British Columbia. Jeannette attended local schools but also received an education in the traditions of her people from her parents and from Okanagan elders.

After earning a diploma in fine arts from Okanagan College, Armstrong was awarded a bachelor's degree in creative writing from the University of Victoria in 1978. She then took a job as a writer and researcher at the En'Owkin Center, a cultural center operated by the Okanagan Nation. One of the center's missions was to develop educational materials for local Indian and non-Indian students about Okanagan history. While working on the project, Armstrong insisted that the material present the Okanagan's past from a Native perspective. She interviewed many elders to make sure that her facts were accurate and refused to accommodate the suggestion of non-Indian school board officials that she hire white consultants. Armstrong later defined her criteria for the work produced by the center: "[I]t's quality, and it's correct, and it's appropriate, and most of all, [it's] Indian!"

Armstrong herself wrote two books for use in middle school classrooms. *Enwhisteetkwa: Walk on Water* (1982) chronicles a year in the life of young Okanagan girl in the mid-19th century, the period in which non-Indians began to settle in Okanagan lands. *Neekna and Chemai* (1984) creates a portrait of daily life among the Okanagan before contact with whites from the perspective of two young girls. *Neekna and Chemai* and three collections of Okanagan legends Armstrong wrote for younger readers were published by the En'Owkin Center's publishing operation, Theytus Books, the first Indian-owned and -operated press in Canada.

Armstrong's best-known work, also published by Theytus, is *Slash* (1985). The novel tells the story of Tommy Kelasket, an Okanagan adolescent who becomes involved in the Indian rights movement of the late 1960s and 1970s. Nicknamed "Slash," Kelasket travels from Canada to the United States and back again, attending sit-ins and demonstrations in an attempt to come to grips with his Native identity. The Indians he encounters display a wide range of responses to oppression, from assimilation into white society to armed protest. After Slash's confusion leads him into alcoholism, he goes home to the Okanagan Reserve. Through his adventures, he becomes convinced that a return to the traditions of the past will create the best future for Indian communities. The product of two years of research, *Slash* was well received and widely read throughout Canada. In 2000, Armstrong published her second novel, *Whispering in Shadows,* which tells the story of a young Okanagan activist.

In the late 1980s, Armstrong embarked on a new ambitious project—the establishment of the first creative writing school in Canada run by and for Natives. Affiliated with the University of Victoria, the En'Owkin International School of Writing opened in 1989 with Armstrong as its director.

Throughout her career, Armstrong has received many honors. Among them was an honorary doctorate in letters, awarded to her by St. Thomas University in New Brunswick in 2000. Three years later, she was given the Buffett Award for Aboriginal Leadership, honoring her work as an author, educator, and community leader.

Further Reading

Armstrong, Jeannette. *Enwhisteetkwa: Walk on Water.* Cloverdale, Manitoba: Friesen Printers, 1982.
———. *Neekna and Chemai.* Penticton, British Columbia: Theytus Books, 1984.
———. *Slash.* Penticton, British Columbia: Theytus Books, 1985.
———. *Whispering in Shadows.* Penticton, British Columbia: Theytus Books, 2000.
Lutz, Hartmut. "Jeannette Armstrong." In *Contemporary Challenges: Conversations with Canadian Native Authors,* 13–32. Saskatoon, Saskatchewan: Fifth House, 1991.

Ashevak, Kenojuak
See KENOJUAK

Ashoona, Pitseolak
See PITSEOLAK

Awashonks (Awashunkes)
(unknown–ca. 1690)   *Wampanoag leader*

As the leader of the Saconet band of the Wampanoag, Awashonks led her people throughout one of

the turbulent eras of their history. The Saconet lived near what is now Little Compton, Rhode Island. By the mid-17th century, their ancestral lands were claimed by the English settlers of the Plymouth colony.

Awashonks was a member of an important Saconet family. But, in accordance with Wampanoag custom, she obtained her political position through her ability to persuade others to support her. She solidified her power by distributing goods among the Saconet. Even so, maintaining her leadership was a struggle. She was challenged not only by rivals within the Saconet but also by the English colonists, who increasingly wanted to exercise control over the Indians in what the English now considered their realm.

Awashonks was firmly anti-English until July 1671. Plymouth leaders called Awashonks and other Indian leaders to a meeting. If they refused to come, the English threatened to send an army to fight them. Awashonks came to the meeting and submitted to their "Articles of Agreement," in which she agreed to surrender guns and Saconet accused of inciting "trouble and disturbance of her peace and ours." She most likely reasoned that she could retain her power more easily with the English as her friends rather than her enemies.

Three years later, Awashonks had her first introduction to the Plymouth court system. There, Mammanuah, a Saconet rival who may have been her son, accused Awashonks of assault. After he had tried to sell land to English settlers, she ordered men to tie Mammanuah up and threaten him. The court found in Mammanuah's favor, possibly just to mollify the English landbuyers. But the court, probably out of respect to Awashonks, fined her a measly £5, far less than the £500 Mammanuah was demanding.

By summer 1675, the relationship between the English and the Wampanoag was more tense than ever. One Wampanoag leader, Metacom (also known as King Philip), was trying to build a military coalition to go to war against the Plymouth settlers. He sent six ambassadors to persuade Awashonks to join up. While hosting the ambassadors, she sent for Plymouth military leader Benjamin Church. Church later wrote that, after a ceremonial feast, she "told [me] that now they were engaged to fight for the English, and [I] might call forth all, or any of them at any time as [I] saw occasion to fight the enemy." In part because of aid provided by Indian leaders such as Awashonks, the English defeated Metacom's forces in King Philip's War (1675–76). After the war, Indian survivors in the region saw their lands overrun by English colonists.

In 1683, Awashonks made her final appearance in the historical record. That year, she was once again called before the Plymouth court. She was accused of helping to kill an infant born to her daughter Betty. She and Betty convinced the court the child was born dead, but Betty was found guilty of fornication. The court also reprimanded Awashonks for having had a woman whipped for announcing Betty was pregnant. The willingness of the Plymouth leaders to chastise Awashonks suggests her political fortunes had fallen since the war. While she had allied herself to the English to bolster her power, ironically their victory eroded her standing among both the English and the Saconet.

Further Reading

Plane, Ann Marie. "Putting a Face on Colonization: Factionalism and Gender Politics in the Life History of Awashunkes, the 'Squaw Sachem' of Saconet." In *Northeastern Indian Lives: 1632–1816,* edited by Robert S. Grumet, 140–165. Amherst: University of Massachusetts Press, 1996.

B

Bedard, Irene
(1967–)   *Inuit-Cree actress*

Best known for playing Native American women of the past and present, actress Irene Bedard was born on July 22, 1967, in Anchorage, Alaska. Her mother was an Inupiat Inuit, and her father was half Cree and half French Canadian. While in Alaska, he worked for the government negotiating Native land rights. When her father decided to go into business for himself, the family moved to Washington State. There, Irene worked in a succession of family businesses, including a hotel and a roller rink. She spent her free time putting on plays for her friends and family.

For college, Bedard headed east to attend the University of the Arts in Philadelphia, Pennsylvania. Studying acting, she appeared in numerous stage productions. After graduation, Bedard moved to New York City, where she cofounded the Chuka Lokali theater group.

Bedard had her big break when she was cast in the lead of the television movie *Lakota Woman: Siege at Wounded Knee* (1994). In the film, she played MARY BRAVE BIRD (also known as Mary Crow Dog), who wrote two books about her participation in the American Indian Movement (AIM) protests during the 1970s. Because of her father's involvement in Native American rights, Bedard had always been interested in American Indian issues. But playing Brave Bird heightened her awareness. As she explained, "For me, it was a major turning point in my understanding of being a Native American and it was really great." She has since founded Guardians of Sacred Lands to help protect areas of religious importance to Indian groups.

In 1994, Bedard also appeared in *Squanto: A Warrior's Tale,* playing the wife of the lead character. On the set, she married musician Deni Wilson. The couple later had a son, Quinn. Billed as Irene Bedard and Deni, they have since formed a progressive rock musical act, with Bedard singing vocals and Wilson playing guitar.

Bedard played her best-known role in *Pocahontas* (1995), an animated Disney feature. She not only provided the voice for the title character, but she also served as a model for POCAHONTAS's appearance and movements. The movie was an enormous success, and Bedard was gratified by her part in creating a popular Native American screen heroine. In one interview, she said, "Of all the Disney female characters, Pocahontas is the strongest.

13

Irene Bedard performs with Ojibwa actor Adam Beach in a scene from *Squanto: A Warrior's Tale* (1994).
(Photo by Attila Dory, © The Walt Disney Company, All Rights Reserved)

She's not waiting for her prince. . . . She is independent and strong-willed."

Since *Pocahontas,* Bedard has appeared in more than 30 films, including *Smoke Signals* (1998) and *The New World* (2005), in which she played Pocahontas's mother. She has also been featured in numerous television shows and had prominent roles in the miniseries *True Women* (1997) and *Into the West* (2005). Throughout her career, Bedard has striven to present nuanced and complex portrayals of Native American women. In 2005, she explained, "[The film industry has] been getting stronger and stronger in the ways of portraying native people in a more realistic light. . . . [A]udiences want to see more of the reality and more of the truth."

Further Reading/Resources

Irene Bedard and Deni. Available online. URL: http://www.nativevoices.net/bedard.html. Downloaded on May 7, 2006.

Schneider, Wolf. "Irene Bedard." *Cowboys and Indians.* Available online. URL: http://www.cowboysandindians.com/articles/archives/1199/bedard.html. Downloaded on June 24, 2005.

Bennett, Ramona

(1938–)   *Puyallup tribal leader, activist, educator*

"It was time for us to get a little bit rowdy," Ramona Bennett has said of the 1970s, when she served as the tribal chairperson of the Puyallup Indians. Her combative brand of activism during this turbulent period helped prevent the dissolution of her tribe.

Bennett was born in Seattle, Washington, on April 28, 1938. She was educated in public school there, but her Indian background made her feel isolated from her fellow students. In 1995, she told interviewer Jane Katz, "My values were different from those of the dominant society; I felt like the odd duck." After graduating from high school, she attended Evergreen State College in Olympia, Washington, where she earned a bachelor's degree in liberal arts. She then pursued and earned a master's degree in education from the University of Puget Sound in Tacoma, Washington. While still in school, she took volunteer jobs with several organizations dedicated to improving the lives of local Indians. Through this work, she found her true calling. As she explained to Katz, "For the first time, I really belonged."

In the 1950s, Bennett moved to the Puyallup Indian Reservation, where her mother had grown up. Located directly east of Tacoma, the small reservation was, in Bennett's words, "a frontier." The desperately poor Puyallups were living in inadequate housing and had very little access to education or health care. The few jobs available to reservation residents were in the shipping and timber industry, which tended to fire Indian workers first when lean profits led to layoffs.

Determined to improve reservation conditions, Bennett was elected to the Puyallup Tribal Council, the tribe's official governing body, in the 1960s. Her spirit and stamina made her a particularly effective advocate for the tribe in its dealings with the federal government. In 1995, she remembered her aggressive approach to demanding the attention of members of Congress: "If I couldn't get an appointment with a congressman, I'd wait outside his door for the bell to ring calling him into chambers to vote. I'd have my papers ready, and when he came out, I'd run with him." One year, Bennett took more than thirty trips to Washington, D.C. The council could not always afford round-trip plane fare, so she sometimes had to make the 3,000-mile trip home by hitchhiking.

One of the greatest problems facing the Puyallup in the late 1960s involved their right to fish in the Puyallup River. Because of the high unemployment on the reservation, many Puyallup depended on fishing for their livelihood just as their ancestors had. Non-Indian commercial fisherman, however, were also setting traps in the river. Conservationists became concerned that the fish population was in danger of extinction, largely because of the overfishing of the commercial concerns. They persuaded the state of Washington to ban the use of fishing traps in the river's waters. This law violated the 1855 Treaty of Point Elliott, which had guaranteed local Indians unrestricted use of their reservation resources.

In 1970, non-Indian law enforcement agents began to crack down on Puyallup fishers who, desperate to feed their families, ignored the ban. The agents harassed the Indians, confiscated their traps, hauled them off to jail, and even tried to run them over with their powerboats. A group of Puyallup, including Bennett, responded by setting up an armed camp on the riverbank. After a 10-week standoff, agents raided the camp and used tear gas and clubs to subdue the protesters. Bennett was assaulted and, with 59 others, taken to jail and accused of inciting a riot. If convicted, she faced a sentence of 35 years in prison.

The case made international news, and the brutal treatment of the Puyallup was denounced around the world. Under pressure from the outraged public, the U.S. Department of the Interior, which oversees reservations, examined the Indians' claims to fishing rights on the river. The morning that Bennett's trial was set to begin, the secretary of the Interior stated that the Puyallup owned the land and its resources and that the agents had been trespassing on the Indians' territory. The case against Bennett was promptly thrown out of court.

The Puyallup scored an even more far-reaching legal victory in 1974 with the landmark ruling in *United States v. State of Washington* (also known as the Boldt decision). In this case, the court found that the Indians of Washington State had a right to one-half of the fish caught in its coastal waters.

In 1972, Bennett was elected the chairperson of the Puyallup Tribal Council, making her one of the few female tribal leaders in the United States. Although traditionally women had had leadership roles in many Indian groups, she frequently had to overcome the sexist attitudes of her colleagues. At a meeting of the National Tribal Chairman's Association, she had to fight to be admitted. When finally given the chance to speak, she loudly demanded that the association devote more attention to the concerns of Indian children, who suffered most from the poor educational facilities and high mortality rates of reservations. On the Puyallup reservation, Bennett made education and health care her highest priorities.

Bennett served as tribal chairperson for eight years before rivals among the Puyallups drove her from office. She has since devoted herself to helping minority children in need. She has served as an educational administrator at the Wa-He-Lut Indian School in Olympia and as the head of the Rainbow Youth and Family Services. This organization concentrates on placing homeless minority children in foster and adoptive homes with adults of the same race. Bennett believes that such an environment provides the best opportunity for troubled youths to develop pride in themselves and their heritage. The mother of five biological and two adopted children, she has often opened her own house to children with nowhere else to go. In honor of her work with children and families, the Native Action Network gave Bennett the Enduring Spirit Award in 2003.

Bennett now sees the revival of the Indian tradition of living in extended families as the best means of improving life for young and old. Although she has no regrets about her past as a militant, she explained to Katz how her ideas about political and social reform have changed with the times: "I used to believe that if we can't get justice, we'll take revenge. But now I know if you walk around looking backwards, you'll constantly slam into things. Now that our tribe is intact, we have the potential to heal."

Further Reading

Bennett, Ramona. "The Puyallup Tribe Rose up from the Ashes." In *Messengers of the Wind: Native American Women Tell Their Life Stories,* edited by Jane Katz, 147–165. New York: Ballantine Books, 1995.
Merryman, Kathleen. "Mother to All Who Need One." *Tacoma Morning News Tribune,* 14 May 1995, SL3.

Big Crow, SuAnne
(1974–1992)   *Lakota Sioux athlete*

"I had thought that Oglala [Lakota Sioux] heroes existed mostly in the past," wrote journalist Ian Frazier in 2000. "But a true Oglala hero appeared in the late 1980s, in suffering Pine Ridge, right under everyone's nose, while the rest of the world was looking the other way: SuAnne Big Crow."

The descendant of a noted Lakota chief and medicine man, SuAnne Big Crow was born on March 15, 1974. She and her two sisters were raised on the Pine Ridge Indian Reservation in South Dakota. Her mother was strict with the girls. One of the few extracurricular activities she would let them participate in was sports. Big Crow emerged as a talented and determined athlete. She ran cross-country and played softball and volleyball. But her favorite sport was basketball. As in many Western reservation communities, high school basketball games were enormously popular on Pine Ridge.

Practicing as much as four hours a day, Big Crow first made the Pine Ridge girls' team in eighth grade. She quickly emerged as a star among the Lady Thorpes, whose name honored the great Sauk and Fox athlete Jim Thorpe. Big Crow made state records for points scored during a single game (67) and for points scored during a season (763).

Big Crow often lectured younger students about the dangers of drugs and alcohol. She also tried to inspire them to succeed despite the anti-Indian discrimination they faced. In one talk, she challenged her audience to "work hard, be dedicated, develop a thick skin, learn to accept criticism but most of all, do it yourself." Big Crow emphasized her own pride in her heritage and her love of Pine Ridge. She once explained to a group of eighth-grade students, "Many people believe that you must leave the reservation in order to have a better life, but I don't believe that. This is my home. I love it. We just need to work together to make this a more prosperous place."

Big Crow backed up her words with action. One such instance occurred during an away game in the non-Indian town of Lead in fall 1988. The Lady Thorpes were waiting to run on the court when they heard the crowd making war whoops and the band playing a faux-Indian drum song, all in an effort to humiliate Big Crow and her Indian teammates. The girls were shaken, and Doni De Cory, a senior who was supposed to lead them onto the court, was too upset to do it. Big Crow, just a freshman at the time, volunteered to take her place.

Big Crow ran into the gym, filled with the noise of drumming and jeers, and stopped dead in center court. She then removed her warm-up jacket and began performing the traditional Lakota shawl dance, using her jacket in the place of a shawl. As she danced, she sang a Lakota song. The audience fell silent. When she finished, she grabbed a ball, ran a lap around the court, and dunked the ball into a goal. The crowd cheered.

Big Crow's gentle act of defiance made her a legend among the Pine Ridge Lakota, who told the story again and again. But it also eased the tensions between the people of Pine Ridge and Lead. As De Cory later explained, "It was funny, but after that game the relationship between Lead and us was tremendous. When we played Lead again, the games were really good, and we got to know some of the girls on the team. . . . What SuAnne did made a lasting impression and changed the whole situation with us and Lead. We found out there are some really good people in Lead."

Toward the end of her senior year, Big Crow was fielding offers of basketball scholarships from several colleges, when she was named as a finalist in South Dakota's Miss Basketball contest. On February 9, 1992, while en route to attend the Miss Basketball banquet, she fell asleep at the wheel. Big Crow was killed after her car crashed.

The news of her death prompted an outpouring of grief in Pine Ridge and beyond. The South Dakota state senate observed a moment of silence to commemorate her life. On Pine Ridge, her mother spearheaded a campaign to establish the SuAnne Big Crow Boys and Girls Club, which includes the Incentive Room—a display of Big Crow's many trophies, awards, and citations meant to inspire young Lakota. Each year, the National Education Association presents an award in her honor to a student, who like SuAnne Big Crow, has promoted "through leadership in specific activities and actions, an appreciation for diversity and the elimination of bigotry and prejudice."

Further Reading/Resources

Frazier, Ian. *On the Rez.* New York: Farrar, Straus & Giroux, 2000.

The Visions of SuAnne Big Crow. Available online. URL: http://www.suannebigcrow.org. Downloaded on May 3, 2006.

Blackjack, Ada
(1898–1983)   *Inuit exploration survivor*

Hailed by the press as the female Robinson Crusoe, Ada Blackjack became famous as the sole survivor of a disastrous Arctic exploration. Born Ada Delutuk on May 10, 1898, in Solomon, Alaska, she married a man named Jack Blackjack. They had one son, Bennett, before Jack died in a drowning accident. Bennett suffered from tuberculosis and, without a husband, Ada had no way of paying for his treatment.

Desperate and destitute, Ada Blackjack signed up for a bizarre adventure. Vilhjalmur Stefansson, a noted author and explorer, was organizing an expedition to Wrangel Island, located 85 miles off the coast of Siberia. By sending a group to colonize the deserted island, he hoped to reclaim the area, then considered part of Russia, for Great Britain. Stefansson recruited four young white men for the adventure. To work for them on the island, he also hired several Inuit families and individuals, including Blackjack.

The group was set to leave on the *Silver Wave* on September 9, 1921, but of the Inuit hired, only Blackjack showed up. At first, she refused to get on the boat, but she was assured they would make a stop along the way to pick up other Inuit employees. The ship, never making the promised stop, arrived on the island seven days later. Blackjack considered returning with the ship. "I thought at first I would turn back," she later explained, "but I decided it wouldn't be fair to the boys."

The expedition was supposed to last two years, but they only brought supplies for six months. Stefansson was sure his men would be able to live off the land. Although they were not experienced hunters, at first they were able to kill enough polar bears, seals, geese, and ducks to supplement their food stores as they waited for a ship with fresh supplies, scheduled to arrive in summer 1922. But blocked from the island by ice, the ship never came.

By fall, the group was starving. Two men decided to set out for Siberia for help. Within a couple weeks, they were back. Probably sick with scurvy, one man, Lorne Knight, had become too ill to continue.

In January 1923, three of the men made another attempt, leaving Blackjack and Knight behind. According to Blackjack, "They promised that they would come back after they got to Nome, with a ship, and if they couldn't get there with a ship they would come over with a dog team next winter. They left with a team of five dogs and a big sled of supplies." The three men were never heard from again.

With Knight bedridden, Blackjack was solely responsible for their survival. She had never hunted before or even shot a gun. But out of necessity she learned quickly. Blackjack became adept at hunting small game and kept herself and Knight alive with the stews she cooked. At the same time, she nursed Knight, trying her best to keep him com-

Ada Blackjack was photographed with four other members of the Wrangel Island expedition in 1922.
(Reproduced from *The Adventure of Wrangel Island* [1925])

fortable and reading the Bible to soothe him. Despite her efforts, Knight died in the spring. She had to chip through the ice to make a grave to bury him.

For months, Blackjack was alone on the island. In addition to finding food, she also struggled to protect herself from predators. She once recalled her terror at stumbling upon a polar bear: "I turned and ran just as hard as I could until I got to my tent. I was just about ready to faint when I got there, too."

On August 19, 1923, her ordeal ended, when a ship was finally able to make its way to the island. After she arrived safely in Nome, she was celebrated in newspapers, although some suggested she bore the blame for Knight's death. The notoriety, however, did little to help her and her family. She married again and had another son, Billy, before getting a divorce. For the rest of her life, she struggled to earn enough to care for her children. Blackjack died in a nursing home on May 29, 1983.

Although she had been hailed as a hero, Blackjack saw herself merely as a survivor. When once asked if she considered herself brave, she replied, "I don't know about that. But I would never give up hope while I'm still alive."

Further Reading

Niven, Jennifer. *Ada Blackjack: A True Story of Survival in the Arctic.* New York: Hyperion, 2003.

Stefansson, Vilhjalmur. *The Adventure of Wrangel Island.* New York: Macmillan, 1925.

Blue Legs, Alice New Holy
(1925–)   *Lakota quillworker*

Almost single-handedly, Alice New Holy Blue Legs has resurrected the dying art of Lakota Sioux quillwork. She was born Alice New Holy in 1925 on the Pine Ridge Indian Reservation near Oglala, South Dakota. After graduating from Oglala Community School, she married Emil Blue Legs. The couple have five daughters.

When Alice Blue Legs was a girl, her mother and grandmother showed her how to decorate cloth and animal skins using dyed porcupine quills. Only after both had died did she realize that few other people knew how to make quillwork designs. As she explained in a 1989 interview, "I never really thought about it being a lost art until it was pointed out to me that my family was one of the few on this reservation—for that matter, on any reservation—still doing it." A traditional Lakota art, quillwork had been dying out ever since non-Indian traders introduced the Lakota to glass beads. According to Blue Legs, "The new trade beads were so much easier to work with, and since they did not require the patience and the artistic talent that quillwork requires, everybody soon switched to using the beads."

Blue Legs decided to save the art of quillwork. She asked for her father's help. He told her what he could remember about how it was done but refused to show her how to handle the quills because he regarded quilling as women's work. Through trial and error, Blue Legs eventually taught herself to collect the quills, dye them using natural minerals, and dry and flatten them. Once the quills were painstakingly prepared, she invisibly sewed them onto skin or cloth using sinew or thread, then folded or wove them to create small beadlike blocks. She used the quills to create geometric and organic designs, just as quill artists of the past had done. Blue Legs did her work at night, after her children were asleep and the house was quiet.

Blue Legs's husband, Emil, also became a skilled quillworker. He is known for his hair roaches, which are often worn by dancers at Indian powwows. Blue Legs passed her knowledge of quillwork onto her daughters as well. For many years, she also shared her art with non-Indians at demonstrations held at schools and museums around the country.

In 1985, Blue Legs was named an Outstanding Folk Artist by the National Endowment for the Arts. The award honored her role in preserving "a singularly North American Indian craft practiced by no other people in the world." The same year, she appeared in the documentary *Lakota Quill-work—Art and Legend.*

Despite her success and recognition, Blue Legs still lives on Pine Ridge in the log house in which she was born. By selling her work, however, she has been able to afford to wire the house for electricity—a great help during those long nights she spends perfecting her art.

Further Reading/Resource

Giago, Tim, Jr. "Lakota Quillwork: Alice New Holy Blue Legs." *Native Peoples* 3 (Fall 1989): 30–34.

Nauman, H. Jane, producer. *Lakota Quillwork—Art and Legend.* Rapid City, S.Dak.: Nauman Productions.Videotape, 27 min., 1985.

Bonnin, Gertrude Simmons (Zitkala-Ša)
(1876–1938)   *Nakota Sioux activist, short story writer, essayist*

Gertrude Simmons Bonnin had enormous success in two careers. Before she was 30, she had established herself as an important writer of both essays and fiction. Through her literary works, she became one of the first American Indians to write about her life without the aid of a non-Indian editor or interpreter. During the second half of her life, she devoted herself to reforming the U.S. government's attitudes toward Indians. On this front, her efforts helped reverse many federal policies that had impoverished reservation communities in the late 19th century.

Gertrude Bonnin was born on February 22, 1876, on the Yankton Sioux Indian Reservation in present-day South Dakota. Her mother, Tate I Yohin Win (also called Ellen), was a Nakota Sioux (also known as Yankton Sioux); her father was a white man who abandoned his family before Gertrude's birth. Tate I Yohin Win soon married John Haysting Simmons, who gave his young stepdaughter his surname.

In her early girlhood, Gertrude was raised according to the traditions of the Nakota Sioux. She later fondly remembered listening to tribal storytellers, who recited old tales that the Nakota had passed down orally for centuries. When she was eight years old, her childhood was interrupted by the arrival of Quaker missionaries on the reservation. They tried to persuade Sioux parents to send their children to a boarding school for Indians that was operated by the Quaker church. Like many other Christian reformers in the 19th century, these Quakers believed that Indian children should learn the English language and non-Indian customs so that as adults they would be well prepared to live among whites.

Many Indian parents wanted their children to learn the ways of their own people and therefore resisted these reformers. Among them was Tate I Yohin Win, who did not want Gertrude to attend a school operated by whites. According to Bonnin, she made the decision to attend the Quaker school over her mother's objections. Nearly 20 years later, Bonnin recorded Tate I Yohin Win's words of warning as she prepared to leave with the missionaries: "[They have] filled your ears with the white man's lies. Don't believe a word they say! Their words are sweet, but, my child, their deeds are bitter. You will cry for me, but they will not soothe you." Fresh in Tate I Yohin Win's memory were the many years of warfare between the Sioux and the United States. With the Indians' military defeat, Americans had taken over most of their tribal territory, leaving many Sioux furious and bitter.

Gertrude soon saw the truth of her mother's words. She was taken by train to White's Indiana Manual Labor Institute in Wabash, Indiana. The teachers at the school were harsh disciplinarians and regularly beat their students. They insisted that the children speak English and punished anyone who broke their rule. Gertrude only knew Sioux, so she had no way to communicate. Silent and lonely, the girl at first found attending boarding school a miserable experience. In time, however, she gradually learned English and became a good student.

After three years at the Quaker school, Gertrude was allowed to return home. To her discomfort, she discovered that her teachers had at least in part achieved their goals. On the reservation, she found that her education in white ways made her feel out of place in Indian society. Yet she realized that she would feel no more comfortable living with whites, who regarded her as an inferior despite her non-Indian manners.

An outcast among both whites and Indians, Gertrude Simmons retreated to the familiar world of the boarding school. Disregarding the pleas of her mother, she returned to Wabash for three years. She then enrolled at Earlham College in Richmond, Indiana, where she studied to be a teacher. At Earlham, Simmons developed into a skilled orator. She was chosen to represent the college at a statewide oratory competition, where students from other schools leveled racial slurs at her. Ignoring their taunts, she got her revenge by delivering the winning speech.

After graduating in 1897, Simmons was invited to join the teaching staff of the Carlisle Industrial Boarding School in Pennsylvania. Founded by Colonel Richard Henry Pratt, the prestigious school was a model for Indian schools throughout the United States. Simmons spent only a year and a half at the job. She was unhappy with Pratt's ideas about Indian education. He believed that Indians should be trained to work as farmers or as menial laborers, but Simmons felt this approach was too limiting. She thought Indians should also be taught academic subjects just as white students were.

After leaving Carlisle, Simmons attended the New England Conservatory of Music in Boston, Massachusetts. There Simmons refined her already considerable talent at playing the violin. Following a year's study, she joined the Carlisle Indian Band on a tour of Europe.

While living in Boston, Simmons also became a successful writer of short stories and essays, which she published under the pseudonym Zitkala-Ša ("red bird" in the Sioux language). Several of her pieces appeared in national magazines, including *Harper's* and the *Atlantic Monthly.* Her favorite subject was one she knew well: the discomfort educated Indians felt in both the Indian and the white

world. Even though she had chosen to continue her schooling, her essays questioned the educational theories of white reformers and accused many of them of hypocrisy. In a piece titled "Why I Am a Pagan" (1902), she explained her own rejection of Christianity despite her teachers' attempts to convert her: "I prefer to their dogma my excursions into the natural gardens where the voice of the Great Spirit is heard in the twittering of birds, the rippling of mighty waters, and the sweet breathing of flowers. If this is Paganism, then at present, at least, I am a Pagan."

Impressed by her enthusiastic readership among cultivated whites, a Boston publisher asked Simmons to write a collection of the Nakota Sioux stories she had heard as a child. Simmons was eager to take on the assignment. She feared that many traditions among her people, as well as among other Indian groups, were in danger of being forgotten. Reservations were run by U.S. government employees, most of whom encouraged and sometimes forced Indians to give up their ways and adopt white customs. By translating her tribe's ancient stories into English and publishing them in book form, she hoped to preserve them for generations to come. Published in the fall of 1901, Bonnin's *Old Indian Legends* was illustrated by Winnebago Indian artist Angel DeCora, who several years later would become a well-respected art teacher at the Carlisle boarding school.

To work on *Old Indian Legends,* Simmons traveled to the Yankton reservation. Her return home put a strain on her relationship with Carlos Montezuma, a Yavapai Indian scholar and physician whom she had met at Carlisle. After a stormy courtship, the two had become engaged, but in August 1901, Simmons broke it off. Both were passionate about working to better the lives of Indian people, but they disagreed violently about how to accomplish their goals. He supported the vocational education Carlisle provided, while she wanted to improve reservation schools and help preserve Indian ways. After he refused to work alongside her on the reservation, she wrote him angrily, "Perhaps the Indians are not human enough to waste your skill upon! Stay in Chicago. Do! I consider my plan a more direct path of my high ideas." Even after the breakup, Simmons and Montezuma remained friends; for decades, their letters to one another kept up their lively, often heated debates about Indian policy.

In 1901, Simmons met Richard T. Bonnin, a Nakota Sioux who worked on the Yankton reservation for the Bureau of Indian Affairs (BIA)—the U.S. government agency that oversaw all official dealings with Indians. Simmons and Bonnin were married the next year and had a child, Richard O. Bonnin, in 1903. The family moved to the Uintah and Ouray Reservation in Utah, where Gertrude and Richard both joined the BIA's staff. For the

This photograph of Gertrude Simmons Bonnin appeared on the frontispiece of *American Indian Stories*.
(Reproduced from *American Indian Stories* [1921; reprinted by the University of Nebraska Press, 1985])

next 13 years, Gertrude Bonnin worked as a clerk and briefly as a teacher. During this time, she largely gave up her writing career, although she did coauthor an opera titled *Sundance* (1913) with non-Indian composer William Hanson. Bonnin shared with Hanson her knowledge of the Plains Indian ritual of the Sun Dance and Indian legends. She also familiarized him with Sioux music by playing traditional songs for him on her violin.

While in Utah, Bonnin grew increasingly disturbed by the poverty and deteriorating living conditions she witnessed on reservations. She shared her alarm in correspondence with a group of educated Indians who in 1911 formed the Society of American Indians. Among the founders were Carlos Montezuma and Iroquois activist MINNIE KELLOGG. This organization supported a variety of Indian causes and took a pan-Indian approach to promoting reforms. Pan-Indianism emphasized the concerns and problems experienced by all Indians, rather than those affecting only individual tribes. The society called for the end of the BIA, whose policies, it maintained, had done Indians far more harm than good. It also advocated that the U.S. government grant full citizenship to all Indian people. In the early 20th century, only some Indians, mostly landowners, were permitted to become U.S. citizens.

In 1916, Gertrude Bonnin was elected secretary of the Society of American Indians. She and her husband moved to Washington, D.C., so that she could lobby for Indian causes with the nation's lawmakers. In addition to drafting the society's correspondence with the BIA, she served as the editor of the society's journal *American Indian Magazine* in 1918 and 1919. Bonnin resigned from the society in 1920. She may have left in protest over pressure from the other leaders to tone down her emotional editorials in the society's magazine. She may also have wanted to show support for her husband, who had staged an unsuccessful campaign for the presidency of the society.

The next year, Bonnin prepared a collection of the autobiographical essays and short stories that she had written in the early 1900s. Her work resulted in the publication of her second book, *American Indian Stories* (1921).

Throughout the 1920s, Bonnin continued to work for Indian policy reforms with several national organizations, including the General Federation of Women's Clubs. This group united women's clubs throughout the country. Their members were often wealthy, socially prominent women seeking to devote their time and money to worthy causes. Employing the oratorical skills she had honed in college, Bonnin frequently lectured these influential women about Indian issues, usually while wearing a buckskin costume to add some drama to her presentations. While involved with the federation, Bonnin worked closely with Roberta Campbell Lawson, a Delaware Indian who later became the organization's president.

In 1921, Bonnin persuaded the leadership of the General Federation of Women's Clubs to form the Indian Welfare Committee. With the help of the Indian Rights Association—another organization with which Bonnin was associated—the committee studied the living conditions on reservations and various injustices committed by the U.S. government against Indian peoples. The committee's research pressured the government to begin its own investigation. The United States hired an independent research firm to study the BIA and Indian reservations. The conclusions of the two-year study were published in 1928 as *Problems of Indian Administration,* popularly known as the Meriam Report, after its editor, Lewis Meriam. The report was highly critical of the BIA and advocated many reforms, such as hiring more Indian employees and spending more funds on Indian education and health, that Bonnin had long endorsed. The Meriam Report led to many important changes in the BIA and its policies in the 1930s.

Bonnin also worked with the Indian Rights Association to investigate the theft of Indian lands in Oklahoma. During the 1920s, oil was discovered on the property of a large number of Indian landowners. Bonnin and other investigators found that many of these Indians had been swindled out

of their land by non-Indian con men. In some cases, the land thieves had murdered Indians in order to gain control of the oil-rich tracts. In 1924, she coauthored an exposé of these crimes entitled *Oklahoma's Poor Rich Indians, an Orgy of Graft and Exploitation of the Five Civilized Tribes, Legalized Robbery.*

Bonnin and her husband helped found a new Indian rights organization, the National Council of American Indians, in 1926. As its president, she stated that the council's wide-reaching goals were to "create increased interest in behalf of the Indians, and secure for them added recognition of their personal and property rights." She became a primary advocate for self-determination—the idea that Indians, not the government, should determine the policies that would affect the social and economic life of Indian communities. Bonnin tried to persuade tribes that they could become self-governing, and thus live entirely free of the BIA, only if their children received better educations. Her message was greeted with limited enthusiasm on most reservations. When in 1938 she died of kidney disease at the age of 61, the National Council of American Indians died with her.

During her lifetime, Gertrude Simmons Bonnin witnessed many reforms in Indian policy that came about in part because of her support. In 1924, all Indians were made U.S. citizens. In 1934, the Indian Reorganization Act (IRA) increased government funding for Indian health care and for reservation schools operated with input by Indian parents. The IRA also allowed tribes to create their own governments and to maintain control over funds for the economic development of reservations. These reforms helped many Indians, but they did not completely solve the problems Bonnin identified. Today many tribes suffer from inadequate health care, limited educational opportunities, and bitter poverty. But as one of the most successful Indian reformers of the 20th century, Bonnin and her career stand as evidence to present and future reformers of the difference one informed and impassioned voice can make.

Further Reading

Bonnin, Gertrude [Zitkala-Ša]. *American Indian Stories.* 1921. Reprint. Bison Books, 2003.

———. *Dreams and Thunder: Stories, Poems, and the Sun Dance Opera.* Lincoln: University of Nebraska Press, 2001.

———. *Old Indian Legends.* 1901. Reprint. Lincoln: University of Nebraska Press, 1985.

Fisher, Dexter. "Zitkala Sa: The Evolution of a Writer." *American Indian Quarterly* 5 (August 1979): 229–238.

Johnson, David L., and Raymond Wilson. "Gertrude Simmons Bonnin, 1976–1938: 'Americanize the First American.'" *American Indian Quarterly* 12 (Winter 1988): 27–40.

Rappaport, Doreen. *The Flight of Red Bird: The Life of Zitkala-Sa.* New York: Dial Books, 1997.

Welch, Deborah. "Gertrude Simmons Bonnin (Zitkala-Ša)." In *The New Warriors,* edited by R. David Edmunds, 35–54. Lincoln: University of Nebraska Press, 2001.

Bosomworth, Mary

See Musgrove, Mary

Brant, Beth

(1941–   ) *Mohawk short story writer, poet, essayist*

"I like to think I am continuing the long journey of being a storyteller that my people first began," Mohawk writer Beth Brant has explained. Born on May 6, 1941, Brant was raised in Melvindale, a suburb of Detroit, Michigan. She and her parents lived with her paternal grandparents, who had moved to the city in search of better job opportunities. However, Beth maintained close ties to her Mohawk relatives through her family's frequent visits to the Tyindenaga Reserve in Ontario, Canada. Through her father's line, Brant traces her ancestry to the distinguished 18th-century Mohawk chief Joseph Brant and his politically powerful sister, Molly Brant.

At 17, Beth Brant left high school without a diploma to get married. She had three daughters before her unhappy marriage ended in divorce. To make a living for herself and her children, Brant worked as a cleaning woman and at other menial jobs.

Brant's life suddenly changed in 1981. On vacation, she was driving through the Mohawk Valley when a bald eagle swooped out of the sky and in front of her car. The eagle, Brant believed, had told her that she must devote herself to writing. Since that time she has produced a large body of short stories, poems, and essays, many of which deal with the struggles of people living outside of mainstream society. Brant is openly lesbian, and her work frequently discusses issues of concern to lesbians and gays as well as to Native American women.

Brant has published two volumes that combine short stories and poetry—*Mohawk Trail* (1985) and *Food and Spirits* (1993). The collections include bittersweet autobiographical tales of her youth, retellings of old Indian legends, and stories of the challenges Native Americans face in the contemporary world. Brant has also edited a highly regarded anthology, *A Gathering of Spirit* (1988). The first collection of literature and art by Native American women, *Gathering* features the work both of established authors and of writers who have often been ignored by the publishing industry. To ensure that anthology included this variety of voices, Brant solicited contributions by running advertisements in tribal newspapers and prison publications.

Brant is equally well known for her essays, which have appeared in many journals and magazines. One of her most notable nonfiction works is "Grandmothers of a New World," in which she reexamines the lives and motives of notable Native American women of the colonial era, such as Pocahontas and Nancy Ward. Some of her essays have been collected in *Writing as Witness* (1994). She has also edited *I'll Sing 'Til the Day I Die* (1995), a compilation of transcribed conversations she had with elders on the Tyindenaga Reserve.

In addition to her career as a writer, Brant has lectured widely at universities throughout the United States and Canada and has organized writers' workshops for Native American women, prisoners, and high school students. To further support the work of Indian women writers, she cofounded an organization named Turtle Grandmother, which maintains a research database of published and unpublished manuscripts by Native women. Brant is also an AIDS activist. Through workshops, she has promoted AIDS prevention in numerous Indian communities.

Further Reading

Brant, Beth. *Food and Spirits: Stories.* Ithaca, N.Y.: Firebrand Books, 1993.
———, ed. *A Gathering of Spirit: A Collection by North American Women.* Ithaca, N.Y.: Firebrand Books, 1988.
———. *Mohawk Trail.* Ithaca, N.Y.: Firebrand Books, 1985.

Brant, Molly (Mary Brant; Mary Degonwadonti)
(1736–1796) *Mohawk tribal leader*

The sister of Mohawk chief Joseph Brant, Molly Brant was perhaps the most politically powerful Native American woman during the late 18th century. During this period, the Iroquois Confederacy (which included the Mohawk, Cayuga, Oneida, Onondaga, Seneca, and Tuscarora tribes) lost much of its lands to European colonists, who also drew the Mohawk into their bloody wars with one another. Through her cunning and knowledge of the white world, Brant worked to save her people from ruin by these destructive outside forces.

Born in 1736 in Canajoharie, a village on the Mohawk River in what is now eastern New York State, Molly Brant was christened with the name Mary Degonwadonti. Like many Mohawk of the period, her parents, Peter and Margaret, had been converted to Christianity by Anglican missionaries. Seven years later the couple had a son, Joseph. Soon after Joseph's birth, Peter died, leaving Margaret alone to provide for their children. In the past, a Mohawk widow in need could rely on relatives and friends for gifts of food and other necessities. However, following the arrival of whites in their lands, Mohawk could no longer afford to be

Molly Brant was pictured on a 1986 Canadian postage stamp.
(© Canada Post Corporation [1986], Reproduced with Permission)

as generous as they traditionally had been. As whites took over their territory, the tribe had difficulty growing enough crops and hunting enough wild game to feed themselves.

Desperate to support her family, Margaret married Nikaus Brant, who was probably of mixed Mohawk and Dutch ancestry. Brant had adopted many of the customs of whites, including living in a single-family, wood frame house and wearing a cloth shirt and pants instead of the Mohawk's traditional buckskin garments. Because of his influence, Molly and Joseph became familiar with the ways of the British colonists who had claimed Iroquois lands for themselves. Nikaus may also have sent Molly to the English school at Canajoharie. During her childhood, she definitely learned there or elsewhere to understand and write the English language.

Among Nikaus Brant's friends was William Johnson, a charismatic Irishman who had come to Mohawk territory at about the time that Molly was born. Eager to make his fortune as a trader, Johnson had gained the confidence of the Mohawk by learning their language and buying their wares at fair prices. Because of Johnson's friendly relationship with the Indians, the British government appointed him superintendent of Indian affairs in 1755. In this official post, he was charged with overseeing trade and with gaining and maintaining allegiances between the English and the Indians.

Legend has it that Johnson fell in love with Molly when at 17 she was challenged to compete in a riding competition between Indian men and British soldiers. This romantic story maintains that Johnson was overwhelmed by the sight of the plucky Molly fearlessly jumping onto the back of a horse ridden by an officer as the animal galloped by. In truth, however, Johnson was a family friend and had probably known Molly for many years. Most likely shortly before or after the death of his first wife Catherine Weissenberg, Brant became Johnson's companion. Although scholars debate whether the couple was ever wed, they probably were married in a Mohawk ceremony and definitely were considered husband and wife by both their Indian and white neighbors. During their many years together, Brant bore either eight or nine children.

There is little doubt that Johnson had great affection and regard for Brant. But he may have married her at least in part for political reasons. His association with her earned him further respect among the Mohawk. As one observer noted, Molly had considerable sway among her people: "One word from her [was] more taken notice of by the [Iroquois] than a thousand from any white man without exception."

Being Johnson's wife, in turn, gave Brant more influence than she otherwise might have had. In traditional Iroquois society, women enjoyed a good deal of economic and political power. Women owned the farmland and the crops it produced. As a consequence, they were in control of most of the food supply, which they could dole out as they saw

fit, thus making men hesitant to discount their wishes for fear of being left hungry. Although women could not serve as sachems (chiefs), they could place a man in office and, if necessary, remove a sachem from his post. Therefore, no sachem could afford to rule without considering the opinions of the women of the tribe. During Brant's childhood, however, the power of Iroquois women was eroding. In order to keep control of their lands, the Iroquois felt an intense pressure to adjust to the presence of non-Indians in their territory. Increasingly, this meant taking on non-Indian ways. Because women in white society at the time had far fewer rights, adopting white customs for Iroquois women usually meant giving up much of the authority they held within their tribes.

Brant had had a small taste of the joys of leadership when, as an 18-year-old, she was chosen to accompany a delegation of elders to Philadelphia, Pennsylvania, where they talked with British officials about various pressing land issues. Sending her on this trip was probably an indication that influential Iroquois were training her for a behind-the-scenes leadership role befitting an impressive young woman. But Brant could see that as a woman, her opportunities to be a traditional tribal leader were rapidly evaporating. Instead she chose to take a different route to power by becoming the wife of a wealthy white man. In their lush mansion, named Johnson Hall, she left the housework to their servants and black slaves. She concentrated on playing hostess to Johnson's many guests and business associates—a role she filled with extraordinary charm and aplomb. She also managed the affairs of their estate. When Johnson was traveling, this job sometimes included taking over his official business as superintendent.

In order to maintain her influence among the Mohawk, Brant also took full advantage of Johnson's wealth. Because of her status as his wife, local merchants gave her unlimited credit, which she used to purchase food and goods for needy Mohawks, possibly without her husband's knowledge. In Iroquois society, the rich gained great respect by redistributing their wealth among the poor. By bestowing gifts on impoverished Mohawks,

Brant showed herself to be a good Iroquois while at the same time ensuring that a large segment of her people were indebted to her.

In 1774, Johnson died, and Johnson Hall became the property of his children from his first marriage. Brant moved back to Canajoharie, taking with her a wide array of luxury goods, including 500 pieces of silver jewelry and a white formal gown. There she established herself as a trader, but she financed most of her lavish entertaining by borrowing from merchants.

Long-growing conflicts between English colonists in North America and the British government finally erupted into violence in 1775. The Iroquois were divided on the question of whom to support during the ensuing American Revolution (1775–83). Most of the Mohawk favored remaining neutral, but Brant—perhaps out of loyalty to Johnson, perhaps out of personal conviction—was a vehement supporter of the British. She housed Loyalists who were fighting for the British cause and provided them with arms and ammunition. She spied on rebel American troops and reported to British soldiers about their whereabouts. She also exhorted the Iroquois youths to join the British troops, as her brother Joseph had done. Because of her position among the Iroquois, the Americans saw her as a substantial threat. An aide of the American general George Washington wrote that on meeting her in 1776, she displayed her characteristic charm by "salut[ing] us with an air of ease and politeness" but warned that "the Indians pay her great respect and I am afraid her influence will give us some trouble." Because of Brant's allegiance to the enemy, a band of American soldiers and their Oneida allies descended on her house—trashing her furniture, robbing her of treasured goods, and humiliating her before she was able to flee to the village of Onondaga. There, in 1777, she addressed a meeting of the Iroquois Council, in which she chastised the confederacy's elders for not providing more support to their old British friends. For a time, she moved to the British-held Fort Niagara, but in 1779, she told the officials there that she wanted to relocate to land held by her Seneca and Cayuga relatives. Knowing her value to

them in soliciting Iroquois support for their cause, the British government instructed Guy Johnson—her former husband's nephew and the new superintendent of Indian affairs—to make her trip as comfortable as possible and to "give her such Presents as [he thought might] be necessary" to keep her well disposed to the British.

After the war ended with a British defeat, Brant, like many Mohawk Loyalists, moved to British-held Canada. She established a home in Kingston, Ontario, near those of three of her daughters and largely retired from public life. In acknowledgment of her unflagging support, the British government paid her more than £1,200 to reimburse her for property she lost during the war and gave her a pension of £100 a year. These funds, in addition to a substantial inheritance she had received following Johnson's death, allowed her to live her final years in comfort. Before her death on April 16, 1796, Brant saw her daughters marry into some of the most elite families of Canada.

Further Reading

Bolton, John, and Claire Wilson. *Joseph Brant: Mohawk Chief.* New York: Chelsea House, 1992.
Carson, James Taylor. "Molly Brant: From Clan Mother to Loyalist Chief." In *Sifters: Native American Women's Lives,* edited by Theda Perdue, 48–59. New York: Oxford University Press, 2001.
Green, Gretchen. "Molly Brant, Catherine Brant, and Their Daughters: A Study of Colonial Acculturation." *Ontario History* 81 (September 1989): 235–250.
Hamilton, Milton W. "Brant, Mary." In *Notable American Women: 1607–1950,* edited by Edward T. James, 229–230. Cambridge, Mass.: Belknap Press, 1971.
Thomas, Earle. *The Three Faces of Molly Brant: A Biography.* Kingston, Ontario: Quarry Press, 1996.

Brave Bird, Mary (Mary Crow Dog, Ohitika Win)
(1953–) *Lakota Sioux activist, autobiographer*

"I am a woman of the Red Nation, a Sioux woman. That is not easy," writes Mary Brave Bird at the beginning of *Lakota Woman* (1990), her autobiographical account of her activism during the Indian rights movement of the early 1970s. In this book and its sequel *Ohitika Woman* (1993), Brave Bird uses the story of her life to illustrate the struggles and challenges reservation women face in contemporary America.

Born in 1953, Mary Brave Bird was reared on the Rosebud Reservation in South Dakota. Her white father abandoned Mary and her mother soon after she was born. Although her mother, Emily Brave Bird, was descended from one of the most distinguished Lakota Sioux families on Rosebud, she did not want her daughter to learn the language or traditions of the Sioux for fear that they would leave the girl ill-equipped for dealing with non-Indians outside the reservation.

Because Emily had to work to feed her family, Mary was raised largely by her grandparents. They, too, were hesitant to teach their granddaughter about Indian ways, but from the behavior and beliefs of these elders Mary gleaned much about the traditional Sioux world. She also learned firsthand about the desperate poverty in which many reservation Sioux lived. She, her older sister Barbara, and her grandparents shared a one-room shack with no heat, electricity, or plumbing and subsisted largely on the meat of wild game animals her grandfather hunted.

When Mary was five, she was sent to St. Francis, a Catholic Indian boarding school that her grandmother and mother had also attended. In *Lakota Woman,* Brave Bird describes the horror of being left at the school "like a small creature from another world, helpless, defenseless, bewildered, trying desperately and instinctively to survive." According to Brave Bird, the students were routinely beaten by their teachers. Many students sought safety by running away, and one of her classmates committed suicide to escape the physical abuse. St. Francis taught Brave Bird little more than a profound suspicion of whites, their religion, and their culture.

As a teenager, Brave Bird began to rebel. After publishing an underground student newspaper reporting the teachers' abuses and getting in a fist-fight with a priest, she quit school in disgust. Brave Bird moved back to Rosebud, where she began hanging out with other aimless young Sioux who could not find work on the reservation. Bored and tired of arguing with her mother, she ran away at 17 and began to drink heavily as she wandered throughout the West with her Indian friends.

This period of rebellion ended in 1971, when on a visit home she attended a ceremonial meeting at the house of Leonard Crow Dog, a medicine man and important spiritual leader among the Rosebud Sioux. At Crow Dog's house, Brave Bird met several members of the American Indian Movement (AIM), an radical organization that had been established in Minneapolis, Minnesota, in 1968. Largely founded by young urban Indians, AIM sought to fight a wide variety of injustices committed against Indians by white society and the U.S. government. Although most of the AIM activists she met knew little about reservation life, in their angry words and fighting spirit she saw a remedy to the defeat and depression that overwhelmed many Rosebud residents. She later wrote, "AIM opened a window for us through which the wind of the 1960s and early 1970s could blow, and it was no gentle breeze but a hurricane that whirled around us."

After the meeting, Brave Bird gave up drinking and threw herself into working for AIM. She and other AIM members jeered in courtrooms as whites accused of beating Indians were set free. They blocked the way of archeologists who tried to dig up ancient Indian burial sites. They provoked fights in the bars of nearby Rapid City, South Dakota, that posted signs reading "No Dogs and Indians Allowed." As an AIM member, she also helped instigate a 1972 multitribal protest called the "Trail of Broken Treaties." Hundreds of Indian activists from across the United States traveled in caravans to Washington, D.C., where they had planned to stage a quiet demonstration to bring attention to their grievances. When government officials gave little attention to their presence, the activists decided to try a more dramatic approach. They stormed the building that housed the Bureau of Indian Affairs (BIA), the agency that conducted all the government's official business with Indian groups. For a week, AIM members occupied the BIA building surrounded by armed FBI agents. The activists finally agreed to leave on the condition that they would not be prosecuted.

On returning home, Brave Bird became involved in another impromptu AIM demonstration. A Sioux man named Wesley Bad Heart Bull had been killed by a white man in Rapid City, whose residents had a reputation for discriminating against Indians. To make sure justice was done, a contingent of AIM members, including Brave Bird, attended the trial. On the courthouse steps, they learned that the killer was charged with second-degree manslaughter rather than murder. Their outrage at the charge erupted into a violent confrontation with the state police. The air was full of tear gas, and the courthouse was set aflame before the riot was quelled.

Almost immediately after the Rapid City incident, the members of AIM answered a call for help from Pine Ridge, a Sioux reservation that bordered Rosebud. Many residents of Pine Ridge were being terrorized by the Indian police force of the reservation government, which was supported by the BIA. Following the orders of tribal chairperson Dick Wilson, heavily armed policemen would wander the reservation in pickups and often shoot into the houses of Wilson's political enemies, many of whom were elders and other traditionalists.

With other young members of AIM, Brave Bird rushed to help her Pine Ridge neighbors. The group initially planned to confront Wilson at his tribal headquarters, but seeing the police's supply of firearms, they feared the tactic would end in a bloodbath. Two elder women suggested that they draw attention to the violent situation at Pine Ridge by taking over the site of the Wounded Knee Massacre as they had the BIA building. Wounded Knee had great symbolic importance to the Sioux. In December 1890, more than 300 Sioux men, women, and children had been massacred there by the U.S. army. In addition to being one of the greatest tragedies of Sioux history, the Wounded Knee Massacre marked the end of the Plains Wars, during which the Sioux and other Plains Indians attempted unsuccessfully to drive white intruders from their lands.

On February 27, 1973, Brave Bird was among some 200 AIM members who took over several buildings at Wounded Knee. Some men in AIM had tried to persuade Brave Bird to stay behind because she was eight months pregnant by an old boyfriend. But Brave Bird had decided that she wanted to give birth at Wounded Knee, no matter what the dangers were. She saw having her baby at the protest site as "a symbol of renewal, a tiny symbol, a tiny victory in our people's struggle for survival."

Soon after the activists had made their stand, Wounded Knee was surrounded by Wilson's police force and the FBI. During the 71-day standoff, the FBI and Indians routinely exchanged gunfire. Activists who were shot relied on healer Leonard Crow Dog to use herbal anesthetics and a knife to remove the bullets. The occupiers had to cope with primitive living conditions and dwindling supplies but were heartened by the sympathetic response of the media and the American public to their message. Amid this chaos, Brave Bird had her first child, Pedro. He was named after Mary's friend and fellow activist Pedro Bissonette, who was later murdered at the hands of Pine Ridge police.

Two Indian men were killed during the Wounded Knee occupation—Frank Clearwater and Buddy Lamont. Lamont was Brave Bird's uncle, and her relatives asked her to leave Wounded Knee to help them plan his funeral. After the FBI agreed that she would not be arrested, Brave Bird and Pedro emerged from the protest site and were immediately whisked off to jail. Brave Bird was interrogated for days but refused to tell the FBI anything. About a week later, an agreement was reached between the protesters and the government that ended the occupation of Wounded Knee. But the incident remained fresh in the minds of many FBI agents, who felt humiliated by the protesters.

After the excitement of Wounded Knee, Brave Bird settled into life as a single mother. To her surprise, she soon found herself courted by medicine man Leonard Crow Dog. Twelve years her senior, Crow Dog was held in awe by Brave Bird. At his insistence, she agreed to marry him by Indian rites. She moved to the lands of the Crow Dog family, where she set about making a home for Pedro and Crow Dog's three older children from a previous marriage.

On Pine Ridge, tensions between AIM and the FBI continued to grow. They culminated in the fatal shooting of two FBI agents, for which the FBI vowed revenge. The occupants of Wounded Knee were among their primary targets. Hundreds of AIM members were arrested, often on trumped-up charges. Many Indians alleged that the FBI was behind the murder of ANNA MAE AQUASH, an AIM activist who had been one of Mary Crow Dog's closest friends.

In September 1973, a SWAT team of 180 men descended on the Crow Dogs' home and arrested Leonard on assault charges. In the subsequent trials, he was found guilty on all counts and sentenced to 23 years in prison. Mary Crow Dog was stunned. When news of the sentence became public, however, she was moved into action. She was supported by many influential people and organizations that saw Leonard as a political prisoner, who was targeted by the authorities because of his role as AIM's moral and religious leader. Among those who came to Mary's aid were Amnesty International, the National Council of Churches, and the famous trial lawyer William Kunstler, who prepared Leonard Crow Dog's appeal.

Leonard was moved to a prison in Lewisburg, Pennsylvania. In order to be closer to him, Mary and Pedro went to New York City, where for a year they lived with writer Richard Erdoes and his wife. Erdoes was interested in the politics of Indian groups in the West and had taken on the role of coordinating Leonard's new defense. For the 22-year-old Mary, living in New York was jarring but exciting. Having only known poverty, she was intrigued by middle-class comforts of electric lights and indoor plumbing. She also began to question her instinctive contempt for whites as her friendship with the Erdoeses deepened.

Hearing Mary Crow Dog's stories of Wounded Knee, Erdoes asked her to collaborate with him to write her autobiography. Erdoes negotiated a contract with his publisher, and together they finished a manuscript titled *Lakota Woman* in 1979. However, fearing that the public would shrink from Crow Dog's radicalism, the publisher rejected their work. The manuscript was shelved until 1990, when Erdoes finally found a new publisher for it. The book was an immediate critical and popular sensation. A best seller, it won a 1990 American Book Award from the Before Columbus Foundation and was made into a TV movie starring IRENE BEDARD. Because of *Lakota Woman*'s success, Crow Dog and Erdoes wrote a sequel, *Ohitika Woman*, which was published in 1993.

Lakota Woman ends with the battle to reduce Leonard's sentence, which was lowered to time served after he had spent two years in prison. *Ohitika Woman* takes up Mary Crow Dog's story in 1977, when she and her husband returned to Rosebud to rebuild their life together. From the beginning, Crow Dog was frustrated living with Leonard's family. The distinguished Crow Dogs were traditionalists. They were hardly welcoming to the young half-white woman who did not know how to speak the Sioux language or perform Sioux rituals. Mary also learned that being the wife of a medicine man was hard work. A Sioux medicine man was expected to be generous, therefore Leonard welcomed anyone in need into their house. Mary had the endless task of feeding and cleaning up after the constant stream of houseguests in addition to caring for the three babies she had by Leonard and the four children they had brought to the marriage. Adding to her stress were financial woes. Leonard often gave away the modest pay he took for his services as a spiritual leader, healer, and lecturer. Although the community needed and welcomed his charity, Mary was angered that their children were sometimes left unclothed and unfed because of Leonard's gestures.

Nearing a nervous breakdown, Mary Crow Dog took her four children and ran away from Rosebud. After living in a series of women's shelters, she settled in a slum in Phoenix, Arizona. Leonard found her and moved to Phoenix so that they could be together. Although they lived together in the city for three years, the marriage continued to disintegrate, and the couple divorced. Mary plunged deeper into despair and turned increasingly to alcohol to cope with her unhappiness. In 1990, she returned to Rosebud, where she continued drinking heavily. A near fatal drunk-driving accident and the suicide of an alcoholic friend finally persuaded her to give up drinking for good. She was given support by Rudi Olguin, whom she married in 1991. The couple later separated, but Brave Bird continued to live in Rosebud.

In *Lakota Woman,* Mary Brave Bird exuberantly depicts the exciting era of the Indian rights movement of the early 1970s. In *Ohitika Woman,* written fifteen years later, she chronicles with unflinching realism both her personal despair and the deepening poverty of reservation communities in the decades that followed. Although the movement failed to bring the sweeping change it promised, the author of *Ohitika Woman* still celebrates AIM and the hope it continues to provide her people. In the book's conclusion, she writes, "AIM will always live in our hearts."

Further Reading

Brave Bird, Mary, and Richard Erdoes. *Ohitika Woman.* New York: Grove Press, 1993.

Crow Dog, Mary, and Richard Erdoes. *Lakota Woman.* New York: Grove Weidenfeld, 1990.

Wise, Christopher, and R. Todd Wise. "A Conversation with Mary Brave Bird." *American Indian Quarterly* 24 (Summer 2000): 282–293.

Bright Eyes

See LA FLESCHE, SUSETTE

Bronson, Ruth Muskrat

(1897–1982) *Cherokee activist, educator*

Ruth Muskrat Bronson devoted her life to helping educate a new generation of Indian leaders. She

Ruth Muskrat Bronson presents President Calvin Coolidge with a book titled *The Red Man in the United States* during the 1923 meeting of the Committee of One Hundred.
(Library of Congress, Neg. no. USZ62-107775)

was born in 1897 in the Delaware district of the Cherokee Nation in Indian Territory. Her childhood was a time of rapid change for the Cherokee. As the United States prepared to incorporate Indian Territory as part of the state of Oklahoma, the federal government dismantled many of the Cherokee's most venerable institutions, including their excellent educational facilities and system of communally owning land. The government's forced assimilation of the tribe into the non-Indian mainstream dealt a severe blow to the Cherokee society and their independence.

Because the Cherokee's own schools had been closed, Ruth Muskrat had to travel to Tonkawa, Oklahoma, to attend boarding school in 1912. She later won scholarships to study at the University of Oklahoma, the University of Kansas, and Mount Holyoke College in Massachusetts. In 1923,

Muskrat became the first Indian woman to graduate from Mount Holyoke.

Even while she was still a student, Muskrat established herself as a public figure. She went to Beijing, China, as the first Indian representative to the annual World's Student Christian Federation conference in 1922. The next year, she served in the Committee of One Hundred, a meeting of one hundred reformers in Washington, D.C. There she met President Calvin Coolidge and delivered a speech in which she insisted that all young Indians needed a good education to bring out their "potential greatness."

After leaving Mount Holyoke, Muskrat became a teacher at the Haskell Institute in Lawrence, Kansas, then the largest Indian boarding school in the nation. While at Haskell, she married John F. Bronson, who wholeheartedly supported her work. The Bronsons had no children of their own, but 10 years later, they adopted a Laguna Pueblo baby, the daughter of a friend of Bronson who had died.

The Bureau of Indian Affairs (BIA), the government agency that oversaw Indian schools, hired Ruth Muskrat Bronson to work in its growing education department in 1930. For several years, she traveled around the Plains states, searching for employment opportunities for Indian boarding school graduates. In 1936, her job took her to the BIA's headquarters in Washington, D.C. There she administered the agency's student loan program. In awarding loans, Bronson showed preference toward students who intended to use their education to serve Indian communities. Before her retirement from the BIA in 1943, the loan program she had overseen had helped to send more than 2,300 Indians to college.

To explain her hopes for the future for Native Americans, Bronson wrote *Indians Are People Too,* which was published in 1944. In the book, she cautioned non-Indians that romanticizing Indian people could be just as destructive as stereotyping them. In the 1940s, she also became involved with the National Congress of American Indians (NCAI), a national multitribal organization dedicated to defending Indian rights. While working as

a volunteer for nearly a decade, she helped establish the NCAI's Washington office. As a leader of NCAI, Bronson opposed the federal policy of termination. Advocates of termination sought to dissolve reservations and assimilate Indian nations into the mainstream society—a mission that no doubt reminded her of the ill treatment of the Cherokees in her youth.

In 1957, Bronson left Washington for the San Carlos Apache Indian Reservation in Arizona. Employed by the BIA's Indian Health Service, she was charged with educating the reservation residents about health hazards and hygiene. But Bronson adopted the additional role of encouraging the San Carlos residents, particularly the women, to take charge of their own health care and other aspects of their lives rather than relying on the BIA for help and advice. She helped initiate Ee-Cho-Da-Nihi, a women's group that created several programs designed to improve living conditions on the reservation.

Bronson and her husband retired to Tucson, Arizona, in 1962. She, however, remained active as a consultant to Save the Children, a charity devoted to helping impoverished youths, until she was paralyzed by a stroke in the early 1970s. After a lifetime of serving others, Ruth Muskrat Bronson died on May 14, 1982, at the age of 85.

Further Reading

Bronson, Ruth Muskrat. *Indians Are People Too.* New York: Friendship Press, 1944.

Harvey, Gretchen. "Muskrat, Ruth (Bronson)." In *Encyclopedia of North American Indians,* edited by Frederick E. Hoxie, 413–414. Boston: Houghton Mifflin, 1996.

Brown, Catharine
(1800–1823)   *Cherokee educator*

One of the earliest Christian converts among the Cherokee, Catharine Brown was born in 1800 in the town of Creek Path in northeastern Alabama. When she was in her late teens, she asked her parents to allow her to attend the Brainerd Mission School in present-day Chattanooga, Tennessee.

The school had been established by the American Board of Commissioners for Foreign Missions. The organization was devoted to converting Indians to Protestantism.

At Brainerd, Brown was schooled in Christianity, quickly learning English well enough to "read the Bible intelligibly," in the words of one missionary. At the same time, she was taught to abandon Cherokee customs in favor of the ways of whites. All students were expected to wear non-Indian clothing and perform manual labor according to the gender roles of white society. Traditionally, Cherokee girls were taught how to farm. But at Brainerd, Brown was encouraged to concentrate on domestic chores, such as housecleaning and sewing cloth clothing.

Brown flourished at the mission school. In January 1818, she became the first Cherokee Indian baptized by American Board missionaries, who praised her progress and discipline. One later wrote that she was "an interesting girl; her complexion blooming; her features comely; her person erect, and of middle stature; her manners easy; her demeanor modest and prepossessing." Brown grew close to other women at the school, leading her own prayer sessions with them at the end of each day.

While adapting to the school, Brown remained concerned with the Cherokee, who were rapidly losing their lands to whites. In one letter, she wrote, "My heart bleeds for my people who are on the brink of destruction." Her own parents decided to move west of the Mississippi River to escape white encroachment. Reluctantly, Brown left Brainerd to return to her family as they prepared to leave their home. But, when her parents postponed their plans, Brown eagerly returned to the mission, possibly because her adoption of Christianity made her feel unwelcome among more traditional Cherokee.

In 1820, Brown again came back to Creek Path, this time to teach. Cherokee leaders there had asked the American Board to establish schools for the children. By adopting some non-Indian ways, these leaders hoped to relieve the pressure whites were exerting on them to leave their homeland.

Brown wrote that "it is truly painful to part with my dear Christian friends" at Brainerd, but felt an obligation to her "poor red brothers and sisters [who] are perishing for lack of knowledge." Brown taught for six months at the Creek Path school for girls. Her classes included 20 girls, several women, and a few African-American slaves owned by prosperous Cherokee.

Soon, Brown's teaching and studies were interrupted by family obligations. She had to help nurse her brother John, who died of tuberculosis. She then took over the care of her elderly parents, for which John had been responsible. While living with them, Brown also became ill with tuberculosis. At first, she turned to traditional Cherokee healers, but as she grew worse, she sought treatment from a white physician. At his home in Limestone, Alabama, she died on July 18, 1823, at the age of 23.

Seeing Brown as an exemplary convert, American Board missionaries wrote about her life. Most notable of their works was Rufus Anderson's *Memoir of Catharine Brown, A Christian Indian of the Cherokee Nation*. Though the book was produced and circulated to raise funds for the board's missionary work, it also documents how Brown, like many other early Indian converts, struggled to reconcile old ways with the new.

Further Reading

Anderson, Rufus. *Memoir of Catharine Brown, A Christian Indian of the Cherokee Nation.* Philadelphia: American Sunday School Union, 1831.

Perdue, Theda. "Catharine Brown: Cherokee Convert to Christianity." In *Sifters: Native American Women's Lives,* edited by Theda Perdue, 204–223. New York: Oxford University Press, 2001.

Buffalo Bird Woman
See WAHEENEE

Burns, Diane M.
(1957–)   *Chemehuevi-Chippewa poet*

The work of poet Diane M. Burns is known best for its deft combination of elements of modern city life with aspects of traditional Indian culture. Born in 1957, Burns was reared by a Chippewa mother and Chemehuevi father. During her childhood, she grew familiar with both Indian traditions as she divided her time between her Chippewa relatives in Wisconsin and her Chemehuevi relations in California.

Burns was educated in several Indian boarding schools—including Wahpeton Indian School in Wahpeton, North Dakota, and the Sherman Institute in Riverside, California—before attending an alternative school in Scarsdale, New York. After graduation, she moved to Santa Fe to study at the Institute of American Indian Arts (IAIA). Because of her distinguished work there, she was awarded the Congressional Medal of Merit. After completing IAIA's two-year program, Burns decided that she wanted to live in New York City. She enrolled at Barnard College at Columbia University and in 1978 was awarded a bachelor's degree in political science.

While still in college, Burns began to write book reviews and articles for various publications. She started writing poetry, however, almost by accident. A friend at the Indian Community House, an Indian center that offers support to Indians living in the New York area, gave Burns's name to the organizers of a poetry reading, who were looking for an Indian writer to feature in their program. Burns later recalled her reaction to their invitation: "They said they were going to give me fifty bucks for this poetry reading, so I said, 'Okay, I'll write some poetry.'" From this inauspi-

cious beginning grew a new career. Soon her poems were frequently appearing in small magazines and journals, such as the *Blue Cloud Quarterly, White Pine Journal,* and *Greenfield Review.* In 1981, Burns published a collection of her work, *Riding the One-Eyed Ford.* The volume was nominated for the William Carlos Williams Award and was named one of the year's 10 best poetry collections by the St. Mark's Poetry Project.

According to Burns, her poetry focuses on "the concept of conformity and nonconformity . . . being part of things and not being part of things." In exploring this theme, she draws particularly on her experiences as a female Indian urbanite: "As American Indians, you always have the feeling of not belonging but you also have this feeling of belonging. As a woman it gets exaggerated. Living in New York it gets more exaggerated." As a member of Poet's Overland Expeditionary Troupe, she has presented her work in numerous schools and galleries. To Burns, reading her poetry to a group is as creative an act as writing. In a 1987 interview, she explained: "I would rather read poetry in front of an audience than almost anything else. I feel the most real when I am doing that because it is really expressing myself and what I am."

Further Reading

Bruchac, Joseph. "That Beat, That Pulse." In *Survival This Way: Interviews with American Indian Poets,* 43–56. Tucson: University of Arizona Press, 1987.

Burns, Diane M. *Riding the One-Eyed Ford.* New York: Contact II Publications, 1981.

C

Callahan, Sophia Alice
(1868–1894)   *Creek novelist, educator*

Sophia Alice Callahan's *Wynema: A Child of the Forest* (1891) was probably the first novel written by an American Indian woman. Born in 1868, Callahan spent her early years in Sulfur Springs, Texas. Her family fled there during the Civil War. They had lived in the Creek Nation in Indian Territory (now Oklahoma), but their trading post and house were destroyed amid the wartime chaos. Like most prominent Creek, Callahan's father was a strong supporter of the Confederacy. He was elected to the Confederate Congress and served as a captain in the Confederate army.

The Callahan family returned to Indian Territory in 1885, when Sophia was 17. Of mixed white and Creek ancestry, she was most likely considered a member of the tribe's elite. Her father was prominent in tribal affairs, and although he experienced periodic financial setbacks, the family had a fair amount of wealth.

The Callahans certainly had enough to fund an expensive education for Sophia. In 1887, she was sent east to attend the Wesleyan Female Institute in Virginia. After 10 months, she returned to the Creek Nation and took a job teaching at the Har-

rell International Institute, a Methodist high school.

While at Harrell, Callahan completed *Wynema,* which was published in June 1891. The story focused on two heroines—Genevieve Weir, a white teacher at a Creek school, and Wynema, a Creek girl who becomes Genevieve's best student. While explaining elements of Creek culture, much of the novel traced Wynema's transformation from a traditional Creek into a well-spoken, educated young woman able to carve out a place for herself in white society. Although Callahan was respectful of Creek culture, she also held Wynema up as an ideal of how Indians could be "civilized" by exposure to mainstream, non-Indian ways.

Like many female writers of her day, Callahan used the narrative to discuss political and social issues. She particularly explored the women's rights and temperance movements, both of which she strongly supported. *Wynema* also touched on contemporary Creek issues, including allegations of the misuse of tribal funds and the U.S. government's campaign to break the Creek lands into individually owned allotments.

Probably drawing on newspaper accounts, Callahan ended the book by delving into a topical Indian controversy that was then national news—

the 1891 massacre of Lakota Sioux in Wounded Knee, South Dakota. In the final lines of *Wynema,* one of her characters expresses her outrage over this event: "Let us pray, my brothers and sisters, that God will open the eyes of the Congress and people of the United States that they change their conduct toward the despised red race, and thus avert the evil sure to come up on us if they persist in their present treatment of the Indians."

The publication of *Wynema* received almost no attention by the literary press. It is unknown whether Callahan was disappointed by its reception. But after its appearance, her immediate ambition was to continue her education. She wrote to a friend, "I think it best to go there [Wesleyan Female Institute] to finish as I have begun there. I am studying on my French & Mathematics, preparing if I go back I shall study nothing but languages & literature & Mathematics. I finished Latin but I shall study it again. . . . When I finish I am going to build up a school of my own."

Callahan's plans were thwarted when, in December 1893, she came down with a sudden and painful attack of pleurisy. The illness took her life on January 7, 1894. An obituary in a Methodist journal hailed her as an excellent teacher, while noting her "literary turn of mind." Although her career and life were brief, she left behind one of the first works to meld Indian issues with the conventions of women's fiction of her time.

Further Reading

Callahan, S. Alice. *Wynema: A Child of the Forest.* Edited and introduced by A. LaVonne Brown Ruoff. Lincoln: University of Nebraska Press, 1997.

Foreman, Carolyn Thomas. "S. Alice Callahan." *Chronicles of Oklahoma* 33 (1955): 306–315, 549.

Campbell, Maria

(1940–) *Métis autobiographer, activist*

"I write this for all of you, to tell you what it is like to be a Halfbreed woman in our country," states Canadian author Maria Campbell in the introduction to her autobiography *Halfbreed* (1973). Through her story, Campbell brought attention to the plight of a frequently ignored and often despised minority in Canadian society.

Campbell was born in April of 1940 in central Saskatchewan. She grew up in a small rural settlement of Métis—people of part-Indian and part-French ancestry often derogatorily referred to as "half-breeds." Unlike many nearby Indian groups, the Métis were not officially recognized as Indians by the Canadian government. Indians who were recognized—known as status Indians—were entitled to land and benefits outlined in past treaties. As non-status Indians, however, the Métis were largely landless and impoverished. As Campbell bitterly recounts in *Halfbreed,* when she was a girl many status Indians held their Métis neighbors and relations in contempt: "We were always the poor relatives, the *awp-pee-tow-koosons* [half-people]. They laughed and scorned us. They had land and security, we had nothing."

Nearby whites also had little regard for the Métis. Mostly recent immigrants from Germany and Sweden, they frightened the young Campbell: "They looked cold . . . and seldom smiled, unlike my own people who laughed, cried, danced and fought and shared everything. . . . They didn't understand us, just shook their heads and thanked God they were different."

Although considered as an outcast by the world at large, Campbell was treated with warmth and affection among the Métis. The oldest in a family of eight children, she was taught by her father to hunt and trap wild animals, while her mother, with little success, tried to interest her in cooking and sewing. The most profound influence on Campbell, however, was her grandmother, Cheechum. Campbell's "best friend and confidante," Cheechum "tried to teach all she knew about living." Above all, Cheechum told her granddaughter to resist seeing herself as whites saw her. She cautioned that these enemies's most powerful tool against her was to make her hate her own people.

When Campbell was 12, her mother died suddenly. Shattered by her death and overwhelmed by the needs of his children, Campbell's father left the family home for days and sometimes weeks at a time. With Cheechum in her nineties, Campbell had to take on the responsibility of caring for her seven younger brothers and sisters. Taught to fear government officials by Cheechum, she worried that welfare workers would place the children in foster homes if they knew of her situation. For three years, she struggled to keep her family healthy and fed while working and going to school.

In desperation, at 15 she married a wealthy white man she did not love. Rather than bettering her lot, the marriage proved disastrous. Her husband had lied about his income, and rather than adopting her siblings as she had hoped, he turned them over to the welfare authorities. After Campbell gave birth to their daughter, Lisa, he abandoned them both.

Campbell then took Lisa and set out for Vancouver, British Columbia, to make her fortune. Like many other Indians in the 1940s and 1950s who wanted to escape rural poverty, she was attracted to city life. Her idealized image of Vancouver included "toothbrushes and pretty dresses, oranges and apples, and a happy family sitting around the kitchen table talking about their tomorrow." She found there, instead, the decay, poverty, and filth of the urban slum. Unable to make a living, Campbell fell into prostitution. And unable to cope with her new profession, she also plunged into drug and alcohol abuse. After several violent relationships and failed attempts to shake her addictions, Campbell tried to kill herself twice. Only after suffering a complete mental breakdown was she able to find a way out of her despair. Once discharged from the hospital, she wandered, destitute and hungry, into a bar. But rather than order a drink, she decided to write a letter to herself "because I had to have somebody to talk to, and there was nobody to talk to." The letter became the beginning of *Halfbreed*.

Halfbreed ends on a note of hope. Through the act of writing her autobiography, Campbell comes to understand herself. And through a new interest in the battle for Indian rights, she learns to envision a better future. In the book's final chapters,

Campbell writes: "I believe that one day, very soon, people will put aside their differences and come together as one. . . . Change will come because this time we won't give up."

A best seller in Canada, *Halfbreed* has had an enormous impact since its publication in 1973. Widely read and revered, it has inspired many Canadian Indian activists to join the Indian rights movement. It has also moved a generation of Indian writers to tell their own stories. Its influence grew with the production of *Jessica,* a play based on *Halfbreed* that starred Cree actress TANTOO CARDINAL in 1982. *Jessica* was coauthored by Campbell and Linda Griffiths, a collaboration discussed by Campbell in *The Book of Jessica: A Theatrical Transformation* (1989), which features the complete text of the play. Campbell also has written several children's books about Métis history and has produced numerous documentaries, including *The Road Allowance People,* about the Métis of Saskatchewan.

A member of the faculty of the University of Saskatchewan since 1998, Campbell has received many honors for her work as a writer and as a political activist. Among the most prestigious is the Molson Prize in the Arts, which the Canada Council awarded her in 2004. The award jury explained its choice by noting that Campbell's "status as a teacher, mentor and inspiration to aboriginal people and all Canadians is unparalleled."

Further Reading

Bataille, Gretchen, and Kathleen Mullen Sands. "The Long Road Back: Maria Campbell." In *American Indian Women: Telling Their Lives,* 113–126. Lincoln: University of Nebraska Press, 1984.

Campbell, Maria. *Halfbreed.* 1973. Reprint, Lincoln: University of Nebraska Press, 1982.

Campbell, Maria, et al. *Our Story: Aboriginal Voices on Canada's Past.* Toronto: Doubleday Canada, 2004.

Cardinal, Tantoo
(1950–) *Métis actress*

Canada's leading Native American actress, Tantoo Cardinal was born on July 20, 1950, in the small rural community of Anzac in Alberta, Canada. With a Cree Indian mother and a white father, Cardinal was considered a Métis, a French word used in Canada to designate people of mixed Indian-French ancestry.

Cardinal was the youngest of the couple's four children. When she was only six weeks old, her father abandoned the family. Her mother then sent the children to live with their grandmother, whom Cardinal now regards as one of the greatest influences of her life. "She taught me how to snare rabbits, catch fish and speak the Cree language," Cardinal explained in a 1991 interview. "She told me what our people were, and what they could one day be again." Her grandmother also gave Cardinal the name "Tantoo"; she read the word on the label of a mosquito repellent she put on the baby's face before taking her out to pick wild blueberries.

After attending grammar school in Anzac's one-room schoolhouse, Cardinal was sent to a high school in the nearby city of Edmonton. She boarded with a white couple and fell in love with their son, Fred Martin. Martin was a college student who was active in the American civil rights movement. Inspired by his political leanings, she became involved in the growing Indian rights movement in Canada. She later remembered attending her first political rally in 1970: "The speaker, wearing this beaded moose-hide jacket, was talking about the Battle of Batoche [the 1885 conflict that marked the end of Métis hero Louis Riel's rebellion against the Canadian government]. It was absolutely electric there." While in high school, she joined United Native Youth, a political organization for young Native Americans. In 1971, she became its president.

Following her graduation, Cardinal and Martin were married. They had one child, Cheyenne, but Cardinal eventually grew restless with her life as a suburban housewife and mother. She and Martin divorced in 1978.

By that time, Cardinal had started appearing in small parts in regional stage and television productions. She landed her first lead role in the 1982 production of *Jessica,* a play about a troubled Indian woman based on *Halfbreed* (1973), the autobiography of noted Métis writer MARIA CAMPBELL. She followed her theater breakthrough with the critically acclaimed Canadian movie *Loyalties* (1986), which tells the story of a conflict between two families—one Indian, one white. Representative of the response to Cardinal's performance was Toronto critic Tom Scott's description of the young actress as "one of the most dimensional, fascinating women to be found in any film this year." Cardinal was nominated for a Best Actress Genie Award (the Canadian equivalent of an Oscar) for her work in this film.

In 1988, Cardinal married an American actor named John Lawlor. The couple had a daughter, whom Cardinal named Riel after the Métis hero. They moved to Los Angeles, where Cardinal began appearing in Hollywood films. Her most high-profile role was that of Black Shawl—the strong Lakota Sioux woman married to medicine man Kicking Bird (played by Native American actor Graham Greene, who, like Cardinal, had emerged as a star in Canada's theater community) in the Academy-Award-winning *Dances with Wolves* (1990). Her other American films include *Legends of the Fall* (1993), *Sioux City* (1994), and *The Space between All Things* (2006). She has also frequently appeared on American television. Tantoo has starred in numerous television movies and miniseries—including *Lakota Woman* (1994), *Grand Avenue* (1996), and *Dreamkeeper* (2003)—as well as playing a recurring role on the series "Dr. Quinn, Medicine Woman."

Cardinal continues to be a frequent player in Canadian film and television as well. She was particularly heralded for her supporting role in *Black Robe* (1991), in which she played a 17th-century Algonquian Indian woman fighting to protect her family from the influences of whites. Cardinal also hosted the six-part television series *As Long as the Rivers Flow* (1991). On camera, she explained that the documentary program's goal was to record "my people's efforts to gain control of their future." In 2004, Cardinal continued to draw attention to the plight of her country's Native peoples by contributing a work of fiction to *Our Story: Aboriginal*

Tantoo Cardinal portrayed Black Shawl in *Dances with Wolves* (1990).
(Courtesy Museum of Modern Art Film Stills Archive)

Voices on Canada's Past, a collection intended to teach students about Canadian history from a native perspective.

Throughout her acting career, Cardinal has remembered her activist roots. She has often insisted on script changes to ensure that the Indian characters she plays are portrayed fairly and realistically. After she was cast in her first major film role in *Marie-Anne* (1979), Cardinal courageously spoke out against the culturally inaccurate representation of Indian women in the film. Her persistence persuaded the director to change the movie's ending twice to address her objections. She also publicly criticized the producers of *Divided Loyalties* (1990)—a Canadian television movie in which she played Molly Brant (the sister of 18th-century Mohawk leader Joseph Brant)—for casting a white actor in the lead. She told *Maclean's* magazine, "I thought we were beyond that," then added, "I

thought about not doing it, but then they would probably have hired a non-Native for my part, too."

As a performer and a watchdog of the film and television communities' representation of Native Americans, Cardinal hopes to increase tolerance and respect for all Indians. "With acting," she has explained, "I have found a way to do my own part to tell my people's story."

Further Reading

Campbell, Maria, et al. *Our Story: Aboriginal Voices on Canada's Past.* Toronto: Doubleday Canada, 2004.
Dwyer, V. "Tantoo Cardinal: An Art with Its Roots in Loyalty." *Maclean's,* 30 December 1991, p. 42.
Johnson, Brian D. "Masks of a Métis Star." *Maclean's,* 20 October 1986, p. 63.

Chipeta
(1843–1924)   *Ute peacemaker*

As the wife of Chief Ouray, Chipeta met with dignitaries in Washington, D.C., during Ute leaders' negotiations with U.S. officials. Born in 1843, Chipeta grew up near present-day Conejos, Colorado. Although she was possibly a Kiowa Apache, she was raised as a Tabeguache (also called Uncompahgre), one band of the Ute people.

In 1859, Chipeta married Ouray, a man of Tabeguache and Jicarilla Apache heritage. The following year, after his father's death, he became the leader of his band. Well versed in English and Spanish, Ouray emerged as an important figure at treaty negotiations with non-Indians. In 1868, he accompanied eight other leaders to meet with negotiators in Washington, D.C. In 1872, Ouray returned to the U.S. capital, this time with Chipeta traveling with him. During the trip, the couple was feted by several officials, including President Ulysses S. Grant.

The next year, during a council with federal treaty negotiators, Ouray agreed to cede 4 million acres of tribal land in exchange for an annual payment of $25,000. Ouray probably believed it was the best deal he could get, but many Ute were upset by the concession. Fueling their discontent was the annual $1,000 pension he was to receive from the government for his help.

In 1875, the government also awarded Ouray 400 acres along the Uncompahgre River near present-day Montrose, Colorado. Ouray's government salary allowed him to build and furnish a large, two-story house. Ouray and Chipeta became known for their hospitality to non-Indian visitors, although Chipeta knew almost no English. William Sanders, a reporter, wrote about meeting Chipeta at their homestead: "Chipeta got used to my presence very soon, and gave rein to her natural vivacity, talking Spanish. . . . Her voice was low and clear and melodious and she talked with a fascinating play of features and gestures."

Chipeta was photographed with her husband, Ouray, during an 1880 visit to Washington, D.C.
(Denver Public Library, Western History Collection, Call no. X-30600)

However, most non-Indians in present-day Colorado were hostile to the Ute. After Colorado became a state in 1876, their ill will only intensified. White settlers and mining companies, both eager for the Utes' landholdings, rallied to remove them from Colorado once and for all. In 1879, the tensions exploded into the violence of the Ute War. During the fighting, several non-Indian women were taken hostage by Ute warriors. Using his negotiation skills, Ouray secured their safe release. Oral history holds that Chipeta might have been involved in the negotiations.

In 1880, Ouray and Chipeta took their final trip to Washington. The press accounts of their visit emphasized Ouray's dignified air and oratory skills but also revealed Washington society's fascination with Chipeta. In one article, female journalist Georgie Davis described Chipeta after meeting with her at her hotel: "She is a stout and comely squaw, gorgeous in a red plaid gown and beaded leggings, her fingers loaded with rings, and wrists with bracelets, a fashionable canvas bag hanging on one side of her belt, and a beaded pouch from the other."

Long in ill health, Ouray died soon after returning. The next year, Chipeta had to leave her elegant home. The federal government forced her and 1,500 other Ute onto a reservation in Utah. There, she lived in poverty, plagued by failing eyesight, stomach ailments, and arthritis. Chipeta died on August 16, 1924, aged 81. The next year, friends of Ouray had her remains transported to Montrose, Colorado. Her body was reinterred in a concrete tomb built on her old homestead. Nearby, a monument was erected to honor Ouray.

Today the homestead is the site of the Ute Indian Museum. Since 2001, an annual Chipeta Day has been held on the grounds. With performances of Ute dancers and Native American musicians, Ute and non-Indians gather to commemorate Chipeta's role in the history of Colorado.

Further Reading

Krudwig, Vickie Leigh. *Searching for Chipeta*. Golden, Colo.: Fulcrum Publishing, 2004.

Waldman, Carl. *Biographical Dictionary of American Indian History to 1900.* Rev. ed. New York: Facts On File, 2001.

Chona, Maria

(ca. 1845–1936)   *Tohono O'odham autobiographer, medicine woman*

In the early 1930s, Maria Chona told her life story to a young anthropologist who had come to Arizona to study Chona's people, the Tohono O'odham (also known as the Papago). The result was *The Autobiography of a Papago Woman* (1936), a landmark in both anthropology and Native American literature.

Although her birth date is unknown, Chona was probably born in about 1845. When she was a girl, the United States acquired the Gadsden Purchase (1853), a small strip of land in what is now southern Arizona and Mexico. As established by the Gadsden Purchase the new boundary between the United States and Mexico ran through the center of Papago territory. Chona's village, Mesquite Root, was on the American side, and her father, Jose Maria, was named its governor by U.S. officials. Otherwise, however, the new boundary had little effect on Chona. Few Americans were willing to venture into the Papago lands because of the forbidding desert environment. Only through hundreds of years of effort were the Papago able to develop the culture that allowed them to survive in a harsh climate where water was scarce.

As a youth, Chona was instructed by her elders in how to be a good Papago woman. They told her old stories of her people and their history and taught her to grind seeds and corn, dig for roots, and haul water. Because the Apache to the east were a constant threat, she was also encouraged to run in foot races. Papago boys needed to be good runners in order to be good warriors. Girls, however, were told that learning to run quickly might save their lives if their village were attacked by their enemies.

Chona took the lessons to heart and feared becoming a "bad" woman. Bad women were lazy, she learned. They visited and gossiped when they should have been spending their time laboring at home. Bad women also talked to young men and did not inform others when they were menstruating. In Papago society, menstruating women were thought to be extremely dangerous. If one looked at a man's bow and arrows, the weapons would be rendered useless. Sometimes, if one touched a man, he would fall dead. To protect the rest of the tribe, menstruating women were sent to a small hut until their menstrual period was over.

Chona accepted the need for her monthly visit to the hut and did not balk at the constant labor that was the lot of a Papago woman. However, she did express regret that her father would not allow her to become a medicine woman. Among the Papago, seeing visions and creating songs gave a person the power to cure. Chona and two of her brothers showed signs of this power, but her father did not want too many of his children to possess medicine. He asked an established medicine man to remove her crystals, which were the source of medicine power. According to Chona, crystals were "little shining things, as long as a finger joint" that grew inside a powerful person's breast. The medicine man performed a ritual to remove her crystals, but before leaving he assured her, "They will grow again, for it is a gift."

When Chona was a teenager, her parents decided she should marry the 17-year-old son of a medicine man. Her mother had taught her to fear all men, so at first she felt awkward with her husband. Following Papago custom, she went to live with his family. She immediately felt comfortable with her new mother-in-law, who had only had sons and therefore welcomed help with the cooking and with making a home. In time Chona came to enjoy her life in their household. Two of her brothers-in-law married, and she liked working with their wives. She also had great affection for her third brother-in-law, Shining Evening, who had chosen to live as a woman. In Chona's eyes, Shining Evening was exceptionally clever. He also was a great help with household tasks because he had the strength of a man.

Chona developed an affection for her husband as well. He became a medicine man and was well paid for his services. Unlike some husbands, he also took her to dances and other tribal get-togethers that Chona enjoyed. She explained that he was proud of her because she had the power to make up songs and wanted her to perform at the Papago's yearly rounds of ceremonies. The most anticipated was a corn dance, where singing ensured that summer rains would water their crops. Participants in the corn dance would drink an alcoholic beverage made from cacti. In this setting, the Papago were encouraged to become "beautifully drunk," but Chona had disdain for non-Indians' whiskey because "it did not bring rain."

During this marriage, Chona had four sons and one daughter, but only the daughter, Crescenza, lived beyond infancy. When Crescenza was about 12, Chona one day returned home from her chores to find that her husband had taken a second wife. As a medicine man, custom held that he could have as many as four wives if he could afford to take care of them. Chona knew that her husband's action was appropriate but she was appalled nonetheless: "I had never thought my husband would do it. You see, we married so young, even before I had really become a maiden. It was as if we had been children in the same house. I had grown fond

Maria Chona gathers yucca in a photograph by anthropologist Ruth Underhill.

of him. We starved so much together." In a rage, Chona took Crescenza and a butcher knife, which she intended to use to kill her husband if he followed her, and returned to her parents' house. Her parents and brothers were not happy to see her and did not understand why she had left her husband. For several days, she waited, hoping her husband would send his second wife away. In the meantime, her family grew impatient with her. They insisted that she get married again and chose her groom—an old but rich horse trader named Chief's Leg. The family was poor and wanted her to marry a man who might help improve their fortunes.

Hesitantly, Chona married Chief's Leg. He immediately took her on her first trip to the nearby town of Tucson and told her she could have anything she wanted from the shops there. She accepted an embroidered shawl, some calico cloth, and a pair of shoes—the first she had ever owned—but the gifts did not make her any happier about her new marriage. "I felt bad," she later explained. "I did not love that old man. I was not fond of him." She continued to hope that her first husband would come back for her, but a year later her brother came to her house to tell her he had died. At the news, she wept so hard that she feared his spirit would take her to the land of the dead. Chona calmed down only after Chief's Leg visited her first husband's grave and threatened to burn his bones if he did not leave Chona alone.

While married to Chief's Leg, Chona had two sons. She also gained the power to cure sick babies through a vision she had when she was ill. In her vision, she was visited by the Virgin Mary and a dead relative, who gave her the ability to harden the soft spot on a baby's head. From watching her first husband, Chona had learned the proper method, which involved pushing into the baby's mouth with her hand, but only a vision could give her the power she needed to cure. Chona was already a powerful woman in her tribe, but her new position as a healer of infants brought her even more respect.

Chona and Chief's Leg were married for some 30 years before his death in the mid-1920s. After

his funeral, Chona promptly received a proposal of marriage but chose instead to live with her grandchildren. After 70 years of caring for others, she was unwilling to lose the measure of independence that age had granted her in Papago society.

In the early 1930s, an anthropologist named Ruth Underhill asked for Chona's help. She was a student of Franz Boas and Ruth Benedict, two great pioneers of American anthropology who taught at Columbia University in New York City. They had sent Underhill to the Papago homeland to perform the first comprehensive anthropological report on the tribe. Chona's age and status made her an excellent source of information on the Papagos' traditional ways.

As the two met to talk about the Papago, Underhill became fascinated by Chona herself. She asked the old woman to tell her about her life with the aid of an interpreter. As Chona spoke, her words were interpreted by a young woman who knew both Papago and English. Underhill pressed the interpreter for more details or clarification, often to the irritation of her willful informant. Chona would sometimes lose her patience and yell at Underhill. The interpreter later recalled an instance in which Chona shouted, "You *mil-gahn* [American], you're so dumb, you don't know anything."

Despite the frustrations on both sides, the collaboration between Underhill and Chona created an autobiography that is still widely read and admired. Underhill brought to the task an editorial talent and flair for language that makes Chona's story as much a work of literature as of ethnography. Chona contributed to the project a powerful story of a woman who, though in some ways limited by her society's rules, was able to achieve her ambitions while living within her tribal traditions. Chona was a good Papago woman, even though she would not stay with her husband when his household became intolerable and even though she violated her father's wishes by becoming a medicine woman late in life. Underhill saw in Chona a strength, a power, and a hint of rebellion that makes her story irresistible and inspirational. As Chona herself remarked, "I am one who knows things, because, even though they took my crystals out, there was always something in me."

Further Reading

Bataille, Gretchen M., and Kathleen M. Sands. "Maria Chona: An Independent Woman in Traditional Culture." In *Native American Women: Telling Their Lives,* 447–482. Lincoln: University of Nebraska Press, 1984.

Underhill, Ruth. *An Autobiography of a Papago Woman.* 1936. Reprint, *Papago Woman.* Long Grove, Ill.: Waveland Press, 1985.

Chrystos

(1946–)   *Menominee poet, activist*

Through her poetry, Chrystos explores the marginalization of both Native Americans and lesbians in American society. Born Chrystos Lieve Snellings on November 7, 1946, she was raised in San Francisco, California. Her childhood was extraordinarily difficult. Her white mother was severely depressed. Her Menominee father was so ashamed of his Indian heritage that he refused to speak his Native language. Adding to her painful home life, as a girl Chrystos was raped by a relative.

As a young adult, Chrystos fell into drug addiction, alcoholism, and prostitution. For more than 10 years, she was continually in and out of mental institutions. She credits her first lesbian lover with helping to free herself from self-destruction and self-hated.

Passionate about political issues involving American Indians, she began writing poetry. By the early 1970s, feminist writer and critic Kate Millett was urging Chrystos to publish her work. Her poems appeared in several influential anthologies, including *This Bridge Called My Back: Writings by Radical Women of Color* (1981) and *A Gathering of Spirit: Writing and Art by North American Indian Women* (1983).

In 1988, Chrystos's first book of poetry, *Not Vanishing,* was published. The collection of 70 poems dealt with the troubles of her youth and early adulthood. Chrystos, however, resists the label "confessional poet," preferring to be known as a political poet. In subsequent collections, including *Dream On* (1991) and *Fire Power* (1995), she has written about an array of issues regarding disenfranchised people, from homelessness to colonialism to genocide. Essentially repudiating her white heritage, Chrystos often writes with heated anger about the abuses suffered by American Indians at the hands of non-Indian society. As she acknowledges, "One of the reasons I annoy people is because I write about real Indian country instead of feathers and bells and that's not pleasant." Equally emotional, though far gentler in its language, is her lesbian erotica, most notably the poems in her 1993 collection *In Her I Am.* She is also the coeditor of *Best Lesbian Erotica 1999.*

Chrystos has won numerous honors for her work. In 1990, she was awarded a grant from the National Endowment for the Arts, which allowed her to complete *Dream On.* She won the Audre Lorde International Poetry Competition in 1994 and the Sappho Award of Distinction from the Astraea National Lesbian Action Foundation in 1995.

A resident of Bainbridge Island in Washington State since 1980, Chrystos often gives lectures and poetry readings at universities across the country. She is also a self-trained artist and is exploring writing stories and novels. In all her work, her aim is the same—to present the truth as she sees it. In Chrystos's eyes, "Telling the truth is powerful medicine. It is a fire that lights the way for others."

Further Reading/Resources

Bealy, Joanne. "An Interview with Chrystos." *Off Our Backs,* September/October 2003.

"Chrystos." Voices from the Gap. Available online. URL: http://voices.cla.umn.edu/vg/Bios/entries/chrystos. html. Downloaded on May 8, 2006.

Chrystos. *Dream On.* Vancouver, British Columbia: Press Gang Publishers, 1991.

———. *Fugitive Colors.* Cleveland, Ohio: Cleveland State University Poetry Center, 1995.

———. *Not Vanishing.* Vancouver, British Columbia: Press Gang Publishers, 1988.

Cobell, Elouise

(1946–   )   *Blackfoot businesswoman, activist*

For more than 30 years, Elouise Cobell has battled the U.S. government for funds stolen from hundreds of thousands of Indians across the country. She is the lead plaintiff in *Cobell v. Norton,* one of the largest class action suits in the history of the United States.

Born in 1946, Cobell was raised on the Blackfoot Indian reservation in Montana. She was one of eight children, living in a modest home without electricity or a phone. At her insistence, she began her education at four years old, attending the reservation's one-room schoolhouse. She later remembered her joy at reading the teacher's Sunday *New York Times* each week: "It would arrive a month late, but it exposed me to a world I never knew existed. It gave me a chance to dream a little."

While growing up, Cobell often heard adults complain about checks they received from the U.S. government. The checks represented royalties held in Individual Indian Money (IIM) accounts. These accounts were first established in the late 19th century, when the federal government divided many reservations into small plots, called allotments, that were assigned to Indian individuals as personal property. However, deeming Indians incompetent to conduct business affairs, the government held these lands in trust. The government was free to lease the lands to timber, mineral, and oil companies without consulting the Indian owners. The income generated by these lands was supposed to be placed in IIMs and then passed along to the landowners.

When Cobell was young, many Blackfoot were baffled by their IIM checks. The federal government sent them with no documentation about how the income was generated. Landowners had no idea who was leasing their land and why. The amounts were often confusing, changing substantially from year to year. Some people with oil rigs on their land received shockingly small sums without explanation.

Still, few people wanted to confront the government on the matter. They distrusted the Bureau of Indian Affairs (BIA), the government agency within the Department of the Interior that is charged with dealing with Indian groups. At 18, however, Cobell started pressing the BIA for answers about her IIM, only to be told she was not "capable" of understanding the accounts. She then decided to study accounting. She once explained, "If someone tells me something can't be done, I get so mad I just have to do it."

Cobell attended Great Falls Community College and Montana State University. In 1968, she left the reservation and moved to Seattle, Washington, where she worked as an accountant for a television station. There she met and married Alvin Cobell, a Blackfoot fisherman. The couple had a son, Turk. In 1970, during a visit to the reservation, Alvin convinced Elouise to move back. Together, they maintained a family ranch.

Six years after their return, Elouise Cobell took on the job of tribal treasurer. In this post, she saw how difficult it was for tribe members to start businesses without any access to capital. To help Blackfoot entrepreneurs, Cobell founded the Blackfeet National Bank in 1987. The institution has grown into the Native American Bank, which counts more than 20 Indian tribes as investors.

As tribal treasurer, Cobell continued to hear tribe members concerns about their IIMs. She was also confused by the Blackfeets' tribal account with the government, which began to show negative interest income. When she went to the BIA for answers, all she got was condescension: "[A]t a meeting with the BIA supervisor, he just stared at me and said, 'Why don't you learn how to read a statement?' It was so humiliating."

But Cobell refused to stop pressing the agency, all the while compiling evidence that the funds meant for IIMs had been stolen or disappeared through incompetent accounting and recordkeeping. She finally was able to secure a meeting in Washington, D.C., with government officials and banking experts. After she outlined her case, banking expert and lawyer Dennis Gingold turned to the officials and said, "I can't believe you guys haven't been sued."

In 1994, Congress passed the Indian Trust Fund Management Reform Act. It was intended to sort out questions about the IIMs, but in fact very little was done to remedy the problem. Frustrated, Cobell contacted Gingold and told him she was ready to sue. With his help, she prepared to sue the U.S. government on behalf of the approximately 500,000 Indians she believed had been defrauded. Warned the suit would cost millions, Cobell began approaching foundations for grant money. In 1997, she was awarded a "genius" grant from the John D. MacArthur Foundation. She put most of the $300,000 award toward legal fees.

In June 10, 1996, *Cobell v. Babbitt* (now known as *Cobell v. Norton*) was filed in Washington, D.C. Judge Royce Lamberth ordered the Department of the Interior to turn over accounting records to the court. When the documents were not delivered, he found Interior Secretary Bruce Babbitt and Treasury Secretary Robert Rubin in contempt of court. The judge was further angered by the discovery that the Department of the Interior had shredded 162 boxes of relevant documents after the trial began. In December 1999, he issued an opinion against the government. Lamberth held that trial had exposed "a shocking pattern of deception. I have never seen more egregious conduct by the federal government."

The case has since moved into its second phase to determine the amount owed to the plaintiffs. For years, the government has tried numerous legal maneuvers to stall the case. BIA officials have also withheld payments due to Indians, blaming the delays on Cobell in an effort to discredit her in Indian country. Lamberth has spoken out against these tactics, condemning "the utter depravity and moral turpitude displayed by [the Department of the Interior's] willingness to withhold needed finances from people struggling to survive and support families on subsistence incomes."

In a 2002 interview, Cobell herself attacked the government's stalling: "The government is going to fight this no matter what, even if it's morally or ethically wrong. That's a real crime in itself. They're in such denial, it's amazing. Congress needs to say

no more money to fight this litigation." Senator John McCain is spearheading just such a campaign to settle the suit through legislation. Although Cobell's accounting suggests the money owed the plaintiffs is as much as $176 billion, the plaintiffs have expressed a willingness to accept a settlement of approximately $27 billion.

In 2000, Cobell's long battle with the federal government earned her the special honor of being named a warrior of Blackfoot Nation—a distinction that is usually reserved for Blackfoot war veterans. Her experience has also inspired a project close to her heart. With Blackfeet educator Roberta Kipp, Cobell has created a bank for Blackfoot elementary school students, which allows them to put money into their own bank accounts. Cobell hopes the bank will teach young tribe members a valuable lesson: "I want these kids to understand the way the world works, and to question everything that comes before them."

Further Reading

Kennedy, J. Michael. "Truth and Consequences on the Reservation—The Eloise Cobell Story." *Los Angeles Times,* 7 July 2002, p. 14.

Maas, Peter. "The Broken Promise." *Parade Magazine,* 9 September 2001, pp. 4–6.

Whitty, Julia. "Accounting Coup." *Mother Jones,* September/October 2005, pp. 56–65.

Cockacoeske (Queen of Pamunkey)
(unknown–1686) *Pamunkey tribal leader*

Perhaps because of her forceful personality, Cockacoeske—hailed as the "queen of Pamunkey" by the Jamestown colonists—is one of the few Indian women discussed in written documents of the colonial era. Though few and brief, the surviving anecdotes about her are telling. Together, they paint a vivid portrait of an uncommonly astute politician, wily negotiator, and staunch defender of her homeland.

In 1607, about 50 years before Cockacoeske began her rule, English colonists founded the Jamestown settlement in the colony of Virginia. At that time, the Indians of the surrounding lands were united under Powhatan, the *werowance* (village leader) of the Pamunkey Indians. By force, Powhatan had taken control of several other area tribes and named himself the leader of a powerful confederacy.

When the colonial leaders and Powhatan first met, both had an interest in becoming allies. The colonists wanted Indian land; Powhatan wanted English trade goods. Although dealings between the two peoples were often strained, Powhatan, with help from his daughter POCAHONTAS, maintained fairly peaceful relations. After his death, however, the occasional raid gave way to open warfare. Broken by diseases contracted from the colonists and by superior European weaponry, the Powhatan confederacy was destroyed. The treaty that ended the war made the Indians subjects of the English.

The colonists soon began to demand that their Indian subjects help them battle other Indian groups considered enemies of Virginia. During one such engagement, Totopotomoy, the Pamunkey *werowance,* was killed. Following the Pamunkey rules of succession the title *weronsqua* (the term for a female *werowance*) fell to his widow, Cockacoeske, herself a descendant of the mighty Powhatan.

Little is known about the first 20 years of Cockacoeske's reign. Her initial appearance in colonial records dates from 1676, when she was summoned to a meeting of the General Assembly, Virginia's governing body. According to an eyewitness who later wrote of the event, she greatly impressed the assemblymen with her regal demeanor. Entering the chambers "with a comportment gracefull to admiration," she was draped in a floor-length deerskin cloak and wore a three-inch woven crown of black-and-white shell beads wrapped around her forehead. On her left was her 20-year-old son, John West, who was named for his father, a politically important English colonel. To her right was an interpreter. As she sat at the head of the council table, she motioned that the interpreter would speak for her, even though Cockacoeske probably knew English almost as well as her native tongue. The interpreter's presence was perhaps a ploy to coax the assemblymen into speaking their minds more freely.

The assembly chairman explained that the colonists wanted Cockacoeske's help. They were trying to put down a rebellion of poor, largely landless colonists, under the leadership of planter Nathaniel Bacon. Bacon's troops were angry at English officials and the colonial leaders, whom the rebels believed were hoarding the colony's wealth. The excuse they gave for rebelling, however, was the government's inadequacy in protecting them from Indian attacks. Using the Indians as a scapegoat, the rebels began slaughtering them randomly, without regard to whether their victims were the colonists' allies or enemies.

After the chairman finished speaking, Cockacoeske responded to his request with a long, stony silence. When he pressed her for an answer, she launched into an angry tirade, screaming over and over "Totopotomoy Chepiack," meaning "Totopotomoy dead." Cockacoeske demanded to know how the colonists could dare to ask her to send more Pamunkey into battle, when in the past they had never bothered to compensate her people for the loss of warriors fallen in their service. As she repeatedly pointed out, even she, the *weronsqua,* had received nothing after the death of her husband.

If the chairman was moved by her grievances, he did not reveal it. Instead, he blandly asked once again how many warriors she would supply. Echoing his indifference, Cockacoeske coldly offered him 12 men, a small fraction of the 150 warriors she had at her disposal.

As bitter as her experience with the assembly was, her dealings with Englishmen would soon become even worse. Several weeks later, her village was attacked by Bacon's troops. As the rebels plundered their homes, the inhabitants ran away in terror, including Cockacoeske, who escaped into the woods. She stayed in hiding for two weeks, nearly starving to death before she gathered the courage to return home.

Soon after the raid, Bacon's Rebellion was squelched, but the defeat gave the Pamunkey little satisfaction. They wanted their lands restored and stolen goods returned. Cockacoeske was particularly incensed; the marauders had made off with her English clothing and other finery she treasured. She petitioned the General Assembly to make restitution to her people, but when they were slow in responding, she took her complaints to officials in the English government. Understanding that the struggling colony could not afford to have a powerful leader such as Cockacoeske as an enemy, these officials insisted that the assemblymen appease this "faithfull friend to and lover of the English."

One result of this effort was the Treaty of Middle Plantation of 1677. Unlike most agreements between whites and Indians, it attempted to be fair to both sides. In the interest of maintaining good relations with Cockacoeske and other Indian leaders of the region, the colonists made many concessions to the tribe's demands. Its signing ushered in an era of relative peace that would last for more than a century.

The treaty also represented a bid by Cockacoeske for even greater power. During the negotiations, she insisted that the treaty identify her as the leader, not only of the Pamunkey, but also of several neighboring tribes. Like Powhatan, she wanted to hold sway over a great confederacy, but unlike her ancestor she chose to use negotiation rather than weapons to realize her ambition.

Cockacoeske's attempt to form her own empire was gutsy, if in the end unsuccessful. The tribes placed under her command resented their loss of independence, especially when she demanded tribute (a tax of goods or food) every spring and fall. Most simply refused to accept her as their ruler, and the English, from whose friendship Cockacoeske derived much of her influence, were careful to steer clear of the conflict. Undaunted, Cockacoeske continued to struggle with her reluctant subjects until her death in 1686. Although some were relieved at her passing, Indians and whites alike owed her a debt for helping pave the way toward an uncomfortable but peaceful coexistence.

Further Reading

Feest, Christian. *The Powhatan Indians.* New York: Chelsea House, 1990.
McCartney, Martha W. "Cockacoeske, Queen of Pamunkey, Diplomat and Suzeraine." In *Powhatan's Mantle: Indians in the Colonial Southeast,* edited by Peter Wood, et al., 173–195. Lincoln: University of Nebraska Press, 1989.
Rountree, Helen C. *Pocahontas's People: the Powhatan Indians of Virginia through Four Centuries.* Norman: University of Oklahoma Press, 1990.

Coocoochee
(ca. 1740–unknown)   *Mohawk medicine woman*

The late 18th century was a time of great change for the Indians of the Northeast. The story of Coocoochee tells of how one Mohawk woman, despite constant upheaval and adversity, was able to carve out a position of authority and influence among her people and in the world beyond.

Coocoochee was probably born about 1740 in a Mohawk village near what is now the Canadian city of Montreal. When Coocoochee was a teenager, the French traders and settlers who laid claim to her homeland began to fight colonists from England for control of eastern North America. The conflict—known as the French and Indian War (1754–63)—ended in defeat for the French. The Mohawks, who were friendly with French traders, were alarmed by the outcome. They were suspicious of the British victors, who generally treated Indians with far less respect than did the French.

During the war years, Coocoochee married a warrior named Cokundiawsaw, and the couple had four children, one girl and three boys. When their youngest son was still an infant, they decided to leave their village and move to lands in present-day Ohio. Like other Mohawk, they had become so frightened and distrustful of the British that they felt they had no choice but to abandon the land of their ancestors. In 1768, the family traveled more than 600 miles to their new home. The journey was no doubt difficult, but they had every confidence that the hardship was worthwhile. In a treaty, the British had promised that this new territory was to be for Indian use only and that whites would be forbidden from encroaching on it.

Like many other Mohawk refugees, Coocoochee and her family were taken in by another Indian tribe. They found a home among the Shawnee in a village headed by a dynamic young leader known to whites as Blue Jacket. Soon after the family had settled in, white colonists began to invade Indian territory about 100 miles to the south. The fighting made Blue Jacket's followers nervous: They began to question the worth of the British government's guarantees that their own land would be theirs forever. The outbreak of the American Revolution (1775–83) confirmed their fears of white interference. Their village, situated between an American and an English stronghold, was sure to be caught in the middle of the conflict. Blue Jacket's followers, including Coocoochee's family, had no choice but to flee their homes in 1777.

They resettled to the south along the Mad River. While there, Coocoochee's husband and her eldest son helped fight the American rebels, whom they regarded as a greater threat to their lands than even the hated British. To Coocoochee's delight, her daughter married and had two children, but to the family's sorrow, her son-in-law was killed in a skirmish with Americans. In 1786, Americans raided their village and burned their homes and fields. Once again Coocoochee's family had to run from white invaders.

Still with Blue Jacket's people, they settled in a village on the Maumee River near present-day Fort Wayne, Indiana. Coocoochee remained there for only three years. The new U.S. government wanted Indians to leave the midwestern territory it had previously promised them so it could open up the lands for settlement by white Americans. In 1790, the government sent in troops to drive the Indians out. Many Indians resisted, including Cokundiawsaw, who died in hand-to-hand combat. Coocoochee and the rest of her family escaped, but they refused to leave the area. They and other militants resettled 60 miles away on the Maumee in an area called the Glaize.

Many more details are known about Coocoochee's life during the period she lived at the Glaize, largely because of the memoirs of Oliver Spencer. A white settler, Spencer was taken captive by one of Coocoochee's sons, White Loon, in July 1792 when Spencer was 11 years old. During his nine months of captivity, he lived with the widowed Coocoochee and her two grandchildren. Like many Indian captives, Spencer was adopted by his captors. Coocoochee soon came to regard him as a son, and he came to see her as his mother.

When Spencer arrived in the village, he was scraped and bruised. Coocoochee immediately began tending his wounds. Through sign language, she told him to bathe in the river, then instructed him to lie in the sun, leaving him there for several hours while she prepared a medicinal drink from barks and roots. She fed him the drink, and within several days, the boy was healed. As Spencer discovered, Coocoochee's knowledge of medicines and healing gave her a special status and unique influence over her neighbors along the Maumee.

As befitting her parent-child relationship with Spencer, Coocoochee diligently saw to his education. She shared with him the same traditional Mohawk stories she told her grandchildren. She taught him about the spirit land, where virtuous Mohawk went after death if they were buried properly. In this paradise, the weather was always pleasant; flowers were always in bloom; and huge melons, pumpkins, and corn grew up in abundance from untended plots. While Spencer lived with her, Coocoochee followed Mohawk custom by exhuming the body of her husband Cokundiawsaw and reburying it according to the necessary rites in order to ensure his passage to the spirit world.

Although Cokundiawsaw had been killed by a white soldier, Coocoochee had no trouble getting along with whites who earned her affection or respect. When her daughter married a white trader, she enthusiastically accepted him into her family, especially after he started giving her gifts as a good son-in-law was expected to do. Spencer also recorded that Coocoochee had special admiration

49

for another white captive, a young man who was exceptionally strong. He repaid her respect by building a special room onto her house where she could perform healing ceremonies. At the Glaize, where Indians of many tribes lived and non-Indian traders visited frequently, Coocoochee's ability to get along with a variety of people often proved to be valuable.

Among Indians, Coocoochee frequently served as a trusted figure of authority. Spencer described a traditional Green Corn Ceremony at the Glaize, during which Coocoochee contributed delicacies to the great feast as Mohawk women traditionally did. But late in the evening, before the men opened a keg of whiskey, they dutifully handed over their knives and weapons to Coocoochee in order to avoid serious violence if a brawl broke out.

According to Spencer, Coocoochee also served as an adviser on matters of war. In one instance, a contingent of 50 Shawnee warriors came to her house. They were planning to join the Miami war leader Little Turtle in a raid on an American supply convoy and wanted her to use her powers to determine whether the raid would be successful. For an hour, she performed rites in her home's spiritual chamber in order to prompt a vision of the outcome. When she walked outside, she spread her arms forward, brought her fingertips together to form a circle, and announced "Meechee!"— "Great" in the Shawnee language. Her prediction was correct, and in the raid the warriors made off with an enormous haul. They thanked Coocoochee for her help by giving her an array of the treasured trade goods they had stolen from the Americans.

However exciting, the raid was only one small victory in a larger conflict between midwestern Indians and Americans. Led by Little Turtle, the Indians of the Maumee Valley had banded together to fight the white settlers in their lands and the American soldiers sent to protect them. But in 1794, in the Battle of Fallen Timbers, the U.S. troops finally overwhelmed the Indian force. After the defeat, Coocoochee most likely once again was forced to flee her home village, but where she went or what became of her is unknown.

What is known about Coocoochee from the historical record reveals that she was a woman of remarkable talents and charisma. Despite her constant displacement, Coocoochee continued to remind the Mohawk of their traditional ways. At the same time, she faced continual change with a courage and adaptability that helped herself, her family, and her people survive the destruction of much of the world they had known.

Further Reading

Tanner, Helen Hornbeck. "Coocoochee: Mohawk Medicine Woman." *American Indian Cultural and Research Journal* 3 (1979): 23–41.

Cook-Lynn, Elizabeth
(1930–) *Dakota Sioux educator, poet, novelist, short story writer, essayist*

"I am me. I exist. I am Dakota. I write." Using these words, author Elizabeth Cook-Lynn described the roots of her creative mission. On November 17, 1930, she was born Elizabeth Bowed Head Irving on the Crow Creek Indian Reservation in South Dakota. Her grandfather was the distinguished Dakota Sioux leader Bowed Head, who on several occasions traveled to Washington, D.C., with Sitting Bull to negotiate treaties on the Sioux's behalf. He also helped write the first dictionary of the Dakota language and with Elizabeth's father served on the Crow Creek Tribal Council. Her grandmother Eliza, in addition to being her namesake, was another powerful influence on her youth. Eliza wrote articles in Dakota about community affairs for Christian newspapers published throughout North and South Dakota.

Raised in a traditional household, Elizabeth became well versed in the oral traditions of the Dakota Sioux. But as a girl she also was fascinated by the written word. She later remembered that she read everything she could find, from John Milton's *Paradise Lost* to *True Confessions* magazine to the Sears catalog. In all her reading, however, she never found a mention of her own people. Cook-Lynn recalled her frustration in a 1987 autobiographical essay: "What happens to a reasonably intelligent child who sees him or herself excluded from a world which is created and recreated with the obvious intent to declare him or her *persona non grata?*" In her case, the realization bred first mistrust and later anger. "That anger is what started me writing," maintains Cook-Lynn.

Elizabeth Irving attended South Dakota State College, from which she graduated in 1952 with a bachelor's degree in English and journalism. The next year, she married Melvin Traversie Cook. They had four children before they divorced in 1970. Five years later, she was remarried to Clyde J. Lynn. Thereafter, she adopted the surname Cook-Lynn, an amalgamation of her two married names.

While raising her family, Elizabeth Cook-Lynn worked as a journalist, editor, and high school teacher. In 1966, she decided to return to school and was awarded a master's degree from the University of South Dakota in Vermillion in 1972. Cook-Lynn was then hired as an associate professor of Native American Studies at Eastern Washington University at Cheney, which granted her emeritus status in 1993. She has since served as a visiting professor and writer-in-residence at universities across the country.

Cook-Lynn began writing poetry and fiction in college. Although her early work appeared in many literary magazines and journals, she contends that she did not feel confident in her ability to write until after she turned forty. National recognition of her work came with the publication of *Then Badger Said This* (1978, reissued 1983), which combines poetry, fiction, and personal remembrances to create a portrait of reservation life. Cook-Lynn has acknowledged that the structure was inspired by *The Way to Rainy Mountain* (1969) by N. Scott Momaday, a Kiowa writer whom Cook-Lynn names as one of her greatest influences. Cook-Lynn has also published a book of short stories, *The Power of Horses* (1990); a novel, *From the River's Edge* (1991); the poetry collections *Seek the House of Relatives* (1993) and *Notebooks* (2007); a collection of three novellas, *Aurelia: A*

Crow Creek Trilogy (1999); and several works of nonfiction, including *Why I Can't Read Wallace Stegner and Other Essays* (1996). She has also served as the editor of the *Wiscazo Sa Review: A Journal of Native American Studies,* which she and anthropologist BEATRICE A. MEDICINE helped found in 1985.

Cook-Lynn has written that the "'real' poets" of the Dakota are "the men and women who sit at the drum and sing the old songs and create new ones." But she also sees written literature as playing a crucial role in the Sioux's present and future. "Writing is an essential act of survival for contemporary American Indians," Cook-Lynn has explained. "I'm not interested in some kind of melancholy reminiscence. . . . I'm interested in the cultural, historical, and political survival of Indian nations, and that's why I write and teach."

Further Reading

Bruchac, Joseph. "As a Dakotah Woman." In *Survival This Way: Interviews with American Indian Poets,* 57–71. Tucson: University of Arizona Press, 1987.

Cook-Lynn, Elizabeth. *Aurelia: A Crow Creek Trilogy.* Niwot: University Press of Colorado, 1999.

———. *From the River's Edge.* New York: Arcade Publishers, 1991.

———. *New Indians, Old Wars: Essays on Fiction, Criticism and Politics.* Champaign: University of Illinois Press, 2007.

———. *Then Badger Said This.* Fairfield, Wash.: Ye Galleon Press, 1983.

———. *Why I Can't Read Wallace Stegner and Other Essays.* Madison: University of Wisconsin Press, 1996.

———. "You May Consider Speaking about Your Art." In *I Tell You Now: Autobiographical Essays by Native American Writers,* edited by Brian Swann and Arnold Krupat, 56–63. Lincoln: University of Nebraska Press, 1987.

Coolidge, Rita
(1944–)   *Cherokee singer*

After great success as a pop singer during the 1970s, Rita Coolidge has returned to her Native American roots as part of the award-winning trio Walela. Coolidge was born in Nashville, Tennessee, on May

1, 1944. Her father was a full Cherokee, while her mother was half Cherokee and half Scottish. In her youth, Coolidge paid little attention to her

Rita Coolidge is pictured here while on tour in London in 1971.
(AP/Wide World Photo)

Indian heritage, although her maternal grandmother often sang songs about her family and their experiences as Cherokee.

Speaking of her family, Coolidge once recalled, "music was a natural part of our lives, just like sleeping and eating." The daughters of a minister, she and her two sisters, Priscilla and Linda, grew up singing in church. All blessed with strong voices, the three girls often sang hymns in close harmony.

When Coolidge was 15, her family moved to Florida. After high school, she entered Florida State University to study art. She started a folk group to earn money for tuition. Hoping to make enough money for graduate school, she moved to Memphis, Tennessee, to work for a jingle company. Encouraged by her employer, she then moved to Los Angeles, California, in search of a performing career.

Coolidge first gained attention by singing backup vocals for rock artists Eric Clapton and Duane Allman on the album *Delaney, Bonnie, and Friends.* She then went on to tour with Joe Cocker and Leon Russell, during which she performed nightly a show-stopping version of Russell's song "Superstar." Coolidge also met singer-songwriter Kris Kristoffersen while singing backup. The two were married from 1973 to 1980. Coolidge and Kristoffersen won Grammy Awards for Best Country Vocal Performance for a Group or Duo in 1973 and 1975. They also appeared together in the film *Pat Garrett & Billy the Kid* (1973).

By the late 1970s, Coolidge had become a successful solo artist. Her 1977 album *Anytime . . . Anywhere* produced three hit singles—"Higher and Higher," "The Way You Do the Things You Do," and "We're All Alone." She also scored a hit with "All Time High," the theme song for the James Bond movie *Octopussy* (1983).

Throughout the 1980s and 1990s, Coolidge's star faded, although she continued to record and tour. One of her songs, "Cherokee Morning Song," caught the attention of Mohawk singer Robbie Robertson. He was compiling the album *Music for Native Americans,* which would serve as the sound track for the television series *The Native Americans.* At Robertson's request, Coolidge recorded the song for the album accompanied by her sister Priscilla and her niece Laura Satterfield. Coolidge was inspired by the seamless blending of their voices: "Those sessions went so well, we knew we had to do something."

What they did was form a new group, Walela, named after the Cherokee word for butterfly. The act's sound combines close harmonies with spare instrumentation, often including Indian drums or flute. Walela's style is an eclectic mix, incorporating Coolidge's background in rock and gospel with Native music and Indian themes. For instance, on their first self-titled CD, the trio sings "Amazing Grace" in Cherokee to the accompaniment of Scottish bagpipes. Released in 1998, *Walela* was an enormous success. At that year's Native American Music Awards, Walela was honored as the best debut group, and their song "The Warrior" was named song of the year. Coolidge was also given a lifetime achievement award. Walela has since followed up with two more well-received CDs: *Unbearable Love* (2002) and *Walela Live in Concert* (2004).

Coolidge continues to perform as a solo artist, most recently releasing a CD of standards titled *And So Is Love* (2005). But working as part of Walela holds a special place for her, allowing her to explore her Cherokee roots and pay homage to her elders. She has explained that Walela's music is meant "to honor our grandmothers, who had strong musical voices. . . . We could feel them around us in the studio as we gave voice to some of the things those old women could never express when they were alive."

Further Reading/Resources

Poet, J. "Walela." *Native Peoples,* May/June 2003, pp. 28–30.

Rita Coolidge Web site. URL: http://www.ritacoolidge. com. Downloaded on May 7, 2006.

Walela. Triloka Records, CD, 2002.

Walela Web site. URL: http://www.walela.com. Downloaded on May 7, 2006.

Cordero, Helen
(1915–1994) *Cochiti Pueblo potter*

Perhaps the most popular Native American potter of her time, Helen Quintana Cordero was born at Cochiti Pueblo in northern New Mexico on July 17, 1915. At 17, she married Fernando (Fred) Cordero, a local political leader who often played drums during ceremonies held in the pueblo. Her early adulthood was devoted to making a home for herself, her husband, and their six children.

As her children grew older, Cordero decided to spend her free time in a creative pursuit. She was inspired by the many artists and craftspeople at Cochiti, most of whom made their living by selling traditional Pueblo crafts to non-Indian tourists and art collectors. In Cordero's words, "Everyone around me was making beautiful things, and I wanted to do something, too."

She first tried her hand at crafting leather items decorated with beadwork, but discovered that the money she could earn from selling her wares barely covered the cost of the materials. Her husband's aunt, known to her as Grandma Juanita, then suggested that she take up pottery-making—an art revered for many centuries among the Pueblo. According to Cordero, Grandma Juanita asked, "Why don't you . . . go back to potteries? You don't have to buy anything; Mother Earth gives it all to you."

Working alongside Fred's cousin, Juanita Arquero, Cordero began making pottery in the late 1950s. Her first efforts were frustrating. Arquero, like many Pueblo women, had been taught to make pots as a child and could work the clay with a confidence and expertise that the novice Cordero admired. She complained that in comparison with Arquero's her pots were "crooked" and "never looked right." Cordero was on the verge of giving up on pottery for good when her friend suggested she try making figurines from clay instead. Small clay figures had been made by their ancestors, but at that time just a few Cochiti potters more than dabbled in them. Non-Indians who collected Pueblo art dismissed the Indians' figurines as tourist curios and were willing to pay very little for them. Pueblo artists who sought to make a decent livelihood from their work, therefore, were compelled to concentrate on pots, which could more often fetch high prices.

Despite its status as a lesser art, Helen Cordero was immediately taken with making figurines. Molding her first clay figure was a revelation: she later told an interviewer that the experience was "like a flower blooming." Eager to see what shapes she could make, she feverishly began experimenting with different forms—including birds, animals, and "little people" that stood about eight inches tall. One of the first times she exhibited her works, these small human figures caught the eye of folk art collector Alexander Girard. He bought all she had to sell, then later commissioned her to make new sculptures to his specifications. One such request was for a large seated figure with several children around it. Girard probably had in mind a particular style of figure known as a "singing mother," which traditionally had been made at the Cochiti Pueblo.

As Cordero grappled with this commission, she kept seeing a mental picture of her grandfather, Santiago Quintana. A leader in the pueblo, Quintana felt strongly that the Pueblo needed to preserve their traditional beliefs and practices. With this eagerness to share his knowledge of Pueblo ways, he was a favorite interview subject of the many anthropologists who studied the Indians' culture in the late 19th and early 20th century. Among the Pueblo, Quintana was known for his love of storytelling, through which he passed along this same knowledge to the next generation. In Pueblo society, storytellers are more than just entertainers; they are also educators. With a crowd of children gathered around them, they tell mythic tales and stories of their people's history. Through these stories, versions of which have been passed along orally over the course of many centuries, children learn what it means to be a Pueblo Indian.

With the voice of her grandfather in her head, Cordero crafted her first "storytelling doll." Unlike the "singing mother" figure type, which usually represents a woman cradling one or two children, her storytelling doll depicted a man with five tiny figures crawling all over him. The doll's mouth was wide open, captured in the midst of telling a tale, as the children—fidgety, yet attentive—clung to the storyteller's head and body while hanging on his every word.

Encouraged by the enthusiastic reception of this sculpture, Cordero began experimenting with the new figure style she had invented. Working through all of its possibilities, she varied the central figure's size from six to 12 inches in height and

Helen Cordero sculpts a storytelling doll in this 1979 photograph.

54

tried adding more and more children. On some sculptures, the storyteller was almost completed covered by as many as 30 small listeners. On each new sculpture, Cordero gave each of the child figures its own unique look, pose, and expression. But soon all her storytellers had a similar face with a round, open mouth and tightly shut eyes. Cordero explained that the face is her grandfather's: "His eyes are closed because he's thinking; his mouth is open because he's singing."

Cordero's storytelling dolls brought her instant acclaim with the public. When they were first exhibited at the craft competition at the 1964 New Mexico State Fair, Cordero took home the prizes for first, second, and third place. The next year, she garnered first prize at the prestigious Santa Fe Indian Market, only the first of many such honors. Soon Cordero was exhibiting her sculptures in galleries and museums, including Phoenix's Heard Museum, where in 1976 she had her first one-woman show. With each honor, Cordero's fame grew, but the demand for her work skyrocketed after one of her storyteller dolls appeared on the cover of *Sunset* magazine in 1972. The number of commissions she received subsequently was so large that she probably was not able to complete them all within her lifetime.

Many other Pueblo potters have reaped their own financial rewards from Cordero's "invention" of the storytelling doll. Capitalizing on Cordero's inability to make enough dolls to fill the overwhelming demand for them among art collectors, a number of Pueblo artists, including some of Cordero's children and grandchildren, have started making their own versions of her figures. Today, nearly 300 potters in 13 different pueblos make storytellers. In their variations on Cordero's figure style, the storyteller often becomes a woman or even an animal, such as a bear or owl, and the number of children represented is sometimes as high as one hundred.

Images of Cordero's storytellers have appeared on cards, posters, and T-shirts. Before her death in 1994, the artist expressed her discomfort with this merchandising of her creation: "They call them Storytellers, but they don't even know what it means. They don't even know it's my grandfather." She was equally ambivalent about her fame. In Cordero's eyes, the attention paid to her did not grant proper credit to the sources of her inspiration: "Grandma Clay . . . she tells me what to do. . . . It's not me, it's the fire, he decides how they'll come out. . . . It's my grandfather, he's giving me these. He was a wise man with lots of stories and lots of grandchildren and we're all there, in the clay."

Further Reading

Babcock, Barbara A. "Clay Changes: Helen Cordero and the Pueblo Storyteller." *American Indian Art* 8 (Spring 1983): 30–39.

Babcock, Barbara A., Guy Monthan, and Doris Monthan. *The Pueblo Storyteller: Development of a Figurative Ceramic Tradition.* Tucson: University of Arizona Press, 1986.

Congdon-Martin, Douglas. *Storytellers and Other Figurative Pottery.* 2nd ed. Atglen, Pa.: Schiffer Publishing, 1999.

Hirschfelder, Arlene. "Helen Cordero: Cochiti Storyteller Dollmaker." In *Artists and Craftspeople,* 45–52. New York: Facts On File, 1994.

Monthan, Guy, and Doris. "Helen Cordero." *American Indian Art* 2 (1977): 72–76.

Crow Dog, Mary
See BRAVE BIRD, MARY

Cuero, Delfina
(ca. 1900–1972) *Diegueño autobiographer*

In her autobiography, Delfina Cuero created, through her own story, a portrait of the Diegueño people during the most difficult period in their history. She was born in about 1900 near the San Diego de Alcadá, a Spanish mission in present-day San Diego, California. Beginning in the late 18th century, many of her ancestors were forced to live and work there.

After the mission system was dissolved in 1834, some California Indian groups received reservations. The Diegueño, however, did not. Though landless, for decades they were able to continue their traditional practice of migrating with the seasons to areas abundant in fish, animals, and wild plant foods.

By the time Delfina was born, this way of life was becoming increasingly difficult, as non-Indians began to establish farms and ranches on the Diegueño ancestral lands. She later explained, "White people kept moving into more and more places and we couldn't camp around those places anymore. We went farther from San Diego, looking for places where nobody chased us away." Eventually, her family had to migrate across the international border to Baja California, Mexico.

In her early teens, Delfina Cuero was dealt a devastating blow when her father abandoned the family. Her mother then insisted Cuero take a husband so they would have a man to hunt for food for them. Cuero married Sebastian Osum, who treated her well. They had five surviving children together.

When Cuero's oldest son was eleven, Osum suddenly died. At a time when all the Diegueño were having trouble feeding themselves, she found herself the sole provider for her family. Survival was a constant struggle. She did domestic work for non-Indians for food and clothing. Often Cuero became involved with non-Indian men who promised to help her but instead abused her. She became so desperate that, to make ends meet, she sold her son into indentured servitude.

Adding to her difficulties, U.S. authorities would not allow her to travel into the United States when, in the 1960s, she wanted to return to California to live among her surviving family members there. Although she was born in the United States, the authorities would not accept she was a U.S. citizen without documentation. She later explained her desire to come home: "I keep praying to God that before I am too old to work for my living I can come back where I belong and be among the few relatives I still have alive, I pray that something will work out so that my children and grandchildren can come back with me to where I was born."

An anthropologist and scholar named Florence Shipek offered to help Cuero. If Cuero would tell her life story to a translator, Shipek would assemble it into an autobiography that Cuero could then submit as evidence of her citizenship. In 1968, *The Autobiography of Delfina Cuero* was published. It remains an important source of scholarship about Diegueño traditions and their struggle to retain their culture in the 20th century.

Cuero's story had the desired effect. She was allowed to return to southern California in 1967. Delfina Cuero remained there until her death in 1972.

Further Reading

Cuero, Delfina. *The Autobiography of Delfina Cuero.* Edited by Florence Shipek. Translated by Rosalie Pinto Robertson. 1968. Reprint, Banning, Calif.: Malki Museum Press, 1970.

Round, Phillip H. "Delfina Cuero: A Native Woman's Life in the Borderlands." In *Sifters: Native American Women's Lives,* edited by Theda Perdue, 187–203. New York: Oxford University Press, 2001.

D

Dabuda
See KEYSER, LOUISA

Dann, Carrie (1934–   ), **Mary Dann** (1924–   )
Shoshone activists

For decades, Carrie and Mary Dann have fought the U.S. government to recognize the land rights of the Western Shoshone. They and their brothers, Richard and Clifford, were brought up on a ranch in north-central Nevada. Their father, Dewey, had first tried his hand at farming, but his white neighbors destroyed his crops by allowing their livestock to wander through his fields. He gave up farming to take up ranching, establishing a ranch that eventually encompassed about 800 acres of land.

As adults, Carrie, Mary, and Clifford took over the family ranch. They worked long and hard—caring for their cattle, breaking wild horses, and mending the fence around their land. In spring 1973, Mary Dann was approached by an official from the Bureau of Land Management (BLM), the federal agency that administers the United States's public lands. He asked Dann for her herding permit. Dann did not have one. Dewey Dann had paid the U.S. government fees for their animals to graze on lands the United States claimed. His children, though, saw no sense in this. They did not accept the United States's claims, convinced instead that the grazing land they used was owned by the Western Shoshone.

The Danns based this belief on the Treaty of Ruby Valley of 1863. In this peace treaty, the Shoshone agreed to allow non-Indians to travel through their homeland, which included about two-thirds of the modern state of Nevada. But the Shoshone did not give away title to their land. Even so, the Indian Claims Commission, which was established to settle all outstanding claims of Indian tribes against the U.S. government, found that the Shoshone homeland belonged to the United States. In 1962, it held that the Shoshone had lost their claim to their land through "gradual encroachment" by non-Indians, although much of the land still remains largely uninhabited.

In 1979, the federal government determined that the proper compensation for the Shoshone land was $26 million, representing $15 per acre based on the prevailing land prices in 1872. The majority of the Shoshone, however, refused to accept this payment. As Carrie Dann explained in 1996, "We don't want any damn money from them. . . . [M]y land is not for sale. . . . [T]hey can't buy my rights. . . . [T]o them the land is real estate, to me it's my Mother."

In 1974, the BLM filed a suit against the Danns, claiming they were trespassing on public lands. For more than 10 years, the Danns battled the government through the courts. At their court appearances, Mary was largely a stoic presence. The outspoken Carrie was more willing to speak her mind. A *New York Times* profile in 2002 held that "Carrie can leap into language so caustic it could wear the enamel off teeth." The suit reached the Supreme Court. In 1985, the Court found in favor of the U.S. government. It concluded that the Shoshone homeland belonged the United States because the Shoshone had received compensation for it: Even though the Shoshone refused the $26 million, it had been accepted on their behalf and placed in an account for them by the secretary of the Interior.

To continue to fight for their land rights, the Danns founded the Dann Defense Project in 1991. (The next year, it was renamed the Western Shoshone Defense Project.) The organization has also actively challenged the right of gold companies to mine and the United States to test nuclear weapons on Shoshone ancestral territory.

The Danns' continuing battle won them support from rights groups representing indigenous peoples from around the globe. They were given the International Rights Livelihood Award in 1993. Their cause has also been taken up by the Inter-American Commission on Human Rights of the Organization of American States and the United Nations Committee on the Elimination of Racial Discrimination.

Despite this international attention, the Danns have paid a heavy price for their activism. In 1992, heavily armed government officials descended on their ranch to confiscate their herds. The raid resulted in a six-day standoff with helicopters hovering over head. Clifford Dann doused himself with gasoline, threatening to set himself on fire, before he was arrested for supposedly assaulting federal officers. The officers removed more than 250 horses. Raids in 2002 and 2003 confiscated

hundreds more horses and heads of cattle. The government is also seeking to collect $3 million from the Danns in fees and penalties.

The Danns' fight divided the Shoshone. While some supported Carrie and Mary, others wanted to accept the government's monetary offer, figuring that the return of their homeland was an impossible dream. In 2005, Nevada congressmen Harry Reid, John Ensign, and Jim Gibbons pushed through legislation that forced the distribution of compensation to the Shoshone. It was signed into law by President George W. Bush. Its sponsors claimed they were only responding to their Shoshone constituents' demands for compensation. (The fund, with interest calculated, amounted to about $140 million, bringing the per capita payment to $20,000.) The legislation, however, also opened the door to the United States's wholesale licensing of mineral rights to the Shoshone's resource-rich lands.

While out mending fences, Mary Dann was killed in an all-terrain vehicle accident on April 22, 2005. Commenting on the tragedy, her niece Patricia Paul took solace in that she died "as she would have wanted—with her boots on and hay in her pocket." Carrie Dann released a statement on the event of her sister's death: "Mary would want us to be strong. She believed in living her life for the protection of her family, the life—the sacred (the land, the air, the water, the sun) . . . We must always remember the future generations and protect the sacred things so that the little ones coming behind us will be OK. The struggle will go on."

Further Reading

LeDuff, Charlie. "Range War in Nevada Pits U.S. against 2 Shoshone Indians." *New York Times,* 31 October 2002, sec. A, p. 18.
Nielsen, Nancy J. "Carrie Dann." *Reformers and Activists.* New York: Facts On File, 1997, pp. 70–77.
Western Shoshone Defense Project. Available online. URL: http://www.wsdp.org. Downloaded on May 19, 2006.

Dat So La Lee
See KEYSER, LOUISA

DeCora, Angel (Angel DeCora Dietz)
(1871–1919)   *Winnebago illustrator, educator, short story writer*

A pioneer in using non-Indian art techniques to represent Indian subjects and designs, illustrator Angel DeCora was born on May 3, 1871. She was reared on the Winnebago reservation in Nebraska by parents from two of the most prominent families among the tribe. They gave her the Indian name Hinook-Mahwi-Kilinaka, which can be translated as "Fleecy Cloud Floating in Place" or "Woman Coming on the Clouds in Glory." It

inspired her nickname "Angel," which she used throughout her professional career.

Angel DeCora briefly attended a local reservation school before she was sent to the Hampton Institute in Virginia when she was twelve years old. This boarding school was dedicated to teaching Indian children to abandon Indian ways and to adopt in their place white beliefs and customs. According to an autobiographical essay written in 1911, DeCora explained that she was taken to Hampton without her or her family's consent. She and five other children were kidnapped by a "strange white man" and put on an eastbound

Angel DeCora paints in the studio of her instructor, Howard Pyle, circa 1897.
(Courtesy of Hampton University Archives)

train. Representatives of Indian boarding schools commonly used this method of "recruiting" reservation students during the late 19th century.

At Hampton, Angel learned to speak English and excelled in both art and music. After attending the school for five years, she was sent home, but her return to the reservation was brief and unhappy. Both of her parents had died, and her years away had left her unfamiliar with reservation life and uncomfortable living among her people. With nowhere else to go, she decided to return to Hampton, where she studied until 1891.

The officials at Hampton were so impressed by Angel DeCora's musical talents that they arranged for her to continue her education in music at Burnham's Classical School for Girls in Northampton, Massachusetts. But soon her interest in painting and drawing led her in a different direction. She decided instead to study art at nearby Smith College, one of the United States's premiere colleges for women. During her four years there, she worked as a custodian to pay for her tuition.

At Smith, DeCora was educated in non-Indian art traditions and history. This training made DeCora highly unusual among Indian artists of the time. Most worked in traditional Indian arts, such as pottery and basketry, that they had learned in childhood from family members.

After graduating with honors, DeCora moved to Philadelphia, Pennsylvania, to attend the Drexel Institute, which offered the best training in book and magazine illustration available. She studied with the famous illustrator Howard Pyle, who immediately saw DeCora's talent. He encouraged her to draw on her Indian heritage for subject matter in her art. DeCora, however, had only hazy memories of her childhood among the Winnebagos. At Pyle's suggestion, she spent the summer of 1897 on the Fort Berthold Indian Reservation in North Dakota, studying and sketching the Arikara, Mandan, and Hidatsa Indians who lived there. From this research and from what she could recall about the Winnebago, DeCora began to draw pictures of everyday Indian life, which was then an extremely popular subject for magazine

illustrations. Her first published works appeared in *Harper's New Monthly Magazine* in 1899. They illustrated two stories she wrote herself, "The Sick Child" and "Grey Wolf's Daughter."

Many non-Indian artists of the period made a livelihood by illustrating sentimental images of traditional Indian life or exciting scenes of Indian warriors or hunters. Usually, these images were based more on the artists' imagination than on the actual experiences of Indian people. DeCora, however, worked to make her depictions of Indians accurate. She was also unusual in portraying Indian women and nontraditional Indians dressed in the style of whites—both of which were rarely included in the works of non-Indian illustrators.

In 1899, DeCora moved to Boston, where she established a studio and continued her education at the Boston Museum of Fine Arts School. Three years later, she relocated to New York City, where she became a professional illustrator specializing in books about Indians and their heritage. Working as a freelance artist, she provided the illustrations for four books: Francis La Flesche's *The Middle Five: Indian Boys at School* (1900), Zitkala-Ša's *Old Indian Legends* (1901), Mary Catherine Judd's *Wigwam Stories Told by North American Indians* (1906), and Natalie Curtis's *The Indian's Book* (1907). DeCora's work on Zitkala-Ša's book resulted in a long friendship with its author, the Sioux activist also known as GERTRUDE SIMMONS BONNIN.

In 1906, DeCora was asked to join the faculty of the Carlisle Industrial Indian School in Carlisle, Pennsylvania. This government-run institution had long been a model for Indian boarding schools across the United States. Like her own school, Hampton, it had sought to teach Indian girls and boys to live like whites. The U.S. government, however, was reconsidering this theory of education. The new commissioner of Indian affairs, Francis E. Leupp, offered DeCora a job at Carlisle because he wanted her help in reforming the school. They agreed that Indian students should be taught to respect their Indian heritage rather than to despise their own people and their culture.

As head of the Carlisle art department, DeCora had her work cut out for her. The program had long been lacking in direction and rigor. According to Leupp, the school's art instruction had concentrated on teaching Indian children "whose own mothers were masters of decorative design, to paint pansies on plush pillows and forget-me-nots on picture frames." DeCora put aside the pillows and frames and gave her students pens and paints, along with an introduction to using these materials based on her many years of art training. Her students were among the first Indian artists to develop expertise in the non-Indian art techniques of drawing on paper and painting on canvas.

DeCora also encouraged her students to experiment with Indian designs and patterns. Many resisted her efforts. Taught by previous teachers to dislike anything Indian, they thought so little of their people that they did not believe that traditional Indians could be artists. As DeCora later said, "When I first introduced the subject—Indian art—to the Carlisle Indian students, I experienced the discouraging sensation that I was addressing members of an alien race." In time, her pupils embraced her teachings and came to share her enthusiasm for researching the designs created by potters, basketmakers, and other traditional artisans.

DeCora spread her message outside the classroom by lecturing frequently. She was also an enthusiastic supporter of the Society of American Indians—an influential organization founded in 1911 by an elite group of Indian intellectuals. At the society's first convention, she delivered a well-received speech about Native American art.

While at Carlisle, DeCora met and married a Sioux student, William "Lone Star" Dietz. The couple collaborated on the book illustrations for Elaine Goodale Eastman's *Yellow Star: A Story of East and West,* a novel about a young Indian woman's difficulty in readjusting to Indian society after attending an all-white school in New England. Dietz also assisted his wife in the classroom until she left Carlisle in 1915. The couple briefly moved to Washington State, but by 1918 they were divorced. DeCora returned to the East—first to Albany, New York, where she worked as an illustrator for the New York State Museum, then to New York City, where she resumed her freelance work. Her renewed art career was tragically cut short on February 6, 1919, when she fell victim to a great worldwide epidemic of influenza.

In one of many published tributes to DeCora, her friend Natalie Curtis recalled DeCora's own description of the goal of her work: "My people are a race of designers. I look for the day when the Indian shall make beautiful things for all the world." In part because of DeCora's encouragement of an appreciation of Native American art, works by Indian artists of the past and present are now treasured by art lovers around the globe.

Further Reading

McAnulty, Sarah. "Angel DeCora: American Indian Artist and Educator." *Nebraska History* 57 (1976): 143–199.

Pfeffer, Wendy. "Angel DeCora Dietz." In *Notable Native Americans,* edited by Sharon Malinowski, 125–126. Detroit: Gale Research, 1995.

Deer, Ada
(1935–) *Menominee activist, tribal leader, educator, public servant*

Few Indian leaders have served their people with as much determination and success as did Ada Deer. As a young social worker, she provided services to American Indians in need. As an activist, she helped ensure the survival of her tribe. As the head of the Bureau of Indian Affairs (BIA), Deer made great strides in improving the relationship between the United States and all Native Americans.

Born on August 7, 1935, Ada Elizabeth Deer grew up on the Menominee Indian reservation in rural northern Wisconsin. The Menominee tribe had lived in this area for more than 5,000 years. The eldest of nine children (only five of whom lived to adulthood), Ada spent most of her youth living with her large family in a one-room log house without heat or running water.

Her father, Joseph, was a Menominee Indian who worked in the reservation's lumber mill, like most of the other men of the tribe. Unfortunately, he also shared with many other Menominees a tendency toward alcohol abuse. A curious girl, Ada asked her father to tell her stories about the Menominee people and the old customs and beliefs, but he avoided answering her questions. Only as an adult did she come to understand why. Joseph Deer had been sent to a government-sponsored Indian boarding school as a boy. There he had been taught by non-Indian teachers to be ashamed of his Menominee heritage and was threatened with beatings if he observed any of his native customs or spoke the Menominee language.

Ada's mother, Constance Wood, grew up in very different circumstances. She was the daughter of wealthy white parents who lived in a beautiful house staffed with servants in Philadelphia. When she was due to marry, Constance rebelled against her family and decided to study to become a nurse. She then took a job with the BIA—the agency of the U.S. government that oversees its dealings with Native Americans. Hired to provide medical services to Indian communities, she was assigned to the Menominee reservation, where she met and married Joseph Deer. Despite her white heritage, Constance Deer became a passionate supporter of Indian rights and enthusiastic student of Indian cultures. Ada Deer in a 1993 speech before the United States Senate named her mother as "the single greatest influence on [her] life."

When Ada was five, her maternal grandfather came to the reservation. He had not arrived for a friendly visit, but rather to persuade his daughter to leave her Menominee family and come home to Philadelphia. Constance Deer refused, and her father left. The brief incident, however, would remain vivid in Ada's memory. Her grandfather had made a point of ignoring her and her brothers and sisters, obviously because he was offended by their Indian ancestry. This early encounter with anti-Indian prejudice taught her a disturbing lesson: "I began to discover that I was different. And for the first time, I sensed that I could be hated and called names because of it."

Attending local schools, she sometimes endured the taunts of non-Indian students. For instance, she later remembered how white girls laughed at her dress at an eighth grade dance. Despite the cruelties of some of her classmates, Ada thrived at school and took seriously her teachers' urgings that she set her sights on college. Her hard work won her scholarships from the Menominee tribe and from the University of Wisconsin. Together, they financed her college education at the university's Madison campus.

The summer before she started college she was awarded a very different type of honor. With encouragement from her mother, she had entered and won a talent search sponsored by Columbia Pictures for the "six most beautiful Indian girls in America." She and the other winners spent a week in Hollywood and appeared in a western, *The Battle of Rogue River*. Bitterly joking about the film, Deer later recalled, "The Indians, of course, were the bad guys."

In 1957, Deer received a bachelor's degree in social work, thus becoming the first Menominee student ever to graduate from the University of Wisconsin, Madison. She then traveled to New York City to continue her studies at Columbia University. Four years later, she was the first American Indian to earn a master's degree in social work from that prestigious institution.

While earning her master's, Deer had proposed to write a thesis about the social and economic difficulties faced by Native Americans. Her professor shot down her proposal, claiming these difficulties did not exist. Deer relented and wrote her thesis instead on communities in New York City's Lower East Side. But from firsthand experience, she knew her professor was wrong, and upon graduation she set about finding solutions to the problems of contemporary Indians.

Her first job as a social worker was at the Edward F. Waite Neighborhood House in Minneapolis. At the time, a large population of Indians lived in the city, in part due to the U.S. government's program of relocation. The policy was designed to encourage reservation Indians to move to urban areas.

62

The officials told Indians that their lives would be much better as city dwellers, but the government had an ulterior motive for promoting relocation. In many of the treaties that established reservation borders, the government promised to make annual cash payments to residents and to provide services such as schools and medical facilities. Wanting to eliminate the expense of these treaty obligations, the United States hoped to use the relocation policy to end the reservation system altogether.

Working in Minneapolis, Deer could see that for many Indians relocation had been a disaster. Uneducated and unskilled, they were not able to find jobs in the city. Away from the reservation, they were left without the financial and social support of their tribe that could help them cope with their troubles. Destitute and desperate, many relocated Indians were plagued by alcoholism and mental illness.

In 1964, Deer took a new job as the community service coordinator of the BIA office in Minneapolis. She found working for the government frustrating. Thirty years later, she described her BIA job to a reporter from the *Minneapolis Tribune:* "I would write memos about what could be done and what should be done. . . . But they just ignored me. I decided to leave."

Over the next few years, she held jobs as a social worker or counselor with a succession of organizations, including Upward Bound, the Peace Corps, and the Minneapolis school system. But increasing she came to see the Menominee as the people who could most benefit most from her attention and training. In 1954, the year Deer had graduated from high school, the U.S. Congress had passed the Menominee Termination Act. Through this law, the federal government was using the Menominee as guinea pigs to experiment with a new Indian policy, known as termination. Through this program, the United States hoped to end its financial obligations to Indian tribes by "terminating" their reservations.

The Menominee were chosen as the test case because, though poor, they were better off than most reservation Indians. By the Wolf River Treaty of 1854, the Menominee had been compelled to cede nearly all of their 9.5-million-acre homeland to the United States. They were able to keep a mere quarter-million acres, but the treaty held that they would have this land for all time. The United States broke treaties with many tribes, but despite the efforts of white settlers and government officials, the Menominee were able to retain control of their reservation for more than one hundred years. However, this relatively large land base, which included lucrative timber lands, made the Menominee a prime candidate for termination in the eyes of the U.S. government. Poorer tribes could clearly not survive the elimination of government services, but officials reasoned that the Menominee might.

As soon as the tribe's termination took hold, these officials were proved terribly wrong. The

Ada Deer was the assistant secretary of the Bureau of Indian Affairs from 1993 to 1997.
(Courtesy Bureau of Indian Affairs)

government quickly closed down the Indians' hospital and most of their schools, facilities the Menominee could not afford to replace. The United States also began collecting income tax from Menominee, which their earlier treaty had prohibited. Many Menominee were unable to pay. In desperation, the tribal government began to sell off land, the little of the tribal homeland that they still owned rapidly becoming the property of non-Indians. In a speech, Deer summed up the effect of termination as "an economic, political, [and] cultural disaster."

In 1970, Deer and other concerned Menominee founded Determination of the Rights and Unity for Menominee Shareholders (DRUMS). DRUMS's immediate goal was to oust the tribal leaders who were selling land. But an offshoot organization, the National Committee to Save the Menominee People and Forest, took on the larger goal of persuading Congress to repeal the termination act. As its vice-president, Deer traveled to Washington, D.C., and presented the Menominee's case to as many members of Congress as she could. Impassioned speeches she gave before committees of both the Senate and the House of Representatives were particularly persuasive. Largely because of her efforts, the government at last admitted its mistake in terminating the Menominee—an admission of error almost unheard of in the history of federal Indian policy. In 1973, President Richard M. Nixon signed the Menominee Restoration Act, which restored the Menominee reservation. The tribe's success inspired other terminated Indian groups to fight the government and in the end led the United States to abandon the policy.

The Menominee Restoration Committee was formed to create a plan for a new tribal government for the reservation. Ada Deer was elected its chairperson and spent two years as the leader of the tribe. Once a tribal constitution was approved, she stepped down, saying that "it was time for new leadership."

In 1977, Deer welcomed the chance to join the faculty of the University of Wisconsin, Madison, as a lecturer, a post she would hold for 15 years. She used her position to establish a scholarship program for Native Americans; create a program to help students from poor, rural backgrounds; and teach the university's first course in contemporary Indian issues. She also was asked to join the boards of directors of a number of organizations. Among them was the Girl Scouts of America, which named her its "Woman of the Year" in 1982.

Throughout the 1980s and 1990s, Deer became increasingly involved in politics, on both the state and national levels. Following two unsuccessful bids for the post of secretary of state of Wisconsin, she served as the vice president of the election committee for Democratic candidate Walter Mondale during his 1984 presidential campaign. In 1992, Deer became the Democratic nominee for a seat in the House of Representatives. Despite high-profile supporters such as Gloria Steinem and Jesse Jackson, she lost to the Republican incumbent.

On the campaign trial, she had become acquainted with then presidential candidate Bill Clinton. After Clinton was elected to the White House in 1992, he invited Deer to join his administration as the assistant secretary of the BIA. No Indian woman had ever held this post before. During the congressional hearing to confirm her nomination, the members of the Senate gave her a standing ovation, an unusual gesture that dramatically demonstrated the admiration she had earned in Washington.

In her position with the BIA, Deer worked to make the agency more efficient and to attack both the social and economic problems that plague Indian communities. Another priority was to give tribes more control over how the funds they receive from the federal government are used. Historically, the BIA often has been seen by Indians as one of their greatest enemies. Deer tried to recast its image—to create a BIA that does not tell Indians how to live, but rather one that serves their efforts to live as they choose.

In 1997, Deer resigned from her post at the BIA. She returned to teaching at the University of Wisconsin, Madison, and in 2000 became the director of the school's American Indian Studies program.

Further Reading

Deer, Ada, with R. E. Simon Jr. *Speaking Out.* Chicago: Children's Press, 1970.

Kidwell, Clara Sue. "Ada Deer." In *The New Warriors,* edited by R. David Edmunds, 239–262. Lincoln: University of Nebraska Press, 2001.

Lurie, Nancy Oestreich. "Ada Deer: Champion of Tribal Sovereignty." In *Sifters: Native American Women's Lives,* edited by Theda Perdue, 223–242. New York: Oxford University Press, 2001.

Ourada, Patricia K. *The Menominee.* New York: Chelsea House, 1990.

Sherrow, Victoria. "Ada Deer: A Menominee Leader Heads for Washington." In *Political Leaders and Peacemakers,* 109–119. New York: Facts On File, 1994.

Deloria, Ella (Anpetu Waste)

(1889–1971)   *Nakota Sioux anthropologist, linguist, educator, novelist*

During a career that spanned nearly six decades, Ella Cara Deloria made great strides toward preserving the customs and language of the Sioux Indians through her pioneering research and writing.

Deloria was born on January 31, 1889, on the Yankton Sioux Indian Reservation in South Dakota. As a baby, she was given the Indian name Anpetu Waste ("beautiful day") because the reservation was engulfed in a snowstorm on the day of her birth. When she was one year old, Ella's family moved to Wakpala, South Dakota, a town on the Sioux's Standing Rock Indian Reservation. Wakpala was the home of the St. Elizabeth's Episcopal Mission, which had been built at the request of Ella's grandfather, Chief François De Lauriers. A spiritual leader among the Sioux, De Lauriers wanted Episcopal missionaries to teach his people about Christianity. Ella's father, Philip Deloria, was ordained as an Episcopal priest and assigned to St. Elizabeth's in 1890. He raised his children as Episcopalians but also taught them to respect traditional Sioux values, which mirrored many Christian principles. As a Sioux and as a Christian, Ella

Ella Deloria poses in the Indian clothing she often wore while lecturing.
(Dakota Indian Foundation)

developed a strong sense of responsibility to her family and to others in need.

An excellent student, Ella Deloria attended the mission school at St. Elizabeth's and, after 1901, the All Saint's School in Sioux Falls, South Dakota. In 1910, she won a scholarship to Oberlin College in Ohio. Two years later, she transferred to Teachers College at Columbia University in New York City, where she was awarded a bachelor's degree in 1915.

While in college, Deloria attracted the attention of Columbia professor Franz Boas, who is now considered the father of American anthropology. Boas was a pioneer in the study and preservation of Native American languages. Because of Deloria's knowledge of several Sioux dialects, he hired her as a research assistant. She was assigned the task of translating thousands of pages of research material written in Lakota Sioux.

Following her graduation, Deloria took a teaching post at All Saint's School, where her younger sister Susan was then a student. Both Ella and Susan left the school to return home in 1919, when their mother became ill. After her death, Ella decided to stay in Wakpala so that she could care for her aging father. To help support her family, she took a job as a health instructor with the Young Women's Christian Association (YWCA). Her mission was to improve the physical education of girls attending Indian schools. Beginning in 1923, she pursued this goal as the physical education and dance teacher at the Haskell Institute, an Indian school in Lawrence, Kansas.

Over the years, Deloria kept up a correspondence with Franz Boas. He repeatedly asked her to return to New York and to her translations of anthropological data. Finally, in 1927, she took Boas up on his offer. For nearly two decades, Deloria worked with Boas and his colleague, Ruth Benedict. In addition to translating Sioux texts, she also began to perform her own fieldwork. Through interviews with elders, she collected a great deal of information about traditional Sioux culture and customs. Encouraged by Benedict, Deloria concentrated on recording the roles and duties of women in Sioux society, an area of study that was often ignored by male anthropologists.

In 1929, Deloria began to publish her findings. That year her first article, which explored the Plains Indian ritual of the Sun Dance, appeared in the *Journal of American Folklore.* Her first book, *Dakota Texts,* followed in 1932. A classic of anthropological literature, the volume collects myths and stories culled from Deloria's interviews. Deloria next collaborated with Boas on *Dakota Grammar* (1941), an analysis of the structure of the Sioux language. Deloria also wrote *Speaking of Indians* (1944), a description of Sioux culture featuring illustrations by Deloria's sister Susan. Originally published by the Young Men's Christian Association (YMCA), the book was intended as a teaching tool for mis-

sionaries sent to minister to her tribe. Deloria believed that their efforts often failed because they did not understand or respect the Sioux's traditional ways.

In another attempt to bring her research to a broader audience, Deloria wrote a novel, *Waterlily,* which told the story of a Sioux woman living in the mid-19th century, the period just before non-Indians began to arrive in Sioux territory. Drawing on her fieldwork, Deloria filled *Waterlily* with details of Sioux life, focusing on the complex network of social obligations Sioux women had to family members and other tribespeople. By presenting anthropological information in the form of a novel, she was perhaps following the example of Zora Neale Hurston, an African-American folklorist and novelist who was also a student of Boas and Benedict. Unfortunately by the time Deloria completed *Waterlily* in the late 1940s, both of her mentors had died. A recommendation by Boas or Benedict probably would have assured the book's publication. But without their support, no publisher was then willing to take a chance on a novel written by a Native American woman. *Waterlily* was not published until 1988, long after Deloria's death.

While working with Boas, Deloria was plagued by financial worries. Her meager salary barely supported her, much less the family members who depended on her. At one point, she and Susan were forced to live in their car while Ella conducted research among the Sioux. After Boas's death, she had to rely on funding from grants and pay from lecturing, teaching, and part-time museum work. Always a slow and careful worker, Deloria found it difficult to find the time to both earn a living and focus on her research and writing. Although her publications were limited to occasional articles, she nevertheless compiled a huge amount of research data in her final years. Up until her death on February 12, 1971, she was hard at work on one of her most ambitious projects, a dictionary of the Sioux language.

With the publication of *Waterlily* and reprinting of many of her nonfiction works, the legacy of Ella Deloria has only recently been fully appreciated. In part because of her research, the traditional life and language of the Sioux are better documented than those of almost any other American Indian group. Her life and work have also served as models to younger Native American scholars who are now working to record tribal histories and cultures from an Indian perspective.

Further Reading

Deloria, Ella. *Dakota Texts.* Lincoln: Bison Books, 2006.

———. *Speaking of Indians.* 1944. Reprint, Lincoln: University of Nebraska Press, 1998.

———. *Waterlily.* Lincoln: University of Nebraska Press, 1988.

Deloria, Philip J. "Deloria, Ella (Anpetu Waste)." In *Encyclopedia of North American Indians,* edited by Frederick E. Hoxie, 159–161. Boston: Houghton Mifflin, 1996.

Demallie, Raymond J. "Deloria, Ella Cara." In *Notable American Women: 1607–1950,* edited by Edward T. James, 183–185. Cambridge, Mass.: Belknap Press, 1971.

Sligh, Gary Lee. *A Study of Native American Women Novelists: Sophia Alice Callahan, Mourning Dove, and Ella Cara Deloria.* Lewiston, N.Y.: Edwin Mellen Press, 2003.

Dick, Lena Frank

(ca. 1889–1965) *Washoe basketmaker*

Famed basketmaker Lena Frank Dick was born in about 1889 in Coleville, California. As a child, she and her two sisters, Lillie and Jessie, were introduced to the traditional Washoe craft of basket making by their mother. As Lena learned to weave, she was further inspired by the many Washoe women who had begun to create versions of traditional baskets to sell to tourists. Among the most skilled of these basketmakers was LOUISA KEYSER (also known as Dat So La Lee). Her works were extremely popular, and the best were hailed as masterpieces by non-Indian art collectors.

As a teenager, Lena Frank was briefly married to George Emm, who left her after the birth of their daughter, Juanita. Soon after, she married Levi Dick, a construction worker whose job provided a steady income for their small family. While raising Juanita, she served as a midwife for many of her neighbors and was an active participant in Washoe ceremonies.

In the early 1920s, Lena Dick started to make baskets for sale. Her first baskets were marketed by Abe Cohn, who displayed the works of the most accomplished Washoe weavers in his store in Carson City, Nevada. The high quality of Dick's work soon came to the attention of a San Francisco collector named Roscoe A. Day. Day pledged to buy all the baskets she could produce, an arrangement that lasted nearly 10 years. His patronage put Dick in a position any artist would envy. Without having to worry about finding buyers for her baskets, she could devote all her time and energy to perfecting her craft.

From the start of her weaving career, Dick was an innovator. She disdained the butterfly and plant motifs that had become popular in Washoe basketry, preferring instead geometric patterns formed in red and black. Like the famous Louise Keyser, Dick concentrated on the *degikup*—a small, sphere-shaped basket. However, the designs woven into Dick's *degikups* were far bolder and more dynamic. She favored decorating her works with vertical columns of V-shapes, diamonds, and triangles. The liveliest combinations gave the impression of living forms growing up toward the basket's opening.

In 1935, failing eyesight ended Dick's career as an artist. She continued to make utilitarian baskets but was forced to abandoned the finely detailed work that had been her trademark. Over the next several decades, many examples of her art found their way into prominent museums. However, Dick's name did not appear alongside them. They were instead mistakenly attributed to Keyser. Owing to Abe Cohn's vigorous promotion of her, Keyser's reputation as the great Washoe basketmaker grew while Dick was largely unknown. But, even as the world at large forgot her contributions to basketry art, Dick remembered. Her granddaughter Marjorie once recalled Dick taking her to the Nevada State Museum and proudly pointing out one of her baskets that was displayed as the work of Keyser.

In the late 1970s, more than 10 years after Dick's death, art scholars rediscovered her and her work. Some 28 existing baskets have been attributed to Dick. Their beauty and superior craftsmanship have finally brought her long-overdue recognition as one of the modern masters of Indian basketry.

Further Reading

Cohodas, Marvin. "Lena Frank Dick: An Outstanding Washoe Basket Weaver." *American Indian Art* 4 (Autumn 1979): 32–41.

———. "Washoe Innovators and Their Patrons." In *The Arts of the Native North American Indian,* edited by Edwin L. Wade, 203–220. New York: Hudson Hills Press, 1986.

Dietz, Angel DeCora

See DeCora, Angel

Dorion, Marie (Dorion Woman)

(ca. 1790–1850)   *Iowa guide, interpreter*

A mythic figure in the history of the American West, Marie Dorion was born into the Iowa tribe in about 1790 in what is now southwestern Arkansas. As a young woman, she became the companion of Pierre Dorion, Jr., and made a home with him in the settlement of St. Louis in present-day Missouri. The son of a Yankton Sioux woman and a French Canadian man, Dorion worked for the St. Louis Fur Company. Like other companies in the fur trade, its employees negotiated with Indian hunters to buy or trade for animal pelts, which the company then sold in Europe for enormous profits.

Many men involved in the fur trade had Indian wives or companions. Few non-Indian women were eager to live in the remote western outposts from which the fur trade operated, whereas Indian women from these regions were accustomed to coping with a harsh environment. During a severe winter or when food was scarce, Indian women knew how to build a warm shelter or where to find wild roots, berries, or game. Because of their knowledge and talents, these women were often held in great esteem by fur traders, who frequently relied on their Indian companions for their very survival.

The respect Pierre had for Marie Dorion was evident when he was hired as an interpreter by the Pacific Fur Company, a fur-trading operation based in Astoria in present-day Oregon. He agreed to join an the expedition traveling from St. Louis to Astoria only on the condition that Marie and their two children, Baptiste and Paul, were permitted to come along. In addition to wanting to keep his family together, Pierre Dorion probably recognized that the men needed Marie's expertise as a guide and interpreter. Although hesitant, the expedition leader relented. Accompanied by the Dorion family, the expedition party set out for the 3,500-mile journey in March 1811.

Traveling largely over land, the trek was physically difficult. For Marie Dorion, it must have been especially grueling after she became pregnant a month into the expedition. According to later accounts, however, she and her children kept up the pace, even as many of the American traders fell behind. While the party was making its way through the Rocky Mountains amid a winter storm, Marie Dorion gave birth to a boy, who died eight days later. Although the travelers had little food, Dorion gathered enough strength to travel some 20 miles the day following the delivery. Finally, after 11 months, they arrived in Astoria on February 15, 1812.

The Dorions remained at the post until July 1813, when Pierre joined a beaver hunting expedition. The family then moved to a small cabin near present-day Kingman, Oregon, some 300 miles east of Astoria. Marie stayed there with the children while Pierre left with the hunters. The following January, one of traders returned to the cabin to tell Marie that all of the other men had been killed during an Indian attack. Despite her efforts to nurse him, the survivor soon died of severe wounds. Dorion and her boys escaped on horseback, riding 120 miles until they were stuck in the mountains

Marie Dorion flees from hostile Indians during the winter of 1814 in a painting by John Clymer.
(John Clymer, *Marie Dorion—Escape 1814,* circa 1982, oil on canvas. Courtesy National Museum of Wildlife Art, Jackson, Wyoming)

by a snowstorm. They remained there for the next 53 days. They survived the ordeal by huddling in a hut Dorion built from branches and snow and by eating meat from their slaughtered horse.

After the spring thaw, Dorion and her sons sought refuge in a Walla Walla Indian village. In April 1814, several Astoria traders found them and escorted them to Fort Okanogan, a trading post in what is now northeastern Washington State. Few details are known about Dorion's life there, although history does record that she lived with a trapper named Venier and had a baby girl in about 1819. She later resettled at Fort Nez Perce, a nearby trading post, where she made a home with Jean-Baptiste Toupin, a French Canadian interpreter. The couple had two children before moving to a farm near present-day Salem, Oregon, in 1841. There Dorion and Toupin were married in a Catholic ceremony. She died nine years later and was buried in the churchyard of a neighboring parish.

No historical records exist that give Marie Dorion's account of her own adventures. But even before her death, celebrations of her courage and fortitude had appeared in books written by several Astorian traders. Their stories of the fur trade made her name familiar to readers in the United States, Canada, and England. She also appeared in *Astoria* (1836), a romanticized account of life at the fur post commissioned from the noted American writer Washington Irving by John Jacob Astor, the wealthy owner of the Pacific Fur Company. Irving spread Dorion's myth further by praising her "force of character that won the respect and applause of the white man."

Further Reading

Carter, Harvey L. "Dorion, Marie." In *Notable American Women: 1607–1950,* edited by Edward T. James, 229–230. Cambridge, Mass.: Belknap Press, 1971.

Irving, Washington. *Astoria.* 1836. Reprint, Lincoln: University of Nebraska Press, 1982.

E

Erdrich, Louise
(1954–   )   *Chippewa novelist, poet, short story writer*

Among the most acclaimed modern Native American novelists, Louise Erdrich uses her work to chronicle the worlds of a wide array of Indian characters. The critical and popular success of her novels has inspired, in the words of author LINDA HOGAN, "a new direction for Indian writers" by encouraging them to tell "the plain stories of people and their lives without pity, judgment, opinion, or romanticism."

Karen Louise Erdrich was born on July 6, 1954, in Little Falls, Minnesota. The eldest of seven children, she grew up in Wahpeton, North Dakota, a small town along the Minnesota border. Her German-American father was a teacher at the Wahpeton Indian School. Her mother, who also worked at the school, was a Chippewa Indian of the Turtle Mountain Band. As a child, Louise frequently visited the nearby Turtle Mountain Indian Reservation, where her grandfather served as the Chippewa tribal chairman.

In a 1985 interview, Erdrich recalled, "Mine were wonderful parents; they got me excited about reading and writing in a lasting way." Both her mother and father were skilled storytellers, who were eager to share their colorful tales about their ancestors. When Louise showed an interest in writing her own stories, her father encouraged her by paying a nickel for every one she finished. Her mother bound her early works in construction paper covers, which, Erdrich later remembered, made her feel like "a published author earning substantial royalties."

After attending the Wahpeton school and a Catholic boarding school, Erdrich applied to Dartmouth College in New Hampshire at her mother's suggestion. Dartmouth, which had originally been founded as a school for Indians, had a distinguished program in Native American Studies. Erdrich was admitted into the Class of 1976, the first Dartmouth class to include women.

When Erdrich began college, she wanted to become a professor. But after she won several prestigious writing prizes, she decided to become a poet instead. After graduating, she returned to North Dakota and took a variety of day jobs—including lifeguarding, working at a construction site, and teaching poetry-writing to prisoners—while she worked on her poetry at night. Erdrich later recalled that, for a writer, these "crazy jobs" proved to be "very useful experiences, although I never would have believed it at the time."

In 1978, Erdrich enrolled in the master's program at Johns Hopkins University in Baltimore. By this time, she had found a subject that consumed her imagination—her Indian heritage. She began using her writing to tell stories about the Chippewa of Turtle Mountain. Deciding that poems did not give her "enough room" for her storytelling, she started concentrating on short stories.

After graduating the next year, Erdrich was hired as a writer-in-residence at Dartmouth. There she renewed her acquaintance with Michael Dorris, an anthropologist of Modoc Indian heritage who directed the college's Native American Studies Program. He soon left for a yearlong research trip to New Zealand, but while he was away they wrote often and exchanged stories they had written. Within a year after Dorris's return, their friendship led to marriage. Together the couple took on the upbringing of three children Dorris had adopted when he was single and eventually added three children of their own to the family.

Following their marriage, Erdrich and Dorris also embarked on a literary collaboration. The cou-

Louise Erdrich is pictured here in 1989.
(Courtesy of HarperCollins, Photo by Michael Dorris)

ple jointly wrote a story titled "The World's Greatest Fisherman," which they submitted to the 1982 Nelson Algren fiction competition. Out of thousands of manuscripts, their story was awarded first prize. The victory gave Erdrich and Dorris enough confidence to try expanding the story into a novel.

The couple began work by creating a number of characters and discussing them thoroughly. In a 1990 interview, Dorris explained this step in their collaborative process: "We get to know the characters very well and talk about them in every situation. If we are in a restaurant, we imagine what so-and-so would order from the menu . . . [so that] when they appear on the page, they have that fullness behind them even though it doesn't all get written about." Once they understood their characters, Erdrich wrote a first draft, which Dorris edited. After working through five or six more drafts, they emerged with a complete manuscript. As a final step in polishing the work, they read it aloud to one another to make sure that each sentence had the right rhythm and effect.

The finished manuscript was published under Erdrich's name as *Love Medicine* in 1984. Composed of 14 self-contained stories, each narrated in the first person by a single character, the novel tells the story of several Chippewa families living on the Turtle Mountain Reservation between 1934 and 1983. The book was widely praised by reviewers, who admired its lyrical prose and skillful melding of humor with tragedy. Among the many prizes it garnered was the prestigious National Book Critics Circle Award for 1984. *Love Medicine* was also a popular success that made an appearance on a number of best-seller lists.

Erdrich and Dorris returned to many of the same characters they developed in *Love Medicine* in their second novel, *The Beet Queen* (1986). This book is set in Argus, a town just outside the reservation, and deals with the interaction of Chippewa and their white neighbors. Also critically acclaimed, *The Beet Queen* allowed Erdrich to explore her mixed ancestry by depicting both Indian and non-Indian characters. Their third novel, *Tracks* (1988)—a "prequel" to the earlier books that takes place between 1912 and 1919—deals with the Chippewa's reconciliation of Catholicism with their traditional religion. The tetralogy of novels was completed in 1994 with the publication of *The Bingo Palace.*

Erdrich has also written three other novels. Officially cowritten with Dorris, *The Crown of Columbus* (1991) is a love story between an Indian scholar and her white lover, who become involved in a search for a relic left in North America by Christopher Columbus. Another best seller, *Columbus* earned Erdrich and Dorris an advance of $1.5 million, the largest amount of money ever paid by a publisher for a novel by a Native American. In 1995, Erdrich and her husband returned to some of the characters from their tetralogy in *Tales of Burning Love,* the story of five women who have all been married to the same man. In 1998, Erdrich published *The Antelope Wife,* a well-received book that deals with the interconnected story of succeeding generations of two families.

In addition to writing fiction, Erdrich is a poet whose work has been published in three collections, *Jacklight* (1984), *Baptism of Desire* (1989), and *Original Fire* (2003). She has also written *The Blue Jay's Dance* (1995), an account of her pregnancies, and *The Broken Cord* (1990), a nonfiction work about fetal alcohol syndrome (FAS) that was published under Dorris's name. Often affecting children of mothers who drank heavily during pregnancy, FAS sufferers are afflicted with birth defects that impair their ability to think abstractly and make reasoned choices. Although the book discusses the prevalence of FAS on Indian reservations and in other impoverished communities, it was inspired by Dorris and Erdrich's own day-to-day experiences caring for their adopted children, who are victims of the syndrome.

The 1990s were a difficult period for Erdrich. In 1992, her eldest son, Abel, was killed in a car accident. The following year, Erdrich and Dorris took one of their other adopted children, Jeffrey, to court after charging him with attempting to extort money from them. The relationship between Erdrich and her husband also began to deteriorate. The couple separated in 1996, and Dorris committed suicide in April of the following year.

Despite these personal problems, Erdrich continues to be an extremely prolific writer. Among her recent works are the best-selling novels *The Master Butchers Singing Club* (2003), *The Painted Drum* (2005), and *The Last Report of the Miracles at Little No Horse* (2001), a finalist for the National Book Award. She is also the author of the young adult novels *The Birchbark House* (1999) and *The Game of Silence* (2005), the latter of which won the Scott O'Dell Award for Historical Fiction. Erdrich lives with her daughters in Minnesota, where, when not writing, she runs Birchbark Books, an independent bookstore.

Further Reading

Bruchac, Joseph. "Whatever Is Really Yours: An Interview with Louise Erdrich." In *Survival This Way: Interviews with American Indian Poets,* 73–86. Tucson: University of Arizona Press, 1987.

Chavkin, Allan, ed. *The Chippewa Landscape of Louise Erdrich.* Tuscaloosa: University of Alabama Press, 1999.

Chavkin, Allan, and Nancy Feyl Chavkin, eds. *Conversations with Louise Erdrich and Michael Dorris.* Jackson: University Press of Mississippi, 1994.

Coltelli, Laura. "Louise Erdrich and Michael Dorris." In *Winged Words: American Indian Writers Speak,* 40–52. Lincoln: University of Nebraska Press, 1990.

Dorris, Michael, and Louise Erdrich. *The Crown of Columbus.* New York: HarperCollins, 1991.

Erdrich, Louise. *The Antelope Wife.* New York: Harper Flamingo, 1998.

———. *The Beet Queen.* New York: Henry Holt, 1986.

———. *Bingo Palace.* New York: HarperCollins, 1994.

———. *The Blue Jay's Dance.* New York: HarperCollins, 1995.

———. *The Last Report of the Miracles at Little No Horse.* New York: HarperCollins, 2001.

———. *Love Medicine.* New York: Holt, Rinehart, & Winston, 1984.

———. *The Master Butchers Singing Club.* New York: HarperCollins, 2003.

———. *Original Fire: Selected and New Poems.* New York: HarperCollins, 2003.

———. *The Painted Drum.* New York: HarperCollins, 2005.

———. *Tales of Burning Love.* New York: HarperCollins, 1995.

———. *Tracks.* New York: Henry Holt, 1988.

F

Fire Thunder, Cecelia
(1946–) *Lakota Sioux tribal leader*

Cecelia Fire Thunder was the first woman elected president of the Pine Ridge Indian Reservation in South Dakota—the second largest reservation in the United States. A Lakota Sioux, she was born Cecelia Apple near the reservation community of Kyle. Although they had little money, the Apples built a comfortable home for their seven daughters. Fire Thunder later recalled, "My parents were nurturing, but my father was very protective. We were never hungry, never afraid." At home, she spoke her native language, learning English only after she began attending a local Catholic school.

In 1963, her family moved to Los Angeles, California. Seeking a better life, the Apples decided to take advantage of the Relocation program—a government policy that encouraged Native Americans to leave reservations and move to urban centers. The government promised reservation residents that jobs were plentiful in cities, but many who relocated were unable to find work. Cecelia's father had more luck, landing a good-paying union job in a factory.

After high school, Cecelia Fire Thunder married and had two children. She divorced and was forced to go on welfare to raise her family. With the help of a social worker, Fire Thunder was admitted to a one-year nursing program. As she once recalled, "My whole life changed. I started earning a pretty good salary, and I began to get involved in some public service work." Fire Thunder helped establish the first free health clinic for American Indians in Compton, California. Moving to San Diego in 1980, she founded another clinic there. Fire Thunder also began to lobby the state legislature for more money for Indian health care.

In 1987, Fire Thunder returned to Pine Ridge, later explaining "it was time to come home." She worked at a hospital, for the tribe, and for the state health department. In her free time, Fire Thunder worked to improve living conditions on the reservation. She was especially active in leading the fight against domestic violence.

Fire Thunder had long thought about making a bid for tribal office. But it was not until 2004 that she felt ready. She once explained her hesitation: "The pain and anger on the reservation is so deep that I knew I would be attacked. I didn't want to run for office until I knew I was strong enough not to take the criticisms personally."

Running for tribal president, Fire Thunder indeed heard plenty of criticism. Her opponent was Russell Means, the flamboyant former head of the American Indian Movement (AIM), a militant Indian rights group, who had since had some success as an actor. During the campaign, Means often noted that Fire Thunder had been seen crying in public. The observation played to a faction on the reservation who opposed the idea of a female president, citing that Lakota leaders had traditionally been male. Even so, by focusing on the issues, Fire Thunder garnered enough support to win the election.

Her first order of business was cleaning up the tribe's troubled finances. Earlier leaders had run up huge debts that were coming due. With the tribe's credit rating in shambles, Fire Thunder took an unconventional approach. She called up the leaders of various tribes with substantial income from the gaming industry. Finally, the Shakopee Tribe of Minnesota agreed to loan Pine Ridge $38 million—enough to pay off the tribe's old debts and to invest in the reservation's own casino.

The deal sparked an impeachment campaign. Fire Thunder's political opponents claimed she had endangered reservation land by putting it up for collateral, a charge she denied. They also held that she did not show proper respect for tribal elders and even that she was not actually a member of the tribe.

In spring 2006, Fire Thunder placed herself in the center of a national controversy. After the governor of South Dakota signed a state-wide ban on abortion, Fire Thunder proposed opening an abortion clinic on Pine Ridge. Because of the Lakota's sovereignty, she held that they are not subject to state law. Her controversial stance led the Pine Ridge tribal council to impeach Fire Thunder in July, although she vowed to fight to win back her position either through the court system or by reelection. Speaking before the American Civil Liberties Union's annual meeting in October 2006, Fire Thunder said she had no regrets over using her political prominence to challenge the abortion ban. She explained, "As a private citizen, as one Indian woman in South Dakota, my voice would not be heard. But as the leader of a great nation, my voice was heard."

Further Reading

Davey, Monica. "As Tribal Leaders, Women Still Fight Old Views." *New York Times,* 4 February 2006. Available online. URL: http://www.nytimes.com/2006/02/04/national/04tribe.html?ex=1296709200&en=b03bc6821914b437&ei=5088&partner=rssnyt&emc=rss. Downloaded on June 10, 2006.

Harlan, Bill. "Tribal Leader Rallies for Abortion Clinic on Reservation." *Rapid City Journal,* 5 May 2006. Available online. URL: http://www.rapidcityjournal.com/articles/2006/03/25/news/top/news02.txt. Downloaded on June 10, 2006.

Hurst, Sam. "Cecelia Fire Thunder: A 'Person of Character.'" *Rapid City Journal,* 19 December 2005. Available online. URL: http://www.rcjonline.com/articles/2005/12/25/news/columns/084hurst.txt. Downloaded on June 11, 2006.

Folwell, Jody
(1942–   )   *Santa Clara Pueblo potter*

Considered the leading avant-garde Pueblo potter, Jody Folwell was born on August 4, 1942, at Santa Clara Pueblo in New Mexico. She was one of nine children born to Michael and Rose Naranjo. Her mother was a noted potter, as is her sister, NORA NARANJO-MORSE.

When Jody was young, her family moved to Taos Pueblo, where she attended high school. She went on to the College of Santa Fe and the University of New Mexico, earning a bachelor's degree in history and political science. In 1961, she married artist Henry Folwell. The couple had three children. While they were growing up, Jody Folwell worked as a kindergarten teacher and a counselor for the Equal Employment Opportunity Commission.

In 1974, Folwell decided she wanted a career that would allow her to spend more time at home. The obvious choice was pottery making. She had grown up watching her mother make ceramics, in the process learning about traditional Pueblo techniques for collecting and processing clay and forming, painting, and firing pots.

Although steeped in these traditions, from the beginning Folwell was moved to innovate. She experimented with new, often asymmetrical shapes. She also played with different colors and firing techniques. Many of Folwell's works displayed a variety of hues and textures on the same piece.

But Folwell's most notable innovations were in her decorations. Favoring the sgraffito method, by which designs are incised into the clay, she adorned her pottery with words and images that often commented on politics. Folwell's pottery also frequently dealt with social issues, including rape and the negative effects of technological advances on society. Folwell also commented on less weighty themes, such as the struggles of married couples and the treatment of stray dogs. In a 2001 interview, she explained the excitement of continually exploring new techniques, shapes, and designs: "An adventure is created with every pot. They are all different from the other. There are no repetitions. Each pot tells its own story."

Initially, Folwell's wedding of the old and new made her work controversial. Although her pottery attracted collectors, she was hesitant to show it in a competitive show, for fear of the response she might get from traditionalists. Finally, in 1979, she entered a pot in the Heard Museum Guild competition. It won first place for contemporary pottery.

She has since won many prizes. Perhaps the most significant for her career was a best-in-show award at the 1985 Santa Fe Indian Market for a pot she made with sculptor Bob Haozous. The prize confirmed for the art world that Folwell was not just able to compete with contemporary artists but also traditional potters. As Folwell once explained, "I think of myself as being a contemporary potter and a traditionalist at the same time. Combining the two is very emotional and exciting to me."

Further Reading

Cohen, Lee M., ed. *Art of Clay: Timeless Pottery of the Southwest.* Santa Fe, N.Mex.: Clear Light Publishers, 1993.

Peterson, Susan. *Pottery by American Indian Women: The Legacy of Generations.* New York: Abbeville Press, 1997.

Francis, Milly
(ca. 1802–1848) *Creek peacemaker*

Like the legendary POCAHONTAS, Milly Francis was heralded by whites for saving the life of an American soldier. Francis was born in about 1802 in a Creek Indian village in what is now Alabama. Her father, Joseph Francis, was a prosperous farmer and a leader among the Creeks. Fearing that American settlers would overtake the Creek homeland, he supported Tecumseh and Tenskwatawa (also known as the Shawnee Prophet). These two Shawnee brothers wanted Indians of all nations to band together to drive whites from their lands by force. Because of his political leanings, Joseph Francis was called Francis the Prophet by the Americans living on the Creek homeland.

Francis's suspiciousness of Americans was well founded. During the War of 1812, forces led by General Andrew Jackson attacked the Creek Nation. Francis and his family fled to Florida, which was then considered Spanish territory. In 1817, warriors among the exiled Creek captured a Georgian military captain named Duncan McKrimmon while he was wandering through their new lands. The warriors took their prisoner back to the village of Miccosukee, where he was tied to a post. Just as they were about to shoot him, Milly Francis, then a teenager, begged the warriors to stop. She asked the Creek to show mercy, and at her insistence, McKrimmon was untied and, briefly, adopted into the tribe. He was later sold as a slave to the Spanish and eventually rejoined the Georgian army. Some anthropologists and historians now believe that McKrimmon was not actually in danger of being killed at the hands of the Creek. They hold that the execution was actually an adoption ceremony, in which Francis's symbolic "rescue" signaled that McKrimmon had been accepted as a member of the tribe.

The following winter, Jackson's troops invaded Florida. They captured and hanged several Indian leaders, including Joseph Francis. The exiled Creek and their lands were ravaged by the warfare. In desperation, a group of starving women and children surrendered themselves to the soldiers at a nearby American stronghold. Living at the post was Captain McKrimmon, who recognized Milly Francis among the refugees. He brought the Creek food and told the other soldiers to extend them every courtesy. Legend holds that McKrimmon asked Francis to marry him, but suspecting that the proposal was made only out of a sense of obligation, she refused and soon returned to her own people.

In the 1820s and 1830s, the American government took control of most of the Southeast, including the territory of the Creek. Like the Cherokee and other large southeastern Indian groups, the Creek tribe was forced by the United States to leave its ancestral homeland and relocate to Indian Territory in what is now Oklahoma. The provisions given to them by government officials for their long journey west were so inadequate that approximately half of the Creek population died of disease or starvation en route.

Widespread allegations about the officials' ill treatment of the tribes removed to Indian Territory prompted the government to initiate an investigation. In 1841, Major Ethan Allen Hitchcock was charged with the task of studying the situation. He discovered that corruption was rife among the officials, many of whom sold the provisions intended for the Indians and pocketed the profits. During his investigation, Hitchcock also discovered Milly Francis, who had probably traveled to Indian Territory in 1828. Since her last encounter with McKrimmon, she had married and given birth to eight children. When Hitchcock met her, she was a poor widow with two young sons and a daughter. The rest of her family probably had died during the Creek removal.

Moved by her plight, Hitchcock alerted his employers in Washington, D.C., about her situation. In 1844, the U.S. Congress voted to issue Francis the Congressional Medal of Honor and an annual pension of $96 for saving McKrimmon. The government agent assigned to the Creek was not told of the honor until four years later. He then sought out Francis, only to find her, by his own description, "in the most wretched condition." Deathly ill with tuberculosis, she was gratified to hear about Congress's action but did not survive long enough to receive either her medal or pension. Milly Francis died on May 19, 1848, and was buried near a marker on the grounds of Bacone College in Bacone, Oklahoma.

Further Reading

Debo, Angie. "Francis, Milly." In *Notable American Women: 1607–1950,* edited by Edward T. James, 660–661. Cambridge, Mass.: Belknap Press, 1971.

G

Glancy, Diane
(1941–   ) *Cherokee poet, playwright, short story writer, essayist, novelist, educator*

"Out of my eight great-grandparents, only one was Cherokee. How can the influence of one be as strong as seven together?" Diane Glancy asked in her 1987 autobiographical essay "Two Dresses." This tension between her white heritage and Indian sensibility has provided the focus of many of the works by this prolific writer.

Glancy was born on March 18, 1941, in Kansas City, Missouri. Her father was one-quarter Cherokee Indian; her mother was of English and German descent. During her upbringing, her parents, particularly her mother, largely ignored Glancy's Indian roots. Although she was reared to think of herself as white, she later claimed that even as a child she always felt out of place in non-Indian society. She found some comfort in visiting her Cherokee grandmother, however. Although her grandmother said very little to her, Glancy remembers that "not speaking, she spoke to me, and it is her quiet influence I feel again and again." She now credits her grandmother with inspiring her interest in words.

In 1959, Glancy graduated from high school in St. Louis and enrolled at the University of Missouri, where she earned a bachelor's degree in 1964. She married and had two children—David (born in 1964) and Jennifer (in 1967)—but she and her husband were later divorced. During the mid-1960s, Glancy moved to Tulsa, Oklahoma, where she worked for the state art council. In this post, she gave speeches to Native American high school students, in which she stressed the importance of education.

In the 1980s, Glancy returned to school to study writing. She received a master's degree from Central State University in Edmond, Oklahoma, in 1983 and from Iowa State University in 1988. Glancy also began to publish a wide variety of works. Although she considers herself primarily a poet, she has published books of short stories, collections of essays, novels, and plays, in addition to numerous volumes of poetry.

Glancy's books and articles have won many awards. She has also served as an artist-in-residence for the Oklahoma State Arts Council and the 1984–87 poet laureate for the Five Civilized Tribes—a group of five large tribes, including the Cherokee, that originally lived in the Southeast.

Diane Glancy is an accomplished poet and professor.
(Reprinted by permission of Holy Cow! Press)

In addition, she has taught poetry at the university level. She is now an associate professor of English at Macalester College in St. Paul, Minnesota.

Although Glancy has written in many different styles and forms, most of her work explores the unique difficulties faced by Native Americans. In her writing, she has confronted social problems and issues, such as alcoholism, illiteracy, and discrimination. Glancy has also frequently used her talents to share her own search for identity as an Indian of mixed ancestry. Her work eloquently evokes what she has described as "the feeling of being split between two cultures, not fully belonging in either one."

Further Reading

Glancy, Diane. *Brown Wolf Leaves the Res and Other Poems.* Marvin, S.Dak.: Blue Cloud Quarterly Press, 1984.

———. *Claiming Breath.* Lincoln: University of Nebraska Press, 1992.

———. *Firesticks.* Norman: University of Oklahoma Press, 1993.

———. *Primer of the Obsolete.* Amherst: University of Massachusetts Press, 2004.

———. *Pushing the Bear: A Novel of the Trail of Tears.* New York: Harcourt Brace, 1996.

———. *Stone Heart: A Novel of Sacajawea.* Woodstock, N.Y.: Overlook Press, 2003.

———. "Two Dresses." In *I Tell You Now: Autobiographical Essays by Native American Writers,* edited by Brian Swann and Arnold Krupat, 169–183. Lincoln: University of Nebraska Press, 1987.

———. *War Cries: A Collection of Plays.* Duluth, Minn.: Holy Cow! Press, 1997.

H

Hale, Janet Campbell
(1946–   )   *Coeur d'Alene novelist, poet, essayist*

In her 1993 book of autobiographical essays *Bloodlines: Odyssey of a Native Daughter,* Janet Campbell Hale notes that "everything one writes is in some way based on his or her own personal vision of life." Throughout her writing career, Hale has used her own experiences to create a unique picture of contemporary American Indian life.

Months before Janet's birth on January 11, 1946, her parents, Margaret and Nicholas Campbell, and her three older sisters moved to California from the Coeur d'Alene Indian reservation in northern Idaho. They made the trip to ensure that she would be born in a hospital. A year before, her mother had given birth to a son, who died in infancy. Their poor reservation community had had no medical facility to give him the care he needed.

The Campbells soon returned to the reservation, but Janet spent most of her youth on the move. Her father, an alcoholic, was often abusive to his wife. During periods when he was drinking heavily, Margaret Campbell would pack up her things and her youngest daughter, sneak out of the house in the middle of the night, and take a bus to the farthest destination she could afford. This constant uprooting was a strain on Janet, who attended 21 schools in three states before dropping out after the eighth grade. An even greater burden was her poverty. Her mother, though highly intelligent, was an uneducated woman who could only find menial work that barely paid a living wage. In *Bloodlines,* Hale recalls their struggle to make ends meet: "We're so poor, Mom and me. . . . I remember being hungry at school, feeling faint. My hands tremble and I sweat, though it isn't warm. My head feels light. Or it hurts. I get headaches a lot when I'm little. Nosebleeds too."

Hale's bitterest memories of her youth, however, revolve around her mother's treatment of her. In Hale's words, she was "a master, an absolute master, of verbal abuse." Angered by her disastrous marriage and the limited opportunities available to an Indian woman of her generation, Margaret Campbell took out her frustration on her youngest daughter. She repeatedly told Janet that she was ugly and stupid, a failure who would never amount to anything. The abuse culminated during her 15th summer, when she was living with both of her parents in Wapato, Washington, on the Yakima Indian reservation. Her mother and father were sharing a house with one of her older sisters. Janet, however, was not allowed inside. She was forced to spend the sweltering summer in a windowless storage shack in the backyard. In those miserable months, she "wrote miles and miles of poetry about God only knows what and fantasized about one day being a writer, a real writer. That would be my last summer at home."

After several aimless years, at 18 Janet Campbell married a white man, who abused her both mentally and physically. At 19 she gave birth to a son, Nicholas Aaron. To protect him, she gathered the courage to leave her husband. Fearing he would try to track her down, she hid out in a squalid hotel in San Francisco, living from welfare check to welfare check. The desire to build a better life for Nicholas inspired her to determine a new course for her life. As she wrote in *Bloodlines,* "For his sake, I told myself, I can imagine a future. I can be more than I was. I can be strong."

From a friend, she learned that she could apply to San Francisco's City College without a high school diploma. After passing the admissions test with an exceedingly high score, she began attending the school tuition-free. The next year, she transferred to the University of California at Berkeley, from which she graduated in 1972. Hale later also attended law school at Berkeley and took graduate courses at University of California at Davis, where she earned an M.A. in English literature in 1984.

In 1972, one of Hale's poems was published in an anthology of works by young Native American writers. Two years later, her first novel, *The Owl's Song,* appeared to good reviews. Written for young adults, the novel tells the story of a poor American Indian teenager whose father and sister are addicted to alcohol. Upon its publication, *The Owl's Song* was praised as one of the first young adult novels to provide a realistic picture of some of the problems besetting contemporary Indians. But while writing the book, Hale had been nervous about how its grittier aspects would be received: "I was afraid of writing something that would offend people. . . . I was torn between writing a novel that was true to

my own vision and one that presented a positive image of Indian people." It was her mother who encouraged Hale to use her writing to tell the truth as she saw it. "What is the point of writing," she asked, "if [you are] going to just write some nonsense to please someone else."

Supporting herself as a college instructor, Hale published a book of poems, *Custer Lives in Humboldt County and Other Poems* (1978), and a second novel, *The Jailing of Cecelia Capture* (1985). Like her earlier fiction, *Cecelia Capture* draws on elements of Hale's life as it tells the story of a 30-year-old Indian woman who is jailed for drunk driving. The novel focuses on the title character's effort to carve out a future for herself as she comes to terms with a difficult past, which like Hale's own is tarnished by poverty and alcoholism. Widely acclaimed, *Cecelia Capture* was nominated for a Pulitzer Prize. In 1999, Hale published a short story collection, *Women on the Run,* that similarly examined the problems confronting Native American women.

Hale's book *Bloodlines* is her most autobiographical. Through a series of essays, Hale recounts her troubled childhood and explores the history of her ancestors, looking for connections between her family's problems and the past. In two heavily researched pieces, Hale reconstructs the worlds of her two grandmothers. Her part-Indian, part-white maternal grandmother proudly traced her ancestry to John McLoughlin, a white fur trader now hailed as the "father of Oregon." Hale discovered that, despite this distinguished lineage, her grandmother, as an Indian woman, was treated shabbily by the same whites who celebrated McLoughlin as a hero.

Hale's paternal grandmother suffered another type of degradation. In 1877, as a young woman, she was a part of a band of Indians led by Chief Joseph, a Nez Perce leader who refused to follow the U.S. Army's orders to withdraw to a reservation. As Chief Joseph's band attempted to escape to Canada, they were hunted by the army for more than 1,700 miles. With the Canadian border in sight, the fleeing Indians were set upon once again by American soldiers. Hale's grandmother was one of the survivors of the bloodbath that ensued.

Through her own story and those of her relatives—living and dead—Hale has explored the pain Indian women have suffered at the hands of abusive men, prejudiced non-Indians, and an often hostile government. But through her own success and her admiration for the women whose stories she tells, Hale also highlights the strength and fortitude that have allowed Indian woman to survive hardship and even prosper in the most bitter circumstances.

Further Reading

Hale, Frederick. *Janet Campbell Hale.* Boise, Idaho: Boise State University, 1996.

Hale, Janet Campbell. *Bloodlines: Odyssey of a Native Daughter.* 1993. Reprint, Tucson: University of Arizona Press, 1998.

———. *The Jailing of Cecelia Capture.* New York: Random House, 1985.

———. *The Owl's Song.* 1974. Reprint, Albuquerque: University of New Mexico Press, 1998.

———. *Women on the Run.* Moscow: University of Idaho Press, 1999.

Hardin, Helen (Tsa-sah-wee-ah, Little Standing Spruce)
(1943–1984) *Santa Clara Pueblo painter*

During her brief career, Helen Hardin was recognized as one of the finest Indian painters to explore the possibilities of modern art. She herself once aptly explained her reputation by citing her ability to "translate the images of Indian cultures into new visual metaphors that speak to all people."

Hardin was born on May 28, 1943, in Albuquerque, New Mexico, but she spent her early years in Santa Clara Pueblo, a nearby Pueblo Indian village where her mother, PABLITA VELARDE, had grown up. There, when Helen was a child, her grandmother performed a traditional naming ceremony. During this ritual, her father, Herbert O. Hardin, gave her the Indian name Tsa-sah-wee-ah, which meant "little standing spruce" in the Tewa

Pueblo language. She would later use this name to sign many of her paintings.

Before starting a family, Hardin's mother had become an accomplished painter. Velarde's works were in what became known as the Traditional Indian Style, which she helped create as a student at the Santa Fe Indian School in the 1930s. Artists working in this style depicted scenes of traditional Indian life using the nontraditional medium of paint on canvas. These paintings became popular with collectors of Indian art and white tourists visiting the Southwest.

While Helen and her little brother Herby (born in 1944) were growing up, Velarde became more and more successful. Her absorption in her work and her husband's resentment of her fame led to a strain in their marriage. The couple separated and, in 1959, when Helen was 16, her parents were divorced. The breakup was difficult for Helen. Living with her mother in Albuquerque, she felt lonely and isolated. Velarde was so devoted to her art that she paid little attention to her daughter. When the two did spend time together, they usually fought.

As a child, Hardin had shown an early interest in art. In imitation of her mother, she painted Indian scenes that garnered her praise and prizes. Recognizing her promise as an artist, *Seventeen* magazine ran a feature on Hardin in 1959. Velarde, however, was less enthusiastic about her talents. She criticized Hardin's paintings and encouraged her daughter to give up art and pursue a career in business instead.

Angered by Velarde's dismissal of her work, Hardin rebelled by developing her own art style. She came to dislike works in the Traditional Indian Style, which she later referred to as "cute little Indian paintings." Instead, she began to find inspiration in the paintings of younger Indian artists, particularly the art of Cochiti Pueblo Joe H. Herrera.

After graduating from high school, Hardin enrolled at the University of New Mexico, but she dropped out following her freshman year. She moved in with her high school boyfriend, Pat Terrazas, and in 1964 gave birth to their daughter.

Hardin named the baby Margarete after Margarete Chase, an art dealer who arranged a one-woman show of Hardin's paintings. She had to paint these works in secret because Terrazas, like her mother, disapproved of her art career.

In addition to his constant discouragement, Terrazas's physical abuse took a toll on Hardin. She later recalled how in 1968 she decided to leave him: "I awoke to the fact that I was twenty-four years old, I was locked into an unhappy [relationship], and I was not painting. I didn't know who I was or what I was. In search of personal freedom, I took Margarete . . . and left the country."

Hardin and her daughter went to visit her father, who was working in Bogotá, Colombia. There she once again began to paint and to her surprise found an enthusiastic audience for her work. In New Mexico, she had assumed that people were interested in her paintings largely because of her mother's reputation. But in Colombia no one had heard of Pablita Velarde. For the first time, she was sure that the praise for her work was earned by her talent alone.

When Hardin returned to New Mexico, she had a new self-confidence and determination. With a fierce intensity, she devoted herself to refining her own unique style. Unlike her mother, who painted with watercolors or with pigments she mixed from pulverized rocks, Hardin used acrylics, which she applied to the canvas in as many as 26 layers to make a variety of effects. The images she created became increasingly abstract. A drafting course in high school had taught her to use a ruler, compass, and protractor with precision. She employed these drawing tools to make repeating geometric forms based on shapes on rock art and pottery made by the Pueblo's ancestors.

Her art also dealt with Pueblo themes, which she often explored in a series of paintings. One series depicted kachinas, the sacred spirits revered by the Pueblo. Another dealt with images of women, drawing on mythic figures among the Pueblo such as Changing Woman. Although Hardin shared with her mother an interest in portraying Indian subjects, her approach and intent were very different. Velarde's highly detailed figures and village scenes were meant to record aspects of Pueblo culture. In contrast, Hardin used her work to communicate the emotions Pueblo objects and ways evoked in her. As she explained, "Rather than painting a subject, I am inspired by that subject to paint what I feel from the idea, the song, the ceremonial, the mask. . . . Traditional art tells its own story. Contemporary art leaves you with a feeling rather than a story."

In 1970, a photograph of Hardin and examples of her art appeared on the cover of the March/April issue of *New Mexico* magazine. The cover brought her work to the attention of a huge audience, and buyers began to clamor for paintings. It also helped make Hardin herself a celebrity in the Indian art world. Admiring her beauty and sense of style, readers were eager to find out where she purchased the jewelry she wore and who had styled her hair. As her reputation soared, she also found personal happiness with Cradoc Bagshaw, a photographer whom she married in 1973.

Throughout the 1970s, Hardin continued to experiment with her art. She had begun to move away from intricate patterns and toward simplified, elegant forms when she was diagnosed with breast cancer in 1981. Treatment appeared to put the disease into remission, but the cancer soon reappeared and spread. On June 9, 1984, the disease took Hardin's life.

At her death at the age of 41, Hardin was recognized as one of the finest and most innovative Indian artists of her generation. She was among the first modern Indian painters to combine her non-Indian art materials and techniques with an Indian sensibility, merging past and present in a new way. "I love my Indian heritage, and I draw on it," she once explained. "I use tradition as a springboard and go diving into my paints."

Further Reading

Culley, LouAnn Faris. "Helen Hardin: A Retrospective." *American Indian Art* 4 (Summer 1979): 68–75.

Hardin, Helen. "Helen Hardin: Tewa Painter." In *This Song Remembers: Self-Portraits of Native Americans in the Arts,* edited by Jane B. Katz, 116–123. Boston: Houghton Mifflin, 1980.

Scott, Jay. *Changing Woman: The Life and Art of Helen Hardin.* Flagstaff, Ariz.: Northland Publishing, 1989.

Harjo, Joy

(1951–   )   *Creek poet, educator, singer*

"I could not live without writing and/or thinking about it," explains Joy Harjo, who is widely considered one of the most skilled poets in the United States. Born in Tulsa, Oklahoma, on May 9, 1951, Harjo maintains that her Creek relatives on her father's side are "the root from which I write." Her great-great grandparents came to Oklahoma, then Indian Territory, when the U.S. government compelled the Creeks to abandon their vast homeland in present-day Alabama and Georgia in the 1830s. Harjo counts among her ancestors the Creek leader Menawe, an instigator of the Red Stick War, in which Creek warriors unsuccessfully battled the U.S. Army to thwart the tribe's forced relocation.

The eldest of four children, Harjo was, by her own description, "high strung and imaginative" as a girl. She later remembered being afraid of the oil wells in her neighborhood, which she imagined to be monsters. At church, she found a focus for her energy when she took to preaching to her friends. Impressed by her own powers of persuasion and attracted to the idea of travel, Joy aspired to become a missionary. She abandoned both her ambition and the church, however, when she heard a minister cruelly insult two Mexican girls.

When Harjo was a teenager, she developed a new goal—to become a visual artist. She attended the Institute of American Indian Art (IAIA), an Indian-operated art school in Santa Fe, where she studied painting. At IAIA, she went to readings by several Indian poets, including Leslie Marmon Silko and Simon Ortiz. Inspired by their performances, Harjo began to experiment with writing poems of her own.

While still a student, Harjo gave birth to her son, Phil. She then enrolled at the University of New Mexico. While working toward a bachelor's

degree, she had a second child, a girl she named Rainy Dawn. Harjo majored in painting until her senior year, when she decided to concentrate instead on creative writing. Harjo later explained the change in her focus: "Language, through poetry, was taking on more magical qualities than my painting. I could say more when I wrote. . . . Poetry-speaking 'called me' in a sense. And I couldn't say no." After graduating in 1976, Harjo continued her education at the University of Iowa, where she earned a master's of fine arts in creative writing two years later. She then began teaching writing first at IAIA, then at several major universities throughout the West. She joined the faculty of the University of New Mexico as a full professor in 1991.

Harjo published her first book of poetry, *The Last Song,* in 1975. This collection plus 48 new

Poet Joy Harjo is also a noted singer and musician.
(Courtesy W. W. Norton, Photo by Paul Abdoo)

85

poems were published as *What Moon Drove Me to This* (1979). The poet later dismissed these works as her "young books," but elaborated, "You could see the beginnings of something, but it wasn't quite cooked."

In her own eyes, Harjo's first mature book was *She Had Some Horses* (1983). This collection was well received, and the poem that gave the book its title is still perhaps her best-known work. She followed this success with *Secrets from the Center of the World* (1989), which combined her prose poems with photographs of the southwestern landscape by Stephen Storm. Her most recent poetry collections are the highly acclaimed *In Mad Love and War* (1990), which won the Poetry Society of America's William Carlos Williams Award, *The Woman Who Fell from the Sky* (1994), and *How We Became Human: New and Selected Poems* (2002). She has also coedited an anthology titled *Reinventing the Enemy's Language: Native Women's Writing of North America* (1997) and written *The Good Luck Cat* (2000), an award-winning children's book.

Harjo maintains that her Creek heritage "provides the underlying psychic structure" of her work. Owing to her "Indian consciousness," many of her poems explore her relationship with nature and display an acute sense of place, be it the Oklahoma of her youth, the Alabama homeland of her ancestors, or the American Southwest in which she has spent much of her adult life. Like many other Indian writers of her generation, Harjo has focused much of her work on her mixed ancestry and the tension of living in non-Indian society while still maintaining ties with the Indian community. Particularly in her later work, Harjo has come to terms with her place in both Indian and non-Indian society. In a essay from 1987, she confidently maintained, "I walk in and out of many worlds. . . . [I have] decided that being familiar with more than one world, more than one vision, is a blessing, and know that I make my own choices."

In additional to poetry, Harjo finds a creative outlet in screenwriting and in music. A graduate of the program in filmmaking at the Anthropology Film Center in Santa Fe, she has written several screenplays for the Native American Public Broadcasting Consortium and for Nebraska Educational Television. She explained in a 1990 interview that she hopes one day to "create a film with a truly tribal vision, viewpoint, in terms of story, camera viewpoints, angles, everything." In the musical arena, Harjo has formed a six-piece band, Poetic Justice, which performs a fusion of rock, blues, jazz, reggae, and poetry. Featuring Harjo's vocals and soprano saxophone playing, the band performs songs based on Harjo's poetry. Their 1996 CD, *Letter from the End of the Twenty-First Century*, includes a version of "She Had Some Horses" and "For Anna Mae Aquash," a tribute to the American Indian Movement activist who was murdered in 1975. Harjo's second CD, *Native Joy for Real*, was released in 2004.

In January 1998, Harjo was one of seven writers awarded 1997 Lila Wallace-Reader's Digest Fund Writers' Awards. Each writer is given a grant of money to partner with nonprofit cultural, educational, and community organizations to foster an exchange of ideas and greater appreciation for contemporary literature. She has also received the 2000 Western Literature Association Distinguished Achievement Award and the 2003 Arrell Gibson Lifetime Achievement Award.

As a teacher, poet, and performing artist, Harjo continues to use her unique vision and voice to present her perceptions to an ever-growing audience. In a 1987 essay, Harjo noted that, despite her grave "responsibility to all the sources that I am," this role gives her "a strange kind of sense [that] frees me to believe in myself, to be able to speak, to have voice, because I have to; it is my survival."

Further Reading

Harjo, Joy. "Family Album." *Progressive*, March 1992, pp. 22–25.

———. *How We Became Human: New and Selected Poems.* New York: W. W. Norton, 2002.

———. *In Mad Love and War.* Middletown, Conn.: Wesleyan University Press, 1990.

———. "Ordinary Spirit." In *I Tell You Now: Autobiographical Essays by Native American Writers,* edited by

Brian Swann and Arnold Krupat, 264–270. Lincoln: University of Nebraska Press, 1987.

———. *Secrets from the Center of the World.* Tucson: University of Arizona Press, 1989.

———. *She Had Some Horses.* New York: Thunder's Mouth Press, 1983.

———. *The Spiral of Memory: Interviews.* Edited by Laura Coltelli. Ann Arbor: University of Michigan Press, 1990.

———. *The Woman Who Fell from the Sky.* New York: W. W. Norton, 1994.

Joy Harjo Web site. URL: http://www.joyharjo.com. Downloaded on October 15, 2005.

Ruppert, Jim. "Paula Gunn Allen and Joy Harjo: Closing the Distance between Personal and Mythic Space." *American Indian Quarterly,* 1983, pp. 27–40.

Scarry, John. "Representing Real Worlds: The Evolving Poetry of Joy Harjo." *World Literature Today,* Spring 1992, pp. 66–68.

Harjo, Suzan Shown

(1945–) *Cheyenne-Muskogee activist, journalist, curator, poet*

For more than 30 years, Suzan Shown Harjo has been an leading advocate for American Indian rights, helping to shape both national legislation and public opinion. Born on June 2, 1945, to a Cheyenne mother and a Creek (Muskogee) father, she spent her first 11 years on a farm in El Reno, Oklahoma. As a teenager, she lived in Naples, Italy, where her father was stationed with the military.

Living in New York City, Harjo found her first career in radio and theater. With her husband, Frank, Harjo coproduced for WBAI-FM "Seeing Red," a radio program dealing with Indian affairs. As the station's literature and drama director, she produced hundreds of radio plays. Harjo also was a founder of the Spiderwoman Theater Company, an improvisational troupe featuring American Indian performers.

The Indian rights movement of the 1970s inspired Harjo to get more involved in government policies toward Indian groups. In 1974, she moved to Washington, D.C., where she worked for several law firms. Four years later, President

Jimmy Carter appointed her a congressional liaison for Indian affairs. In this capacity, Harjo helped draft legislation that called for the protection of tribally held lands.

From 1984 to 1989, Harjo was the president of the National Congress of American Indians, the largest Indian advocacy organization in the United States. At the time, Indians were facing severe cuts in the federal funding for housing, health care, and education by the Reagan administration. Harjo also sought to help Indian groups through the Morning Star Initiative, which she founded in 1984. Among its goals were the protection of sacred lands and the development of policies regarding the proper use of Indian names and symbols. Harjo's work helped shape hundreds of pieces of legislation, including the National Museum of the American Indian Act of 1989 and the Native American Graves Protection and Repatriation Act of 1990. Her efforts have also led to the return of approximately 1 million acres of land to the Cheyenne, Lakota Sioux, Arapaho, and other Indian peoples.

Since 1992, Harjo has been the lead plantiff in *Harjo et al. v. Pro Football, Inc.,* a lawsuit brought by her and six other Indians before the U.S. Patent and Trademark Office. The suit aims to stop the owner of the Washington football team from using the name "Redskins." In 1999, a three-judge panel found unanimously in favor of Harjo and her co-plaintiffs. The Redskins owner won an appeal to the U.S. District Court, but the trademark office's original decision was upheld by the Court of Appeals in 2005.

Harjo is a frequent lecturer on topics relating to Indian affairs and has appeared on numerous national television programs, including *Oprah* and *Larry King Live.* She also writes a regular column for *Indian Country Today,* the leading American Indian newspaper in the country. Harjo's writings have often stirred up controversy among both Indians and non-Indians. In 2005, she set off a heated debate in Indian country over her condemnation of fry bread, a favorite food among many Indians that Harjo complains is not only not traditionally Indian but also unhealthy for a population plagued by obesity and diabetes.

Devoted to preserving Indian culture, Harjo is also active in the arts. From 1990 to 1996, she served as a founding director of the National Museum of the American Indian. She has curated several exhibits, including the 1998 show "Gifts of the Spirit: Works by Nineteenth-Century and Contemporary Native American Artists" at the Eitljorg Museum in Indianapolis, Indiana. Harjo is a highly regarded poet as well. In 2004, she was named the Eric and Barbara Dobkin Native American Artist Fellow at the School of American Research.

Further Reading/Resources

Gamarekian, Barbara. "Working Profiles: Suzan Harjo, Lobbying for a Native Cause." *New York Times,* 2 April 1986, sec. A, p. 24.
"Suzan Shown Harjo." Indian Country Today—Authors. Available online. URL: http://www.indiancountry.com/author.cfm?id=26. Downloaded on April 28, 2006.

Harris, LaDonna
(1931–   )   *Comanche activist, public servant*

In 1970, activist LaDonna Harris founded Americans for Indian Opportunity. This national multitribal organization is devoted to developing the economic opportunities and resources of Indians throughout the United States.

On February 15, 1931, Harris was born in Temple, Oklahoma, to a Comanche mother and Irish-American father. They had difficulty coping with the hostility that they encountered as a mixed-race couple and separated soon after LaDonna's birth. She was thereafter reared by her maternal grandparents. Owners of a prosperous farm and ranch, they gave her a traditional Comanche upbringing. Under their care, LaDonna was educated in the customs of their tribe but did not learn English until she started school.

While in high school, she met Fred Harris. Though the son of a poor white farmer, he had high ambitions and set his sights on a career in politics. The two were married after graduation, and LaDonna went to work to help put Fred through law school. With limited time and money, the young couple struggled to raise two daughters, Kathryn and Laura, and one son, Byron.

In the early 1960s, Fred Harris was elected to the Oklahoma state senate. As his wife, LaDonna Harris developed influential contacts and political savvy that helped her act on her own dream—helping to improve the lives of Indians in her home state. In 1965, she organized a meeting of representatives of 60 tribes in Oklahoma, the state with the largest and most diverse Indian population. Out of the gathering emerged an urgent sense that Oklahoma tribes needed to improve their economies in order to overcome the ill effects of discrimination and poverty. With this mission in mind, Harris founded Oklahomans for Indian Opportunity, the first intertribal organization in the state.

After her husband was elected to the U.S. Senate in 1965, Harris moved to the nation's capital, where she continued her efforts on behalf of Oklahoma Indians. While in Washington, D.C., she also established herself as crusader for the rights of children and the mentally ill. Because of her passion, intelligence, and political instincts, she was asked to contribute her expertise to a variety of national organizations and committees, including the National Rural Housing Conference and the National Association of Mental Health. Impressed by her reputation, President Lyndon Johnson invited her to chair the National Women's Advisory Council of the War on Poverty in 1967. Harris was also asked to join the National Council of Indian Opportunity. She hoped that this post would allow her to continue her work in developing tribal economies but was disappointed by the inaction of the Nixon administration that succeeded Johnson's in 1968. Frustrated by the bureaucracy of Washington, Harris resigned and in 1970 founded Americans for Indian Opportunity (AIO), a national organization dedicated to the economic growth of Indian communities throughout the United States.

While serving as AIO's president, Harris devoted time to other issues of interest to her. As a representative of the Inter-American Indigenous Institute, she traveled around the globe to study the plight of native populations on other continents. Her devotion to feminist causes led President Gerald Ford to appoint her to the U.S. Commission on the Observance of International Women's Year. Under President Jimmy Carter, the Office for Economic Opportunity welcomed her services as an adviser. During the Carter years, Harris also worked with the Council for Energy Resources Tribes. This council monitored and advised tribes regarding the development of mineral and other natural resources on their lands.

Fred Harris left the Senate in 1975. After he staged an unsuccessful bid for the Democratic candidacy in the 1976 presidential election, the Harris family relocated to New Mexico. LaDonna Harris reestablished Americans for Indian Opportunity in her new home before running her own national campaign in 1980 as a candidate for vice president with the Citizen's Party, which was founded as a liberal alternative to the Democratic and Republican establishment.

As Chief Executive Officer of Americans for Indian Opportunity, Harris continued to expand the organization's goals to meet the current needs of Indian groups. One of AIO's most important efforts is the "American Indian Ambassadors" program, which provides one-year fellowships for Native American students with demonstrated leadership potential. The participants are instructed in tribal values and modes of government and sent to foreign countries, where they can observe other indigenous governmental systems firsthand. Speaking of this unique program in 1994, Harris explained, "In today's changing world, it is time for Native Americans to define ourselves . . . what kind of new leaders we need for the 21st century."

In 2002, LaDonna Harris passed the position of CEO of AIO to her daughter Laura. However, she remains active in the organization by serving as the president of its board of directors. Her 50-year career as one of the countries leading Indian activists and leaders was honored in 2004 in Washing-

LaDonna Harris served as the president of Americans for Indian Opportunity until 2002. (Courtesy LaDonna Harris)

ton, D.C., as part of the events held for the opening of the National Museum of the American Indian.

Further Reading

Anderson, Gary C. "LaDonna Harris." In *The New Warriors,* edited by R. David Edmunds, 123–146. Lincoln: University of Nebraska Press, 2001.

Harris, LaDonna. *LaDonna Harris: A Comanche Life.* Lincoln: University of Nebraska Press, 2000.

Kasee, Cynthia R. "LaDonna Harris." *Notable Native Americans,* edited by Sharon J. Malinowski, 183–185. Detroit: Gale Research, 1995.

Nielsen, Nancy J. "LaDonna Harris." *Reformers and Activists.* New York: Facts On File, 1997.

Heth, Charlotte
(1937–   ) *Cherokee ethnomusicologist, educator*

As both a scholar and teacher, ethnomusiologist Charlotte Heth has worked to preserve the rich musical heritage of American Indian peoples. A member of the Cherokee tribe, she was born in Muskogee, Oklahoma, in 1937. Heth earned a bachelor's and master's degree in music at the University of Tulsa before receiving her Ph.D. in ethnomusicology at the University of California, Los Angeles, in 1975.

Heth became a professor at UCLA in 1974. From 1976 to 1987, she also served as the director of the university's American Indian Studies Center. Heth has taught at Cornell University as a visiting professor and acted as the president of the Society of Ethnomusicology.

Heth's research into Indian music and dance began with an analysis of the Cherokee Stomp Dance, the subject of her doctoral dissertation. She has since made in-depth studies of Cherokee hymns and the Iroquois Condolence Ceremonies, in addition to her continuing research into the history and ceremonial traditions of the Cherokee-Natchez town of Medicine Spring. In order to preserve Native American musical traditions for future generations, Heth also has produced many videotapes and CDs. Heth's work emphasizes that traditionally, music and dance were associated with nearly every aspect of Native American life. In *Selected Reports in Ethnomusicology,* which she edited in 1980, Heth explains that Indians in the past and present have made use of music "for public ceremonies and social occasions as well as for private and semi-public activities such as curing, prayer, initiation, hunting, influencing nature, putting children to sleep, storytelling, performing magic, playing games, and courting."

Heth has also been involved in numerous projects designed to introduce Indian music to the broader public. In 1987, she served as a musical consultant to *Roanoak,* a well-received television series produced by the Public Broadcasting Service. She has been an adviser to the American Folklife Program of the Smithsonian Institution and served as the assistant director of public programming at the National Museum of the American Indian (NMAI) in Washington, D.C. from 1994 to 1999. Now retired, Heth continues to lecture on and research a wide array of topics relating to American Indian music, dance, and musicology.

While at the NMAI, Heth edited the museum's first major publication, *Native American Dance: Ceremonies and Social Traditions* (1992). In its introduction, she summed up the significance of the subject to which she has devoted decades of research: "The importance of American Indian dance is found not only in its impact on modern society, but also in the traditions and values it expresses to and for the Indian peoples. This oral tradition has survived solely because the music and dance were too important to be allowed to die."

Further Reading

Heth, Charlotte, ed. *Native American Dance: Ceremonies and Social Traditions.* Washington, D.C.: National Museum of the American Indian, Smithsonian Institution, 1992.

Meredith, Howard. "Charlotte Heth." In *Notable Native Americans,* edited by Sharon J. Malinowski, 189–190. Detroit: Gale Research, 1995.

Hill, Roberta (Roberta Hill Whiteman)
(1947–   ) *Oneida poet, educator*

Best known for her 1984 collection *Star Quilt,* poet Roberta Hill was born on February 17, 1947, in Baraboo, Wisconsin, and reared in the nearby city of Green Bay. Her father, Charles Allen Hill, was a member of the Oneida tribe, one of the six tribes of the Iroquois Confederacy. The Oneida had lived in western New York State until the years following the American Revolution (1776–83), when they were driven from their homeland by non-Indians. As the tribe dispersed, one group of Oneida, which included Hill's ancestors, settled in Wisconsin. Roberta's mother, Eleanor Smith Hill, traced her Indian ancestry to a branch of the Choctaw that lived in Louisiana.

Roberta Hill had, in her own words, a "hard childhood" marred by the deaths of her grandmother and mother when Roberta was five and nine, respectively. Growing up as an Indian in a largely white community also was a source of tension and pain. In a 1995 interview, Whiteman recalled bitterly the taunts leveled at her by white children at school. Her parents endured discrimination as well. The couple found that realtors were unwilling to sell them a house in a white neighborhood, and her father could not get a job at a public school, despite his solid credentials as a math teacher.

Roberta found some comfort in the family's frequent visits to the Oneida Indian Reservation, where her father had grown up. Among friends and relatives there she found a sense of belonging and a welcome relief from the hostilities with non-Indians. She particularly treasured hearing Oneida stories from her grandmother and father. Whiteman later explained, "When my father told us stories about the Oneida . . . we knew it was special, it was something for us to hold in our hearts, and to think about in hard times."

When Roberta's grandmother died, she left her son's family two volumes of English poetry by William Wordsworth and William Shakespeare. Roberta spent many hours reading and studying the books. Her childhood enjoyment of these poems led her to start writing her own in secret. Despite her love of words, she did not consider a career as a writer. As long as she could remember, her father had insisted that she earn a medical degree like her grandmother. Using a combination of Western medicine and traditional tribal curing practices, her grandmother had doctored the Oneida on the reservation for several decades.

At her father's insistence, Roberta Hill entered the premedical program at the University of Wisconsin after graduating from high school. She disliked her courses, particularly those that required an expertise in math. She struggled with the material until, following Charles Hill's death in 1970, she allowed herself to admit that she had little interest in being a doctor. Hill graduated with a major in creative writing and psychology and con-

tinued her education at the University of Montana. There she studied with poet Richard Hugo, who saw her talent and encouraged her to take her poetry seriously.

After graduating with a master's degree in 1973, Hill began to publish her poems in magazines and anthologies. She also taught in the Poets-in-the-Schools program in seven states before taking a position with the faculty of the University of Wisconsin, Eau Claire. While teaching American literature there, Hill married the Arapaho artist Ernest Whiteman in 1980. The couple had three children—Jacob, Heather, and Melissa—before divorcing.

In 1984, under the name Roberta Hill Whiteman, she published her first book of poetry, *Star Quilt,* after more than eight years of work on the

Roberta Hill credits her talents as a poet to her powers of observation.
(Reprinted by permission of Holy Cow! Press)

volume. Featuring illustrations by her husband, the book was praised by critics for its simple yet eloquent language. Hill's poems were also acclaimed for their use of precise and telling details. The poet credits her powers of observation—an "intense love for looking at things, earth and sky and people"—for this aspect of her work. The poems in *Star Quilt* intertwine a variety of subjects, including family life, love, the natural world, and the Oneida's past and present. Her second volume of poetry, *Philadelphia Flowers,* appeared in 1996.

Now a professor of English and American Indian Studies at the University of Wisconsin at Madison, Hill has recently completed a biography of her grandmother, Lillie Rosa Minoka-Hill. She was the second American Indian woman to earn a medical degree in the United States. Through this project, Hill hopes to use her talent as a writer to educate the young members of her tribe. As she has explained, "I want the next generation to grow up knowing what their people went through so they will understand why it's so important to recover their traditions and language."

Further Reading

Bruchac, Joseph. "Massaging the Earth: An Interview with Roberta Hill Whiteman." In *Survival This Way: Interviews with Native American Poets,* 323–35. Tucson: Sun Tracks/University of Arizona Press, 1987.

Katz, Jane, ed. "Let Us Survive: Roberta Hill Whiteman, Oneida." In *Messengers of the Wind: Native American Women Tell Their Life Stories.* New York: Ballantine Books, 1995.

Whiteman, Roberta Hill. *Star Quilt.* Duluth, Minn.: Holy Cow! Press, 1984.

———. *Philadelphia Flowers.* Duluth, Minn.: Holy Cow! Press, 1996.

Hogan, Linda

(1947–   ) *Chickasaw poet, novelist, short story writer, essayist, educator*

"Outside was my church, my place of vision and dreaming," poet and novelist Linda Hogan once wrote about her love of nature as a child. Her desire to protect the Earth and its inhabitants has been the primary guiding force in her work and in her support for antinuclear and pacifist policies and organizations.

Linda Henderson was born in Denver, Colorado, on July 16, 1947. Her family shuttled between a working-class neighborhood in Denver, where her father worked as a carpenter, and the Indian community in rural Oklahoma where he had grown up. Her father was a member of the Chickasaw, a tribe that originally had lived in the Southeast but was forced by the U.S. government to relocate to Indian Territory (now Oklahoma) in the 1830s. Her mother's ancestors were German immigrants who had come to Nebraska as homesteaders several decades later. According to Hogan, her mixed-race background "created a natural tension that surfaces in my work and strengthens it."

Linda Henderson was a poor student. Only at her mother's insistence did she stay in school long enough to earn her diploma. Henderson did not even consider continuing her education beyond high school. She later recalled, "It was never mentioned to me that I might go to college, or even what it was." Instead, she married Pat Hogan in 1972. Before the couple divorced in 1982, they adopted two daughters, Sandra Dawn Protector and Tanya Thunder Horse. Linda Hogan also worked as a nursing-home aide, dental assistant, secretary, and other low-level office jobs. While employed as a teacher's aide in a school for handicapped children, she began to experiment with writing poems during her lunch hour. She had little familiarity with literature; from her high school classes she had been given the impression that "all poetry was written by dead people, and, that it all had to do with ravens that say 'Nevermore.'" Nevertheless, she felt compelled to put her words and emotions on paper. "Something about the process of doing that writing tapped into my own life in a way I couldn't have done without the writing," Hogan has explained.

In the mid-1970s, Hogan started attending college at night at the University of Colorado at Boulder. In her creative writing classes, both her teachers and the other students discouraged her from writing about her Indian heritage and experiences among her Chickasaw relatives. They were uncomfortable with the material, particularly because her stories and her light-skinned appearance did not conform to their preconceptions about Indians and Indianness. Intimidated by the academic setting, Hogan put aside her old work and tried to write about subjects more acceptable to her professors. But she dates her emergence as a true writer from the moment she decided to trust her instincts. She returned to writing about the subjects that were most important to her and, while still attending college, to determine the course of her own education by reading works not assigned in her classes. Her biggest influences included GERTRUDE SIMMONS BONNIN, Audre Lorde, Meridel Le Sueur, and Tillie Olson.

Hogan graduated in 1978 with a master's degree in English and creative writing. After participating in the Poets-in-the-Schools programs in Colorado and Oklahoma, Hogan taught at Colorado College and the University of Michigan. In 1989 she became a member of the faculty of the University of Colorado at Boulder.

Hogan's poems began appearing in journals and magazines in 1975, but her first collection, *Calling Myself Home,* which included heavily revised versions of her earliest works, was not published until 1979. She has since produced four more books of poetry: *Daughter, I Love You* (1981), *Eclipse* (1983), *Seeing through the Sun* (1985), and *The Book of Medicines* (1994). All have been well received by critics. *Seeing through the Sun* was also awarded the American Book Award by the Before Columbus Foundation in 1986 and *The Book of Medicines* was a finalist for the National Book Critics Award in 1994.

Hogan is also well regarded as a writer of fiction. *That Horse,* published in 1985, is a collection of short stories about Hogan's Chickasaw roots on which she and her father collaborated. These stories and her poems from *Calling Myself Home* were reprinted together as *Red Clay* in 1991. Hogan's first novel, *Mean Spirit,* appeared in 1990. One of

Linda Hogan, pictured here in 1996, has written in numerous genres.
(Courtesy W. W. Norton, Photo by Douglas Kent Hall)

three finalists for the 1991 Pulitzer Prize, it tells the story of an Indian woman's murder in Osage territory in the 1920s. During that period, many Indians were swindled or killed by non-Indian con men when oil was discovered on the Indians' lands. *Solar Storms* (1995), her second novel, presents a Native American woman's search for her roots, and *Power* (1998), her third novel, tells a coming-of-age story about a 16-year-old Indian girl in Florida. Hogan has also written a play, *A Piece of Moon* (1981), which was awarded the Five Civilized Tribes Museum Playwriting Award, and two screenplays, *Aunt Moon* (1986) and *Mean Spirit* (1986).

Hogan has recently turned her attention to nonfiction. She has authored the essay collection

Dwellings: A Spiritual History of the Living World (1995) and coauthored *Sightings: The Gray Whales' Mysterious Journey* (2002). Hogan also recounted her difficult youth and struggles with her Indian identity in *Woman Who Watches over the World: A Native Memoir* (2001). For this book, Hogan won a Wordcraft Circle Writer of the Year Award. She has also coedited several anthologies, including *The Sweet Breathing of Plants: Women Writing on the Green World* (2001) and *Face to Face: Women Writers on Faith, Mysticism, and Awakening* (2004).

Hogan maintains that all her work grows from her Chickasaw upbringing. After she began writing, she realized the enormous influence that the tribe's storytelling traditions had had on her use of words. Hogan once explained, "My ideas and even my work arrangement derives from that oral source. It is sometimes as though I hear those voices when I am in the process of writing." Even more important to Hogan's work is her spirituality, drawn from the respect she was taught to have for nature by her Chickasaw elders. Interviewed in 1985, Hogan stated, "If you believe that the earth, and all living things, and all the stones are sacred, your responsibility really is to protect those things. I do believe that's our duty, to be custodians of that planet."

Further Reading

Bruchac, Joseph. "To Take Care of Life." In *Survival This Way: Interviews with American Indian Poets,* 119–133. Tucson: University of Arizona Press, 1987.

Coltelli, Laura. "Linda Hogan." In *Winged Words: American Indian Writers Speak,* 71–86. Lincoln: University of Nebraska Press, 1990.

Cook, Barbara J., ed. *From the Center of Tradition: Critical Perspectives on Linda Hogan.* Boulder: University Press of Colorado, 2003.

Hogan, Linda. *Dwellings: A Spiritual History of the Living World.* New York: W. W. Norton, 1995.

———. *Mean Spirit.* New York: Atheneum, 1990.

———. *Power.* New York: W. W. Norton, 1998.

———. *Red Clay: Poems and Stories.* Greenfield Center, N.Y.: Greenfield Review Press, 1991.

———. *Seeing through the Sun.* Amherst: University of Massachusetts Press, 1985.

———. *Solar Storms.* New York: Scribner, 1995.

———. "The Two Lives." In *I Tell You Now: Autobiographical Essays by Native American Writers,* edited by Brian Swann and Arnold Krupat, 232–249. Lincoln: University of Nebraska Press, 1987.

———. *The Woman Who Watches over the World: A Native Memoir.* New York: W. W. Norton, 2001.

Hopkins, Sarah Winnemucca

See WINNEMUCCA, SARAH

House, Donna

(1954–) *Navajo ethnobiologist, environmental scientist*

"Plants were here way before people. They know you, have a relationship with you," Donna House explained to the *New York Times* in 2004. Through her work as an ethnobiologist, she has devoted herself to illuminating the cultural and spiritual connections between humans and the plant world.

In 1954, House was born in Washington, D.C., where her father worked as a guard at the Pentagon. But she spent most of her youth in Oak Springs, Arizona, a small rural community on the Navajo Indian Reservation. As a girl, she often accompanied relatives as they gathered sacred plants, which they used to make natural medicines.

With her early fascination with nature, House was drawn to science lessons in school. At the University of Utah, she intended to study medicine, inspired by her desire, in her words, to become "a supercontemporary Navajo," but she changed plans when she could not overcome her aversion to dissecting animals. She chose instead to study environmental science with a concentration in botany.

As an environmental scientist, House has worked with many organizations to help them protect endangered plants, including the National Park Service, Fish and Wildlife Service, and the Navajo Nation. For eight years, she was an adviser to the Nature Conservancy, providing her expertise on the conservation of Indian-held lands.

Through her work, House has developed close ties with tribal elders, which allows her to bring attention to their concerns about how their land should be used.

House has been involved with several environmental groups. She was particularly active in efforts to restrict oil development in El Huerfano Mesa in New Mexico. An area sacred to the Navajo (Dineh), the mesa contains Navajo burial sites and remains a source for plants of ceremonial importance to her tribe. House's environmental concerns have also informed an art installation she produced in collaboration with Winnebago (Ho-Chunk) artist Truman Lowe. In 2006, the work was displayed as part of the "Between the Lakes" exhibition at the Madison Museum of Contemporary Art in Wisconsin.

House is also well known in the field of ethnobiology—the study of the cultural uses of plants. In 2000, she was hired to use her expertise to design the landscape surrounding the new National Museum of the American Indian on the Mall in Washington, D.C. Working as part of team of architects and designers, she sifted through ideas presented by hundreds of tribal leaders. She also consulted with local botanists and even took a canoe trip down the Potomac River to better understand the plant life indigenous to the region.

Four years of research produced a landscape that combines meadowlands, forests, wetlands, and croplands. The habitat includes more than 30,000 individual plants, including buttercups, wild rice, and fields of tobacco, squash, and corn.

As with all of House's work, the landscape displays her effort to keep alive an understanding of the natural world that Indian peoples traditionally passed along from generation to generation. As House has explained, "I respect [that] knowledge. I want to keep that ethos and knowledge continuing."

Further Reading

Brown, Patricia Leigh. "A Native Spirit, Inside the Beltway." *New York Times,* 9 September 2004. Available online. URL: http://www.nytimes.com/2004/09/09/garden/09HOUS.html?ei=5070&en=fbe12001060c4f14&ex=1161576000&adxnnl=1&adxnnlx=1161444075-13bBiCZgur8cv5Dcw+X/HQ. Downloaded on April 27, 2006.

National Museum of the American Indian. Available online. URL: http://www.nmai.si.edu. Downloaded on April 26, 2006.

 Humishuma
See MOURNING DOVE

J

Jemison, Alice Mae
(1901–1964)   *Seneca-Cherokee activist*

A tireless crusader for Indian rights, Alice Mae Jemison was one of the leading Native American activists during the 1930s. She was born on October 9, 1901, in the small town of Silver Creek, New York, near the Cattaraugus Indian Reservation. The reservation was occupied by the Seneca, one of the six tribes of the Iroquois Confederacy.

Alice's father, Daniel A. Lee, was a Cherokee Indian who worked as a cabinetmaker. However, she was shaped more strongly by her mother's Seneca roots. Traditionally, the Seneca traced their ancestry through their mother's line, therefore Alice considered herself more Seneca than Cherokee. The association would give her a sense of confidence throughout her political career. In Iroquois society, men were leaders, but women often wielded the greatest power. From behind the scenes, elder women often told male leaders what to do. If these men did not do as the women advised, the women had the power to take away their position. Familiar with a political structure in which women held great sway, Alice never questioned her right to voice her opinion. This background gave her an advantage over many

non-Indian women of her day, in whom American society discouraged any hint of political ambition.

At a young age, Alice was instilled with a keen respect for hard work. Her conservative parents also taught her to revere the traditions of the Iroquois and to distrust interference by non-Indians in tribal affairs. These beliefs, along with the generally antigovernment views of many residents of western New York at that time, dictated many of her political positions as an adult.

Smart and industrious, Alice longed to be lawyer, but her family did not have the financial resources to fund her dream. Several months after graduating from high school, she instead married LeVerne Jemison, a Seneca steelworker. The couple separated in 1928, leaving Alice Jemison fully responsible for the care for their two children, Jimmy and Jeanne, and her aging mother. To support her family, she took any work she could find and often held several jobs at the same time. During this period, she labored as a beautician, housekeeper, dressmaker, factory worker, door-to-door saleswoman, farmer, and theater usher.

Her most satisfying job was as a part-time secretary to Ray Jimerson, the president of the Seneca Nation. In this challenging and multifaceted position, Jemison could finally put her intelligence to good use. Her talents were particularly valuable when in 1930 the Seneca government came to the defense of two young Seneca women who were accused of murdering the wife of Henri Marchard, an internationally famous sculptor who lived in nearby Buffalo. The Marchard case turned into a media circus. The prosecutor frantically tried to push the case through the legal system, hoping that a speedy trial would lead to a quick conviction. To bias the jury against the defendants, he also fed stories to the local press that tapped into many non-Indians' prejudices against Indian women. In newspaper reports, the two defendants were condemned as promiscuous, and one was even accused of being a witch. The sensational stories were soon repeated in the national press to the disgust of Indian people across the United States.

Alice Jemison set about challenging the allegations against the Seneca women by writing her own newspaper stories about the case. She came to the defense not only of the accused but of all Indian people. The titles of her articles included "Present Crime Poor Example of True Indian" and "Indian Today Is Not Murderous." Largely on the strength of these pieces, she was hired to write a syndicated column from 1932 to 1934.

During the Marchard trial, Jemison also received a valuable education in political lobbying. To garner support for the defendants, she wrote letters to prominent figures, including Vice President Charles Curtis, who was of Kaw and Osage Indian descent. Because of Curtis's intervention, the prosecutor's plan to rush through the trial was foiled. In the end, one defendant was acquitted, and the other, after pleading guilty to manslaughter, served one year in jail.

Jemison then turned her skills toward a new goal: dismantling the Bureau of Indian Affairs (BIA), the government agency charged with overseeing the United States's official dealings with Indian people. Throughout its history, the BIA had been accused of corruption. It had also promoted several policies that were meant to "protect" Indians but that had ultimately helped to make them the poorest minority group in the nation. Many

Indian people resented the BIA, but conservative Iroquois such as Jemison despised the agency and blamed it for nearly all of the problems of Native Americans.

Following his election to the presidency in 1932, Franklin D. Roosevelt was set to appoint a new commissioner to head the BIA. Jemison joined a campaign to promote the appointment of attorney Joseph W. Latimer, who published a newsletter that bore on its masthead the slogan "The Only Good Bureau Is a Dead Bureau." Jemison echoed these sentiments in a newspaper article that appeared on April 18, 1933: "Abolish this bureau with its un-American principles of slavery, greed and oppression and let a whole race of people, the first Americans, take their place beside all other people in this land of opportunity as free men and women."

Roosevelt ignored the Latimer campaign and instead selected John C. Collier to head the BIA. The appointment was a great blow to Jemison. Collier was a political liberal who wanted to use his position to strengthen tribal governments, promote economic development in Indian communities, and preserve Indian traditions. Although Jemison herself saw these as worthy goals, she disagreed wholly with Collier's impulse to achieve them through increased government involvement in Indian affairs.

The passage of the Indian Reorganization Act of 1934 put Collier's plans into motion. Jemison was incensed by the legislation; she immediately began a campaign for its repeal and called for Collier to be ousted from his position. Her vehicle for voicing her demands was the American Indian Federation. She joined this organization in 1935 as its official spokesperson and the editor of its newsletter, *The First American*. The federation was a national association of influential Indians, who had widely varying ideals about Indian policy. The only thing its members shared was a burning hatred of the BIA.

Throughout the late 1930s, Jemison eloquently denounced Collier and his agency in articles, lectures, and appearances before Congress. Completely dedicated to her mission, she made her arguments with a ferocity that was hard to ignore. Often, however, her passion led her to make inflammatory attacks and overblown claims. She was particularly irresponsible in her characterizations of Collier. In congressional hearings, she frequently resorted to name-calling, declaring that Collier was a communist and an atheist to discredit him.

Collier and his supporters were just as eager to defame Jemison. They often denounced her as a fascist, largely because of her position with the American Indian Federation. Some members of the organization were sympathetic to Adolf Hitler's Nazi Party in Germany. Assuming her guilty by association, her political enemies branded her the "Indian Nazi" and even spread a rumor that she was a Nazi spy with the code name "POCAHONTAS."

Jemison added fuel to the fire by publicly opposing the Selective Service Act of 1940. This law called for young American men to be drafted in the military in preparation for the United States's involvement in World War II (1941–45). Jemison claimed that the law could not legally be applied to the Seneca. According to past treaties, the Iroquois were a separate nation with a separate government; therefore, she held that only the Iroquois Nation could send its citizens to war. Jemison was not suggesting that the Seneca should not join the war effort, but that the decision to do so was theirs, not the federal government's. Still, her position exposed her to allegations that she was unpatriotic and un-American, particularly damaging charges in the tense climate of the era.

During the war years, Jemison evaded more attacks on her character by keeping a low political profile. On the verge of financial ruin, she was compelled to take full-time work with the Bureau of the Census. Afraid of jeopardizing her government job, she refrained from lambasting the BIA and instead focused her energies on the wrongdoings of New York State in its dealings with the Iroquois. In the early 1950s, however, she renewed her campaign against the BIA in a series of savage articles she wrote for a new version of *The First*

American newsletter. She continued to lobby for the recognition of Indian rights until her death from cancer in Washington, D.C., on March 6, 1964.

Despite her unflagging zeal, Jemison's efforts to destroy the BIA ultimately failed. However, the cause was revived after her death. In the 1970s, the leaders of the Indian rights movement launched their own crusade against the agency, employing the same highly charged rhetoric and confrontational tactics that Jemison pioneered.

Further Reading

Hauptman, Laurence M. "Alice Lee Jemison: A Modern 'Mother of the Nation.'" In *Sifters: Native American Women's Lives,* edited by Theda Perdue, 175–186. New York: Oxford University Press, 2001.
———. "Jemison, Alice Mae Lee." In *Notable American Women: The Modern Period,* 379–380, edited by Barbara Sicherman and Carol Hurd Green. Cambridge, Mass.: Belknap Press, 1980.
———. "The Only Good Indian Bureau Is a Dead Indian Bureau: Alice Mae Jemison, Seneca Political Activist." In *The Iroquois and the New Deal,* 34–55. Syracuse, N.Y.: Syracuse University Press, 1981.

Johnson, Emily Pauline (Tekahionwake)
(1861–1913)   *Mohawk actress, poet, short story writer, essayist*

"I am a Redskin, but I am something else, too—I am a woman." With these words, the narrator of Emily Pauline Johnson's "As It Was in the Beginning" (1911) begins to tell her story. However, this proud declaration just as easily could been spoken by any number of Johnson's defiant heroines, or even by Johnson herself. As an internationally famous performer, poet, and fiction writer, Johnson dedicated her talents to presenting a sympathetic picture of Indian women, thus giving a voice to a minority all too often silenced in her day.

Born on March 10, 1861, Emily Pauline Johnson (known as Pauline to her family) grew up on the Six Nations Reserve near Brantford, Ontario, in Canada. Following the American Revolution

(1775–83), the British government granted this lush tract of land to the Mohawk Indians, who had allied themselves with the English during the conflict.

Pauline's father, George, was a well-to-do Mohawk leader and interpreter who had been educated in English-run schools. On his side, she traced her ancestry to one of the original founders of the Iroquois Confederacy, a powerful league of Indian nations including the Mohawk that had been formed in the late 16th century. The lineage of her mother, Emily, was no less distinguished. A white women from an upper-class English family, she was a cousin of William Dean Howells, a celebrated poet of the era.

Initially, neither Emily's nor George's family approved of their marriage. At that time, unions between Indians and non-Indians were considered inappropriate, if not scandalous. For the couple, however, the similarities in their tastes and upbringings far outweighed the differences in their backgrounds. In her story "My Mother" (1909), a fictionalized account of her parents' marriage, Pauline Johnson later recalled the shared interests that brought her mother and father together: "They loved nature—the trees, best of all, and the river, and the birds. They loved the Anglican Church, they loved the British flag, they loved Queen Victoria [of England]. . . . They loved music, pictures, and dainty china, with which George filled his beautiful home." The Johnson house near Brantford, known as Chiefswood, was in fact so impressive that it earned Pauline's father a new name among the Mohawk—Onwanonsyshon, or "He Who Has the Great Mansion."

The essay, however, went on to explain that the most important bond between George and Emily Johnson was that "these two loved the Indian people." According to Canadian law, Pauline's mother became a Mohawk when she married Pauline's father. But in Pauline's estimation, Emily Johnson was also an Indian "by the sympathies and yearnings and affections of her own heart." From her youngest days, her mother's example taught Pauline that her own status as an Indian was wholly compatible with her position as a refined and cultured woman.

Pauline's early education, likewise, stressed both Indian and non-Indian beliefs and ways. Before she started school, she taught herself to read, and by twelve she had pored through all of the volumes in her family's large library of English and American classics. At the same time, her father and grandfather shared with her the Mohawk legends and stories of their history. She would come to consider these ancient tales to be as important a part of her literary heritage as the English masterworks she read so avidly.

In addition to her love for literature, Pauline discovered a passion for acting while performing in school plays and pageants. As a teenager, she decided to become a professional actress. Her parents greeted the idea with little enthusiasm. They were far more encouraging when she turned to writing poetry, an ambition they considered more in keeping with her social station than a career on the stage.

In 1884, the Johnsons fell on hard times following George's death from injuries he had sustained years before. (On several occasions, he had been severely beaten by white traders, angered by his opposition to the sale of liquor on the reserve.) Without his earnings to draw on, the family soon was forced to sell Chiefswood and many of the cherished treasures it contained.

Determined to at least earn her own keep, Pauline Johnson began publishing her poems in small newspapers and journals. There she took to signing her works "Tekahionwake," the Indian name of her great-grandfather. Although her status as a published poet made her a local celebrity, the money she received from the sale of her work was meager at best.

To Johnson's relief, she fell into a new, more lucrative career in 1892, when Frank Yeigh, a former classmate, asked her to read some of her poems at a recital he was organizing. The program was to feature a number of readers well known in Canada's literary circles. Yeigh invited Johnson to read in the hope that her appearance would lend a little novelty to the evening's entertainment.

True to Yeigh's expectations, Johnson's debut was a great success. After overcoming a bout of nerves, she delivered a spirited performance, which according to newspaper reviews of the program stole the show from the more experienced readers. Flattered by the reviewer's praise, Johnson happily accepted Yeigh's suggestion that she become a professional recitalist and take him on as her manager.

For the next few years, Johnson continually toured cities and towns throughout Canada. At each performance, she recited a variety of poems, many of which celebrated the beauty of nature and the wonders of the Canadian countryside. But at Yeigh's urging, Johnson always included several of her poems about Indians, which were proven crowd-pleasers. Yeigh suspected that many patrons of her shows paid the admission to see a genteel Indian woman. To customers taught by the popular press to regard Indians as savages, Johnson's composure and sophistication made her a genuine curiosity.

To cash in on the audience's fascination with Johnson's Indian heritage, Yeigh billed her as a "Mohawk Princess." Although Johnson was the daughter of an important political leader, she was by no means considered a "princess" among the Mohawk. Instead of reflecting her true position in her tribe, the title was merely a marketing tool concocted to appeal to non-Indians' romanticized views of Indian women. This "princess" stereotype, then prevalent in many forms of popular entertainment, was typified in the myth of POCAHONTAS. In such stories, young Indians were depicted as beautiful, innocent maidens, uncorrupted by the modern world but eager to be at the service of white men.

If Johnson felt uneasy about playing to this stereotype, her discomfort did not prevent her from dressing the part. She fashioned her own "Indian" performance costume consisting of a buckskin dress, a bear-claw necklace, woven bracelets of wampum (shell beads), and a feather in her hair. Johnson wore this outfit, which cobbled together elements of the traditional garb of a variety of tribes, during the first part of her program. After an intermission, she appeared in a glamorous evening gown, an ensemble that felt much more natural to her than her supposedly Indian dress.

In form, her Indian poems likewise were designed to appeal to the expectations of a non-Indian audience. They resembled the romantic, often melodramatic style common in the work of the period's most popular poets. What made Johnson's Indian verses unusual and memorable was instead their content. Through these poems, she often told the story of an Indian woman confronting the prejudice of her non-Indian peers. While in most representations, Indian women were then depicted as either violent or passive, Johnson's characters were generally intelligent, passionate, and defiant when their people or culture was threatened in any way.

One of her audiences' favorite verses was "A Cry from an Indian Wife." During her performance, she acted out the role of its narrator, an Indian woman who is sending her husband into battle during the Riel Rebellion of 1885. During this conflict, which would have been fresh in the memories of her listeners, three hundred Indians in Saskatchewan, Canada, fought 8,000 Canadian troops in an unsuccessful attempt to retain control of their ancestral homeland.

The poem traces one Indian woman's conflicting emotions about the rebellion. She vacillates between rallying her husband to fight and worrying about the fate of the government soldiers, of whom, she concedes, "all are young and beautiful and good." Finally, she solves the quandary by remembering the Canadians' complete disinterest in the Indians' point of view:

> They never think how they would feel to-day,
>   If some great nation came from far away,
> Wresting their country from their hapless braves,
>   Giving what they gave us—but wars and graves.

At the poem's conclusion, the Indian wife instructs her husband to "go forth, nor bend to greed of white men's hands, / By right, by birth we Indians own these lands."

Another popular portion of Johnson's act was her dramatization of "A Red Girl's Reasoning," the story of a beautiful Indian woman married to a dashing young Canadian official. The couple is idyllically happy until the wife casually mentions that her parents were wed by Indian rites. The husband is scandalized; in his eyes, if her parents were not married in a Christian church, she is illegitimate. Disgusted by his lack of respect for Indian customs, she leaves him, declaring "I tell you we are not married. Why should I recognize the rites of your nation when you do not acknowledge the rites of mine?"

In April 1894, Johnson arrived in London, where she performed in drawing rooms throughout the city to great acclaim. In the process, she came to know the cream of London society and used her new position as an international celebrity

Emily Pauline Johnson is shown dressed for a performance, circa 1900.
(The Brant Museum & Archives)

to land a contract with the Bodley Head, England's premier publisher of poetry. A year later, Johnson's first volume of poems, *The White Wampum*, appeared to good reviews. However, the income it generated was a disappointment. Exhausted by her grueling touring schedule, she had hoped to be able to give up show business and live off her book's profits.

Instead, financial difficulties forced Johnson to return home and embark on a tour through the western provinces, where she appeared mostly in rural areas and small towns. The audiences she encountered there were much more vocal in their prejudices against Indian people than her city patrons were. Disgusted and angered by their smallmindedness, Johnson responded by proclaiming her Indianness frequently and loudly. In much of her publicity material, she insisted on being photographed in profile to emphasize her nose, her one facial feature that most whites recognized as Indian-like.

During her 1894 tour of the United States, Johnson was even more offended by the crude remarks she heard from her audiences there. Following a trip through Michigan, Johnson angrily told the press that everyone she met in the state was "very uncultured, very ignorant, very illiterate," an assessment that, however snobbish, encapsulated her opinion of most Americans.

In 1902, Johnson published her second book of poems, *Canadian Born*. When reviewers complained that the new poems were technically clumsy and lacked the honest emotion of her earlier works, Johnson became so discouraged that she gave up writing poetry for good. Instead, she began to write short stories about Indian life, which magazines were eager to buy. After finally retiring from performing in 1909, Johnson became a regular contributor to *Mother's Magazine.* Her stories for the magazine, which were later published in a collection titled *The Moccasin Maker* (1913), were largely tales of struggle and triumph with Indian women as their heroines. Johnson also wrote children's tales about Canadian trappers and mounties for *Boy's World* and her own versions of the legends of Pacific Coast Indians for the *Vancouver Province*.

On March 7, 1913, Johnson died from breast cancer at the age of 51. In her will, she directed that "no tombstone or monument be raised in my memory, as I prefer to be remembered in the hearts of my people and my public." For many years, Johnson did live on through her work. Seen to promote Canadian nationalism, her poetry became a standard part of high schools' literature lessons: For several generations, nearly every Canadian student had to commit at least one of Johnson's poems to memory. However, her work—old-fashioned in style and often melodramatic in tone—has since gone out of favor. She is now known more for the story of her life, in which, much like her characters, she had to endure great hardships and overcome prejudice before emerging as a heroine.

Further Reading

Gerson, Carole, and Veronica Jane Strong-Boag, eds. *E. Pauline Johnson, Tekahionawake: Collected Poems and Selected Prose*. Toronto: University of Toronto Press, 2002.

Johnson, E. Pauline. *Flint and Feather: The Complete Poems of E. Pauline Johnson*. 1912. Reprint, Toronto: Hodder and Stoughton, 1969.

———. *The Moccasin Maker*, 1913. Reprint, Tucson: University of Arizona Press, 1987.

Keller, Betty. *Pauline: A Biography of Pauline Johnson*. Vancouver: Douglas & McIntyre, 1981.

Sonneborn, Liz. "Emily Pauline Johnson: Mohawk Actress." In *Performers*. New York: Facts On File, 1995.

Strong-Boag, Veronica Jane, and Carole Gerson. *Paddling Her Own Canoe: The Times and Texts of E. Pauline Johnson*. Toronto: University of Toronto Press, 2000.

Juana Maria (Lost Woman of San Nicholas Island)

(unknown–1853)   *last survivor of the Chumash of San Nicholas Island*

The last living member of her tribe, Juana Maria was born on San Nicholas Island, which lies 75 miles west of present-day Los Angeles. As early as 1602, white explorers knew of the island and its inhabitants, who were members of the Chumash tribe. But because rough waters made traveling to the San Nicholas difficult, the Indians there were left relatively undisturbed until the early 19th century. At that time, priests at the mission at Santa Barbara took an interest in claiming the Indians as converts. Rather than hazard the trip to the island, the priests enlisted the help of the then Mexican government of California, which decided to relocate the San Nicholas Indians to the mainland.

In 1835 or 1836, the Indians boarded a ship headed for California. As soon as it set sail, a young woman discovered that her baby was still on the island. In a panic she jumped overboard and swam back to the island. An impending storm prevented the ship from turning around to retrieve her and her infant. The mission priests later issued a $200 reward for the woman, but few people were willing to venture out to the remote island to search for her. Occasionally, bands of hunters looked for her while stalking otters and seals, but years passed without a sighting.

At last in 1853 a crew of hunters led by Captain George Nidever came upon the woman, sitting with her dog outside a house she constructed from whale bones. The hunters brought her aboard the ship and took her to Santa Barbara. By the time she arrived, however, there were no longer any of her people left at the mission. During her 18-year-long disappearance, they had all been killed by non-Indian diseases to which they had no natural immunities.

In Santa Barbara, one mission priest, Father Gonzales, developed a friendship with the woman, who was baptized and given the name Juana Maria. Because no living person knew her language, she could talk with him only by using sign language, which proved ineffective for communicating any details about her life alone on the island. She lived at the mission only seven weeks when she, like the rest of the San Nicolas Indians, died of disease. She left behind several pieces of her clothing and a basket, but her meager possessions were all later either lost or destroyed. The sad and strange story of the lost woman of San Nicholas Island has been told in several works of fiction, most notably Scott O'Dell's *Island of the Blue Dolphins,* a young adult novel that won the 1960 Newbery Award.

Further Reading

O'Dell, Scott. *Island of the Blue Dolphins.* Boston: Houghton Mifflin, 1960.

Jumper, Betty Mae Tiger
(1923–) *Seminole tribal leader*

The first female tribal chief of the Seminole tribe of Florida, Betty Mae Tiger Jumper was born in 1923 in a chickee (a traditional Seminole dwelling) near the small village of Indiantown in Florida. Her mother was a full Seminole, and her father was a white trapper. Betty Mae's Seminole grandparents disapproved of the mixed-race marriage and raised the girl as a traditional Seminole. They did not want her to attend school or learn English, but after seeing a comic book, the young Betty Mae was determined to learn how to read. Against her grandparents' wishes, she went to a nearby day school for several years before moving to Cherokee, North Carolina, to attend an Indian boarding school. Graduating in 1945, she became one of the first Seminoles to receive a high school diploma.

Betty Mae Tiger continued her education at the Kiowa Indian Hospital in Oklahoma, where she studied nursing for a year. She then returned to Florida, where she pioneered improvements in the health care provided to the residents of the three Seminole reservations. In honor of her work, the tribal medical center in Hollywood, Florida, is named for her. While working as a nurse, Tiger married Moses Jumper, an old friend and classmate. The Jumpers raised two sons and one daughter.

In 1957, the Seminole tribe organized a formal government according to the guidelines of the Bureau of Indian Affairs. In its first election, Betty Mae Jumper was named a member of the Seminole Tribal Council. After serving in this post for two years, she joined the tribe's board of directors. In

1967, she was given an even greater honor: The Seminole people elected her as their tribal chief, the first woman voted into such a high position in any American Indian tribe. As the leader of the Seminole, Jumper concentrated on improving the tribe's economy, housing, medical, and educational facilities. She also helped found United South and Eastern Tribes (USET), in which the Seminole joined forces with the Cherokee, Choctaw, and other major southeastern tribes to solve common social and economic problems.

After completing a four-year term, Jumper retired from politics to become the full-time director of Seminole Communications. At that time, she began to publish the Seminole tribal newspaper, *Alligator Times,* later renamed the *Seminole Tribune.* This organization continues to publish the *Tribune,* which is regarded as Indian country's most colorful newspaper. She also oversees the Seminole Print Shop, which in 1980 published Jumper's history of Christianity among the Seminoles, . . . *and with the Wagon Came God's Word.* Jumper and her family are devout Baptists.

In recent years, Jumper has lectured widely about Seminole history and culture and has toured nationally as a storyteller. Every summer she is a featured speaker at the Florida Folk Festival in White Springs, where she recounts traditional stories of the Seminole people. She collected a number of these tales in her popular book *Legends of the Seminoles* (1995). With coauthor Patsy West, she also wrote an autobiography, *A Seminole Legend: The Life of Betty Mae Tiger Jumper* (2001).

In recognition of her contribution to the preservation of Florida's folklore, the Florida Department of State honored her with its Folklife Heritage Award in 1994. The following year, Jumper was inducted into the Florida Women's Hall of Fame by Governor Lawton Chiles and awarded an honorary degree from Florida State University. In 1997, Jumper received two more honors: She was given the first Lifetime Achievement Award from the Native American Journalists Association and was named Woman of the Year by the Florida Commission on the Status of Women.

Further Reading

Kasee, Cynthia R. "Betty Mae Tiger Jumper." In *Notable Native Americans,* edited by Sharon J. Malinowski, 219–221. Detroit: Gale Research, 1995.

Jumper, Betty Mae. *. . . and with the Wagon Came God's Word.* Hollywood, Fla.: Seminole Tribe, 1980.

———. *Legends of the Seminoles.* Sarasota, Fla.: Pineapple Press, 1995.

Jumper, Betty Mae Tiger, and Patsy West. *A Seminole Legend: The Life of Betty Mae Tiger Jumper.* Gainesville: University Press of Florida, 2001.

K

Kauffman, Hattie
(1955–   )   *Nez Perce journalist, news anchor*

Hattie Kauffman has made her mark as the most visible Native American journalist in television. Born in Grangeville, Idaho, Kauffman spent her early years on the Nez Perce Indian reservation. She was the middle child of seven children born to her Nez Perce mother and white father.

When Hattie was a girl, her parents, in search of work, moved the family to Seattle, Washington. Without the support of neighbors that they had had on the reservation, they struggled to get by. As Kauffman later recalled, "On the reservation, you can be poor but you can still go hunting or you can still go to grandma's house . . . [P]eople still share." In Seattle, however, the family was "lost in the city," suffering what Kauffman has called her "starvation years."

Throughout her youth, Kauffman's mother insisted her children get an education. Kauffman tried to quit high school once, but her mother refused to let her. After graduating, she headed to Minneapolis to attend the University of Minnesota, unsure about what she wanted to study.

As a freshman, she attended a meeting of the school's American Indian Student Association. A representative from a local radio station told the group it was looking for a student reporter for a five-minute program on Indian news. When no one volunteered, Kauffman raised her hand and blurted out, "I'll do it!"

At the time, the American Indian Movement (AIM), an Indian rights organization founded in Minneapolis, was staging protests across the country. The situation gave Kauffman, even as a rookie reporter, the opportunity to work on important stories. "It was a real exciting time," she once recalled. "I interviewed [AIM leaders] Dennis Banks and Russell Means. I tried to get on a bus and go to Wounded Knee [the site of a 1973 AIM protest]. I didn't get in. I wanted to ask, why are you here, what's going on?"

Even though Kauffman had stumbled into journalism, she later explained how it allowed her to make good use of her natural curiosity: "[As a child,] my nickname was 'How Come?' My grandfather named me that because I was always asking, 'How come I have to come in; how come I have to go to bed? How come?' I think it all started back then."

Impressed by her work on the radio, the Minneapolis television station WCCO-TV approached Kauffman, offering her a scholarship to the University of Minnesota's journalism school. Kauffman, though, was not ready to commit herself to a career in journalism. She turned down the scholarship and graduated with a degree in political science. After three years of teaching school, however, Kauffman was finally ready to give reporting a try. She called up WCCO-TV and took them up on their offer.

Kauffman began her television career in 1981, when she was hired as a reporter by KING-TV in Seattle. Two years later, she was promoted to weekend anchor. During her six years at the station, Kauffman received four Emmy Awards for her reporting.

Despite this success, she initially was not sure she was cut out for television reporting. In Nez Perce culture, asking personal questions was considered inappropriate, so she found interviewing people in the middle of a crisis difficult. She was almost ready to quit after her first story, which involved talking with grieving friends of a dead construction worker. As she recalled, "I didn't feel right about it . . . There was that moment of 'Awgh!—what am I doing? I don't want to do this.'"

With time, Kauffman became much more comfortable in interviews. She attributes her Indian heritage in part with her skill at getting the story. She once explained, "We [Native Americans] are culturally suited [to reporting]. We are a culture of story tellers."

In 1987, Kauffman was hired by ABC as a reporter for *Good Morning America*. While there, she inadvertently made history. In February 1989, she happened to be in Honolulu, Hawaii, when an airplane crashed nearby. Although she officially worked for the entertainment division of ABC, she was called on to submit a story for the evening news. Her quick reporting proved a scoop for ABC, when no other network was able to pull together a report from Hawaii. Her report also became landmark—the first report ever delivered on a national newscast by a Native American.

The next year, Kauffman left ABC for CBS. From 1990 to 1999, she was a correspondent for

CBS This Morning, while contributing to the prime-time news program *48 Hours* and occasionally filing in for vacationing anchors. Since 1999, she has been the national news correspondent for the network's *Early Show*. While with CBS, she has covered a wide variety of stories, from consumer reports to celebrity interviews. But she still prefers the excitement and challenge of breaking news. Among the national news stories she has covered are the Oklahoma City bombing and the death of John F. Kennedy, Jr.

Throughout her career, Kauffman has promoted a higher profile for American Indian reporters. In 2000, speaking to the Tribal Leaders Summit and Presidential Candidate Forum, she explained, "There needs to be more [American Indian] people working in television and in the media, not just in Native American newspapers and Native American radio, but in the regular media."

Further Reading/Resources

"Interview with Hattie Kauffman." *Native America Calling.* Available online. URL: http://www.nativecalling.org. Downloaded on April 22, 2006.

Trahant, Mark N. *Pictures of Our Nobler Selves.* Nashville, Tenn.: The Freedom Forum First Amendment Center, 1995.

Kellogg, Minnie (Laura Cornelius Kellogg)
(1880–1947)   *Oneida activist*

Among the most controversial figures in modern Native American history, Minnie Kellogg was hailed as a brilliant advocate for Indian rights by her supporters. In the eyes of her detractors, however, she was nothing but a swindler, tainted by a scandal that in the end spelled her ruin as a political leader.

Born Laura Miriam Cornelius on September 30, 1880, Minnie was raised on a farm on the Oneida Indian Reservation in Wisconsin. Among her ancestors were several of the greatest 19th-century leaders among the Oneidas, one of the six tribes of the Iroquois Confederacy. Her hardworking parents instilled in their daughter a respect for the Iroquois culture and pride in her distinguished lineage. They also taught her to value education as the road to self-improvement and self-sufficiency.

As a girl, Minnie Cornelius attended Grafton Hall, a private finishing school sixty miles away from her family's farm. The school was very different from those attended by most Indian students at the time. The U.S. government then supported a program through which Indian girls and boys were sent—sometimes against their parents' will—to boarding schools hundreds or even thousands of miles from their reservations. There they were taught to abandon all Indian customs and to adopt the ways of whites. Children who did not comply were often beaten. Many others died at school from malnutrition and disease. The environment at Grafton Hall was far more congenial. Although Minnie, the only Indian in the school, received a traditional non-Indian education there, she was not made to feel ashamed of her Indian ancestry by her teachers or fellow students. In fact, she graduated with honors after composing a senior essay titled "The Romans of America," which celebrated Iroquois culture by comparing it with the civilization of ancient Rome.

After leaving Grafton in 1898, Minnie Cornelius spent two years traveling through Europe. She then attended many of the United States's finest colleges and universities, including Barnard College, Stanford University, Cornell University, and the University of Wisconsin. Her course of study was aimless, reflecting a pattern of restlessness and instability that would resurface throughout her life. After ten years of study, she still had not earned a degree.

A caption in her Barnard yearbook, however, hinted that even while in school she had decided on a new path. It stated that "her heart's desire" was "to uphold the honor of her ancient race." Cornelius had a reputation among Indian intellectuals as a highly educated, articulate woman. Her talents, along with articles she had written about Indian issues, brought her to the attention of a new breed of educated Indian leaders who wanted to see massive reforms in the United States's policies toward Native Americans.

At the time, Indians across the nation were suffering from the consequences of the federal government's policy of allotment. Traditionally, Indian groups had shared their land, rather than privately owning individual plots as whites did. Even when they were confined to reservations, Indians continued to hold their land in common. This custom disturbed government officials who wanted Indians to assimilate into the larger culture. It also troubled non-Indian settlers, who hungered for access to Indian lands. To please both, the Congress passed the General Allotment Act in 1887. This law forced Indian groups to divide their land into small plots that were assigned (or allotted) to qualified tribe members as their private property. Any surplus land left over after all allotments were assigned was opened to settlement by whites.

Almost immediately after the allotment policy was implemented, millions of acres of Indian land passed into the hands of non-Indians. Surplus allotments counted for some of the dramatic loss of Indian land. But unscrupulous non-Indians were the cause of much more. Con men flocked to reservations. They knew they could easily trick new Indian landowners—many of whom were uneducated and unfamiliar with the concept of private property—into selling their plots for absurdly low prices. The Oneida land base in Wisconsin was particularly decimated by these scams. When the reservation was allotted in 1892, it measured 65,000 acres. When the allotment policy was abandoned in 1934—just 41 years later—it comprised less than 90.

Largely because of the government's allotment and assimilation policies, at the beginning of the 20th century most Indians were exceedingly poor. Seeking to reverse the lot of all Indian people, Minnie Cornelius became one of the founders of the American Indian Association (soon renamed the Society of American Indians) in 1911. She was also named its secretary.

At the organization's first national convention, Cornelius demonstrated her oratorical skills by delivering a stirring speech. She questioned the very notion of assimilation—that Indians would benefit by becoming more like whites. Cornelius told her audience, "I cannot see that everything the white man does is to be copied," then noted one area in which she felt Indians could well improve upon the ways of whites—economic development. At the time, reformers were attacking the brutal conditions under which many Americans worked, including unsafe and unsanitary facilities and unregulated child labor. Cornelius went on to insist that Indians could improve their financial situation and still "avoid the things that are killing off the majority of the laboring population in the country of the whites." She proposed that Indians work toward building reservation-based industries. Following the Indian tradition of communal ownership, all workers would have a share of the business and of the profits produced by their cooperative labor. Such

industries would also allow Indian groups to become self-sufficient, finally free of dependence on wages or charity from whites.

Cornelius's speech was well received. A reporter from the *New York Tribune* wrote that she was "a woman of rare intellectual gifts" and "one of the moving spirits in the new American Indian Association." Her prominence in this group, however, did not last much longer. Philosophically, she had strong disagreements with her fellow founders. Most believed that traditional Indian ways should be tolerated, but certainly not encouraged. They saw that Indians were experiencing such a state of crisis that old modes of thinking were best abandoned. Always a dedicated defender of Indian cultures, Cornelius believed that any strategy for dealing with current problems had to respect and help preserve ancient traditions. She once summed up her position with the words, "I am not the new Indian. I am the old Indian adjusted to new conditions."

Cornelius's personality was another cause of her falling out with the society. Throughout her career, she had trouble sharing the limelight and working with others toward a common goal. She could also be impulsive and was prone to using questionable judgment. In 1913, she and Orrin Kellogg, a non-Indian lawyer whom she had married the year before, were arrested for impersonating federal agents while investigating alleged wrongdoings on the Osage Indian Reservation. Although the couple was cleared of the charges, the embarrassing incident made the other founders of the society more eager than ever to distance themselves from Minnie.

Despite this setback, Minnie Kellogg was able to further her reputation as a leading crusader for Indian rights with the publication of *Our Democracy and the American Indian* (1920). The book was an condemnation of the Bureau of Indian Affairs (BIA), the agency of the federal government that supervised the United States's official dealings with Indian peoples. She charged that the BIA's policies had impoverished Indians, destroyed many of their cultural traditions, and demolished

This photograph of Minnie Kellogg is from the frontispiece of *Our Democracy and the American Indian* (1920).
(General Research Division, The New York Public Library, Astor, Lenox and Tilden Foundations)

their traditional structure of leadership. Her most savage words were saved for the BIA's Indian boarding schools, which Kellogg held responsible for many of the problems Indian people faced. Kellogg urged her Indian readers to call for dissolution of the BIA: "Our solidarity will be threatened by them just so long as you do not wake up and refuse to allow them to represent you."

In the 1920s and 1930s, Kellogg changed her focus from national issues to problems closer to home. She came to concentrate her reform efforts exclusively on the situation of Iroquois. Her goals, however, became more and more grand. She still held that economic self-sufficiency was the best road to improving the lives of the Iroquois. But she also decided that the Iroquois could only become self-sufficient if their original land base and system of leadership were restored. Though perhaps noble, these aims were too high even for someone as ambitious as Kellogg to hope to achieve.

She began her mission by launching a lawsuit against the government with the help of her husband and her brother. Through litigation, she hoped to force the government to return to the Iroquois their original homeland in western New York State—an estimated 6 to 15 million acres of prime land. To finance this venture, she asked the Iroquois people for help. Traveling from reservation to reservation in the United States and Canada, she lectured on how her plan would once again bring glory to the Iroquois people. Beaten down by years of poverty, the Iroquois were eager to hear her message. They were also impressed by its delivery. Traditionally, Iroquois leaders were the best orators, so her skill as a speaker brought her special respect. In an era when fewer and fewer Indians were learning to speak their native tongues, her mastery of the Oneida language did as well. She also endeared herself to elders by employing traditional Iroquois oratorical techniques—she often spoke in metaphors, reminded her audience of the Iroquois's greatness, and praised the elders for their wisdom.

Others were won over to her cause not by her lofty speeches but by her description of what her lawsuit would mean to them. From her presentation, many Iroquois were persuaded that winning the lawsuit was a sure thing. She also told them that they would receive a portion of the settlement only if they gave her a donation, which was patently untrue. Many Iroquois, wooed by Kellogg's fine words and guarantees of financial gain, gave Kellogg money; some even surrendered their life savings to her care. Other Iroquois, however, were suspicious of Kellogg. In time, most Iroquois communities were bitterly divided between Kellogg supporters and Kellogg detractors.

In 1927, Kellogg finally succeeded in bringing a land claim case to trial, but it was eventually dismissed on a legal technicality. She experienced an even more devastating setback the same year when she, her husband, and her brother were arrested for fraud in Canada. They were accused of soliciting $15,000 under false pretenses from Iroquois living in Quebec and Ontario. Although Kellogg was cleared of all charges at the subsequent trial, the incident reinforced what some of her supporters had come to suspect—that they would never see any of the money and land Kellogg had promised them. She continued to ask for donations, but as time passed and she failed to bring any more suits to trial, her guarantees sounded more and more hollow. As Oneida leader Oscar Archiquette bitterly recalled in a 1970 interview, "Her last haul of money from the poor Oneidas in Oneida, Wisconsin, was perhaps in 1928 or so when she told her victims that they would be getting lots of money before the snow falls. The snow has fallen many times, but not the money." In the end, Kellogg collected and spent several hundred thousand dollars from the Iroquois and never returned a cent.

By the early 1930s, Kellogg's personal reputation was in shambles. However, her many ideas about Indian policy reform were at last being taken seriously. Through the Indian Reorganization Act (IRA) of 1934, the BIA's relationship to Indian tribes was completely overhauled. Allotment was abolished, the Indian boarding school program was dismantled, and programs were created to help Indians establish reservation-based businesses. The

IRA's reforms almost immediately brought much-needed money into many Iroquois communities, which spelled the end of Kellogg's fund-raising efforts. Kellogg had relied on presenting herself as the Iroquois's friend and the government as their enemy. But as people saw that she was funneling cash out of the community while the government was funneling it in, they arrived at a new conclusion about who their true enemy was. Disgraced and reviled, Kellogg retreated from public life. In 1947, she died in New York City while living on welfare.

The tragic career of Minnie Kellogg contains many ironies. She was dedicated to leading her people to financial self-sufficiency, but in the end many Iroquois lost all the money and assets they had by funding her schemes. She longed for the day all Iroquois people would again be united under a traditional system of leadership, but her reservation visits succeeded in factionalizing every community into those who supported her and those who did not. Yet Kellogg did leave behind one enduring legacy: She taught her people that they could fight for their rights in court. Although true court victories are still rare, the Iroquois today continue to look to the legal system as their best means for righting the government's past wrongs.

Further Reading

Hauptman, Laurence M. "Designing Woman: Minnie Kellogg, Iroquois Leader." In *Indian Lives: Essays on Nineteenth- and Twentieth-Century Native American Leaders,* edited by L. G. Moses and Raymond Wilson, 158–179. Albuquerque: University of New Mexico Press, 1985.

Kenojuak (Kenojuak Ashevak)
(1927–)   *Inuit printmaker*

Kenojuak is one of the leading artists of Cape Dorset, a small Inuit settlement in the Canadian Arctic that is renowned internationally for its printmakers. The daughter of a hunter and fur trader, she was born on October 3, 1927, on Baffin Island in the Northwest Territories. When she was six, her father Ushuakjuk was murdered by enemies in a nearby hunting camp. Kenojuak and her younger brother were then sent to live with her grandmother Koweesa.

From Koweesa, Kenojuak learned to sew traditional Inuit clothing from sealskins. During these lessons, the girl was taught to adorn the items she made with inset designs. To create an inset design, she first cut a simple shape out of a sealskin. She next lay the cut skin over another smaller skin dyed a contrasting color. Kenojuak then sewed the pieces together so the color of the second skin could be seen through the cut-out section of the first.

At 19, Kenojuak married a hunter named Johnniebo. Following Inuit custom, her husband was chosen by her relatives. Kenojuak disliked the match, however, and after the wedding displayed her anger by throwing rocks at Johnniebo whenever he approached her. Eventually, though, her feelings for him softened. Before his death in 1970, the two would raise 16 children (five of them adopted) and collaborate on some of Kenojuak's works.

In 1952, Kenojuak was diagnosed with tuberculosis. In her remote village, she had only minimal access to medical care, so she had to move hundreds of miles to the city of Quebec for treatment. During the three years she spent in a Quebec hospital, she learned several new crafts, including dollmaking and beadwork.

When Kenojuak returned to Baffin Island, she began to sell her handiwork through a program established by Alma Houston, the wife of writer and adventurer James A. Houston. He had been a frequent visitor to Inuit communities in northern Canada since the 1940s. Houston was so impressed with the small carvings the Inuit made that he organized several exhibits of them. Non-Indian art collectors shared his enthusiasm and clamored to buy Inuit artwork. For their part, the Inuit were eager to sell their carvings and began to make these and other items specifically for sale. Because much of their hunting territory had been taken over by non-Indians, the Baffin Island Inuits were having a hard time making a living from hunting as they had in the past. Growing ever poorer, they welcomed a chance to earn a cash income from their art.

In the late 1950s, Houston introduced print-making to the Inuit at the Baffin Island community of Cape Dorset. He showed them that they could etch a design on a slab of soapstone—the soft stone they already used for their carvings—paint the raised image, and then press a piece of paper on the paint to create a print. The residents of Cape Dorset immediately took to this new art technique, perhaps because it created patterns on paper that reminded them of the inset designs of their clothing.

With Houston's encouragement, Kenojuak became the first female printmaker at Cape Dorset. She generally only draws the designs for her prints. A carver then translates the image onto a slab of soapstone, to which a printer applies paint and paper. Although she usually does not create her own print slabs, she is an accomplished carver of soapstone sculptures.

Most Cape Dorset artists use printing to create scenes of everyday life or fantastic scenes featuring mythological creatures. Kenojuak, however, favors simple shapes representing animals and humans. Birds are particularly prevalent in her work. She has explained that her birds have no symbolic meaning for her. They are her favorite subject merely because she is fond of them. She remembers warmly that she enjoyed watching and chasing after birds when she was a young girl.

Kenojuak has no set idea about where she is heading with a drawing when she sits down with pencil and paper. In a 1980 interview, she explained her technique: "I may start off at one end of a form not even knowing what the entirety of the form is going to be; just drawing as I am thinking, thinking as I am drawing. . . . And rather what I do is I try to make things which satisfy my eye, which satisfy my sense of form and colour." Whereas the prints of other Inuits tend to feature realistic details, Kenojuak's graphic designs concentrate on capturing the basic shape of an animal. Some are so abstract that the animals they represent are difficult to identify. Kenojuak is also unique in her eagerness to experiment and innovate. Throughout

Kenojuak was awarded the Order of Canada in 1967.
(*Kenojuak Ashevak, 1968*, Photo by/Gift of Norman E. Hallendy, McMichael Canadian Art Collection Archives)

her career, she has delighted in using color in new ways and in overlapping and intersecting shapes to create new effects.

Kenojuak's first published print, *Rabbit Eating Seaweed,* appeared in the annual collection of Cape Dorset prints in 1959. In the years that followed, she was singled out as one of the best Inuit printmakers within non-Indian art circles. Her fame spread even wider when the National Film Board of Canada produced *Eskimo Artist—Kenojuak,* a 1962 documentary of her life and working methods. Since then, her work has appeared in many exhibits in the United States, Canada, and Europe. Most notably, she was honored in 1986 with a 25-year retrospective of her career at the McMichael Canadian Art Collection Gallery in Kleinburg, Ontario.

The Canadian government has repeatedly paid tribute to Kenojuak's contributions to art. In 1967, she was awarded the Order of Canada, the highest honor given to civilians by that country. Five years later, she became a member of the Royal Canadian Academy, Canada's most distinguished organization for the arts. Twice Kenojuak's works were reproduced on Canadian postage stamps: *The Enchanted Owl* (1960) on a six-cent stamp in 1970 and *Return of the Sun* (1961) on a 17-cent stamp in 1980. She received honorary degrees from Queens University and the University of Toronto in 1992 and the Lifetime Aboriginal Achievement Award in 1995.

Kenojuak maintains that economic concerns have been the driving force behind her work. As she has explained, "the main reason why I create things is because of my children, my family." Her career has brought her a steady and sizable income, which has caused some friction between her and some other Inuit, particularly Inuit men who are having trouble supporting their families. But, in addition to the pleasure in being able to provide for her family, she also admits to a second motivation guiding her printmaking, one as simple and elegant as her work—"to make something beautiful, that's all."

Further Reading

Blodgett, Jean. *In Cape Dorset We Do It This Way: Three Decades of Inuit Printmaking.* Kleinburg, Ontario: McMichael Canadian Art Collection, 1991.

———. *Kenojuak.* Toronto: Firefly Books, 1985.

Roch, Ernst, ed. *Arts of the Eskimo: Prints.* Barre, Mass.: Barre, 1975.

Walk, Ansgar. *Kenojuak: The Life Story of an Inuit Artist.* Manotick, Ontario: Penumbra Press, 1999.

✦ Keyser, Louisa (Dabuda, Dat So La Lee) (ca. 1850–1925) *Washoe basketmaker*

The most famous of all Indian basketmakers, Louisa Keyser was probably born in about 1850, although some scholars date her birth as early as 1835. Known as a child and young adult by the name Dabuda, she lived in a Washoe Indian village near the town of Sheridan in western Nevada's Carson Valley.

Survival had always been difficult in the Washoe's desert homeland. Traditionally, their lives were consumed with searching for the little food available in their harsh environment. However, during Dabuda's youth, the Washoe faced even greater obstacles. Non-Indian settlers flocked to the region in the late 19th century and took control over the Washoe's best land. At the same time, larger Indian groups, such as the Northern Paiute, invaded the Washoe territory after non-Indians displaced them from their native territories. Soon, the Washoe's homeland was so reduced that they could no longer live off their land by hunting wild animals and gathering berries and roots, as they traditionally had. To make a livelihood, they were eventually forced instead to perform menial labor for non-Indians for meager wages. Men usually found jobs as ranchhands and farmhands, whereas women could only find far lower paying work as domestics.

In about 1871, Dabuda began working as a laundress and cook for white families in California and Nevada. She married a Washoe man named Assu, and the couple had two children before his early death. Dabuda's children also died young. She was left without a family until 1888, when she married Charley Keyser, a young craftsman of partial Washoe descent. Following Charley's lead, Dabuda took an English name and thereafter called herself Louisa Keyser.

Like all Washoe females, Keyser as a child had learned the basic techniques of basket making. In traditional Washoe society, baskets had many uses. They were cradles for babies, carriers for the plant foods women gathered, plates and bowls that held the meals they cooks, and storage containers for leftovers. But when Keyser grew older, fewer and fewer Washoe women spent time making baskets. Most were so busy with wage work that they began to use metal containers, tins, and other goods manufactured by non-Indians in place of the baskets they had crafted for their family's use.

Just as basketry was becoming a lost Washoe art, women found that their old, worn-out baskets were valued by non-Indian tourists. Desperately in need of more income, impoverished Washoe eagerly sold their families' old baskets to local storeowners, who in turn sold them to tourists at a much greater price.

One of these storeowners was Abe Cohn, who ran a large clothing shop called The Emporium in Carson City, Nevada. Keyser knew Cohn's parents, for whom she had once worked, and decided to approach him with samples of basketry work she made for sale. In 1895, she showed him four whiskey bottles covered with woven willow weeds. Cohn hired Keyser on the spot—to do his family's laundry. But he also encouraged her to continue her weaving. His wife, Amy, who pushed for him sell Indian wares in the store and could recognize good work, saw that Keyser was an excellent craftsperson whose brand-new baskets could fetch higher prices than the used ones the Cohns had been selling.

The Cohns asked Keyser to make more and more baskets, and in time, she was working as a basketmaker full time. As an employee of the Cohns, she gave them ownership of every basket she made. In exchange, they paid for her food, housing, and medical care. Eventually, the Cohns built a small house for Keyser and her husband next to their own.

Keyser made several types of baskets, including cone-shaped *singams* and *monkeewits,* the Washoe baskets traditionally used for carrying and storing food. But her favorite style—the *degikup*—was of her own invention. Her *degikups* were small spherical baskets made from cream-colored willow twigs, blackened fern roots, and red birch bark. With a piece of glass, she carefully scraped these materials to make thin threads about 1/30th of an inch wide. The threads were then coiled around willow twigs and interlocked to stitch the coils together. Most of her baskets were decorated with geometric red-and-black shapes scattered at even intervals over the vessel's light tan surface. The work was difficult and painstaking. Keyser often spent months on a single basket. Late in her career, when she began to experiment with making larger *degikups,*

her best, most intricate baskets required more than 50,000 stitches and took as long as a year to complete.

Although other Washoe women started making new baskets for sale, Keyser's achievements as an artist were unequaled. Most basketmakers concentrated on quantity rather than quality. Tourists, who generally could not distinguish good work from bad, would pay the same price for a shoddily produced basket as for one carefully made. Therefore, for women for whom basket making was primarily a means of putting food on their family's table, it made economic sense to create as many baskets as possible, even if a speedy output resulted in sloppy work. Keyser, on the other hand, was encouraged by the Cohns to take the time to create baskets of the highest quality and to experiment with innovative shapes and designs. Assured of financial support by her patrons, Keyser had the luxury of treating her basket making as an art rather than as a business.

Keyser also did not have to adapt her baskets to the tastes of the marketplace. As more Washoe women became professional basketmakers, they increasingly had to compete for potential customers. To make their wares stand out, some wove showy, even gaudy designs into their baskets. However, as an employee of the Cohns, Keyser did not have to worry about finding a buyer for each of her works. As a result, she was free to make the simple, elegant patterns she preferred.

Soon after starting to work for the Cohns, Keyser became well known among Indian art collectors and enthusiasts. Her superior artistry certainly helped bring her acclaim, but Keyser's fame was largely due to her patrons' promotion campaign. Amy Cohn created a brochure about Keyser and gave it to everyone who bought one of Keyser's works. She also distributed photographs of the artist surrounded by examples of her basketry and lectured widely, telling her audience Indian legends and stories about Keyser. Her non-Indian customers loved to hear Cohn's tales. The stories, which mirrored those told about Indians in the popular press, assured customers that they were buying authentic Indian baskets from a "real" Indian.

What the customers did not realize is that the stories about Keyser and the Washoe people were hatched entirely in Amy Cohn's imagination. Even though the *degikup* was Keyser's own invention, Cohn routinely claimed that it was a traditional Washoe ceremonial basket. She even made up a detailed description of the ceremony in which it was used. Among Cohn's other favorite fictions was that Keyser was considered a "princess" among the Washoe and that the designs she wove on her baskets were symbols with secret religious meanings. To capitalize further on non-Indians' romanticized views of Indians as exotics, Cohn often gave

Louisa Keyser poses with examples of her basketry, circa 1910.

(Nevada Historical Society)

Keyser's baskets overblown titles, such as "Myriads of Stars Shine over the Graves of Our Ancestors."

The Cohns went so far as to give Keyser herself a new name. After 1900, her baskets were marketed as the work of "Dat So La Lee," a Washoe nickname that meant "big hips," possibly given to her by a prominent customer. Most likely, Keyser did not appreciate her new name. Like most women of her tribe, she was physically large, weighing approximately 250 pounds. She was made to feel self-conscious about her size only when, as part of her employment with the Cohns, she was expected to spend the summer working on her baskets outside their second store, the Bicose, in the resort area of Lake Tahoe. This marketing gimmick of allowing passersby to stop and gawk at Keyser while she worked made her feel uncomfortable, especially when members of her audience spat out unkind remarks about her appearance and weight. She was so disturbed by these comments that she once asked Abe Cohn if she could have a corset—a then-popular close-fitting women's undergarment designed to make the wearer's waist appear smaller. Cohn refused and added to her embarrassment by repeatedly telling the story of her request in a tone that ridiculed the very idea that an Indian woman would think herself fit to wear a gentlewoman's garment. In public forums, Abe Cohn frequently depicted Keyser as childish, vain, and dim-witted, reflecting then-common stereotypical views of both women and Indians.

Despite the abuse Keyser endured from the Cohns, they never belittled her talents as an artist. Their promotion of her, in fact, was largely responsible for elevating Indian basketry from a craft to an art in the eyes of non-Indian experts and scholars. The Cohns recognized many of her works as masterpieces and priced them as an art dealer might price a painting of an acknowledged master. Although most collectors were scared off by the amount of money the Cohns were asking for Keyser's work, some of her baskets sold for phenomenal sums even during her lifetime. In 1930, five years after her death, one basket was purchased for

$10,000. In the 1990s, her best works have garnered prices of about $250,000.

Neither Keyser nor her heirs, of course, ever received a penny of this money. Her arrangement with the Cohns did not allow her to benefit directly from the sale of her work. It did, however, offer certain opportunities that helped her to develop as an artist. Although living away from other Washoe on the Cohns' property undoubtedly caused Keyser some emotional strain, it helped her forge her own unique style of basket making. Isolated from her people, she could ignore or alter traditional Washoe basket-making techniques without worrying about offending her tribe. Through her association with the Cohns, she also was able to study the basketry of other Indian people sold in her patrons' stores. She was particularly influenced by the work of the Pomo Indians of California. Their ornate decorative basketry moved Keyser to see that baskets could be more than utilitarian objects. And

however unfair her financial arrangement with the Cohns was, it did allow her to focus on her art and dedicate all of her time and energy to it.

It is because of the Cohns' relentless promotion of her wares that decades after her death Keyser remains perhaps the most famous basket weaver in the world. But it is because of her own devotion to the art of basketry that she is now almost universally considered to be the greatest of all Indian basket makers.

Further Reading

Cohodas, Marvin. "Dat So La Lee's Basketry Designs." *American Indian Art* 1, Autumn 1976, pp. 22–31.

———. "Washoe Innovators and Their Patrons." In *The Arts of the Native North American Indian,* edited by Edwin L. Wade, 203–220. New York: Hudson Hills Press, 1986.

Hirschfelder, Arlene. "Dat So La Lee: Washo Basket Maker." In *Artists and Craftspeople,* 1–8. New York: Facts On File, 1994.

L

LaDuke, Winona
(1959–) *Ojibwa activist, novelist, essayist*

One of the most prominent young Indian activists, Winona LaDuke is spearheading the efforts of the Mississippi band of the Ojibwa to retrieve ownership of their reservation in Minnesota. Her training as a activist started early. Her Ojibwa father, Vincent LaDuke, and white mother, Betty Bernstein, were both passionate supporters of the Indian rights movement of the 1970s.

Winona was born in an Indian neighborhood in Los Angeles, where Vincent LaDuke often worked as a movie extra. But when she was a young girl, the family frequently paid visits to White Earth Indian Reservation in rural northern Minnesota, where her father had grown up. Betty and Vincent LaDuke agreed that their daughter should be raised with an understanding and respect for her Indian heritage.

When Winona was five, her parents were divorced. She moved with her mother to a predominantly white neighborhood in Ashland, Oregon, where Winona experienced prejudice for the first time. Her classmates taunted and threatened her because of her appearance. "I was the darkest person in my school. You just don't fit in," LaDuke explained to *People* magazine in 1994.

A good student, LaDuke was recruited by Harvard University in 1979. She describes her time at the school a "transformative experience." Through contact with a group of fellow Indian students, LaDuke became more informed about various Native American causes. She became particularly concerned about the increasing environmental damage to Indian reservation lands instigated by corporate and government forces. During her time at Harvard LaDuke spent a summer in Nevada, during which she worked on a campaign to stop uranium mining on Navajo lands. The same year, she traveled to Geneva, Switzerland, to offer expert testimony before a United Nations conference about the exploitation of Indian lands.

After graduating from Harvard with a degree in native economic development, LaDuke moved to the impoverished White Earth Indian Reservation in 1982. Even though her impressive college credentials could earn her a job just about anywhere, she never entertained the idea of settling anywhere else. "Ever since I was a little I wanted to come back and work in the Indian community," she explained in an interview in 1995.

LaDuke spent her first year at White Earth working as the executive director of the reservation high school. She left this post to organize an effort to launch a lawsuit against the U.S. government to win back land illegally taken from the Ojibwa in past treaties. While in Toronto to attend a Native American conference in 1986, she met Randy Kapashesit, a Cree Indian activist. They married two years later and had two children before separating in 1992.

When the Ojibwa land claim suit was dismissed, LaDuke refused to give up the dream of restoring the ownership of White Earth to her people. The reservation had been established in 1867 by a treaty that promised the land would be the Ojibwa's forever. White Earth then consisted of 837,000 acres of forests, marshlands, and lakes. Over time, however, government policies allowed lumber companies and non-Indian swindlers to take control of more and more of the reservation. By 1934, Indians owned only 7,890 acres—less than $\frac{1}{100}$th of the original reservation. The loss of their land base was devastating to the Ojibwa. As LaDuke has explained in *Harper's Bazaar* magazine, "Our land reaffirms us, makes us who we are, gives us the instructions to form our lives. If you lose control of your land, you lose your essence."

To help return the Ojibwa's land to them, LaDuke founded the White Earth Land Recovery Project (WELRP). Initially funded by a $20,000 grant from Reebok, the organization began to solicit contributions to buy up reservation land and finance further land claim suits. LaDuke also asked for donations of land. Concentrating on obtaining lands of special importance to the tribe, such as burial grounds, WELRP has restored more than 1,000 acres. LaDuke hopes to bring a total of 30,000 acres under Ojibwa control by the year 2010.

WELRP has also created a variety of programs aimed at reviving traditional Ojibwa culture. The organization operates Native Harvest, which sells traditional Ojibwa foods, such as wild rice and maple syrup, over the Internet and at its store and café in Ogema, Minnesota. Through WELRP, LaDuke has also initiated an effort to revive the Ojibwa language. In recent years, few young people on the reservation have learned to speak their Native tongue. LaDuke's program concentrates on providing classes in Ojibwa to preschoolers. She expects that these children when they become adults will be equipped to pass along their knowledge to both older and younger generations and thus keep the language alive.

To help other Indian women achieve the same type of successes in their own communities, LaDuke became the cochairperson of the Indigenous Women's Network (IWN) in 1989. The organization helps fund local efforts to improve the quality of Indian life. To solicit money for the organization, LaDuke organized the 27-city "Honor the Earth" tour in 1995. This series of concerts, starring the folk rock duo the Indigo Girls, raised close to $250,000 for the cause. IWN also made headlines later in the year by sending a delegation to the United Nations Women's Conference in Beijing, China, where LaDuke was featured as a speaker. In 1997, *Ms.* Magazine honored LaDuke's work by naming her Woman of the Year.

LaDuke has written about Native rights for many publications. In 2002, her most important writings were collected in *The Winona LaDuke Reader.* LaDuke is also the author of *All Our Relations: Native Struggles for Land and Life* (1999) and *Recovering the Sacred: The Power of Naming and Claiming* (2005). She published her first novel, *Last Standing Woman,* in 1997.

Recognized as an advocate for international indigenous rights, LaDuke was asked to run as the Green Party candidate for vice president in 1996 and 2000. She ran her campaign alongside the party's presidential nominee Ralph Nader, a leading environmentalist and the leader of the public interest law movement. The ticket received .7 percent of the vote in 1996 and 2.7 percent in 2000.

LaDuke has sometimes butted heads with the White Earth tribal council, the official governing body of the reservation. She has refused to turn over to the council control of the reservation land purchased by WELRP. As an explanation, she says that her organization has "a cultural and environmental agenda" that "often runs counter to the tribal council's focus on economic development and gambling." LaDuke also believes that the best hope for improving conditions in poor reservation communities is grassroots efforts conceived by local residents. As she explained to *The Ethnic Newswatch* in 1996, "Someone needs to speak up for community work and community people and show that these struggles are bottom-line in the communities. Our future generations are at stake."

Further Reading

Bowermaster, Jon. "Earth of a Nation." *Harper's Bazaar* 126 (April 1994): 101–102.

LaDuke, Winona. *The Winona LaDuke Reader: A Collection of Essential Writings.* Stillwater, Minn.: Voyageur Press, 2002.

Paul, Sonya, and Robert Perkinson. "Winona LaDuke: Native American Econological Activist." *Progressive* 59 (October 1995): 36–40.

Rosen, Marjorie. "Friend of the Earth." *People* 42 (November 28, 1994): 165.

White Earth Recovery Project and Native Harvest. Available online. URL: http://www.nativeharvest.com. Downloaded on October 30, 2005.

Marguerite La Flesche was a proponent of education for the Omaha.
(Nebraska State Historical Society Photograph Collections)

La Flesche, Marguerite (Marguerite Picotte, Marguerite Diddock)

(1862–1945) *Omaha educator, civic leader*

Throughout her life, Marguerite La Flesche was driven to aid and serve the Omaha people. The daughter of Omaha leader Joseph La Flesche, she was born on the tribe's reservation in Nebraska in 1862. She shared with her father the belief that non-Indian education was crucial to the Omaha if they were to survive as a tribe.

After attending local schools, she and her sister Susan La Flesche headed east in 1879 to continue their education at the Elizabeth Institute for Young Ladies in New Jersey. Ten years earlier, her older sister Susette La Flesche had gone to the same school. During their three years there, Marguerite and Susan studied a standard curriculum of reading, writing, and arithmetic, while also taking classes in philosophy, physiology, and literature. While at the Elizabeth Institute, Marguerite developed a lifelong love of reading.

Marguerite and her sister returned to the reservation in 1882. For a year, Marguerite taught at the Presbyterian Mission School there. In 1884, she and Susan left on another adventure. They traveled to Hampton, Virginia, to enroll in the Hampton Normal and Agricultural Institute. Originally a school for African Americans, Hampton was a centerpiece in the federal government's program to assimilate promising young Indian men and women into white society through education and introduction to non-Indian ways. Both of the La Flesche sisters took the "normal" course of study—that is, they were trained as teachers. Marguerite graduated in 1887. At her commencement ceremony, she read her award-winning essay titled "Customs of the Omahas."

121

Susan stayed in the East to attend medical school. Marguerite, however, decided to return home, where she was offered a job as a missionary. She instead married Charles Picotte, a half-Sioux Hampton student with whom she developed, in Susan's words, "a mutual admiration society." They settled on the Omaha reservation, taking over the management of the family homestead after Joseph La Flesche's death in 1888.

Picotte died suddenly in 1891. Left to fend for herself, Marguerite began teaching at a school run by the federal government near the Omaha agency. For a time, she also served as a "field matron." She visited Omaha families in their homes and provided whatever aid they needed—from teaching them to cook non-Indian food to caring for the ill.

In 1895, Marguerite La Flesche married Walter Diddock, a non-Indian teacher. The couple had five children. The Diddock family was instrumental in the establishment and development of the town of Walthill, Nebraska. There, Marguerite and Walter built a large frame house. It was furnished with the amenities she had enjoyed in the East, including a bathroom, then a luxury in rural Nebraska.

While raising her children, Marguerite emerged as a tireless community leader. She belonged to numerous civic organizations, including the Walthill Women's Club and the Missionary Society, often offering her house as a meeting place. With Susan, who lived nearby, she also sponsored lectures and concerts. Marguerite was particularly passionate about the library she helped establish on the reservation. While most of her projects appealed only to the more assimilated Omaha, Marguerite also reached out to more traditional tribe members. She often acted as an interpreter during funerals and other events. Marguerite and Susan also counseled young couples on the advantages of legal marriage, often organizing the weddings themselves.

After Walter Diddock's death in 1928, Marguerite became somewhat more reclusive, although she remained involved in community affairs throughout her life. In 1945, at the age of 83, she

died at the Susan Picotte Memorial Hospital, which was named in her sister's honor.

Further Reading

Diffendal, Anne P. "The LaFlesche Sisters: Victorian Reformers in the Omaha Tribe." *Journal of the West,* January 1994, pp. 37–44.

Green, Norma Kidd. *Iron Eye's Family: The Children of Joseph La Flesche.* Lincoln, Neb.: Johnsen Publishing Company, 1969.

La Flesche, Rosalie (Rosalie Farley)
(1861–1900)   *Omaha businesswoman*

The daughter of Omaha chief Joseph La Flesche, Rosalie La Flesche was born in Nebraska in 1861. The years of her youth were a period of transition for her tribe. Omaha contact with non-Indians was increasing. Joseph La Flesche held that their survival as a tribe would depend on their ability to adapt to and interact with white society. He insisted that all his children learn English and receive a non-Indian education.

Rosalie attended Presbyterian Mission School on the Omaha reservation. Unlike her well-known sisters—SUSAN LA FLESCHE, SUSETTE LA FLESCHE, and MARGUERITE LA FLESCHE—Rosalie did not travel east to continue her education. Instead, she stayed on the reservation and taught at the mission school. In 1880, she married a fellow teacher, Ed Farley.

In 1884, the Omaha reservation was allotted—divided into small plots (called allotments) that would be held as private property by tribe members. Once all the allotments were doled out, there was still a large amount of unallotted lands. White ranchers let their cattle graze in this area, and the animals often wandered onto the homesteads of Omaha farmers, destroying their fields.

The Omaha were reluctant to fence in their farms. But they embraced another idea suggested by anthropologist Alice Fletcher, a close friend of Rosalie and her family. Fletcher said the tribe should place a fence around the unallotted land and charge white cattlemen a fee to use it for grazing. The plan would not only solve the problems of wandering cattle but also raise money for the tribe.

Ed Farley signed on to manage this grazing area. In 1884, he leased 18,000 acres from the tribe. All income made from the venture would be split between Farley and the Omaha.

The business was highly successful, largely because of Rosalie's work. While Farley cared for the cattle, she kept the books. Because she knew English and the Omaha language, she was also able to negotiate with both white cattlemen and the Omaha tribal council. Rosalie also became an informal banker, managing funds paid by the federal government to individual Indians unfamiliar with non-Indian financing dealings. Individual Omaha would often borrow money from merchants and other white-owned businesses in anticipation of these government payments. On payment day, Rosalie made sure that the creditors received no more money than they were due.

Rosalie La Flesche also often stepped in to help Omaha having personal problems. In her journal, she recounted one instance when a woman came to her after being beaten by her husband. Rosalie took her to a lawyer and translated the woman's story. With the lawyer's aid, they arranged for the husband's arrest.

La Flesche also was welcoming to non-Indian guests. Her sister Susette was a journalist who often gave lectures to philanthropists interested in helping Indian peoples. On Susette's recommendation, they often came to visit Rosalie and her family. Rosalie also aided Fletcher and other anthropologists who wanted to study and preserve the Omaha's traditional ways.

After a lengthy illness, Rosalie La Flesche died on May 9, 1900. Her funeral was attended by throngs of friends and acquaintances, both Indian and non-Indian. Reporting her death, the *Omaha Bee* declared, "Mrs. Farley never severed her relations to the tribe . . . [She] was one of its most influential personages. . . . She was a woman of rare business qualifications . . . [who] conducted large enterprises successfully. . . . But her influence among the Omaha was not due to her sagacity. . . . She was the resource of the poor, the sick and the improvident, her life was a benediction, truly she was one of the most remarkable women of the state."

Further Reading

Diffendal, Anne P. "The LaFlesche Sisters: Victorian Reformers in the Omaha Tribe." *Journal of the West,* January 1994, pp. 37–44.

Green, Norma Kidd. *Iron Eye's Family: The Children of Joseph La Flesche.* Lincoln, Neb.: Johnsen Publishing Company, 1969.

Rosalie La Flesche was an important business leader among the Omaha.
(Nebraska State Historical Society Photograph Collections)

La Flesche, Susan (Susan Picotte)
(1865–1915)   *Omaha physician*

Susan La Flesche was the first American Indian woman to become a physician trained in Western medicine. By the time she was born on June 17,

1865, her father Joseph had served as the principal chief of the Omaha Indians for more than a decade. During that time, he had commanded great influence over the tribe. Although he respected Omaha ways, he told his people that the time had come for them to assimilate into non-Indian society. In an 1854 treaty that Joseph La Flesche signed, the Omaha had been compelled to give most of their lands in present-day Nebraska to the United States. In La Flesche's eyes, the only way the powerless and land-poor Omaha could prosper in a country dominated by whites was to adopt their customs and beliefs.

Joseph La Flesche practiced what he preached. He and his wife, Mary, were enthusiastic Christian converts and supported the Presbyterian and Quaker missionaries who came to live among the Omaha. La Flesche also rejected the traditional Omaha dwelling, the earth lodge, and founded a small settlement of frame houses similar to those of whites. Many conservative Omaha did not approve of La Flesche's innovation. They spoke dismissively of his settlement as the "Make Believe White Man's Village."

The element of white culture that the La Flesches most passionately advocated was education. They insisted that their four daughters and one son receive the best schooling possible. The La Flesche children were all trained to be leaders. Susan's oldest sister, SUSETTE LA FLESCHE, proved to be particularly successful. As an adult, she garnered a national reputation as an Indian rights activist.

The youngest of the five children, Susan began her education at local Presbyterian mission schools. At 13, she was sent to the Elizabeth Institute for Young Ladies, a finishing school in New Jersey that Susette had attended. After graduation, Susan briefly returned home to teach at a mission school before enrolling at the Hampton Institute, a Virginia college for Indians and African Americans, in 1884. A distinguished student, she was asked to give a speech at her graduation ceremony two years later. Reflecting her father's assimilationist beliefs, she told the crowd, "We who are educated have to be pioneers of Indian civilization. We have to pre-

pare our people to live in the white man's way, to use the white man's books, and to use his laws if you will only give them to us."

In the audience was Alice Fletcher, a family friend of the La Flesches and a noted ethnologist who studied Indian cultures. She later remembered that Susan "looked well, spoke clearly and every one was delighted with her." Fletcher was so impressed by the young woman that she brought Susan to the attention of acquaintances in the Connecticut Indian Association. This group of non-Indian women and men was dedicated to teaching Indians to live like whites and saw Susan as an ideal vehicle to spread their message.

To Susan's delight, the association agreed to send her to medical school. Her decision to become a doctor was a daring one. At the time, very few American women were practicing physicians. The Omaha society in which she was reared provided her with even fewer models for her chosen career. In this tribe, traditionally only men could be healers.

In fall 1886, Susan La Flesche began her medical studies at the Women's College of Medicine in Philadelphia. As always, she immediately excelled in her classes. She had a much more difficult time adjusting to the new and unfamiliar social world in which she found herself. Raised in the rural Midwest, La Flesche had to learn how to get about in a large eastern city. She also had to become accustomed to socializing exclusively with whites for the first time. Bright and vivacious, she soon had friends who took her to parties, museums, plays, and other social activities enjoyed by young, sophisticated citydwellers. They also taught her to dress in the latest styles and to wear her long hair piled in a bun as most well-bred white women then did.

Although La Flesche quickly mastered her new social environment, she was often homesick. After graduating first in her class in 1889, she eagerly returned to the Omaha reservation, where she was hired by the federal government to be the reservation's physician. In this post, she served as the only doctor for some 1,300 Omaha, most of whom

Susan La Flesche graduated from medical school in 1889.
(Archives and Special Collections on Women in Medicine, Drexel University College of Medicine)

lived on isolated farms scattered throughout the reservation. Often working from dawn to well after sundown, she spent every day traveling over many miles of unpaved roads in a horse and buggy to reach her patients. Her efforts helped contain epidemics of influenza, smallpox, and diphtheria. In addition to providing medical care, La Flesche also tried to teach those she treated about preventing disease through improved hygiene and sanitation.

La Flesche's grueling schedule finally caught up with her in 1893. She told the government that she had to quit her job to care for her ailing mother. But in truth her own health was also failing. An infection left her bedridden for weeks before her condition slowly began to improve. She was still recovering when she surprised her family by announcing her engagement to Henry Picotte, a half-Sioux, half-French man with a reputation for drinking heavily. Over her parents' objection, they married in 1894 and soon moved to the town of Bancroft, Nebraska. The couple had two sons, Caryl and Pierre.

Despite continuing bouts of ill health, La Flesche Picotte opened a private practice in Bancroft that treated Indians and non-Indians alike. At the same time, she worked for a variety of charitable causes. She also frequently lectured on the reservation and beyond about health issues and the merits of Christian living. Like her father, she was a particularly passionate advocate of temperance and the prohibition of alcohol. La Flesche Picotte recognized a rise in alcohol abuse among the Omaha and launched a partially successful campaign to outlaw the sale of liquor in reservation towns.

Unfortunately, her efforts did not save her husband, who died of alcohol-related illness in 1905. Left alone to support her aging mother and two young sons, La Flesche Picotte welcomed an offer of a salary and housing from the Presbyterian Board of Home Missions in return for serving as its missionary to the Omaha. She then moved to the newly established town of Walthill. There her elegant house, appointed with modern luxuries, such as a furnace and indoor plumbing, became an informal social center. She welcomed Omaha to borrow books and magazines from her extensive library; these publications provided many with their first introduction to life outside the reservation. The personal example of the stylish, glamorous doctor, who still dressed in the latest Eastern fashions, also inspired many young Omaha women to adopt the values of non-Indian middle-class society.

While continuing her extensive charity work, La Flesche Picotte became increasingly involved in the political affairs of the tribe. Although she was not a formal Omaha leader, she was often drafted to represent the tribe in its dealings with white authorities. Her fluency in English, poised manner, and familiarity with non-Indian ways made her a particularly effective liaison between the Omaha and government officials. These white men felt more comfortable negotiating with La Flesche Picotte than they would have been with someone with a more traditionally Indian appearance and demeanor.

In one such instance, La Flesche Picotte was asked to travel to Washington, D.C., as part of an Omaha delegation. The delegation was protesting the U.S. government's treatment of Omaha who owned land on the reservation. Beginning in 1882, the government had divided the reservation into small plots that were then assigned (or allotted) to individual Indians. The Indian landowners, however, were given very little control over their property. Believing all Indians to be too uneducated to manage their own land, the federal government held these plots in trust for 25 years. During this time, the Omaha could not sell or lease their property.

In 1910, just as the trust period was ending, the United States decided to extend the trusts for another 10 years. The Omaha were outraged. Compared to most Indians and to many non-Indian westerners, they were quite well educated. The tribespeople felt insulted that the government still deemed them incompetent to handle their own business affairs.

La Flesche Picotte had written letters to many officials to protest the trust extension. She thus was a natural choice to serve in the Washington delegation formed to argue the Omaha's case in person. However, she declined the invitation, feeling too ill to travel. Omaha officials begged her to change her mind; some even said they would carry her onto the train if she still refused to board of her own accord. She finally relented, recognizing, as she wrote to an old college friend, that "the Omaha depend on me so." Weak and exhausted from the trip, she met with the Secretary of the Interior and convinced him to grant the Omaha the same rights to their property that non-Indian landowners had.

A more personally satisfying success came in 1913, when La Flesche Picotte saw the opening of a hospital in Walthill for both Indians and whites in the area. For many years, she was the driving force behind a campaign for the hospital's construction. On September 15, 1915, her life ended fittingly in this facility, after a long and painful illness resulting from an infection of her facial bones.

La Flesche Picotte's death was a great blow to the Omaha, who had come to rely on both her medical advice and her personal counsel. The *Walthill Times*

had to run an extra page to accommodate the many tributes to her that flooded its offices. One long-time friend summed up her achievements with the words, "Hardly an Omaha Indian is living who has not been treated and helped by her, and hundreds of white people and Indians owe their lives to her treatment, care and nursing."

Throughout her life, Susan La Flesche Picotte was singled out for praise by white reformers, who saw her as a shining example of what Indians could do if they abandoned traditional ways and learned to live like whites. She herself promoted many non-Indian customs to her tribe. But she saw these, not as replacements for Omaha ways, but rather as complements to them. Although she gained much of her status among whites because she shared many of their beliefs and values, she always proudly considered herself an Indian. Appropriately, her funeral was presided over by a Presbyterian minister, but the final prayer was offered by an Omaha elder speaking in the language of her people.

Further Reading

Clark, Jerry E., and Martha Ellen Webb. "Susette and Susan La Flesche: Reformer and Missionary." In *Being and Becoming Indian: Biographical Studies of North American Frontiers,* edited by James A. Clifton, 137–159. Chicago: Dorsey Press, 1989.

Green, Norma Kidd. *Iron Eye's Family: The Children of Joseph LaFlesche.* Lincoln, Neb.: Johnsen Publishing, 1969.

Mathes, Valerie Sherer. "Dr. Susan LaFlesche Picotte: The Reformed and the Reformer." In *Indian Lives: Essays on Nineteenth- and Twentieth-Century Native Americans,* edited by L. G. Moses and Raymond Wilson, 61–90. Albuquerque: University of New Mexico Press, 1985.

Tong, Benson. *Susan La Flesche Picotte, M.D.: Omaha Indian Leader and Reformer.* Norman: University of Oklahoma Press, 1999.

La Flesche, Susette (Inshtatheamba; Bright Eyes; Susette Tibbles)
(1854–1903)   *Omaha activist*

A passionate Indian rights advocate, Susette La Flesche Tibbles was born into a prominent Omaha family on the tribe's Nebraska homeland in 1854. When she was just old enough to walk, she was given her Indian name—Inshtatheamba—during a traditional naming ceremony. At age five, she traveled with her family to witness her first buffalo hunt, an important event for a child in an Omaha tribe. The Omaha revered the buffalo and relied on the animal both for food and for the materials used to make their houses and clothing.

Susette was among the last Omaha to enjoy a traditional childhood. In the year she was born, the tribe was pressured by the U.S. government to surrender more than 5 million acres of hunting territory. They were left with only a small reservation. As principal chief of the Omaha, Susette's father, Joseph La Flesche, had been present at the negotiations. Recognizing that the Omaha had little political power, he told his people that they would prosper only if they assimilated, or adopted the ways of whites, as U.S. officials advised. In his own attempt to assimilate, La Flesche became a Christian and moved into a wooden house like those built by non-Indians. He also insisted that his children attend white-run schools, so that they would be prepared to deal with whites effectively when they grew up.

Susette first attended mission schools on the new reservation. There missionaries taught their young Indian students how to speak English and how to behave like proper Christian girls and boys. Susette later remembered her early education with bitterness. Although she did not object to learning white customs, she fiercely resented her teachers' insistence that Indian ways were inferior.

In 1872, she traveled to New Jersey to complete her schooling at the Elizabeth Institute for Young Ladies. This finishing school offered her a better education than that available to most girls, Indian or white, in the West. By studying at Elizabeth, she became the first Omaha to leave the tribe's homeland to go to school. Her youngest sister, SUSAN LA FLESCHE, however, would soon follow her example. Several years later, she would attend Elizabeth, then go on to medical school, where she would earn the first doctorate of medicine ever awarded to an Indian woman.

After graduating with honors, Susette La Flesche returned home and tried to secure work as a teacher at a reservation school operated by the U.S. government. She did not get the job, but two years later she discovered that reservation schools were required to hire qualified Indian teachers for available posts if they applied. In a rage, she fired off an angry letter to the Commissioner of Indian Affairs: "It is all a farce when you say you are trying to civilize us, then, after we educated ourselves, refuse us positions of responsibility and leave us utterly powerless to help ourselves. Perhaps the only way to make ourselves heard is to appeal to the American public through the press. They might listen." Her threat worked, and she was promptly given a teaching post. But even more important for her future career, she also learned from that incident the power she could wield by speaking out.

This lesson soon served her well when she became involved in the trial of Ponca chief Standing Bear in 1879. The Ponca, a tribe closely related to the Omaha, also had traditionally lived in Nebraska, but in 1877 were forced by the United States to move to Indian Territory (now Oklahoma). Miserable in their new lands, a band led by Standing Bear returned to Nebraska, where they were given land by their Omaha kin. The U.S. Army tracked down the defiant Indians. Although they had committed no crime, they were locked up in jail as the army made preparations to sent them back to Indian Territory. The injustice gained the attention of a young editor at the *Omaha Herald,* Thomas H. Tibbles. He publicized their plight, which led several lawyers to volunteer to help the Ponca. In the case *Standing Bear v. General George Crick,* they argued that Indians were people, hence according to the law they could not be imprisoned without just cause. The judge agreed and the case made history: It marked the first time in American law that Indians were legally recognized as human beings.

Like many Indians and non-Indians alike, Susette La Flesche was outraged by the trial. Following Tibbles's lead, she wrote articles about the wrongs committed against the Ponca. She also testified in court on the Indians' behalf.

After the trial, Tibbles persuaded Standing Bear to go on a speaking tour in the East. There the cause of Indian rights had become fashionable among wealthy, educated non-Indians, so Tibbles knew that the chief could draw large audiences with his story. He also asked Susette and her half-brother Francis to come along as translators.

An energetic speaker, La Flesche herself was soon a star attraction. Wearing an Indian-style dress and calling herself "Bright Eyes," the translation of her Indian name, she lectured audiences in Boston, Pittsburgh, New York, Chicago, and Washington, D.C., about the injustices Indians

Susette La Flesche lectured on various American Indian causes.

(Nebraska State Historical Society Photograph Collections)

had suffered at the hands of the federal government. Her success on stage made her a national celebrity. She was praised by many luminaries of the day, including Henry Wadsworth Longfellow, who said that in her he saw Minnehaha, the Indian heroine of his famous poem "Hiawatha."

In addition to gaining fame for herself, La Flesche also brought attention to the Indian causes in which she believed deeply. In her speeches, she called for the government to grant Indians citizenship. She also advocated the allotment of reservation lands. Traditionally, Indian land was held in common. This system of land ownership, La Flesche felt, allowed the government to take control of large amounts of Indian territory, as the Omaha's and Ponca's recent histories had borne out. By dividing reservation land into small, individually owned plots called allotments, she thought Indians could have a better chance of holding on to the legal title to their lands.

Following their eastern tour, La Flesche and Tibbles married and settled in Nebraska. Both continued to write articles and lecture about a wide variety of causes. Indian rights, however, remained a primary focus of their work. In 1886, the couple repeated their previous success on a 10-month lecture tour through England and Scotland. They also worked together on impassioned reports from the site of the Wounded Knee Massacre, where more than 300 Sioux women, men, and children had been slaughtered by army soldiers in 1890.

Often in ill health, Susette La Flesche Tibbles returned to Nebraska to spent her final years quietly before her death on May 26, 1903. Despite her efforts, she saw conditions for Indians deteriorate further toward the end of her life. The U.S. government had initiated a policy of allotting Indian lands, in large part due to the insistence of reformers such as La Flesche Tibbles. Allotment, however, only contributed to the theft of Indian land as white swindlers tricked many Indians, new to land ownership, out of their plots. La Flesche Tibbles's greatest achievement instead lay in her example to later Indian advocates. Through her unflagging insistence on the legal and moral right of Indians to be treated humanely, she was a model activist for those who followed.

Further Reading

Clark, Jerry E., and Martha Ellen Webb. "Susette and Susan La Flesche: Reformer and Missionary." In *Being and Becoming Indian: Biographical Studies of North American Frontiers,* edited by James A. Clifton, 137–159. Chicago: Dorsey Press, 1989.

Green, Norma Kidd. *Iron Eye's Family: The Children of Joseph LaFlesche.* Lincoln, Neb.: Johnsen Publishing, 1969.

———. "Tibbles, Susette La Flesche." In *Notable American Women: The Modern Period,* edited by Barbara Sicherman and Carol Hurd Green, 379–380. Cambridge, Mass.: Belknap Press, 1980.

Lang, Naomi (Maheetahan)
(1978–)   *Karuk athlete*

The first American Indian woman to participate in the Winter Olympics, Naomi Lang was born on December 18, 1978, in Arcata, California. Her father was a member of the small Karuk tribe. When she was a baby, he gave her the Indian name Maheetahan, meaning "Morning Star."

Naomi's parents divorced, and her mother moved with her and her older brother, Daniel, to Allegan, Michigan. When Naomi was eight, her mother took her to an ice show featuring skaters dressed as Smurfs, popular cartoon characters Naomi loved. Entranced by the show, she told her mother, "I want to do that. I want to skate." Naomi had already taken ballet lessons for five years, giving her skills that helped her pick up skating fast. Her coach urged her to start competing. She won her first skating competition at age nine.

Three years later, Naomi Lang took up ice dancing, which helped her combine her skating and dancing talents. She wanted to compete, but had trouble finding a partner, since few men entered the sport. Lang finally paired up with John Lee. In 1995, they won the national championship at the novice level. The next year, competing at the junior level, they took home a silver medal.

Naomi Lang and Peter Tchernyshev perform at the 2002 World Figure Skating Championships.
(AP/Wide World Photos)

The partnership dissolved, however, when Lang's mother was no longer able to afford her skating expenses. But soon she received a letter from Peter Tchernyshev, a 30-year-old ice dancer whose grandfather had been a champion skater in Russia during the 1930s. Tchernyshev had seen Lang at the 1996 nationals and invited her to tryout to be his partner, promising to pay her expenses if it worked out. From the start, it was clear they would make a great team. "Our look was good on the ice," Lang once explained. "Our leg lines matched, our sizing matched. But I was coming up from the junior level, so I knew I would have to work hard."

After working together for nine months, Lang and Tchernyshev headed for the nationals. In 1997, they placed fifth; in 1998, they placed third.

The following year, they began a historic winning streak, becoming the third ice dancing team in the United States to place first five years in a row.

In 2002, their standing won them a spot on the U.S. Olympic team. At the Winter Olympics in Salt Lake City, Naomi was one of five athletes chosen to participate in a tribute to the five Native tribes of Utah during the games' opening ceremonies. Because Tchernyshev had only recently become a U.S. citizen, he and Lang were dubbed by the press the "New American and the Native American." They placed 11th in the competition, an impressive showing for an American ice dancing team.

Two years after the Olympics, Lang and Tchernyshev tried for their sixth consecutive national win, but at the last minute, they had to withdraw because Lang had injured her Achilles tendon. Soon afterward, they decided to end their competitive career together. At the same time, Lang announced that she was pregnant. She gave birth to her daughter, Lillia, in August 2004. Lang has since appeared with Tchernyshev in professional ice shows. She has also indicated a desire to coach ice dancers and perhaps instruct American Indian skaters of the future. As Lang once explained, "I'm proud to be Indian and competing in sports. I have worked and am working very hard to make something of myself. I want to help young Native kids make something of themselves."

Further Reading/Resources

Fleming, Gretchen. "Naomi's Dream Comes True." *Grand Rapids Press,* 3 February 2002. Available online. URL: http://www.ice-dance.com/users/naomiandpeter/news_inprint_002.html. Downloaded on May 1, 2006.

Naomi Lang & Peter Tchernyshev Online. URL: http://www.ice-dance.com/users/naomiandpeter. Downloaded on May 1, 2006.

Lawson, Roberta Campbell
(1878–1940)   *Delaware (Lenni Lenape) civic leader*

A national leader in the American women's club movement, Roberta Campbell was born on Octo-

ber 31, 1878, in Alluwe, Indian Territory (now Oklahoma). Her father, J. E. Campbell, was a white rancher originally from Virginia. Roberta's mother, Emma Journeycake, was a member of one of the most distinguished families among the Delaware (Lenni Lenape) Indians. Emma was the daughter of Charles Journeycake, a beloved chief of the Delawares and the founder of Alluwe's Indian church. He also helped to establish Bacone College, which was at the time one of the few Indian colleges in the United States.

Roberta and her younger brother had a privileged childhood. Her wealthy parents showered them with toys and employed a private tutor for their education. Rare for rural Indian Territory, their comfortable house even had such amenities as a tennis court and a piano. Among their few neighbors who enjoyed a similarly lavish lifestyle were the Rogerses, a well-to-do Cherokee family. Their youngest child, Will Rogers—who would become an internationally famous humorist—was among Roberta's closest childhood friends.

After studying music at Hardin College in Mexico, Missouri, Campbell married lawyer Edward B. Lawson in 1901. The couple moved to the nearby town of Nowata and had one son. The Lawsons quickly established themselves as financial and civic leaders in their community. Edward founded the First National Bank and the Lawson Petroleum Company. Roberta spearheaded the construction of a town library and park.

The Lawsons' growing oil business required the family to move to the city of Tulsa. In this more cosmopolitan setting, Roberta Lawson thrived. She became a leader in various clubs for socially prominent women and was eventually named the president of the Oklahoma Federation of Women's Clubs. Women's clubs were then among the only organizations through which women could affect social and political change. Lawson also served as the director of the Oklahoma Historical Society, as a member of the board of regents of the Oklahoma College for Women, and as the only female trustee of the University of Tulsa. At the request of her friend Will Rogers, in 1931 she took on as well the task of administering funds he had collected for Oklahoma drought relief. The hefty profits of her husband's oil company gave Lawson the financial freedom to devote herself to her civic good works. However, the fierce determination and energy she brought to these projects was all her own.

In 1935, Lawson rose to national prominence when she was named the president of the General Federation of Women's Clubs. At the time, this organization had a membership of 3 million, making it the largest association of women in the world. She held the office for three years, during which she organized a number of campaigns built around the theme "Education for Living." During her administration, the General Federation put its power behind such progressive causes as vocational training for women and the prevention of the spread of venereal disease.

Roberta Campbell Lawson served as the president of the General Federation of Women's Clubs.
(Courtesy of the Oklahoma Historical Society, Neg. no. 8547)

Amid her club activities, Lawson found time for a hobby. After her move to Tulsa, she began to amass a huge collection of Indian paintings, musical instruments, and artifacts, which she carefully catalogued. Her interest in music also inspired her to study Indian musical traditions and transcribe Delaware songs that, without her efforts, most likely would have been lost to history. In a series of lectures, she performed these songs and recounted Delaware legends told to her by her grandfather. She also published the fruits of her research and experiences on the lecture circuit in *Indian Music Programs for Clubs and Special Music Days* (1926).

On December 31, 1940, some two years after Lawson retired from the General Federation, she died of leukemia in Tulsa. Her vast and valuable store of Indian paraphernalia was donated to the city's Philbrook Art Center, where it is now housed as the Roberta Campbell Lawson Collection. In 1992, Lawson was posthumously inducted into the Tulsa Hall of Fame.

Further Reading

Debo, Angie. "Lawson, Roberta Campbell." In *Notable American Women: 1607–1950,* edited by Edward T. James, 376–377. Cambridge, Mass.: Belknap Press, 1971.

Gridley, Marion E. "Roberta Campbell Lawson: Leader of Three Million Women." In *American Indian Women,* 88–93. New York: Hawthorn Books, 1974.

Lee, Bobbi
See MARACLE, LEE

Lewis, Lucy M.
(ca. 1895–1992)   *Acoma Pueblo potter*

A native of the Acoma Pueblo in New Mexico, Lucy M. Lewis was heralded as one of the greatest Indian potters of her generation. She was probably born in the 1890s, although she never knew her exact birthdate. By watching her female relatives at work, as a girl Lucy learned to make pottery in the traditional manner. She also followed their example in selling her work to help supplement her family's small income from farming and ranching. During her childhood, Acoma Pueblo women began to sell their handcrafted pottery to non-Indian tourists traveling through the American Southwest. With her mother, Lucy rode on horseback for 17 miles into Grants, New Mexico, and hawked her wares for a nickel or dime apiece to passengers at the town's railway station.

When Lucy was still a teenager, she married Toribio Luis (later changed to Lewis), with whom she had nine children. In addition to taking care of her large family, she planted gardens and raised chickens, turkeys, and other livestock to keep them fed. Despite her efforts, the Lewises were desperately poor and frequently hungry. All free moments she devoted to making small pots for the tourist trade to bring more money into the household. To ensure that she profited from the time spent, she often made these pots quickly and with little attention to craftsmanship. She later recalled that she could paint more than a hundred of these tourist trinkets in a single day.

Over time, Lewis came to devote more care to the quality of her pottery. Like other Acoma potters, her works were molded from clay by hand, then painted with white slip, a coating made by mixing light-colored clay with water. On this white surface, she then painted black and orange figures and designs using a brush made from a yucca leaf. She often used the bird and flower motifs then popular with customers and potters alike. But on some pots she painted abstract patterns of her own invention that were inspired by similar designs on pieces of broken pottery that she found on the ground near her home. Lewis particularly favored what have become known as fine-line designs, in which an outlined form—such as a zigzag shape— is filled in with a series of closely spaced parallel lines.

In 1950, one of her fine-line pots brought Lewis and her talents to the attention of the growing number of art traders and collectors dealing in southwestern Indian pottery. She won a blue ribbon for the pot, which she entered in an art compe-

tition at the Gallup Inter-Tribal Indian Ceremonial in Gallup, New Mexico. Lewis was one of the first Acoma potters to dare to exhibit her work. Traditionally, Pueblo society frowned upon any behavior that made one person stand out from the crowd. Living in a desert environment where mere survival was a constant struggle, they believed that they could stay strong only if individuals valued the common good over their own desires. Pueblo artists from groups that lived closer to Santa Fe, New Mexico, the art center of the Southwest, had already begun to chip away at this convention by seeking recognition for their talents. Following their lead, Lewis further shocked the Acoma by deciding to sign her name on the bottom of her pots, on which she had previously written only the name of her pueblo.

After her success at the Gallup competition, Lewis's work was eagerly sought after by collectors. As she exhibited more of her works, her fame spread and she won more and more prizes. In 1958, she was honored at Santa Fe's annual Indian Market—the most prestigious Indian art exhibition—with the Outstanding Exhibit Award. Lewis was given the prize by Laura Gilpin, a well-known photographer. In talking to Lewis, Gilpin discovered that she had never seen the Museum of New Mexico's extensive collection of Indian pottery. The photographer promptly arranged a trip to the museum, where Lewis was surprised to find some of her unsigned works on display. She was even more excited at seeing whole pots painted with the same designs she had studied from the small shards she had unearthed herself. Lewis learned that these vessels had been made by ancient Indians, including the direct ancestors of the Pueblo.

Lewis's fascination with this collection led her to mimic some of her ancestors' pottery-making techniques and decorations. But her imitation was far from slavish. Although she borrowed ideas from both ancient and contemporary potters, the hallmark of her work was her love of innovation. One of her most popular designs—the "heart-line" deer, on which the heart of a black deer is marked with a brilliant orange triangle—emerged from her own imagination. Likewise, on some pots she deviated from the standard all-over patterns of the Pueblo by painting a small black figure in a large patch of white—a dramatic effect that was later adopted by other potters. Lewis also pioneered the creation of clay miniatures among the modern Acomas.

Lewis continued to make pottery until her death on March 28, 1992. Her work today can be seen in the permanent collections of major museums throughout the world, among them the Smithsonian Institution in Washington, D.C. She also left behind a living artistic legacy. Four of her daughters, including noted contemporary potters Delores and Emma Lewis, learned the art of pottery-making just as their Pueblo ancestors had thousands of years ago—by carefully watching a master.

Further Reading

Fauntleroy, Gussie. "Great Women Potters of the Past." *Native Peoples,* September/October 2001, pp. 26–27.
Peterson, Susan. *Lucy M. Lewis: American Indian Potter.* Tokyo: Kodansha International, 1984.

Locklear, Arlinda
(1951–)   *Lumbee lawyer*

The first Native American woman to argue a case before the U.S. Supreme Court, Arlinda Locklear has devoted her career to helping Indians obtain legal recognition of their rights. Locklear was born in 1951 into one of the most prominent families of the Lumbee, a tribe of Indians native to Robeson County in central North Carolina. She graduated from the College of Charleston in 1973 and was awarded a law degree from Duke University three years later.

Locklear began her law career as a staff attorney with the Native American Rights Fund (NARF). In this capacity, she represented Indian tribes throughout the country in a variety of suits. Her first appearance before the Supreme Court came in 1983 in the case of *Solem v. Barlett,* in which she

successfully defended the right of Sioux courts to try their own people for illegal acts committed on their reservations. Two years later, she won her second Supreme Court case, *Oneida Indian Nation v. County of Oneida.* In this trial, she persuaded the justices that the State of New York should surrender control of certain lands that traditionally had belonged to the Oneida tribe.

In addition to land claim suits, Locklear garnered a reputation as an expert in recognition procedures and litigation. The U.S. government formally recognizes more than 500 different Indian groups, but some 100 more are seeking this official acknowledgment. Recognition can mean a great deal to a tribe. Only a recognized group can obtain funds from the U.S. government for programs to finance Indian-run businesses, health care facilities,

Arlinda Locklear was the first American Indian woman to argue a case before the U.S. Supreme Court.
(Photo courtesy of the University of North Carolina at Pembroke)

and schools. In poor Indian communities, these funds provide people with one of the few means for improving their lives. Almost as important, recognition gives an Indian tribe the respect of the United States and of other Indian groups. As Locklear has said, "The problem is, in Indian country, if you lack the status of federal recognition, you are very plainly treated like a second-class Indian."

At the NARF, Locklear helped many groups—including the Tunica-Biloxis, the Houmas, the Gay Head Wampanoags, and the Indiana Miamis—apply for recognition, a process that often requires many years and costs hundreds of thousands of dollars. In 1987, she left this post and established a private practice so that she could devote more of her time to her most important client—her own tribe. Although North Carolina recognized the Lumbee in 1885, the United States does not regard them as an official tribe.

When Locklear's husband died, leaving her with two children to raise on her own, she joined the firm of Patton Boggs LLP. She later returned to her private practice and continues to participate in the Lumbees' 100-year fight for federal recognition. On their behalf, Locklear has testified before Congress several times in an effort to persuade the House of Representatives and the Senate to pass a bill formally recognizing the Lumbee. If Locklear succeeds, the Lumbee will become the largest federally recognized Indian tribe in the United States.

Further Reading

Brown, Cynthia. "The Vanished Americans: Unrecognized Tribes." *Nation* 257 (October 11, 1993): 384.
Tpkunesh. "Arlinda Faye Locklear." In *Notable Native Americans,* edited by Sharon Malinowski, 244–245. Detroit: Gale Research, 1995.

✵ Loloma, Otellie Pasivaya
(1922–1992)   *Hopi sculptor, potter, educator*

Both as a potter and an art teacher, Otellie Pasivaya Loloma has had an enormous influence over several generations of Indian artists. Born in 1922, she was raised on Second Mesa on the Hopi Indian Reservation in northeastern Arizona. Although craftswomen on Second Mesa were known best as basketmakers, Pasivaya was intrigued by working with clay. As a girl, she enjoyed sitting with her grandmother in her family's orchards and molding tiny clay toys.

Pasivaya did not receive any formal training in pottery making until 1945, when she won a scholarship to study ceramics at the School of the American Craftsman at Alfred University in Alfred, New York. She was hesitant to leave Second Mesa but in the end decided that the offer was too exciting to refuse. At the school, she met fellow ceramics student Charles Loloma, who in the 1960s would spearhead a renaissance in modern Indian jewelry. Otellie and Charles married in 1947.

After leaving Alfred University, the Lolomas moved to Scottsdale, Arizona. The couple opened a studio and a shop at the Kiva Craft Center, an emporium where several noted Indian artists sold their work. They developed a reputation with Indian art collectors for their beautiful ceramic work, which they dubbed "Lolomaware." The Lolomas' healthy sales placed them among the first Indians to become successful in both the art and business worlds.

Otellie and Charles Loloma moved back to Second Mesa in 1962 and were divorced three years later. Having attended classes at the College of Santa Fe and Northern Arizona University, Otellie decided to concentrate on teaching art. She joined the faculty of the Institute of American Indian Arts (IAIA) in Santa Fe in 1962, the year it was founded. Loloma would remain on the teaching staff of this prestigious Indian-run art school until her retirement in 1988. In addition to classes in painting and ceramic sculpture, Loloma frequently taught a course in Hopi dance. She performed with her students at the White House and at the 1968 Olympics in Mexico.

Loloma showed an unusual devotion to her students, many of whom considered her a friend as well as a mentor. As she once explained, "If I'm going to make a creative artist out of them, I've got to be working close with them. . . . I'd rather have them come out of my class knowing something than me going out and doing my own exhibits." Despite a demanding teaching schedule, however, Loloma did find time for her own art. Her pottery and clay sculptures were characterized by her joy in bringing together the old and the new. She often employed the time-honored Hopi methods of coiling and molding clay, but she was just as comfortable with using a potter's wheel. Although Loloma sometimes incorporated nontraditional materials such as turquoise and leather into her clay artworks, she maintained that the ideas behind her sculptures were drawn from her people's culture. In a 1975 interview, she explained that Hopi ways and legends were "like the seed" that "[gave] their strength to make the plant grow."

Loloma's work is today found in museums and private collections throughout the United States. Shortly before her death in 1992, the National Women's Caucus for Art honored her long and distinguished career as an artist and teacher with its award for Outstanding Achievement in the Visual Arts.

Further Reading

Hammond, Harmony, and Jaune Quick-to-See Smith. *Women of Sweetgrass, Cedar, and Sage.* New York: Gallery of the American Indian Community House, 1985.
Monthan, Guy, and Doris Monthan. *Art and Indian Individualism: The Art of Seventeen Contemporary Southwestern Artists and Craftsmen.* Flagstaff, Ariz.: Northland Press, 1975.

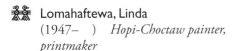

Lomahaftewa, Linda
(1947–   )   *Hopi-Choctaw painter, printmaker*

"My paintings contain the history of my people," artist Linda Lomahaftewa has said about her work. Born in Phoenix, Arizona, on July 3, 1947, Lomahaftewa was surrounded by Indian art and artists from her birth. Her father carved kachinas, small figures that represent spirit beings that are sacred to the Hopi. Her mother was a skilled craftswoman accomplished in quilting, ribbonwork, and bead-

work. Linda's sister and three brothers also enjoyed making traditional Indian crafts. Like Lomahaftewa, her brother Dan grew up to become a master painter and printmaker.

Linda divided her childhood between Phoenix and Los Angeles, California. As a teenager, she boarded at the Phoenix Indian School and at Santa Fe's Institute of American Indian Arts (IAIA), which is today a two-year college, but then offered high school classes. A member of the institute's first class, Lomahaftewa graduated in 1964. Her teachers encouraged her to continue her art education, so she applied to the San Francisco Art Institute, from which she received a bachelor's degree in 1970 and a master's in 1971. At the time, San Francisco was a hotbed of Indian rights activism, but Lomahaftewa concentrated on her schoolwork. "I chose to be a student and to help [Indians] in whatever way I could with my artwork," she later remembered.

Living in San Francisco, however, did have an effect on her work: "The city was such a new place for me that most of what I thought about was back home, the Southwest." Initially, most of her paintings were abstract experiments in color and form. But instinctively she began incorporating symbols and designs from Hopi culture in her work. In doing so, Lomahaftewa began to feel more assured as an artist and confident enough, in her words, "[to] unlearn European styles and techniques which predominate in art schools."

Hopi motifs have since appeared in most of Lomahaftewa's work. She is guided in her choice of colors, shapes, and forms by her memory of traditional Hopi designs and the southwestern landscape. Lomahaftewa's research, however, also informs her imagery. A favorite image—the parrot—emerged from her study of the Hopi fascination with the bird. Long ago, the Hopi treasured the parrots and parrot feathers they obtained through trade with Mexican Indians. Lomahaftewa's monotype print *Awatovi Parrots* (1987) resulted from her interest in the mural paintings found in the kiva (a religious structure used by the Hopi) at Awatovi. Lomahaftewa has also been

135

inspired by petroglyphs, carvings or engravings left on rocks by ancient Indian artists. She draws or photographs petroglyphs she finds in Hopi territory and then refigures these images in her own compositions.

Possibly Lomahaftewa's most famous work is her "Cloud Maiden" series of paintings. Because of their popularity, she has created more than thirty works inspired by these supernatural beings, who bring water to the Hopi. Lomahaftewa attributes her attraction to cloud maidens to her membership in the Hopi Water Clan.

More recently Lomahaftewa has experimented with new forms and with drawing on her own personal history for the themes in her work. Her *Honamie* (1990) originated with a photograph of her great-grandfather. Lomahaftewa combined photocopying and collage with printmaking techniques to transform the image into a work of art.

Lomahaftewa's paintings are in the permanent collections of several major museums and have been featured in more than forty exhibits. Among these shows was "Looking for Beauty in the Future"—a 1992 two-person exhibit at the Galleria Posada in Sacramento, California, that showcased her paintings alongside those of her brother Dan. Lomahaftewa has won numerous prizes for her work, including the HELEN HARDIN Award for Excellence at Santa Fe's 1988 Indian Market.

In addition to her recognition as an artist, Lomahaftewa is also well regarded as an art teacher. She taught at California State College and the University of California, Berkeley, before joining the faculty of the Institute of American Indian Arts in 1976. Although she sees the values of learning the basics, she tries to free her students to find their individual vision. "I don't think that you need to always follow [the rules] in drawing or painting," she explained in a 1994 interview. "You need to know how to work your own style."

Further Reading

Abbott, Lawrence, ed. *I Stand in the Center of the Good: Interviews with Contemporary North American Artists.* Lincoln: University of Nebraska Press, 1994.

Indyke, Dottie. "Linda Lomahaftewa." *Southwest Art* 31 (March 31, 2003): 42–44.

Lost Bird
See ZINTKALA NUNI

Lovelace Nicholas, Sandra
(1948–) *Maliseet activist, politician*

Sandra Lovelace Nicholas is one of Canada's leading advocates for Native women's rights. She was born on April 15, 1948, on the Tobique Reserve in New Brunswick. She attended St. Thomas University for three years and earned a degree in residential construction from Maine Northern Technical College.

In 1970, she married Bernie Lovelace, a non-Indian American, and moved with him to California. The couple divorced, and Sandra returned to the Tobique Reserve. There, she found that she and her four children had lost their Indian status. No longer classified as Indian by the Canadian government, they were not eligible to receive the housing, health care, and education available to other reserve residents.

Lovelace lost her Indian status due to a provision in the Indian Act. First passed in 1869, this law and later revisions defined the relationship between the Canadian government and that country's Native peoples. According to the Indian Act, if a Native woman married a non-Indian man, she and her children relinquished their Indian status. However, if a Native man married a non-Indian woman, his status remained intact.

Beginning in the mid-1970s, several Native women's groups began to challenge this provision in the Indian Act. Lovelace joined the fight in 1977. In July 1979, she and other women from Tobique protested the act by marching 100 miles from Oka (a town near Montreal) to the Canadian capital of Ottawa. Lovelace also took the matter before the Human Rights Committee of the United Nations. "We, the Native women, feel no one should have the right to discriminate," she declared. "I think even God would agree with me."

In 1981, the United Nations ruled that, by discriminating against Native women, Canada was in breach of the International Covenant on Civil and Political Rights. The ruling placed pressure on the Canadian government to revise the Indian Act. But the government was also pushed on the other side by the traditional male leadership of some Native groups, who opposed the idea. After four years, Canada finally acted. The Indian Act was revised to allow Native women to retain their Indian status after marrying a nonnative.

For her role in removing the act's discriminatory clause, Lovelace received several honors. She was awarded the Order of Canada, Canada's highest civilian honor, in 1990. The following year, she was given the prestigious Governor General's Award in Commemoration of the Persons Case. The award celebrates contributions to society that have promoted the equality of women in Canada.

On September 21, 2005, Canadian prime minister Paul Martin named Sandra Lovelace Nicholas to the Senate, as a representative of Nova Scotia from the Liberal Party. Phil Fontaine, national chief of the Assembly of First Nations, a leading national Indian rights group, praised the appointment: "Sandra is a longtime activist, who has been committed to advancing the rights of First Nations women. . . . The recognition of the accomplishments of First Nations people in Canada is important, but this appointment also helps advance First peoples in the country."

Further Reading/Resources

"Sandra Lovelace." *Famous Women in Canada.* Canadian Studies at Mount Allison University. Available online. URL: http://www.mta.ca/faculty/arts/canadian_studies/english/about/study_guide/famous_women/sandra_lovelace.html. Downloaded on June 2, 2006.

"Sandra M. Lovelace Nicholas." Parliament of Canada. Available online. URL: http://www.parl.gc.ca/common/senmemb/senate/isenator_det.asp?senator_id=2792&sortord=N&Language=E&M=M. Downloaded on June 2, 2006.

Lowry, Rhoda Strong
(1849–1909)   *Lumbee outlaw*

Nicknamed the "Queen of Scuffletown," Rhoda Strong Lowry has been a legendary figure in Southern history for more than a century. Born in 1849 in North Carolina, she was probably the daughter of a Lumbee woman and a white man who called himself John Strong. Her mother probably died when Rhoda Strong was still a girl, leaving her in the care of her father. He was rumored to be from Virginia, from which he fled after committing murder.

When Rhoda Strong was young, the Lumbee Indians were suffering greatly at the hands of their white neighbors. An 1835 state law prohibited the Lumbee from voting and from owning guns. Without guns, they were unable to hunt, which aside from farming was their primary means of obtaining food. They were also defenseless against the Home Guard, a police force that frequently assaulted and stole from the Lumbee.

The Home Guard also tried to take control of Lumbee land. One tactic was to plant a white person's possessions on the property of a Lumbee landowner and then accuse the landowner of stealing it. The landowner was then forced to sell his land to pay restitution for his so-called theft.

In 1864, probably because of such trumped up charges, two respected Lumbee men—Allen Lowry and his son William—were arrested and executed without a trial. Lowry's youngest son, Henry Berry Lowry, was incensed. Only 16 at the time, he vowed to avenge their deaths.

Henry soon made good on his threat. Leading a gang of disaffected, angry young Lumbee men, he initiated a 10-year campaign of violence that became known as the Lowry Wars. His gang killed at least 16 whites and stole from many others, usually giving away the fruits of their crimes to Lumbee families in need.

Rhoda Strong undoubtedly heard stories about Henry's gang. Not only were they famous among the Lumbee, but Henry was also Rhoda's cousin. Nothing is known about their courtship, but on

December 7, 1865, the two married. In the middle of the wedding feast, the Home Guard showed up to arrest Henry. Legend has it that Rhoda visited the jail with a cake for her new husband. Inside was a file, which Henry used to free himself.

Several other stories recount Rhoda's efforts to help Henry escape. In 1872, Henry was imprisoned, facing execution. Rhoda supposedly came to the jail dressed in long flowing shirt. Flirting with the jailer, she convinced him to take off his gun belt. She then pulled an iron bar from under her skirt, bashed the jailer in the head, grabbed his keys, and set Henry free.

Despite these tales, Rhoda Lowry probably did not participate in the Lowry gang's crime spree. More likely, she spent most of her time at her home in the Indian community of Scuffletown (now Pembroke, North Carolina). There, like most Lumbee women, she tended a farm while raising her three children. Henry was often away, hiding from the law in nearby swamps. He and his men, however, frequently visited Rhoda, which always prompted a huge feast and celebration. If they needed to make a quick getaway, the gang members could crawl through a 60-yard tunnel built in the back of the house.

Even if she was not running with the gang, just being married to an outlaw put Rhoda in harm's way. In 1871, the leader of the Home Guard kidnapped Rhoda and the wives of other gang members, in hopes of pressuring Henry Berry Lowry to surrender. Instead, Lowry threatened to murder whites in retaliation. He declared "the Bloodiest time will be here that ever was before—the life of every man will be in jeopardy." His vow set off such a panic in white neighborhoods that the Home Guard had little choice but to release Rhoda and the other Lumbee women.

By this time, the Lowry gang's exploits were national news. Reporters from across the country came to North Carolina to find out more. Many wrote about Rhoda Lowry as a glamorous figure, nearly always highlighting her extraordinary beauty. Characteristic of the media attention on Rhoda, one correspondent wrote, "This young woman is remarkably pretty; her face oval, of a very light color; large dark, mournful looking eyes, with long lashes; well shaped mouth with small even teeth . . . combined to make her a very pleasant object to gaze at." However, the reporter also added, with astonishment, that "SHE SMOKES A PIPE AND RUBS SNUFF."

Observers of the Lowrys also often commented on their deep affection for each other. One wrote, "She is truly devoted to her robber lord. . . . She looks on him as a persecuted man and a hero, instead of a felon and a bandit. . . . I must add also that her husband is exceedingly fond of Rhody, and idolizes his children."

The Lowry Wars came to an end in 1874. Following a botched robbery, Henry Berry Lowry disappeared. With a $45,000 bounty on his head, he possibly realized he could survive only by going into hiding permanently. Other stories spread about Lowry's fate. Some held he accidentally killed himself when his rifle discharged. Others maintained that he faked his own death.

After her husband's disappearance, Rhoda Lowry led a quiet life, tending to her farm and caring for her children and grandchildren. One grandson later explained, "Rhody never married again. She lived well, always had money." When she died in 1909 at 60 years old, he explained she was "still beautiful."

Throughout her later years, visitors would seek her out from time to time, sharing rumors that Henry had been spotted in New York or Florida or some other faraway location. Rhoda Lowry, however, refused to discuss what had happened to Henry, giving no clue as to whether she knew his whereabouts. For her legendary loyalty to her husband and to her people, she is still honored by the Lumbee.

Further Reading

Pugh, Eneida Sanderson. "Rhoda Strong Lowry: The Swamp Queen of Scuffletown." *American Indian Culture & Research Journal,* Spring 2002, 67–81.

Smith, Margaret Supplee, and Emily Herring Wilson. *North Carolina Women: Making History.* Chapel Hill: University of North Carolina, 1999.

⚜️⚜️ Lozen (Woman Warrior)
(ca. 1848–1890)   *Apache warrior*

Lozen is the only Apache woman known to have devoted herself fully to the life of a warrior. She was born in the late 1840s in the Apache homeland, which then included portions of what is now northern Mexico and the states of New Mexico and Arizona. At an early age she learned to ride and train a horse and to use a gun and knife as weapons. Young Lozen also earned the admiration of her band by winning foot races with her male peers.

When Lozen reached puberty, she decided to acquire supernatural powers from the mountain spirits. Following Apache tradition, she climbed the Sacred Mountain (Salinas Peak in the San Andreas range) and fasted there for four days and nights. To reward her courage, the mountain spirits were said to have given her two great powers—the ability to heal wounds and to determine the location of Apache enemies. Eyewitnesses later recorded her method of finding enemy forces. She raised her face to the sky, outstretched her arms, and slowly moved in circle while singing a prayer. When she was facing a foreign army, her hands would begin to tingle or, as some witnesses claimed, her palms would turn purple.

According to Apache legend, at about the same time that Lozen received her powers, she met a young Seneca Indian chief from New York, where his people's lands were being overtaken by whites. While looking for western lands where the Seneca might relocate, he was taken in by Lozen's band. Lozen supposedly fell deeply in love with the chief and was heartbroken when he left to continue his search. The despondent Lozen then vowed never to marry and instead to become a warrior.

Although the story may be true, it may also have been developed over time to help explain Lozen's unique role among the Apache. Other Apache women joined war parties but generally only to provide support for their husbands. Women sometimes helped their relatives in battle. More often, however, their responsibilities were to set up camp, cook, and nurse the wounded. By becoming a warrior herself, Lozen was disregarding the traditional roles assigned to women by her tribe. But apparently the Apache respected her unusual choice to become a fighter, perhaps because at the time her band desperately needed warriors with Lozen's skill and bravery.

In the early 1870s, the Apache had been forced onto reservations by the U.S. government. On the reservation, the food supplies were small and disease was rampant. But even worse to many Apache was the boredom of confinement within reservation borders. In the past, the Apache spent the year traveling through a large expanse of land, where they hunted wild game and warred with their enemies. Reservation life had little appeal to a people accustomed to the freedom and excitement of the traditional Apache way of life.

Lozen was part of a band of Apache who fled the San Carlos Reservation in 1877. They were led by Victorio, who was either Lozen's brother or cousin. The members of Victorio's band were considered rebels by both the U.S. Army and Mexican forces. As the renegades moved through their traditional territory, they were constantly in danger of attack from these enemies. In their skirmishes with foreign soldiers, Lozen was considered one of the band's most valuable warriors. Victorio himself once explained, "Lozen is as my right hand. Strong as a man, braver than most, and cunning in strategy, Lozen is a shield to her people."

After three years on the run, Victorio's band was decimated by Mexican soldiers in the Battle of Tres Castillos. Approximately half the band was killed, including Victorio. At the time of the massacre, Lozen was helping to guide a pregnant Apache woman to her home in present-day New Mexico. Some of Victorio's warriors held that if she had been among them, her power to locate the enemy would have prevented the band's defeat.

Lozen briefly stayed with the remnants of Victorio's band before joining a group of rebel Apache headed by Geronimo. She quickly developed a reputation as a superior warrior among her new companions. One Apache battle story tells of her crawling into the line of fire to retrieve a dropped bag of bullets sorely needed by the underarmed Indians. For this and many other acts of bravery, Lozen was called "the Woman Warrior" by Geronimo's men.

Relentlessly pursued by American and Mexican forces, Geronimo and his small band had little choice but to surrender in 1886. The great leader sent Lozen and Dahteste, another distinguished Apache woman warrior, to arrange a meeting with U.S. military officers. That Geronimo entrusted this crucial mission to Lozen demonstrates his respect for her. He may also have suspected that the American soldiers would be less threatened by female messengers.

After their surrender, the members of Geronimo's band were placed in manacles and put on a train to Florida. There they were held as political prisoners at Fort Marion for a year. They were then sent to Mount Vernon Barracks in Alabama, where small food rations, unhealthy living conditions, and tuberculosis led to the death of one out of every four prisoners. Among the casualties was Lozen, the great woman warrior of the Apache, who had dodged so many white man's bullets only to fall victim to a white man's disease.

Further Reading

Aleshire, Peter. *Warrior Woman: The Story of Lozen, Apache Warrior and Shaman.* New York: St. Martin's Press, 2001.

Ball, Eve, with James Kaywaykla. *In the Days of Victorio: Recollections of a Warm Spring Apache.* Tucson: University of Arizona Press, 1970.

Buchanan, Kimberly Moore. *Apache Women Warriors.* El Paso: Texas Western Press, 1986.

Moore, Laura Jane. "Lozen: An Apache Woman Warrior." In *Sifters: Native American Women's Lives,* edited by Theda Perdue, 92–107. New York: Oxford University Press, 2001.

Lubo, Nancy Youngblood
See YOUNGBLOOD, NANCY

Lubo, Ramona
(ca. 1865–1922)   *Cahuilla basketmaker*

The model for the heroine of Helen Hunt Jackson's 1884 novel *Ramona,* Ramona Lubo was a native of what is now San Diego County in California. A Cahuilla Indian, she was a skilled basketmaker, as were many of the women of her tribe.

The most dramatic incident in her early life—and the one that brought her to Jackson's attention—was the brutal killing of her husband, Juan Diego. Diego was known to have spells during which he acted erratically. During one of these episodes, he took a ride on a horse that belonged to a white man, Sam Temple. When Temple discovered Diego had taken his animal, he shot

Ramona Lubo displays a basket in a photograph taken by author George Wharton James in 1899.
(Milstein Division of United States History, Local History & Genealogy, The New York Public Library, Astor, Lenox and Tilden Foundation)

Diego 22 times in the chest. At Temple's trial, the white jury accepted the defendant's dubious claim that he had acted in self-defense. The only witness to the murder, Ramona was not allowed to testify under American law because she was an Indian.

Jackson read newspaper accounts of the case while traveling through southern California as an investigative reporter in 1881. During the trip, she became fascinated by the history of California Indians and visited nearly every Indian settlement between Santa Barbara and San Diego, including the Cahuilla reservation.

Earlier that year, Jackson had published *A Century of Dishonor*, which chronicled the discrimination and injustices endured by American Indians over the previous century. To Jackson's irritation, the book was not widely read. She was looking for another way to bring the plight of Indians to the attention of the American public, and in California, she found it. Inspired by her research, Jackson began work on a new book, a novel set on and near the Camulos ranch in the Santa Clara Valley. She hoped the book could bring the same attention to the plight of Indians as Harriet Beecher Stowe's famous *Uncle Tom's Cabin* (1852) had for the trials of black slaves.

The novel, *Ramona*, was an immediate success. It tells a romantic story of a beautiful young half-Mexican, half-Indian woman who falls in love with and marries an Indian man named Alessandro. The villains in the story are white settlers, who take over the homeland of Alessandro's people. Displaced and impoverished, Alessandro is driven mad and makes off with the horse of a white man, who then guns Alessandro down as his wife looks on.

Soon after publication, fans of *Ramona* began to flock to the real Camulos ranch. To capitalize on their interest, the ranch owners sold postcards and other souvenirs to tourists that advertised the ranch as the home of Ramona. As "Ramona's home" drew more and more visitors, a pageant based on the book became an annual event in the nearby town of Hemet and attracted even more tourists to the area.

One of *Ramona*'s biggest fans was writer and lecturer George Wharton James. While researching his book *Through Ramona's Country* (1908), he discovered accounts of Juan Diego's death and recognized him as the inspiration for Jackson's Alessandro. James went on a search for Diego's widow, whom he found on the Cahuilla Indian Reservation. A shy woman, Ramona Lubo reluctantly answered James's questions and even honored his request that she take him to her husband's grave. Overwhelmed with emotion, she fell over the grave and began to weep. James had brought along a camera, but hesitated to use it because, as he later wrote, "it seemed a sacrilege to take a photograph of her at this moment." Nevertheless, James overcame his sense of propriety long enough to take the picture, which he reproduced on postcards and sold.

Largely because of this image and James's book, Ramona Lubo herself became a tourist attraction. Streams of visitors to southern California wanted to meet the "real Ramona" and have their pictures taken with her. Lubo was able to make a modest income from these tourists by selling them her baskets, but she was never comfortable with the celebrity thrust upon her.

Enthusiasm for the story of Ramona continued long after Lubo's death from pneumonia on July 21, 1922. The novel has been filmed four times, and the Ramona pageant still brings throngs of tourists to Hemet every year. Despite *Ramona*'s lasting appeal, Helen Hunt Jackson, who died a year after the book's publication, surely would have been disappointed by its reception. The portions of the story dealing with the mistreatment of Indians were largely ignored by fans of the book. Instead, they concentrated on its romantic, mythic view of California's past.

Similarly, those who sought out Ramona Lubo could see only the myth, not the person. In their eyes, she was a pretty, youthful heroine, instead of an old woman left widowed and poor by her husband's murder. Even the graves of Diego and Lubo reveal the persistence of this fantasy. On Diego's grave marker, "Alessandro, Ramona's martyred spouse" is carved below his name. Lubo's tombstone bears only one word: "Ramona."

Further Reading/Resources

May, Antoinette. *The Annotated Ramona.* San Carlos, Calif.: Wide World Publishing / Tetra, 1989.

Ryan, Teya, producer. *Ramona: A Story of Passion and Protest.* Princeton, N.J.: Films for the Humanities, 28 min., 1988.

M

Mankiller, Wilma
(1945–)   *Cherokee tribal leader, activist*

Wilma Mankiller was the first woman to be elected principal chief of the Cherokee Nation. During the 10 years she served as chief, Mankiller was a symbol and an inspiration to Indian women. Many have since followed in her footsteps by seeking political offices within their tribal governments.

Mankiller was born in Tahlequah, Oklahoma, the capital of the Cherokee Nation, on November 18, 1945. Her mother, Irene, was of Dutch-Irish ancestry. Her father, Charlie, was a full Cherokee whose ancestors came to Indian Territory (now Oklahoma) in 1838 on what the Cherokees called *Nunna Daul Tsunyi* (roughly translated as "the Trail of Tears"). This route was traveled by many Cherokees after the U.S. government confiscated their vast southeastern homeland and forced them to relocate to the West. Traveling mostly on foot with little food and few supplies, nearly one-fourth of the Cherokee population died of starvation and disease on the Trail of Tears.

The sixth of 11 children, Mankiller was raised on Mankiller Flats, a tract of land allotted to the Mankiller family in the 1890s. The family eked out a living by hunting and farming, and lived in a four-room house with no heat or running water that was built by Wilma's father. Although Wilma never went hungry, her family was desperately poor. In her autobiography, *Mankiller* (1993), she remembered walking six miles to and from school in the dead of winter while wearing a dress her mother made from a flour sack.

When Mankiller was ten, her father decided to move the family to San Francisco, California. He was persuaded to leave Mankiller Flats by officials with the Bureau of Indian Affairs (BIA), the body of the federal government that oversees the United States's dealings with Indian nations. The BIA representatives visited the Mankillers' house and told Charlie about their relocation program, which promised rural Indians good jobs and better housing if they moved to a large city. Relocation was the dominant federal Indian policy of the late 1940s and 1950s. The United States no longer wanted to assume the costs of maintaining reservations or paying for services guaranteed to Indian groups in past treaties. The BIA hoped that if enough Indians moved to cities, tribal nations would disintegrate, leaving the government free to renege on its financial obligations to them.

When the Mankillers arrived in San Francisco, they discovered that the BIA had greatly exaggerated

143

the benefits of city life. Charlie Mankiller found work in a rope factory, but his salary could barely keep the family fed. They could only afford a cramped apartment in a dangerous neighborhood. In their effort to escape rural poverty, they found themselves living in an urban slum. In Oklahoma, they at least had had the support of friends and relatives and the stabilizing influence of Cherokee traditions. In San Francisco, they were impoverished and alone.

Wilma was particularly devastated by the family's move to the city; she later described it as her personal "trail of tears." With no preparation for urban life, she was frightened of her new surroundings. In *Mankiller,* she recalled that nearly everything about the city was unfamiliar to her—from neon lights to elevators to telephones. Even worse than her sense of dislocation was the scorn of her peers at school. Because of her dark skin, Oklahoma accent, and unfashionable clothes, she was often ridiculed by her classmates. Ill-equipped by her rural education to keep up in her studies, Wilma lost all interest in school. Instead the San Francisco Indian Center became the focus of her world. This organization provided a place where relocated Indians could meet and exchange information about how to cope with the trials of city living. Wilma's father shared her enthusiasm for the center. When she was a girl, she saw him lobby the organization to use its resources to establish a free health clinic for Indians. Mankiller's interest in politics and instinct for organizing people around a common cause grew from listening to and watching her father at work.

In summer 1963, Mankiller graduated from high school. Because no one in her family had ever gone to college, she did not consider continuing her education. She was instead content to take a dead-end clerical job that at least gave her some pocket money. Soon she met Hugo Olaya, a handsome young man from a wealthy Ecuadorian family. They married in November 1963, and almost immediately, they started a family. With the birth of two girls, Felicia and Gina, Mankiller settled into the roles of homemaker and mother.

Mankiller's marriage provided her with financial security for the first time in her life. But this did little to quell a gnawing sense of uneasiness that she began to feel after several years. Bored and restless, she started taking classes in social work at San Francisco State College and to her surprise found that she now enjoyed studying and going to class. Her husband was less pleased by her return to school. He made it clear to Wilma that he did not want her to pursue any interests outside of caring for their children and home.

Much to his dismay, Mankiller also continued to frequent the Indian Center. Her involvement with the people there drew her into the burgeoning Indian rights movement. Inspired by the civil rights movement of the early 1960s, young Indians, mostly in urban areas, were speaking out against the historical mistreatment of tribes by the U.S. government. To make sure their message was heard, they began organizing formal protests and demonstrations. One of the most dramatic was the occupation of Alcatraz, a small island off the coast of San Francisco that years earlier had housed a high-security federal prison but was then abandoned. On November 20, 1969, 89 protesters calling themselves the "Indians of All Tribes" took possession of the island and demanded that the government build an Indian cultural center on the site. When reports of the demonstration reached the public, many more Indians came to Alcatraz to join in the protest. At one point, more than 1,000 protesters were occupying the island. They remained there in a standoff with the authorities until they were finally removed by the police 19 months later. In that time, the protest had become international news.

The Alcatraz occupation changed the course of Mankiller's life. In her autobiography she wrote, "[It] excited me like nothing ever had before. It helped to center me and caused me to focus on my own rich and valuable Cherokee heritage." The protest also revealed her skill as an organizer. While several of her brothers and sisters joined the demonstration, she remained in San Francisco where, working out of the Indian Center, she raised much-needed funds and supplies for the protesters.

Just as she was discovering a purpose, Mankiller suffered a devastating loss—the death of her father from kidney disease. Grieving, she threw herself into volunteer work in the Indian community. In a poor neighborhood in East Oakland, Mankiller founded and directed the Native American Youth Center. She also became involved in the legal battle of the Pit River Indians of northern California, who were fighting for control of tribal land claimed by the Pacific Gas and Electric Company.

Mankiller's activism and growing independence further soured her relationship with her husband. In 1974, the couple divorced, and three years later, Mankiller with her two daughters moved back to Tahlequah. As a single mother, she welcomed the support offered by the tight-knit community and wanted to give her children a better sense of their Cherokee roots.

Mankiller was hired by the Cherokee Nation as an economic stimulus coordinator charged with encouraging Cherokee to study environmental and health science. At first she had trouble adjusting to working within a bureaucratic atmosphere because of her past as a grass-roots activist. But soon her experience made her a valued employee. In San Francisco, Mankiller had funded many of her activist efforts by applying for grants. Her skill at writing an effective grant proposal helped her bring a great deal of money into the Cherokee Nation for social and economic programs.

Once she was settled in Tahlequah, Mankiller decided to go back to school. She took classes to complete her bachelor's degree in social work and then enrolled in the graduate program in community planning at the University of Arkansas, Fayetteville, about an hour's drive from her home. In November 1979, on the way home from a morning class, Mankiller was in a terrible car accident. Another automobile, attempting to pass a row of cars, moved into Mankiller's lane and struck her car nearly head-on. At impact, Mankiller's face was smashed, and her legs and ribs were shattered. Admitted into a hospital in serious condition, Mankiller began the long road to recovery. Her face was rebuilt through plastic surgery, and she

regained use of her legs after 17 operations. Surgeons, however, could not help her overcome her grief when she learned that the other car's driver, who had been killed in the crash, was her best friend, Sherry Morris.

While Mankiller was convalescing, she realized that she was losing control of her muscles throughout her body. Her doctors were at a loss to explain why. Mankiller herself discovered the answer while watching the annual muscular dystrophy (MD) telethon on television. The catalog of symptoms described by one MD sufferer on the program were identical to her own. Mankiller was then tested and diagnosed with myasthenia gravis, a form of MD that can lead to paralysis if left untreated. Through surgery and steroid therapy, Mankiller was cured.

Surviving a near-fatal accident and illness was difficult for Mankiller, but as she explained in her autobiography, the experience also helped to focus her life. During her long convalescence, she had the time to study Cherokee history and tribal issues, which renewed her resolve to work toward bettering their community. Mankiller also maintained that she developed a "Cherokee approach" to life during the process of healing. She worked toward, in the words of Cherokee elders, "being of good mind." According to Mankiller, "That means one has to think positively, to take what is handed out and turn it into a better path."

In December 1980, Mankiller returned to her job at the Cherokee Nation determined to make a difference. She founded the Cherokee Nation Community Development Department and threw herself into the organization's first project—the revitalization of the Cherokee community of Bell. The residents of Bell were among the poorest Cherokee. Many lived in substandard housing, and none of their homes had running water. Mankiller planned and found funding for the construction of a 16-mile-long water line and the renovation of some 20 houses. An important element of her program was to recruit volunteers from Bell to help with the work. Drawing on Cherokee traditions of cooperation and shared labor, Mankiller hoped to build the confidence of the demoralized residents as they rebuilt their community.

The Bell project was a great success and earned Mankiller the respect of many Cherokee. It also brought her in contact with Charlie Soap, a volunteer with whom she developed a close friendship. Over the course of several years, she and Soap slowly fell in love. They married in October 1986.

Well known as a hard worker and skilled organizer, Mankiller was approached by the Cherokee's principal chief Ross Swimmer with an offer in 1983. He wanted her to run on his ticket for the post of deputy chief in the upcoming election. No woman had ever served as deputy chief, so Mankiller initially had difficulty seeing herself in the job. But she reconsidered her decision when she realized that, as deputy chief, she could be a more effective advocate for the poor: "Many Cherokees were forced to put up with poor housing, rising medical costs, and educational deficits. I realized I was being given an opportunity to create change for Cherokee families."

Sinking all of her savings into the campaign, Mankiller steeled herself for accusations that she was too liberal to lead the Cherokee, many of whom had conservative leanings. To her surprise, however, her opponents only wanted to discuss her gender. They said that electing a female deputy would be an affront to God and would make the Cherokee a laughingstock among other Indian groups. Despite receiving hate mail and death threats, Mankiller continued to campaign with enthusiasm. In a close vote, she and Swimmer won the election.

Mankiller had won over many voters, but she still had to contend with a distrustful tribal council, which continued to question her ability to lead. In time she learned to work with the council. But just as she began to feel somewhat comfortable in the job, she was presented with a new challenge. Swimmer was asked to head the Bureau of Indian Affairs in Washington, D.C., in 1985. When he resigned from his post as leader of the Cherokee Nation, Mankiller became the new principal chief, the first woman to ever hold this job among the Cherokees.

As she finished the two years left in the term, Mankiller came to be regarded as an excellent chief. But the true tests of her popularity were the 1987 and 1991 campaigns, in which she ran for reelection. In the first election, in a run-off vote, she narrowly emerged the winner. But, in the second election, by winning an astonishing 82 percent of the popular vote, Chief Mankiller finally proved that she had become fully accepted as the leader of the Cherokee people.

While serving as principal chief, Mankiller suffered a new threat to her health. She had inherited kidney disease from her father and after repeated hospitalizations her life was saved by a kidney transplant in 1990. In part because of her health problems, Mankiller declined to run for reelection in 1995. She received chemotherapy for lymphoma—a form of cancer possibly caused by drugs taken for her kidney ailments. The lymphoma went into remission, but in 1999, she was diagnosed with breast cancer. A year earlier, she required a second kidney transplant.

Despite these difficulties, Mankiller has remained in the public eye. Mankiller continues to lecture widely, emphasizing the need for solutions to the social and economic problems in American Indian communities. She has also compiled *Every Day Is a Good Day: Reflections of Contemporary Indigenous Women* (2004), which includes essays from 19 Indian women about modern American life. Among the many honors Mankiller has received after leaving politics is the Presidential Medal of Freedom, which was presented to her by President Bill Clinton in 1998.

Through her trailblazing work, Wilma Mankiller has helped to transform not only the political world of the Cherokee but other tribal governments as well. Her example made female politicians more acceptable to other Indian groups. Just as important, she also has demonstrated to younger Indian leaders how they can work effectively within a tribal government and still maintain their activist ideals.

Further Reading

Agnew, Brad. "Wilma Mankiller." In *The New Warriors,* edited by R. David Edmunds, 211–238. Lincoln: University of Nebraska Press, 2001.

Mankiller, Wilma, ed. *Every Day Is a Good Day: Reflections by Contemporary Indigenous Women.* Golden, Colo.: Fulcrum Publishing, 2004.

Mankiller, Wilma, and Michael Wallis. *Mankiller.* New York: St. Martin's Press, 1993.

Sherrow, Victoria. "Wilma Mankiller: First Woman Chief of the Cherokee." In *Political Leaders and Peacemakers,* 120–129. New York: Facts On File, 1994.

Maracle, Lee (Bobbi Lee)

(1950–) *Métis autobiographer, novelist, short story writer, poet, activist*

In her writings, Lee Maracle addresses the pain racism and sexism has inflicted on Native American women. Born on July 2, 1950, she grew up in a poor neighborhood in North Vancouver in British Columbia. Her mother struggled to keep Lee and her seven siblings clothed and fed. But she often found time to take them to meet elders of the Squamish tribe, to which Lee's father belonged. Maracle later wrote, "Among the elders I visited in the first years of my life, there was a quiet and deep respect for thinking which extended to men, women and children." Their wisdom gave Maracle "an outlook which defied everything that existed in the outside world."

That "everything" included the discrimination she faced in Canada as a Métis—a person of Native and French descent. The Métis were often looked down on by Indians and non-Indians alike. Many also suffered from devastating poverty. Maracle reacted by rebelling. She dropped out of school after eighth grade and embraced the 1960's counterculture. Traveling throughout North America, she became involved with drugs and alcohol.

In the 1970s, Maracle decided to redirect her anger into affecting social and political change. She gravitated toward the Red Power Movement and joined a circle of Indian activists in Vancouver. While taking a class in oral history, Maracle recorded an account of her life and the social injustices she saw around her. After the 80 hours of tape were transcribed, her words were edited to create her first book, *Bobbi Lee: Indian Rebel* (1975). Like Maria Campbell's *Halfbreed,* Maracle's autobiography was one of the first books published in Canada to explore the sorrows of Métis life.

Maracle has remained an activist, but increasingly, she has turned to writing as a means to promote her social and political goals. As she once explained, "I think all artists worth their salt can spark revolution and I hope that I contribute a little bit to social change in my writing. I think that's what writing is all about, it's about conflict, transformation and redemption so it has to have that edge."

In her second book, *I Am Woman: A Native Perspective on Sociology and Feminism* (1988), Maracle combined prose and poetry to explore her struggles as a woman in a sexist society. She has also written a collection of stories (*Sojourner's Truth,* 1990), a book of poetry (*Bent Box,* 2002), a young adult novel (*Will's Garden,* 2002), and three adult novels (*Sundogs,* 1992; *Ravensong,* 1993; and *Daughters Are Forever,* 2002). Her adult novels meld Indian oral history with Western literary structures to tell the stories of Native American women trying to reconcile Indian traditions with the modern world. Maracle has also contributed to numerous anthologies, including *Telling It: Women and Language across Cultures* (1990), which she coedited.

Also involved in acting, Maracle served as the cultural director of the Centre for Indigenous Theatre from 1998 to 2000. Her daughter, Columpa Bobb, a noted actor and playwright, has performed and taught at the theater. Maracle has also lectured and taught at many institutions, including the En'owkin Centre, the University of Waterloo, and Western Washington University. In 2003, she was named writer-in-residence at the First Nations House at the University of Toronto. Through her teaching and writing, Maracle strives to "change the way Canada feels about [the Métis]." In a 2005 interview, she assessed her success: "I think I contributed significantly through my stories, people started reading and seeing who we are."

Further Reading

Lutz, Hartmut. *Contemporary Challenges: Conversations with Canadian Native Authors.* Saskatoon, Saskatchewan: Fifth House Publishers, 1991.

Maracle, Lee. *Bobbi Lee: Indian Rebel.* Expanded edition. Toronto: Women's Press, 1990.

———. *Daughters Are Forever.* San Diego, Calif.: Polestar Book Publishers, 2002.

———. *Sundogs.* Penticton, British Columbia: Theytus Books, 1992.

Martinez, Maria
(ca. 1887–1980) *San Ildefonso Pueblo potter*

During her lifetime, Maria Montoya Martinez was recognized as one of the greatest ceramicists in the world. Her success as a potter ushered in the modern Native American arts industry, which today brings income and honor to Indians from tribes throughout the United States.

In the late 1880s, Maria Montoya was born at San Ildefonso Pueblo, then a small farming community in what is now north central New Mexico. The second eldest of five daughters, Maria was baptized as a Catholic but otherwise was reared as a traditional Pueblo girl. When she was about seven, her aunt, Tia Nicolasa, introduced her to pottery making. In the past, Pueblo women had been expected to make the pots and other vessels their families used for cooking, carrying food, and hauling water. During Maria's youth, however, this duty was less and less important. As more Pueblo were able to obtain manufactured pots from non-Indian traders, pottery making was becoming less common and less revered.

Maria learned to make pottery as her ancestors had hundreds of years before. The potter began by flattening a clay ball with her hands to create a shallow, curved base. She then formed the vessel's sides with a long coil of clay, which, starting at the base, she wrapped in overlapping layers using a circular motion. The potter smoothed the sides with her hands, then used a gourd to help shape the pot's curves inside and outside. After the clay was dry, the pot's surface was polished with a smooth stone.

The potter next applied a coat of slip—a white paint formed from ground clay and water, polished the surface a second time, and passed the vessel to a male artist, who used vegetable dyes to paint red and black designs on its sides. The completed pot was then placed in burning coals for firing.

Maria attended day school at San Ildefonso and spent two years at the St. Catherine's Indian School in Santa Fe. As a young teenager, she considered a career as a teacher but after returning to her pueblo she decided instead to marry. She and longtime acquaintance Julian Martinez were wed in 1904. They spent their honeymoon in St. Louis, where, as part of a troupe of Pueblo dancers, they performed at the World's Fair. Martinez also held pottery-making demonstrations for the crowd.

Back in San Ildefonso, the Martinezes started a family, which eventually would include four sons. Julian earned their livelihood as a farmer, but to supplement the family income he took a job working for archaeologist Edgar Lee Hewitt of the University of New Mexico in 1907. Hewitt was heading an excavation of Frijoles Canyon, a site that had been occupied by Pueblo ancestors, the Anasazi. He drafted Julian and several other locals to help him with the dig and eventually hired Maria as a cook for the laborers.

When the crew unearthed pot shards, Hewitt encouraged Julian to make sketches of the designs painted on them. Knowing of Maria's skill as a potter, the archaeologist also asked her to attempt to replicate Anasazi pots based on a few shards they had found. Martinez took the task extremely seriously. The shards were thinner and more polished than the pottery she was accustomed to making. Through careful observation, she realized that the clay used to make them had been mixed with a very fine sand. Trial and error allowed her to mix a clay of a similar consistency. When she finished molding the pots, Julian reproduced his sketches in paint on their surface. Pleased with the authenticity of the Martinezes' Anasazi-style pots, Hewitt bought their work and encouraged them to make more.

To further their study of ancient pottery, Julian Martinez took a job as a janitor at the Museum of

New Mexico, where Hewitt's finds were exhibited. He and Maria examined the museum's artifacts and experimented with a variety of techniques and materials until they could duplicate them. The couple was particularly intrigued with shards with a shiny black surface. They had no idea how the Anasazis were able to so darken clay until Julian observed that black spots appeared on their pottery whenever wind blew up smoke during the firing process. He correctly theorized that the smoke had turned the clay black. He and Maria found that they could create a black surface on their own pots, if during firing they tossed powdered dung on the flame to produce a huge smoke cloud. Through more experimentation, Julian discovered that he could create an interesting effect by painting a design with slip before firing a pot by this new method. A pot painted and fired in this way had a slick black surface except where Julian had applied slip. His slip designs also appeared in black but had a matte texture. This black-on-black style of decoration became a trademark of the Martinezes' work.

During the years the Martinezes were perfecting their pottery techniques, tourism in the Southwest was booming. By car or train, easterners could travel to the region in comfort for the first time. Accustomed to crowded urban areas, many were attracted to open expanses of the West. These tourists were also fascinated by the Pueblo, Navajo, and other tribes living in New Mexico and Arizona. Most Indians in the East were fairly assimilated into non-Indian society. In the Southwest, however, many Indians still lived in traditional communities. Their unfamiliar appearance and customs seemed exotic to non-Indian easterners.

With the help of Hewitt, the Martinezes began selling their wares to these travelers, who deemed an authentic Indian pot an ideal keepsake of their western adventure. Their black-on-black pottery was particularly popular with art collectors as well as tourists. By the early 1920s, the Martinezes' work was featured in several prominent private and public collections.

At first, Maria Martinez did not sign her pottery. Signing a work of art was a non-Indian custom that the Pueblos did not observe or necessarily respect. Such self-promotion was frowned upon by the Pueblos, who traditionally held that the needs of the group were always more important than the needs of an individual. But as high demand drove up the price of her work, Martinez hesitantly acquiesced to her customers' requests that she authenticate their purchases with her signature.

Brisk sales of the Martinezes' pottery made them among the wealthiest residents of San Ildefonso. In 1924, they became the first San Ildefonso Pueblo to own a car, but such indulgences were rare for the couple. Like most traditional Pueblo, they had little interest in material things. Maria freely gave away her profits to those in need. She also was generous with her knowledge of pottery making, which in light of her success had become a valuable commodity. At San Ildefonso and at the Indian school in Santa Fe, Martinez taught other Pueblo the techniques she and her husband had invented and perfected. Her students were able to make a substantial living by selling their wares, but they discovered they could increase their profits if Maria signed their work, which she eagerly did when asked. Most likely, Martinez did not believe she was being dishonest by signing the work of other potters. She felt so closely linked to her Pueblo friends and relatives that she probably considered any pot produced at San Ildefonso as one of her own.

In 1943, Julian Martinez died after years of battling alcoholism. Maria then looked to Santana Martinez, the wife of her son Adam, to paint her work. This collaboration continued until 1956, when her son Tony, also known as Popovi Da, began to work with her. Well regarded by art collectors and experts, Popovi Da's painting revived many of the red-and-black designs favored by ancient potters.

By the 1950s, Maria Martinez's work had become internationally acclaimed. She was given several honorary doctorates and accepted four invitations to visit the White House. The American Institute of Architects awarded her its prestigious Craftsmanship Medallion in 1954. In the same

Maria Martinez displays her pottery with her husband, Julian.
(Photo by Wyatt Davis, Courtesy Palace of the Governors (MNM/DCA), Neg. no. 4591)

year, the French government granted her the Palmes Académiques for her contributions to the world of art. In addition to these official honors, Martinez played host to ceramicists from around the world who traveled to San Ildefonso to meet the Pueblo master.

After nearly a century of life, Maria Martinez died in her home pueblo in 1980. At the time of her death, her enormous talents and huge body of work had already made her the most famous Indian artist in history. But ever modest and self-effacing, Martinez drew less satisfaction from her international reputation than from her success in sharing her gifts with others. Interviewed in 1979, she explained, "My Mother Earth gave me this luck. So I'm not going to keep it. I take care of our people." Because of her teaching efforts, today scores of distinguished San Ildefonso Pueblo potters—including her grandson Tony Da and great-granddaughter Barbara Gonzeles—work in the Martinez tradition.

Further Reading

Marriott, Alice. *Maria: The Potter of San Ildefonso.* Norman: University of Oklahoma Press, 1945.

Peterson, Susan. *The Living Tradition of Maria Martinez.* New York: Kodansha International, 1989.

Spivey, Richard L. *The Legacy of Maria Poveka Martinez.* Santa Fe: Museum of New Mexico Press, 2003.

McKay, Mabel

(1907–1993) *Pomo-Wintun medicine woman, basketmaker*

Famed for both her healing and her basket making skills, Mabel McKay was born on January 12, 1907, near Nice in northern California. She was raised by her grandmother, who recognized early that Mabel had special power. A sickly child, Mabel often fell into a trancelike state and talked in her sleep. Her grandmother recognized that Mabel was being visited by spirits during her dreams.

By the time Mabel was in her teens, she was having several dreams or visions a day. She later explained she had to quit school because the spirits' voices made it impossible for her to concentrate. Their messages to her were often disturbing and cryptic. In one dream, a spirit said, "I put these things to you, and you have to sort them out." In another, she was told, "You have to learn many bad things so you know what to do when the time comes."

Through her contact with the spirits, McKay developed healing powers. She believed the spirits also allowed her to weave baskets. McKay once explained, "[M]y basket-making goes with my healing. When I am asked to make a basket for a person, I put that person's name down in my book and I pray on it. I cannot finish the basket until the prayer is answered."

The basketry of the Pomo is world famous for its beauty and craftsmanship. McKay's grandmother, mother, and aunts were all accomplished basketmakers. McKay's baskets, however, were especially spectacular. While praying and singing, she collected the materials for her works—willow shoots, sedge roots, redbud shoots, and bulrush shoots. She often wove feathers into her baskets, adding one to every other stitch. Bursting with yellow, green, and orange feathers, McKay's baskets were as colorful as they were delicate. She was also adept at creating miniature baskets. Some were so

small their decorative designs could only be seen using a magnifying glass.

Throughout her life, McKay was eager to share her knowledge with others. She gave classes in weaving and lectures in traditional Pomo ways and beliefs at colleges and universities. For decades, she also demonstrated basket making at the California State Indian Museum in Sacramento. Her baskets are displayed in museums throughout the United States. Well known internationally as both an artist and as a religious leader, McKay was sought out by many dignitaries, including Pope John Paul II, who asked to meet her during a California visit.

At the end of her life, McKay collaborated with scholar Greg Sarris, who had known McKay as a teenager, to create an as-told-to autobiography, *Mabel McKay: Weaving the Dream* (1994). After a long illness, Mabel McKay died on May 31, 1993. She was buried in a Pomo cemetery next to her dear friend ESSIE PARRISH, another noted traditional healer.

Further Reading

Johnson, Troy R. *Distinguished Native American Spiritual Practitioners and Healers.* Westport, Conn.: Oryx Press, 2002.

Sarris, Greg. *Mabel McKay: Weaving the Dream.* Berkeley: University of California Press, 1994.

Medicine, Beatrice

(1924–2005) *Lakota Sioux anthropologist*

Throughout her career as a professor and scholar, Beatrice Medicine promoted the interpretation of anthropological data about Indians from an Indian perspective. A Lakota Sioux, she was born on August 1, 1924, on the Standing Rock Indian Reservation in South Dakota. Her interest in Sioux culture led her to study anthropology at the University of South Dakota, from which she received a bachelor's degree. Medicine went on to graduate school at Michigan State University and the University of Wisconsin, Madison, which awarded her a doctorate.

When her education was complete, Medicine taught anthropology at many colleges and universities, including Dartmouth College, Stanford University, the University of Washington, and the University of British Columbia. While teaching at San Francisco State College, she also served as the director of the school's Native American Studies Program. When Medicine retired in the early 1990s, she was an associate professor at the University of California, Northridge.

Medicine contributed articles to more than 60 scholarly journals. She also wrote *Native American Women: A Perspective* (1978) and coedited *The Hidden Half: Studies of Plains Indian Women* (1983), a collection of papers delivered at a 1977 symposium on the role and status of women in Plains Indian cultures. Medicine's contribution to the volume explores the phenomenon of female warriors in traditional Plains society and uses the existence of these warrior women to counter the stereotype of Native American women as drudges or slaves. In 2001, the University of Illinois Press published *Learning to be an Anthropologist and Remaining "Native,"* a collection of her most noteworthy essays.

Like much of Medicine's writings, the essay challenges the past interpretations of non-Indian anthropologists, which were often made without an accurate understanding of Indian societies or worldviews. Medicine's work often points out the irony that Native American cultures are perhaps the most studied but least understood by scholars. In a 1985 newspaper interview, Medicine noted the truth in the joke that an Indian family is defined as a "mother, father, children and anthropologist." As one of the few Native Americans to study and teach anthropology at a university level, Medicine used her knowledge of Indian societies to reinterpret anthropological data particularly as they related to Native American women, whose roles in society have all too often been ignored or dismissed as unimportant by male anthropologists.

Medicine always maintained her close ties to her people. While working as a professor, she raised her son, Ted Gardner, as a traditional Lakota Sioux and frequently returned to the reservation for ceremonies and other events. Her tribe honored Medicine in 1977 by naming her a Sacred Pipe Woman during a revival of the Sun Dance ritual. After her retirement, Medicine moved back to Standing Rock. There, she was instrumental in the establishment of a new public school and served on the board of the Wakpala-Smee School District. Following emergency surgery, Medicine died in a North Dakota hospital on December 19, 2005. She was 81 years old.

Further Reading

Medicine, Beatrice. *Learning to Be an Anthropologist and Remaining "Native": Selected Writings.* Urbana: University of Illinois Press, 2001.
———. *Native American Women: A Perspective.* Austin, Tex.: National Educational Laboratory, 1978.
———, and Patricia Albers, eds. *The Hidden Half: Studies of Plains Indian Women.* Washington, D.C.: University Press of America, 1983.
Zimmerman, Karen P. "Beatrice A. Medicine." In *Notable Native Americans,* edited by Sharon J. Malinowski, 271–272. Detroit: Gale Research, 1995.

Medicine Flower, Grace (Grace Tafoya, Wopovi)
(1938–)   *Santa Clara Pueblo potter*

One of Santa Clara Pueblo's most distinguished potters, Grace Medicine Flower was born Grace Tafoya on December 13, 1938. As an infant, during a traditional naming ceremony, her mother gave her the name Wopovi, meaning "medicine flower" in the Tewa Pueblo language. After attending a pueblo day school, Grace graduated from high school in 1957. She married and began studying to become a secretary. But in 1962 she returned to Santa Clara, deciding to devote herself full time to pottery making.

The decision was hardly surprising. Medicine Flower was a member of the Tafoya family, many of whom were legendary potters. The best known of all was MARGARET TAFOYA, Medicine Flower's aunt. But her parents, Camilio Tafoya and Agapita

Silva, were also well regarded. Medicine Flower once described their collaboration: "My mother and father worked at pottery together. They made bowls and ollas. He sculpted horses out of clay and incised his designs onto the surface of the pottery. He was one of the first male potters in the pueblo. They sold their work on the portal in Santa Fe. That was our income; that's how we lived."

In her earliest pottery lessons, her mother merely gave her a piece of clay and told her to "make it beautiful." Over time, she learned about each painstaking step in making pottery the traditional way. Like her ancestors, Medicine Flower collects her own clay, dries it in the sun, and sifts it to remove impurities. She then builds a pot from coils of clay, which she smooths with a gourd. To the formed pot, she applies slip, a coat of clay mixed with water, and polishes the pot with stones she inherited from her mother. Finally the pot is fired outdoors.

Medicine Flower is best known for decorating her pots using the sgraffito method—a technique she and Joseph Lonewolf, her brother and sometime collaborator, perfected beginning in the 1970s. Before firing, she uses a knife or sharpened nail to carve incised designs. The decoration method is extremely difficult; any mistake in carving the freehand design will destroy the pot. Medicine Flower is especially famed for her delicate decorative motifs, including butterflies, dragonflies, and flowers. To complement her floral patterns, she sometimes abandons the traditional reds, tans, and blacks of Pueblo pottery, favoring instead to fire her pots to a light pastel green or purple.

At the beginning of her career, Medicine Flower received a great deal of attention for her miniatures, which could measure as small as $3/8$ inch. More recently, however, she has tried her hand at larger vessels and experimented with different decoration techniques—in her own words, "combining elements, deep carving with sgraffito, sculptured rims, even rims with carved basket-weaving elements." She sees these experiments as necessary to her growth as a potter: "Potters must push them-selves to advance their art. . . . I like to try new ideas. This is the exciting part of my work."

Much sought after by collectors, Medicine Flower's work has won numerous prizes at the Santa Fe Indian Market, the Gallup Inter-Tribal Indian Ceremonial, and other shows of Indian art. But the approval most important to Medicine Flower is that of the Clay Lady, the spirit of past generations that is inhabited in the clay. As Medicine Flower has explained, "[E]very day I pray to the Clay Lady before I work with the clay. I ask her to make it beautiful."

Further Reading

Dillingham, Rick. *Fourteen Families in Pueblo Pottery.* Albuquerque: University of New Mexico Press, 1994.

Katz, Jane. *This Song Remembers: Self-Portraits of Native Americans in the Arts.* Boston: Houghton Mifflin, 1980.

Modesto, Ruby
(1913–1980)   *Cahuilla medicine woman*

In her autobiography, medicine woman Ruby Modesto shared her knowledge of the healing arts of the Cahuilla people. In 1913, she was born on the Martinez Reservation in southern California's Coachella Valley. Her mother was from the Serrano tribe, but Ruby was raised in the traditions of her Cahuilla father.

At 10, Ruby began attending school, where she learned English. But her most important education came from her relatives, especially her grandfather Francisco. Francisco was a *net,* a clan leader responsible for preserving Cahuilla history, culture, and ceremonial life. He oversaw the last Cahuilla kiva, an underground chamber where ceremonies and council meetings were held.

Francisco was also a *pul,* a medicine man. He taught Ruby about Umna'ah, the creator of the Cahuilla people. She also learned that a person could not choose to become a *pul.* Instead, Umna'ah determined who would have this power while they were still in the womb. Most *pul* were men, although sometimes a woman was recognized as having the power to heal.

A *pul's* power came from a spirit helper. Usually, the helper came to the *pul* in a vision induced by ingesting jimsonweed. But Ruby, at 10 years old, achieved her power in a different way. She later recounted, "I Dreamed to the 13th level." In this deep sleep, she encountered her spirit helper, the eagle Ahswit. Ruby remained in a comalike sleep for days before her uncle, also a *pul,* was able to wake her up.

Ruby Modesto married and had three children. While taking care of her family, she also became a medicine woman, achieving her full power only as an adult after the death of her mother. She was skilled in the use of sacred plants to cure illnesses and ailments. But she specialized in casting out demons. Modesto had long attended a Moravian church on her reservation. But she came to see being a Christian as inherently incompatible with being a *pul* because Christianity suggested "a pul gets power from the devil and I don't believe that way." Although a *pul* could use his or her power for evil, Modesto insisted "[i]t's my choice everyday to use the power in a way that is helpful."

Modesto devoted much of her energy to preserving Cahuilla ways. On the reservation, she taught classes in the Cahuilla language. At local colleges, she also gave lectures about her tribe. Modesto also worked with anthropology student Guy Mount, who sought her out in 1976. Together, they wrote *Not for Innocent Ears: Spiritual Traditions of a Desert Cahuilla Medicine Woman.* Modesto had come to feel it was time to pass along her spiritual knowledge to non-Indians, although she doubted their ability to take it in. She wrote, "Very few white people know how to See, nor are they willing to learn. It's too bad, because I think our vision is true and these healing methods would be used to help many people, Indians and non-Indians alike." The book was published shortly after Modesto's death on April 7, 1980.

Further Reading

Johnson, Troy R. *Distinguished Native American Spiritual Practitioners and Healers.* Westport, Conn.: Oryx Press, 2002.

Modesto, Ruby, and Guy Mount. *Not for Innocent Ears: Spiritual Traditions of a Desert Cahuilla Medicine Woman.* Angelus Oaks, Calif.: Sweetlight Books, 1980.

Walker, Paul Robert. "Modesto, Ruby." *Spiritual Leaders.* New York: Facts On File, 1994.

Mountain Wolf Woman (Xehaciwinga)
(1884–1960)   *Winnebago autobiographer*

Over the course of five weeks in early 1958, a 74-year-old Winnebago Indian known as Mountain Wolf Woman dictated the story of her life to anthropologist Nancy Lurie. The result was *Mountain Wolf Woman, Sister of Crashing Thunder,* one of the classic works of Native American autobiography.

Mountain Wolf Woman was born in 1884 during a period of rapid change for the Winnebago. Natives of the Green Bay area of Wisconsin, the Winnebago had been forced to relinquish their homeland to the United States by treaty in the early nineteenth century. Beginning in 1837, the tribe was uprooted and relocated to a series of reservations—first in Iowa, then in Minnesota and South Dakota. Finally, in 1865, they were granted a permanent reservation in Nebraska. These many moves were enormously disruptive to Winnebago society. But the transition from living on their own territory to confinement on a reservation was even more devastating. Like other Indians removed to reservations, the Winnebago were compelled to give up their traditional way of living and adopt the values and ways of their white neighbors.

Some of the Winnebago stubbornly refused to leave their Wisconsin home. Even though they were removed from their lands by the U.S. Army time and time again, they always returned. Mountain Wolf Woman's family was among this group. In her autobiography, she recounts that in 1874 the United States gave up trying to keep these persistent Winnebagos out of Wisconsin and allowed each adult to claim a 40-acre tract of farmland. The settled life of the farmer, however, held little appeal for most tribe members. Traditionally, the Winnebago had spent much of the year hunting and gathering wild plants, traveling seasonally wherever the best foods could be found.

Mountain Wolf Woman's father had no interest in claiming a plot of land. A member of the Thunder Clan, he declared, "I do not belong to the Earth and I have no concern with land." Her mother, though, welcomed the stability that owning land could give their family and registered for a tract at Black River Falls. There her husband built the log cabin where Mountain Wolf Woman spent much of her youth.

As a baby, Mountain Wolf Woman acquired her name after coming down with a mysterious illness. In desperation, her mother took her to see a wise elder, known as Wolf Woman, and begged her for a cure. Wolf Woman replied, "My life, let her use it. . . . I will give my name to my own child. She will reach an old age." The infant recovered and was known thereafter as Xehaciwinga, a Winnebago word that meant to make a home on a bluff or a mountain as a wolf does.

The youngest of six children, Mountain Wolf Woman grew up as a traditional Winnebago girl, moving from camp to camp and helping her family by picking berries and gathering wild roots. Her fondest early memories were of ceremonial feasts and dances and of myths and sacred stories her father recited to her from memory. She also remembered that "there were not many white people around at that time," but this situation was changing. Increasingly, non-Indians were moving into the Winnebago lands, and the tribe was coming to depend on wages they received as berrypickers and hunters working for white employers.

Seeing that more contact with whites was inevitable, one of her brothers insisted that Mountain Wolf Woman attend school in order to learn English. At nine years old, she was enrolled at an Indian school in Tomah, Wisconsin, but after two years her parents took her out of class so that she could once again join them on their seasonal migrations. As a teenager, she was briefly sent to a Lutheran mission school, where she earned the envy of her classmates as the owner of a new invention called a bicycle, a gift from her brother. Soon,

however, she reluctantly left school for good when her mother declared that the time had come for her to marry. According to Winnebago custom, a husband had been selected for her by her family without her consent.

The marriage was not a happy one. In her autobiography, Mountain Wolf Woman referred to him only as "that man" and explained that she left him soon after their second child was born. Her brother found a new husband for her, a man named Bad Soldier with whom she was already friendly. A devoted couple, they had nine children and remained married until his death in 1936.

With her family, Mountain Wolf Woman moved frequently in search of better work or to be closer to friends and family. This unsettled way of life was familiar from her youth, but also reflected an ability to adapt easily to new circumstances. Like many of the Winnebagos of her generation, Mountain Wolf Woman by necessity learned to cope with cultural change by combining the best of both old and new ways.

Some white customs she readily adopted and supported. For instance, after her own disappointment with being forced to leave school, she was heartened to see more Winnebago children receiving a non-Indian education. She also welcomed the end of arranged marriages. Remembering her bitter experience with her first husband, she allowed her daughters to choose their own mates. However, she mourned the passing of many Indian customs. While in her seventies, she was particularly alarmed by Winnebago children's treatment of tribal elders: "'Respect those old people,' mother and father used to say to us. That is what we used to do. We respected the old people, but today they do not respect the old people."

Her adaptability to new and different ways was perhaps best illustrated in her approach to religion. Mountain Wolf Woman participated in traditional Winnebago ceremonies, such as the scalp dance and the medicine dance. But at the same time, she was a practicing Christian. As a young woman, she also joined the Native American Church, a religion that combines elements of Indian and Christian

155

spiritual rituals. Its ceremonies center around the sacrament of peyote, the fruit of a type of cactus that causes hallucinations when eaten. At the recommendation of her sister, Mountain Wolf Woman first took peyote to relieve childbirth pains. But after attending several peyote meetings, she became an enthusiastic convert. Her autobiography provides an account of one dramatic vision she had under the influence of peyote, in which Jesus appeared and she herself turned into an angel. Her devotion to the Native American Church made her a radical in the eyes of more traditional Winnebago. After her conversion, she lived only among peyotists because other Winnebago, in her words, "hated the peyote people."

Mountain Wolf Woman also became adept at dealing with representatives of the U.S. government. Past treaty negotiations committed the government to providing certain funds and services to Indian people who, usually unwillingly, had ceded their lands to the United States. The government, however, was not always eager to honor these obligations. Enterprising Indians such as Mountain Wolf Woman had to learn to deal with the government bureaucracy if they were to receive the benefits due to them. In *Mountain Wolf Woman,* she describes her successful efforts to persuade officials to come to the aid of a poor, elderly neighbor. She also recounts her skillful resolution of a family crisis. Discovering her daughter's marriage has broken up, Mountain Wolf Woman, who was then well into her seventies, agreed without hesitation to take a bus to Portland, Oregon, pick up her daughter's children, and bring them back to Wisconsin to live with her. Through negotiations with the social workers in both Wisconsin and Oregon, she was able to fund the trip for herself and her grandchildren. Like a good traditional Winnebago woman, Mountain Wolf Woman put her family first. But, as the story illustrates, she often met her responsibilities in a very nontraditional manner.

A sense of obligation to family also led Mountain Wolf Woman to record the story of her life. In 1945, she adopted anthropologist Nancy Lurie as a niece. When, 13 years later, Lurie asked her to relate her autobiography, Mountain Wolf Woman felt she could not say no to a family member. Taking her first airplane trip, she traveled to Lurie's home in Ann Arbor, Michigan. There she dictated her story into a tape recorder, first in the Winnebago language, then in English. On November 9, 1960, several months before Lurie's edited version appeared in print, Mountain Wolf Woman died in her sleep from pneumonia at the age of 76.

Lurie found Mountain Wolf Woman an ideal subject for an autobiography; she affectionately described her as "witty, empathic, intelligent, and forthright." But the anthropologist had another reason for wanting to set down Mountain Wolf Woman's story. Lurie saw it in part as a companion to the famous autobiography of her brother Sam Blowsnake. Published in 1920 under the pen name Crashing Thunder, this book was the first autobiography written by a Native American.

Mountain Wolf Woman collaborated with anthropologist Nancy Lurie on her successful autobiography
(Courtesy Milwaukee Public Museum)

Characteristic of the role Winnebago men played in their society, Blowsnake's story was full of adventure and bluster. In contrast, Mountain Wolf Woman's book represents in style and content the concerns of traditional Winnebago women. Modest and often self-mocking, she tells of ordinary occurrences, of small triumphs and failures, of relatives and friends. Before the publication of *Mountain Wolf Woman,* few traditional Indian women had been asked by scholars about their lives because their stories were thought to be uninteresting. By showing the drama of the everyday, however, Mountain Wolf Woman demonstrated the value in preserving women's autobiographies. Largely because of her example, many Native American women have since been inspired to share their own.

Further Reading

Bataille, Gretchen, and Kathleen Mullen Sands. "Culture Change and Continuity: A Winnebago Life." In *American Indian Women: Telling Their Lives,* 69–82. Lincoln: University of Nebraska Press, 1984.

Blowsnake, Sam. *Crashing Thunder: The Autobiography of an American Indian,* edited by Paul Radin. 1926. Reprint, Ann Arbor: University of Michigan Press, 1999.

Mountain Wolf Woman. *Mountain Wolf Woman, Sister of Crashing Thunder: The Autobiography of a Winnebago Indian,* edited by Nancy Oestreich Lurie. Ann Arbor: University of Michigan Press, 1961.

Mourning Dove (Christine Quintasket, Humishuma)

(ca. 1885–1936)   *Colville-Okanagan novelist, activist*

The first Native American woman to write a novel, Mourning Dove, by her own account, was born in a canoe while her mother was crossing the Kootenai River in northern Idaho in about 1885. Known as Christine (or Christal) Quintasket in her youth, the girl was the eldest surviving daughter of an Okanagan Indian father, Joseph, and a Colville Indian mother, Lucy. The family settled on a farm along the Kettle River in northeastern Washington

State. The Quintaskets were leaders among local Indians, largely because of the distinguished lineage of Christine's proud and demanding mother.

By the time Christine was born, most of the Colville of Kettle River, including the Quintaskets, had converted to Catholicism, although they still practiced their traditional religion. At age 10, she was sent to a Catholic mission boarding school in Ward, Washington. The unfamiliar setting and sometimes brutal treatment of the students upset the girl. Within a few months, ill from anxiety, she was sent home to her parents.

While Christine was gone, the Quintaskets, a poor but generous family, had taken in two friends who had no place to live—an old Indian woman named Teequalt and an Irish-American teenager known as Jimmy. Both were great influences on Christine. Teequalt was a traditionalist who refused to adopt the ways of whites who had settled in the homelands of many Indian groups in eastern Washington. She taught Christine about old Indian customs and prepared her for puberty in the traditional manner by helping the girl search for a spirit guide.

Jimmy, on the other hand, introduced Christine to the world of books. He was a fan of pennydreadfuls, cheap and popular mass-produced novels that featured crudely written adventure stories. Jimmy read his collection to Christine and her younger siblings and patiently taught them to read some simple words. Christine Quintasket later remembered that the first printed English word she was able to recognize was "Kentucky," the setting of one of the tales Jimmy shared with her.

With a new enthusiasm for books, Quintasket returned to school. She attended the school at the mission and one at a nearby Indian agency for a total of about three years. Her education was then interrupted by the death of her mother in 1902. Accepting the responsibility of caring for her younger brothers and sisters, Quintasket took her mother's place in the family for two years.

In 1904, her father married again, this time to a woman who was little older than Christine. Perhaps uncomfortable with the situation, Quintasket left home to join the staff of the Fort Shaw Indian School in Montana. While working there, she met Hector McLeod, an amiable Flathead Indian. She and McLeod soon married, but the union was never happy, possibly because of McLeod's heavy drinking. The two separated not long after their wedding, but they were not officially divorced until 1917.

In 1912, when Quintasket was probably in her late twenties, she decided to make a fresh start. She moved to Portland, Oregon, where she knew no one, and set out to become a writer. She began work on her own penny-dreadful—the story of a romance between a white man and a woman of part-Indian and part-white ancestry. Quintasket completed a draft, but, having only a limited command of written English, she was disappointed in the result. Quintasket stashed the manuscript away in the bottom of her trunk, but she refused to bury her desire to write. As a symbol of her determination, she adopted a pen name, Morning Dove. She later changed the spelling of her pseudonym to Mourning Dove and sometimes went by Humishuma, the Okanagan word for the bird. The mourning dove was a important figure in the stories that elders had recited to her when she was a child. The wife of Salmon, the mythic Mourning Dove heralded the return of salmon to the area rivers every spring with her song.

With her renewed commitment to being an author, Mourning Dove moved to Calgary in Alberta, Canada, and enrolled in business school in 1913. There she studied composition and learned how to type. The instruction she received proved valuable, although the experience was otherwise bitter. The only Indian in the school, she was frequently taunted and humiliated by her white classmates.

In summer 1915, Mourning Dove traveled to Walla Walla, Washington, to attend the annual Frontier Day celebration. There she met Lucullus Virgil McWhorter, who would have an enormous influence on her both personally and professionally. McWhorter was the founder of the *American Archaeologist* magazine and an enthusiastic amateur

scholar interested in Indian cultures. He was well known and well liked among the Yakima Indians, a large tribe in central Washington, because he had helped them demand payment for land they sold or leased to whites. Mourning Dove warmed to McWhorter so much that she sheepishly agreed to show him her manuscript. After reading the novel, he agreed that it was weak but encouraged her to revise it and even offered his services as an editor. In a letter McWhorter wrote her that November, he explained the glory that awaited her if she only took his advice: "I see a future of renown; a name that will live through the ages." Desperate to become a published author and desperately insecure about her talents, Mourning Dove was thrilled by McWhorter's confidence in her and her work. She began to send him all of the material she wrote and then revise it according to his suggestions. This literary friendship and collaboration would last for the rest of Mourning Dove's life.

To earn her keep, Mourning Dove took jobs as a housekeeper or more often as a migrant laborer. Many area Indians relied on the meager earnings that they could make from wage work on farms and in orchards. The labor was backbreaking and the hours were long, but, as they lost their traditional lands to white settlers, they had few other means of earning a living.

Mourning Dove would often work ten hours in the fields before retiring to a tent, where she would write long into the night. The demanding schedule left her exhausted and chronically ill. Unusually nervous and prone to irrational fears, Mourning Dove frequently fell victim to ailments that were probably rooted in psychological as well as physical fatigue.

Adding to her stress was the scorn many of her Indian neighbors had for her literary ambitions. Traditionally, Indians' stories were passed along orally from generation to generation. Thus Mourning Dove's desire to write stories down, as white people did, was held in great suspicion. Her way of life was also deemed inappropriate by Indians and whites alike. For a young woman, living without a husband or children, to spend every free moment writing was considered to be bizarre, if not subversive, behavior.

Perhaps responding to outside pressures, in 1919 Mourning Dove married Fred Galler, an Indian man with whom she had a stormy relationship. Galler was frequently unemployed, so the union did little to improve Mourning Dove's financial situation. The marriage also left her desire to write undiminished. Although a wife, Mourning Dove still refused to take on the wifely roles of caring for a home and family.

As the years past, Mourning Dove grew more and more eager to see her novel in print. In addition to acting as her literary adviser, McWhorter had become her agent, taking on the duties of negotiating with publishers on her behalf. In 1922, 10 years after she had started work on her novel, she finally received a contract from Four Seas, a publisher in Boston, Massachusetts. But even after the contract was signed, McWhorter continued to ask Mourning Dove for more revisions.

He also pushed her to set aside the manuscript to work on another project he had insisted she take on—collecting and translating into English the stories and myths told by the Colville elders. Mourning Dove was hesitant to work on the collection. She saw herself as a novelist and wanted to devote her little writing time to fiction. McWhorter, however, persuaded her that the project would both preserve Colville traditions and make her famous. Once convinced, however, Mourning Dove found working on the collection frustrating. The elders of the tribe, already distrustful of the novelist in their midst, did not want Mourning Dove to write down their stories and were therefore unwilling to share them with her. She had to gather much of her material by attending funerals, where traditionally mourners would relieve their grief by talking well into the night. At these large gatherings, she could listen to the elders' tales unnoticed.

But Mourning Dove had a still greater obstacle to overcome in compiling the collection—the advice and queries of Hester Dean Guie, a newspaper editor whom McWhorter had asked to prepare Mourning Dove's legends for publication. Both Guie and McWhorter badgered Mourning Dove with endless questions and requests. Guie particularly was a stickler for accuracy and consistency. He asked her to provide more and more details about any tribal custom she mentioned in passing. Uncomfortable with the project and the approach of her editors, she became increasingly discouraged with her career. Adding to her vexation was her publisher, Four Seas, which seemed to be doing nothing at all with the manuscript of her novel. In her letters to McWhorter, she began to refer to the firm first dismissively as "Four Ponds" and later angrily as "Four Liars."

After a five-year wait, Mourning Dove finally saw her novel published as *Cogewea: The Half-Blood* (1927). The book told the story of three sisters of mixed Indian and white ancestry. One sister marries a white man and adopts white ways; another adamantly holds on to Indian traditions. The third, Cogewea, tries to live in both the white and Indian worlds but has trouble fitting into either. Much of the plot deals with Cogewea's love life. She rejects a suitor of mixed ancestry for a white man, but when he proves despicable, she returns to her "half-blood" lover. Like much of the popular fiction Mourning Dove admired, *Cogewea* is melodramatic and its language is often overwrought. It is also marred by many insertions written by McWhorter, who wanted to use the novel to educate whites about Indians. McWhorter frequently interrupted the story with passages about Indian history and culture and occasional meditations on how they had been mistreated by whites.

Despite its flaws, *Cogewea* was a popular and critical success. It sold well and received generally good reviews in western newspapers. It also earned Mourning Dove the respect of her tribespeople, who were impressed by her newfound fame outside the reservation. Mourning Dove enjoyed the attention and used the opportunity to take for the first time a more public role among the Colville. She started giving lectures to a variety of groups and became active in several clubs for Indian women. Mourning Dove also became involved in tribal politics, particularly in a battle to force a white-owned

This photograph of Mourning Dove appears on the frontispiece of her novel *Cogewea: The Half-Blood.* (Reproduced from *Cogewea: The Half Blood* [1927; reprinted by the University of Nebraska Press, 1981])

days picking apples and hops to make a living. The stress of constantly working took its toll on her already nervous disposition. In general ill health and disoriented, she was admitted to the state hospital in July 1936. On August 8, she died of what her doctors termed "exhaustion from manic depressive psychosis." She left behind several partial manuscripts, including fragments of an autobiography, which were edited and published in 1990.

Christine Quintasket, as Mourning Dove, overcame enormous hardships to become one of the first Native Americans to write and publish fiction in English. Because of her lack of education and the intrusiveness of her editors, her works did not, in the end, give her the lasting literary reputation she craved. But they did provide models to many later Indian novelists, who later became as masterful storytellers with written language as their ancestors had been with the spoken word.

Further Reading

Garceau, Dee. "Mourning Dove: Gender and Cultural Mediation." In *Sifters: Native American Women's Lives,* edited by Theda Perdue, 108–126. New York: Oxford University Press, 2001.

Miller, Jay, ed. *Mourning Dove: A Salishan Autobiography.* Lincoln: University of Nebraska Press, 1990.

———. "Mourning Dove: The Author as Cultural Mediator." In *Being and Becoming Indian: Biographical Studies of North American Frontiers,* edited by James A. Clifton, 160–182. Chicago: Dorsey Press, 1989.

Mourning Dove. *Cogewea: The Half-Blood.* 1927. Reprint, Lincoln: University of Nebraska Press, 1981.

———. *Coyote Stories.* 1933. Reprint, Lincoln: University of Nebraska Press, 1990.

Sligh, Gary Lee. *A Study of Native American Women Novelists: Sophia Alice Callahan, Mourning Dove, and Ella Cara Deloria.* Lewiston, N.Y.: Edwin Mellen Press, 2003.

lumber mill located on the reservation to hire Indian workers. In 1935, she became the first woman elected to the Colville Tribal Council.

Mourning Dove followed up *Cogewea* with the publication of *Coyote Stories* (1933), which featured 27 of the legends she had collected. Many of the stories featured the character of Coyote, a trickster whose misadventures traditionally taught Indian children lessons about proper behavior. Heavily edited by Guie and McWhorter, many of Coyote's less savory antics were removed from the final manuscript so as not to offend a white readership.

Coyote Stories furthered Mourning Dove's reputation but had little effect on her financial situation. Her writing and political activities took more and more of her time, yet she still had to spend her

Musgrove, Mary (Coosaponakeesa, Mary Matthews, Mary Bosomworth)
(ca. 1700–ca. 1763)   *Creek trader, interpreter*

One of the most important and colorful figures in the early history of Georgia, Mary Musgrove was born with the name Coosaponakeesa in about

1700. She was reared in Coweta, a large Creek Indian village located along the border dividing present-day Georgia and Alabama. Her mother was a prominent Creek woman whose brother, Brim, was a leader in the tribe. Coosaponakeesa's father was one of the European traders who had started to arrive in Creek territory in the late 17th century.

When Coosaponakeesa was 10, her father sent her to a school run by Christian missionaries in the English colony of Carolina. There she was converted and given the baptismal name "Mary," which she used for the rest of her life. At school, she also learned to speak English, a skill that would prove enormously useful in the changing world of the Creeks.

During Mary's youth, English, French, and Spanish traders and settlers began to overrun the lands of the Creek. In some ways, the arrival of these Europeans benefited the Indians. From them, the Creek obtained manufactured goods such as metal pots and tools that were more durable than comparable objects that the Creek had traditionally made from stone and wood. In exchange for these goods, the Indians gave deerskins to the foreign traders, which they sent back to Europe to be made into leather goods. The Creek prospered by participating in this trade network. By the beginning of the 18th century, the Creek population had grown to nearly 8,000, making it the largest Indian group in what is now the southeastern United States.

But trading with Europeans also hurt the Creek and their society. They came to rely so heavily on European goods that, eager to ensure a steady supply of them, the Indians were willing to retain friendly relations with Europeans and their governments at any price, including a loss of political independence. Trade also increased warfare among tribes. In addition to deerskins, English traders were eager to buy captives that the Creek had taken in battle with other groups. These captives were then sold as slaves to large farm owners in the growing English settlements in Carolina. In time the Creek began to wage war on weaker Indian tribes for the sole purpose of taking captives whom

they could later trade away. Many small tribes were destroyed by this constant warfare.

In 1715, one group—the Yamasee—had had enough. Because the English had kidnapped many of their women and children, Yamasee warriors rose up and killed hundreds of English settlers. English soldiers put down the uprising, but authorities in colonial Carolina were shaken by the massacre, so much so that they outlawed the Indian slave trade in 1717.

Soon after the Yamasee War, Mary left school and came home to Coweta. There at about 16 she married a white trader named John Musgrove. The Musgroves lived in Carolina for several years, but by 1732 they had returned to Creek territory and established a trading post in the village of Yamacraw. The post was an extremely successful enterprise. Historical records indicate that local Indians traded them more than 1,200 pounds of deerskins a year. The couple was prosperous enough to keep a small herd of cattle and maintain a modest plantation on which they grew food crops.

In 1733, the English government decided to establish a new colony, Georgia, to the south of Carolina. James Oglethorpe was dispatched to Creek territory as the leader of Georgia, which would be populated mostly by English prisoners who had been jailed because they were unable to pay their debts. Oglethorpe knew that founding a colony among the Creek would be difficult. Although the Indians welcomed traders, they did not want more European settlers taking over their lands. Oglethorpe was also aware that he would be hard-pressed to rally support from the tribe in battling the English colony's Spanish enemies, who had founded settlements in present-day Florida. The large and powerful Creek had avoided allying themselves formally to England, France, or Spain. This policy, advocated by Mary Musgrove's influential uncle, Brim, allowed them to stay friendly with all these nations, while remaining beholden to none.

When Oglethorpe arrived in what would become Georgia, one of the first Creek he met was Mary Musgrove. He eagerly enlisted her as his interpreter because of her fluency in English. But even more important he found in Musgrove an indispensable aide in dealing with the Creek. She encouraged her tribespeople to welcome the English. Because of her wealth and high social position as Brim's niece, Musgrove held considerable influence over even the more militant Creek. Her support of Oglethorpe allowed his colonists to settle in Creek territory with a minimum of resistance from the native residents.

Musgrove also helped the English colony grow and thrive. From her plantation, she offered stores of food desperately need by the newcomers. Over time, the supplies used by the colonists amounted to a debt of £800, which they never paid. Musgrove also became involved in the Georgians' battles with the Spaniards to the south. She rallied Creek warriors to fight alongside Oglethorpe's troops in several battles. At the request of her English employer, she even established a second trading post, Mount Venture, along the Altamaha River close to Spanish-held lands. From here, she spied on the Spanish and alerted the Georgians to their activities. Musgrove paid a price for her support of the English. Both of her trading posts were destroyed during the war between the English and Spanish forces.

Initially, Musgrove's efforts to help the Georgians increased her influence and furthered her position among the Creek and the colonists alike. But in 1743 she lost her greatest advocate when James Oglethorpe returned to England. As a parting gesture of gratitude, he gave her the diamond ring from his own finger and £200. He may also have promised to give her £2,000 more in payment for her services.

Oglethorpe's departure was not the only blow to Musgrove's status. After the death of her first husband in 1740, she had promptly married Jacob Matthews, a white man who had been her indentured servant. By all accounts, Matthews was a drunk and a blowhard. Gaining power through his union with Mary only made him more arrogant and uncontrollable. Georgia officials grew weary of his outrageous and violent behavior. In disgust,

one colonial official wrote that he found it pointless "to foul more Paper in tracing Jacob Matthews through his notorious Debauches." The antics of Mary's husband tarnished her reputation among the Georgians.

Mary's third marriage, however, turned her into a full-fledged villain in the colonists' eyes. Matthews died in 1742, and four years later, she wed Thomas Bosomworth, a former minister who had come to Georgia to make his fortune. The couple built a new trading post, but Bosomworth had even bigger dreams. He wanted to raise cattle, a business that required a great deal of land and money. The Bosomworths hatched a scheme that involved defrauding both the Creek and the colonists. As their first step, Mary met with her cousin Malatchee and several other Creek leaders in 1747. She persuaded them to sign an agreement naming her the owner of three islands in Creek territory— St. Catharine's, Ossabaw, and Sapelo—and a sizable tract of hunting land north of the colonial town of Savannah. All the chiefs except for Malatchee later claimed that they had been led to believe they were signing a list of grievances that Mary Bosomworth was volunteering to take up with English officials.

With their land grant in hand, the Bosomworths bought a herd of cattle on credit and built a ranch on St. Catharine's Island. To get the money to pay off the creditors, Mary approached Georgian authorities and insisted that they owed her for her service to the colony. She suggested that if they did not give her the funds she requested, she would use her influence among the Creeks to organize an Indian rebellion. When the colonists were unresponsive, she, her husband, and Malatchee led a contingent of Creek warriors into Savannah in July 1747. Surrounded by a small army, Mary Bosomworth declared that she was the "Queen of the Creeks" and intimated that if her demands were not met she would turn her warriors loose on the town.

Ever afraid of Indian revolts, the town's officials treated their unexpected visitors with care. The Bosomworths and Malatchee were invited to several dinners with Savannah's leaders, who tried to assess the seriousness of the threat posed by the Creek party. When Malatchee confided that he thought Thomas Bosomworth was a liar, the Georgians began to question whether Thomas and Mary actually had the influence over the warriors that they claimed. Behind the Bosomworths' backs, they talked with the Creek, presented them gifts, and discovered that the men had no true allegiance to their so-called queen. When Mary came to sense her power was in question, she staged an ugly scene in front of the authorities. According to one eyewitness, she "rushed into the Room, in the most violent outrageous and unseemly manner, that a Woman Spirited up with Liquor, Drunk with Passion, and disappointed in her Views could be guilty of." The Georgians put the hysterical Mary in the guardhouse, and Thomas's and Malatchee's veneer of haughtiness crumbled. They blubbered apologies, begged for forgiveness, and blamed the entire fiasco on Mary. Humiliated and defeated, the Bosomworths skulked out of Savannah after terrorizing the town for nearly a month.

The episode filled Mary with bitterness. Accustomed to Oglethorpe's esteem, she was angered by the contempt that the Georgians now felt for her. Back in Creek territory, she immediately started talking ill of the English in an attempt to turn her people against them. She also asked more Creek leaders to sign agreements to legitimize her land claims. Some Creek complained to colonial officials about her efforts to gain control of land that rightfully belonged to the entire tribe. When they started talking about killing the Bosomworths' cattle, the Georgians took action to prevent a violent scene. Representatives of the colony legally purchased the three islands from the Creek in 1751.

Desperate for money to pay their creditors, the Bosomworths turned to the English government for help. In 1750, they submitted to the English Board of Trade a pile of documents that they held supported their land claims and their demands for compensation for Mary's service to the colony.

Years passed, and eventually Mary and Thomas sold a small tract of land to finance a trip to England, where they pled their case in person. Eager to end the affair, the Board of Trade settled with the Bosomworths in 1759. The couple was given St. Catharine's and £2,100 generated by the sale of the other two islands. The Bosomworths then returned to St. Catharine's, where they built a great mansion and maintained a ranch. Mary died there in about 1763; soon afterward, Thomas married her chambermaid.

According to the portrait of Mary Musgrove left by history, she was an exceedingly opportunistic, self-serving, and unscrupulous person. Although her story is perhaps more dramatic than most, these characteristics hardly made her unique among Indians living in the days of colonial America. As foreign settlers poured into their lands, many eastern Indians had to cope with rapid and often devastating change. With the arrival of colonists, the economies and political structure of tribal communities were forever transformed. Frequently, much of their traditional cultures was also destroyed, sometimes within a few years. As the old rules of conduct disappeared, they were left to create new rules for themselves. With their very survival as the prize, unsurprisingly, some were willing to do whatever was necessary to emerge as winners in the colonial power play into which they had been thrust.

Further Reading

Coulter, E. Merton. "Mary Musgrove, 'Queen of the Creeks': A Chapter of Early Georgia Troubles." *Georgia Historical Quarterly* 11 (March 1927): 1–30.

———. "Musgrove, Mary." In *Notable American Women: 1607–1950,* edited by Edward T. James, 605–606. Cambridge, Mass.: Belknap Press, 1971.

Green, Michael D. "Mary Musgrove: Creating a New World." In *Sifters: Native American Women's Lives,* edited by Theda Perdue, 29–47. New York: Oxford University Press, 2001.

Todd, Helen. *Mary Musgrove: Georgia Indian Princess.* Savannah, Ga.: Seven Oakes, 1981.

N

Nampeyo
(ca. 1860–1942) *Hopi potter*

Before Nampeyo, non-Indians generally saw Indian pottery wares only as quaint souvenirs of the American Southwest. Her mastery and innovation, however, moved art lovers and collectors throughout the world to think of her craft in a new way. After Nampeyo, the finest examples of Native American pottery were regarded not just as charming curios but as important works of art.

A Hopi Indian, Nampeyo was born in about 1860 in the Pueblo village of Hano in what is now northern Arizona. She was given her name during a ceremony held soon after her birth. Nampeyo means "snake girl," a nod to her father's membership in the Snake Clan.

Little is known about Nampeyo's early life, but the historical record does indicate that she learned about pottery from her grandmother. Pueblo girls traditionally were taught this skill by watching their elders work and by trying their own hand at making miniature pots. As Nampeyo discovered, the first step to making a pot was collecting clay. Nampeyo may have gathered her clay about three miles from her home near the ruins of Sityatki, a Pueblo village that had been destroyed about 250

years earlier. The collected clay was then ground, softened with water, and mixed with pulverized stones or shards of old pottery. A ball of the prepared clay was pounded into a rounded base. Then the sides of the pot were built up by spiraling a coil of clay up from the base. Frequently wetting her hands with water, the potter molded the shape of the vessel and smoothed the clay. The molded pot was covered with slip—a thin paint mixed from water and a small bit of clay. After being polished with a smooth pebble, the pot was then painted with brown and red pigments made from ground stones. For a brush, the painter used a leaf of the yucca plant that was chewed on one end. To harden the clay and allow the paints to take on their true color, the pot finally was fired in a kiln of heated rocks or animal dung.

Pottery making had been a respected skill among the Pueblo and their ancestors for nearly 2,000 years. But when Nampeyo was a young woman, it was rapidly becoming a lost art. When she was young, most women had stopped decorating their pots. They only made vessels for utilitarian purposes, such as carrying water and cooking food. Even these basic pots were becoming obsolete. Non-Indian traders in the Pueblo territory offered the Indians metal pots and china bowls. As these manufactured items became available, many Pueblo women abandoned the laborious process of making their own pots.

In 1875, when Nampeyo was about 15, a team of government surveyors studying the Southwest as part of the U.S. Geological Survey arrived in Hano. With them was a noted photographer named William Henry Jackson. Nampeyo's brother took in the visitors, and Nampeyo helped serve them a meal. Jackson, apparently somewhat taken with the young woman, took two photographs of her that later would be reprinted around the world. In the pictures, her hair was wrapped in two large coils, one on each side of her head. To the Pueblo, the hairstyle meant that she was old enough to marry.

After a customarily long engagement of several years, Nampeyo did marry a man named Kwivioya, but they never lived together. In 1881, she

William Henry Jackson photographed Nampeyo outside her home in 1875.
(Photo by William H. Jackson, Courtesy Palace of the Governors (MNM/DCA), Neg. no. 49806)

wed a second time, to a man named Lesou. The couple had at least five children and stayed together until Lesou's death in 1932. Some scholars believe Lesou guided Nampeyo's career as a potter. Although the level of his involvement is debated, he clearly took an interest in Nampeyo's pottery and encouraged her in her work.

In 1891, archaeologist Jesse Walter Fewkes arrived at the old village of Sityatki. He hired about 15 Pueblo men, including Lesou, to help excavate the ruins there. The team found many shards and some whole pots that the village residents had made hundreds of years before. Lesou brought some of these artifacts home to show his wife, who was excited by their beautiful painted designs. She started visiting the excavation site, where she borrowed pencils and paper to sketch the patterns on the pots Fewkes's workers unearthed.

Nampeyo possibly was already familiar with Sityatki designs from potsherds she had found years before. But definitely after the village was excavated, she began an organized study of her ancestors' pottery decoration. She also started to create versions of these designs on her own pots. Nampeyo never slavishly copied the patterns on the older works; instead, she used them as a source of inspiration. She also adapted some of the shapes of the Sityatki artifacts. The potter's favorite shape was a wide, squat water jar with a nearly flat top and an open mouth. She usually placed her decoration in a thick band circling the shoulder of the jar and sandwiched between two black horizontal stripes. During an interview with anthropologist Ruth Bunzel, Nampeyo explained her standard plan for painting this band: "The best arrangement for the water jar is four designs on top, two and two. . . . The designs opposite each other should be alike."

Nampeyo was a quick and hard worker. She was soon selling the many pots she produced to a number of traders. For large pots, traders generally paid her about two to five dollars, but they could resell them for far more. Even tourists unfamiliar with Indian pottery would pay top dollar for the superior artistry of her work. The popularity of Nampeyo's work worried Fewkes. He feared that she had so captured the spirit of Sityatki works that "unscrupulous traders" were driving up prices by telling their customers that Nampeyo's pots were prehistoric artifacts.

One of the earliest admirers of Nampeyo's art was Walter Hough of the Smithsonian Institution. While visiting Fewkes's dig site in 1896, he met Nampeyo and saw her work. He bought several pots for the collection of the U.S. National Museum. In an article in *American Anthropologist* magazine, Hough wrote that Nampeyo's pottery had "attained the quality of form, surface, fire change, and decoration of the ancient ware which give it artistic standing."

The *Chicago Tribune* offered even higher praise when in 1910 it described Nampeyo as "the greatest maker of Indian pottery alive." She and Lesou were invited to the midwestern city in 1898 and 1910 to demonstrate pottery making at the Chicago Coliseum. They also made several trips to the Grand Canyon. There Nampeyo made pots before an audience at a luxury hotel managed by the Fred Harvey Company. The company's chain of hotels and restaurants catered to easterners who traveled to the Southwest on the Santa Fe Railroad. To capitalize on the tourists' desire to have an "authentic" western experience, Fred Harvey establishments often hired Indians and cowboys to entertain their customers. The promotional materials the company used to tout Nampeyo as a star attraction made her face and name familiar to non-Indians throughout much of the United States.

In Hano, the attention paid to Nampeyo and her pottery bred resentment in some of her neighbors. But her success also inspired others to imitate her work. Many women in Hano began to making pots in the Sityatki style for sale to traders. Among them were Nampeyo's four daughters—Annie, Cecelia, Fannie, and Nellie.

In 1920, William Henry Jackson, who had photographed the young Nampeyo nearly 50 years earlier, suggested to a friend traveling through Pueblo country that he visit the famed potter. The friend tracked down Nampeyo, but sadly reported back to Jackson that she had gone blind. Despite her loss of sight, Nampeyo continued to work with the help of her family. She could still mold a pot by relying solely on her sense of touch to achieve the proper shape. She then passed along her work to Lesou or to one of her daughters for painting.

On July 20, 1942, Nampeyo died in her home in Hano. During her 70-year career, she had played an important role in helping to popularize Indian pottery. Following her example, hundreds of Pueblo potters—including nearly 75 members of her own family—have been able to make a substantial living by selling their wares. But as the first Native American to be regarded as an artist, Nampeyo not only brought her people a new source of income—her artistic mastery also gave them a new source of pride and respect in the non-Indian world.

Further Reading

Ashton, Robert, Jr. "Nampeyo and Lesou." *American Indian Art* 1 (Summer 1976): 24–33.

Blair, Mary Ellen, and Laurence Blair. *The Legacy of a Master Potter: Nampeyo and Her Descendants.* Tucson, Ariz.: Treasure Chest Books, 1999.

Hirschfelder, Arlene. "Nampeyo: Hopi Potter." In *Artists and Craftspeople,* 9–15. New York: Facts On File, 1994.

Kramer, Barbara. *Nampeyo and Her Pottery.* Albuquerque: University of New Mexico Press, 1996.

McCoy, Ronald. "Nampeyo: Giving the Indian Artist a Name." In *Indian Lives: Essays on Nineteenth- and Twentieth-Century Native American Leaders,* edited by L. G. Moses and Raymond Wilson, 43–57. Albuquerque: University of New Mexico Press, 1985.

Naranjo-Morse, Nora
(1953–   ) *Santa Clara Pueblo potter, printmaker, poet, filmmaker*

Both a noted visual artist and poet, Nora Naranjo was the ninth of 10 children in a Pueblo family known for its artistic talents. Born in Espanola, New Mexico, near the Pueblo village of Santa Clara, she spent most of her youth in the town of Taos, where her father served as a Baptist missionary. After graduating from high school, 16-year-old

Naranjo left home and began to travel with no particular goal in mind. She worked odd jobs—including sorting mail in Washington, D.C., and selling fireworks in South Dakota—while she struggled with finding a way to reconcile her vision of herself as a modern American woman with her Pueblo upbringing. After this period of exploration, she decided to return to Santa Clara, where her parents had retired. At the pueblo, she met and married Greg Morse, with whom she had two children, twins named Eliza and Zakary. She also attended the College of Santa Fe, from which she received a bachelor's degree in social welfare in 1980.

With her return to Santa Clara, Naranjo-Morse became intrigued by the work of her mother Rose and her sisters, Dolly, Tessie, and Jody, all of whom were accomplished potters. Following their example, she began to work in clay in 1976. Like many Pueblo women, she had learned the basic techniques of creating pottery as a girl by watching her mother at work. Naranjo-Morse remembers once waking up in the middle of the night and finding her mother in deep concentration as she molded a storage jar. "I'll never forget the way she looked, so involved and happy," Naranjo-Morse has explained.

Naranjo-Morse discovered her own passion for pottery as soon as her sister Jody reintroduced her to handling clay. As Naranjo-Morse has recalled, "I put my hand on the clay and held it with three fingers. It was the first time I ever felt a connection with something greater than myself. I became addicted immediately. I had come home."

Naranjo-Morse's first forays into creating pottery were frustrating. She was embarrassed by her early efforts, which looked amateurish in comparison with the perfectly shaped, symmetrical works of her mother and sisters. Wanting to carve her own path, Naranjo-Morse gave up trying to imitate their pottery and instead started to mold small figures of animals and people. By making figurines, she was following in the tradition of ancient Pueblo potters. She was also inspired by contemporary artists, including sculptors Henry Moore and HELEN CORDERO, whose "storytelling dolls" had

revived an interest in figurative pottery among the Pueblos during the 1960s and 1970s.

Although Naranjo-Morse differed from her relatives in her choice of pottery forms, she did follow their lead in using Santa Clara clay as the primary material in her pottery. Like them, she also prepared it in the traditional manner. The laborious process of digging, hauling, drying, and purifying clay can take more than a month, but only by performing this work herself does Naranjo-Morse feel as if she has shown proper respect to *Nan chu Kweejo,* the "Clay Mother" who provides the gift of clay to Pueblo potters.

Many of her early works were playful depictions of Pueblo clowns and village scenes. She had a particular fondness for creating small adobe (mud brick) pueblos, the multistoried complex of dwellings in which the Pueblo Indians traditionally lived. Complete with tiny ladders connecting the stories to one another, these miniatures were based on her memories of her childhood in Taos. "I love the ladder," Naranjo-Morse has said. "I remember going up and down them constantly as a little girl, real proud, feeling real secure. To me, a ladder against an adobe wall is beautiful, knowing it will take you up, up, up." To house their family, Naranjo-Morse and her husband built their own adobe dwellings, whose 17-foot walls were constructed from 5,000 clay bricks.

Naranjo-Morse's best-known works are the sculptures of the "Pearlene" series. A comic figure often dressed in short, tight skirts and purple sneakers, Pearlene is a character that represents, in the words of American Indian poet JOY HARJO, "the wild thing in all of us." For Naranjo-Morse, creating Pearlene became a means of "trying to figure out my place and, being a modern Pueblo woman, trying to find out where I belonged." She often placed Pearlene in situations in which she had found herself as a way of making sense of her own experiences. For instance, after a trip to Las Vegas, Naranjo-Morse created a particularly humorous piece titled *Pearlene Teaching Her Cousins Poker* (1987). In her eyes, the "idea of this modern Pueblo woman teaching her traditional cousins the art of the game verged on the ridiculous." Soon after crafting this sculpture, Naranjo-Morse decided to stop making Pearlenes in response to a businessman's proposal that she construct a mold from which he could mass-produce plastic versions of the character for sale. She refused his offer, then made one final Pearlene before saying good-bye to her alter ego. "As a human being and as an artist," she has explained, "I couldn't just let [Pearlene] become ordinary or overdone."

The popularity of Pearlene helped to build a following for Naranjo-Morse's work among art collectors. Her figurative pottery has been exhibited in galleries from New York to San Francisco and has won numerous prizes and awards. A dynamic speaker, Naranjo-Morse has lectured widely and has presented demonstrations of her pottery techniques in Germany and Denmark. As a participant in a project sponsored by the Museum of Northern Arizona, she has also appeared in "Separate Visions," an educational videotape that illuminates how contemporary Native American artists meld traditional Indian beliefs with the realities of their lives in the modern world.

Naranjo-Morse herself explored this theme in her 1992 book *Mud Woman: Poems from the Clay.* Described by the author as "a volley between words and clay, clay and words," the volume combines her own poems with photographs of her pottery. Naranjo-Morse, who has written poetry since she was fifteen, got the idea of bringing together her words and art when she realized how interrelated they were. Noting that most books about Pueblo pottery have been written by non-Indian anthropologists or historians, she has said that she also "wanted to talk about the direct experience, like when a piece breaks after you've spent six months on it, or how it feels to go sell a form you've spent months working on and caring for."

In recent years, Naranjo-Morse has been creating installations and monotype prints, as well as experimenting with combining metal with adobe to create large sculptures that would easily break if made from clay alone. Naranjo-Morse has also created environmental landscape art, including

Numbe Whageh (Our Center Place), a permanent installation at the Albuquerque Museum. The piece was conceived as a commentary from an American Indian perspective on the 500th anniversary of the arrival of Don Juan de Oñate in New Mexico—an event that marketed the beginning of the subjugation of the Pueblo people by the Spanish.

Always eager to work in new media, Naranjo-Morse has recently delved into filmmaking. Working in video, she had directed several short films, including *I've Been Bingo-ed by My Baby* (1997) and *Clay Beings* (2003). In 1997, Naranjo-Morse herself became the subject of a film. With six other artists, she appeared in *Inspirations,* a documentary made by director Michael Apted that explores the origins of the creative spirit.

Further Reading/Resources

Abbott, Lawrence. "Nora Naranjo-Morse." In *I Stand in the Center of the Good: Interviews with Contemporary North American Artists,* 197–208. Lincoln: University of Nebraska Press, 1994.

Apted, Michael, and Eileen Gregory, producers. *Inspirations.* Chatsworth, Calif.: Home Visions Entertainment. DVD, 100 min., 2002.

Lichtenstein, Grace. "The Evolution of a Craft Tradition: Three Generations of Navajo Women." *Ms.* 11 (April 1983): 59–60, 92.

Naranjo-Morse, Nora. *Mud Woman: Poems from the Clay.* Tucson: University of Arizona Press, 1992.

Trimble, Steven. "Brown Earth and Laughter: The Clay People of Nora Naranjo-Morse." *American Indian Art* 12 (Autumn 1987): 58–65.

Natawista

(1825–1893)   *Blood peacemaker, interpreter, trader*

Respected by whites and Indians, Natawista helped maintain peace during the early years of contact in what is now southern Montana. She was born in 1825 in the Blood Indian homeland in present-day Alberta, Canada. When she was 15, Natawista traveled south with her father Men-Es-To-Kos to Fort Union, a trading post that had been established at

Natawista was respected among both Indians and whites.
(Montana Historical Society, Helena)

the confluence of the Missouri and Yellowstone rivers by the American Fur Company in 1829. Probably in hopes of maintaining a good relationship with Blood traders, the head of the post, Alexander Culbertson, asked to marry Men-Es-To-Kos's teenage daughter. Natawista and Culbertson were wed by Indian rites in 1840. During their 20 years of marriage, the couple would have five children.

After her wedding, Natawista settled at Fort Union and occasionally accompanied her husband to the headquarters of the American Fur Company in St. Louis, Missouri. In 1845, the Culbertsons moved up the Missouri to establish a new trading post, Fort Benton. There Natawista developed a reputation as an excellent hostess to non-Indian visitors to the fort. She also soothed relations between the whites at the post and the Indians in the region, including the Blood, Blackfeet, Piegan, and Gros Ventre (Atsina). In her dealings with these tribes, Natawista probably was aided by her powerful family. Her brother had become the chief of the Blood, and her cousin was the leader of the Piegan.

In 1847, Isaac Stevens, the governor of Washington Territory, appointed Alexander Culbertson to a Pacific Railroad surveying expedition through Indian lands. Stevens most likely hired Culbertson because he knew that Natawista would accompany him. By communicating the party's peaceful intent to the Indians it encountered, she did in fact prove instrumental to the surveyors' success.

The Culbertsons' involvement in trade made them rich. By 1858, they had amassed enough wealth to retire to a mansion in Peoria, Illinois. While living there, Natawista was a consultant to anthropologist Lewis Henry Morgan, to whom she explained the kinship networks of the Blackfeet and Gros Ventres. Also in Peoria, Natawista became known for her love of expensive gowns and jewelry. These extravagant tastes and some poor investments in time depleted the couple's fortunes. In the late 1860s, they were forced to return to trading on the upper Missouri to make a living.

Several years later, Natawista apparently became disillusioned with her husband and with living among whites. She left Culbertson and went home to Blood territory, where she lived with her nephew until her death in 1893.

Further Reading

Bredin, Renae Moore. "Medicine Snake Woman." In *Native American Women: A Biographical Dictionary*, edited by Gretchen M. Bataille, 173–174. New York: Garland, 1993.
Waldman, Carl. *Who Was Who in American Indian History*. New York: Facts On File, 1990.

Nicolar, Lucy (Princess Watahwaso)
(1882–1969)   *Penobscot entertainer, activist, basketmaker, businessperson*

Performing as Princess Watahwaso, Penobscot entertainer Lucy Nicolar used her business savvy and personal charisma not only to build a successful career but also to open up economic and political opportunities for her tribe.

Nicolar was born on June 22, 1882, on the Penobscot reservation on Indian Island, located across the Penobscot River from Old Town, Maine. Her highly educated father was a leader in the tribe and a well-known lecturer and writer on Penobscot culture.

Like many Penobscot women, Nicolar's mother was a skilled basket weaver. She was also adept at marketing her work to the tourist trade. By the time Nicolar was a teenager, she and her two sisters traveled up and down the east coast. At a variety of shows and exhibits, they demonstrated basket making and sang and danced wearing Indian garb.

Lucy stood out among the entertainers at this show, as one journalist noted: "Lucy is a young miss of marked beauty, and wherever she goes with baskets and Indian exhibits, many a young American who looks upon the Indian maiden feels that the land of the Penobscot must be 'the land of handsome women.'"

Lucy was also smart and determined. At 14, she realized that the Catholic school on Indian Island offered a poor education. She lobbied instead to attend the non-Indian high school at Old Town and became the first Indian student enrolled there. Her academic success caught the attention of Montague Chamberlain, an administrator at Harvard College. He soon hired her as his assistant and moved her into his family's home in Boston. Soon, Nicolar—now calling herself Princess Watahwaso (meaning "Bright Star")—became a fixture at high-society events in Boston and New York.

Wanting a career as a performer, Nicolar developed a concert act with her singing and retelling Indian legends. After a brief first marriage, she wed her manager Tom Gorman. With his help, she landed a contract with the Redpath Lyceum to perform on its chautauqua circuit from 1917 through 1919. Chautauquas featured musical acts and lectures by well-known writers and political leaders. After her stint on the circuit, Nicolar returned to New York and made several popular recordings.

In the 1920s, Nicolar went back on the road, this time traveling with an act she put together with a troupe of younger Indian performers, including MOLLY SPOTTED ELK. One number fea-

tured Nicolar singing "Indian Love Song" with Bruce Poolaw, a Kiowa rodeo star about 20 years her junior. With the onset of the Great Depression, finding audiences for her traveling show grew more difficult. Adding to Nicolar's troubles, Gorman ran off to Mexico, taking with him much of her earnings.

On a visit to Indian Island in 1930, Nicolar decided to return home for good. She and Poolaw moved into a large modular house she had moved there from Chicago, Illinois. In 1937, they were married. Together, they organized several elaborate Indian pageants to bring tourists to the reservation. They also built a large tourist shop, full of baskets, moccasins, and other wares made by Penobscot artisans.

A brochure advertises a concert by Lucy Nicolar, who performed under the name Princess Watawaso.
(University of Iowa Libraries)

After settling on Indian Island, Nicolar also turned her considerable energy to helping the Penobscot people. With her sister Florence, she revived the Wabanabi Women's Club, an organization originally founded by her mother. The club pushed for the Old Town High School to admit all Penobscot reservation students. Angry that Nicolar was sending students away from its own school, the local Catholic church expelled her from its congregation. In retaliation, Nicolar helped found a Baptist church on the island.

Nicolar also led a campaign to persuade the state to build a bridge from the island to the mainland. She insisted that, without a bridge, the Penobscot were isolated, unable to explore employment and educational opportunities. After decades of bringing attention to the issue, she attended the bridge's dedication in 1950.

Nicolar just as tirelessly lobbied for repealing a state law that prohibited reservation Indians from registering to vote. The law was finally changed in 1953. The following year, Nicolar became the first Indian on a reservation to vote in a Maine state election.

On March 27, 1969, Lucy Nicolar died at the age of 86. The obituary in the *New York Times* recalled the passion and persistence that made her extraordinary performing career as Princess Watawaso possible. Later in life, however, Nicolar found just as much satisfaction from her second career—that of willful and effective advocate for the Penobscot people.

Further Reading

McBride, Bunny. "Lucy Nicolar: The Artful Activism of a Penobscot Performer." In *Sifters: Native American Women's Lives,* edited by Theda Perdue, 141–159. New York: Oxford University Press, 2001.

Niro, Shelley

(1954–)   *Mohawk photographer, filmmaker, painter, installation artist, sculptor*

Through her art, Shelley Niro explores the struggles of contemporary Indians to establish a sense of identity and community. She was born in 1954 in Niagara Falls, New York, but was raised on the Six Nations Reserve near Brantford, Ontario. Creativity was an important part of her early home life. Many people on the reserve were artisans, including her parents, who made and sold beadwork at Indian festivals. Niro and her siblings also competed to see who could tell the best stories, put on the best plays, and sing the best songs.

Niro attended Cambrian College in Sudbury, Ontario, to study classical music but soon left to marry and raise a family. In her spare time, she began to create artwork, all the while harboring doubts over her talents. As she once explained, "I questioned whether I could say something that meant something. Finally I got to an age where I thought, 'If I don't get over it. I can't call myself an artist.'" Niro enrolled at Ontario College of Art and was heartened by her teachers' encouragement. She graduated with honors in 1990 with a major in painting and sculpture. Seven years later, Niro earned a master's in fine art from the University of Western Ontario.

In 1991, Niro created her photograph series *Mohawks in Beehives.* The series includes photographs of her three sisters, posing dressed in loud clothes and flashy makeup and hairstyles. In these playful, humorous images, the subjects look strong and knowing, challenging preconceptions of Indian women as weak victims of a hostile society. The series immediately made Niro one of the most notable up-and-coming artists in Canada.

Niro uses a wide variety of techniques for embellishing her art photography. She sometimes hand-tints black-and-white photographs, mixes painting with photography to create multimedia pieces, and inscribes phrases and sentences onto photographs that act as commentary on the images. Niro frequently groups images in diptichs or triptichs, inviting the viewer to read them as a sequence. Recently, she has used large photographs to create installations. In *Grand View* (2004), she combined several views from Whiteface Mountain in New York, showing the traditional lands of the Mohawk from a variety of perspectives. In *Shirt*

(2004), she employed multiple images of an Indian woman wearing a shirt baring different phrases to explore the injustices committed to Indian peoples during the colonization of North America.

Given the storytelling aspect of her photograph series, it is hardly surprising that she is also a distinguished filmmaker. Her first short was *It Starts with a Whisper* (1993). The film combines realistic and absurd elements to tell the story of Shanna, a young woman who comes to terms with her Indian identity during a road trip.

Even more ambitious is *Honey Moccasin* (1993), a 45-minute film starring Métis actress TANTOO CARDINAL. The film takes place on a contemporary Canadian reserve where all of the traditional Indian dance paraphernalia has been stolen, forcing the reserve residents to redefine their ideas about Indian identity. Niro again combines disparate elements, juxtaposing performance art with a mystery story and adding hints of comedy throughout. According to Niro, "The film gets mixed up with historical notions that are quite heavy . . . [and that] might turn a lot of people off . . . I think that's where humour comes in. It pulls them in a little bit and gets them to wait for the punchline."

Niro's work has been exhibited in museums and galleries throughout the world. Recently, it has appeared in such celebrated shows as the Canadian Museum of Civilization's *Reservation X: The Power of Place* and the National Museum of the American Indian's *Continuum 12.* Speaking of her drive to explore new subjects and media, Niro has explained, "The good side is I'll never run out of things to do. But the bad side is I'll probably never finish all the places that I've started."

Further Reading

Indyke, Dottie. "Shelley Niro." *Southwest Art* 34 (March 31, 2005): 42, 44.

Martin, Lee-Ann. "Shelley Niro: Flying Woman." In *After the Storm,* edited by W. Jackson Rushing III, 61–67. Indianapolis, Ind.: Eiteljorg Museum of American Indians and Western Art, 2001.

Ryan, Allan J. "I Enjoy Being a Mohawk Girl: The Cool and Comic Character of Shelley Niro's Photography." *American Indian Art,* Winter 1994, pp. 45–53.

 Nuñez, Bonita Wa Wa Calachaw
See WA WA CHAW

Obomsawin, Alanis
(1932–) *Abnaki filmmaker, singer*

One of Canada's most renowned documentary filmmakers, Alanis Obomsawin was born in Lebanon, New Hampshire, but grew up on the Odanak Reserve outside of Montreal, Quebec. When she was nine, her family moved to nearby Trois-Rivières, where the Obomsawins were the only Indian residents. Adjustment to this new environment was difficult for Alanis. In addition to her ignorance of non-Indian culture, she knew only a little English and no French and was therefore unable to speak with other children. The discrimination and sense of isolation she experienced as an Indian child among a non-Indian population would influence much of her later work.

Before turning to the medium of film, Obomsawin pursued a career as a professional singer. Following her New York City singing debut in 1960, she toured throughout Canada and the United States, where she appeared at folk festivals and in schools and museums. Her performances featured many of her own compositions with lyrics written in Abnaki, her native language. She included some of these songs on her 1988 album, *Bush Lady.*

In 1967, Obomsawin began working on her films with the National Film Board of Canada. Her early documentaries were celebrations of Native American art and culture. Among these works are *Christmas at the Moose Factory* (1971), which focuses on the artwork of Cree Indian children, and *Mother of Many Children* (1977), which deals with the storytelling traditions of Indian women. As a recognition of the cultural importance of these films, Obomsawin was awarded the Order of Canada, the government's highest honor, in 1983.

Obomsawin's subsequent documentaries continued to explore Native American issues but were far more political in their content and perspective. For instance, her 1984 film *Incident at Restigouche* is a sympathetic account of the plight of Indian fishermen in Quebec, who were the victims of a violent police raid after they refused to give up fishing rights to their native territory. Equally critical of the Canadian government's policies toward Indians are Obomsawin's features *Richard Cardinal: A Cry from a Diary of a Métis Child* (1986), an expose on the failures of the child welfare system, and *Poundmaker's Lodge: A Healing Place* (1987), an examination of the treatment of Indian drug and alcohol abusers.

Perhaps Obomsawin's most politically charged film is *Kanehsatake: 270 Years of Resistance* (1993), which was named best Canadian feature at the 1993 Toronto Film Festival. The documentary focuses on the Oka crisis—a 78-day standoff between Mohawk activists and Canadian police that became international news in the summer of 1990. The showdown was sparked by a plan of the mayor of Oka, Quebec, to expand a municipal golf course into a neighboring pine forest. Local Mohawks, whose traditional lands had included the forest, responded by arming themselves and occupying the site. Living among the protesters, Obomsawin used a video camera to shoot eyewitness footage of the dramatic confrontation. But as the film's title indicates, her documentary explores not only the incident itself but also its historical context. The film offers a detailed account of the centuries of illegal land-grabbing that resulted in the tribe's loss of most of their ancestral lands around Montreal. Obomsawin has explained that her goal in making *Kanehsatake* was "to show what the Mohawk people were like and why they took the stand they did." Obomsawin continued to explore the ramifications of the Oka crisis in *My Name is Kahentiiosta* (1995) and *Rocks at Whiskey Trench* (2000).

Obomsawin's recent works include *Is the Crown at War with Us?* (2002), the story of a Micmac community's battle for fishing rights, and *Our Nationhood* (2004), an account of the Micmac people in Quebec and their fight for access to their traditional lands. Like her other productions, it reveals her long-standing commitment to present Indian issues from an Indian perspective.

Further Reading

Case, Barry. "Behind the Barricades." *Maclean's,* 31 January 1994, pp. 58–59.

Lealand, Brett A. "Alanis Obomsawin." In *Notable Native Americans,* edited by Sharon Malinowski, 292–293. Detroit: Gale Research, 1995.

Lewis, Randolph. *Alanis Obomsawin: The Vision of a Native Filmmaker.* Lincoln: University of Nebraska Press, 2006.

Ockett, Molly (Marie Agathe)
(ca. 1740–1816)   *Abnaki healer*

During the mid-18th century, Molly Ockett was hailed as a "Great Indian Doctress" by the Indians and whites of what is now western Maine. Ockett was born in about 1740, while her family was camped along Saco River. There, the Abnaki of Pigwackets village gathered every spring to collect shellfish. In the winter, the Pigwackets Abnaki headed for hunting grounds. They spent the rest of the year in their palisaded village, where they tended fields planted with corn.

The years of Ockett's youth were difficult for the Abnaki. For many years, they had been allies of the French, who settled areas to the west in the St. Lawrence River valley. Many Abnaki traded with the French, learned the French language, and, under the tutelage of French missionaries, adopted the Catholic religion. Ockett's name was an Abnaki pronunciation of Marie Agathe, the Christian name she was given at her baptism.

By the 1740s, English settlers to the east were beginning to encroach on Abnaki lands. Afraid the French were too far away to protect them, a group of notable Pigwackets Abnaki warriors (possibly including Ockett's father) decided to shift allegiances. They supported the English in fighting the French in King George's War (1744–48). During the conflict, the warriors' wives and children were sent to Boston, Massachusetts. Ockett was among them. She spent four years living with the English there, learning their language and their ways.

When Molly was a teenager, another conflict—the French and Indian War (1754–63)—broke out between the English and the French. This time, the English were no longer interested in Indian alliances. They sent troops into Abnaki territory to slaughter the Indians there. One group, including Ockett, fled to a Catholic mission in Canada. The English attacked it in 1759, but Ockett managed to survive, supposedly by hiding behind a bush when the troops swarmed in.

After the French and Indian War ended with an English victory, Ockett returned to her village. In

1764, she married an Abnaki named Piol Susup. They had one daughter, Molly Susup. Several years later, Ockett took up with another man, Jean Baptiste Sabattis. They had three children together; it is unclear whether they married.

As time passed, more and more settlers claimed land in Abnaki territory. Near Pigwackets, the English build the town of Fryeburg. Generally, the settlers there tolerated the Abnaki in their midst. By then, greatly overnumbered by non-Indians, the Abnaki posed little threat. In addition, the Abnaki were useful trading partners. They offered the English animal furs, baskets, and other crafted items in exchange for clothing and food.

Ockett was an excellent hunter and often traded pelts to the English. But she had an even more valuable commodity to sell—her knowledge of herbal remedies. When English settlers were injured or became ill, they hired her to prescribe and make medicines from wild plants and animal products. Ockett's formidable talents as a healer soon won her respect among both her Indian and non-Indian neighbors. By 1772, in search of better farmland and hunting grounds, Ockett moved some 30 miles to the north, near the town of Bethel. Because of her healing skills, she was welcomed there, and her daughter, Molly, was even allowed to attend school with English children.

Several English writers left stories about Ockett, some bordering on legend. For instance, the Hamlin family supposedly moved her into their home to care for an ailing infant. Ockett cured the baby, who grew up to be Hannibal Hamlin, vice president of the United States in the Lincoln administration.

In his memoir, a non-Indian named Henry Tufts praised Ockett for treating him for a knife wound, although he was less than enthusiastic about the taste of her medicines: "My kind doctress visited me daily bringing new medical supplies, but my palate was far from being gratified with some of her doses. . . . Nevertheless, having much faith in the skill of my physician, I continued to swallow with becoming submission every potion she prescribed. Her means had a timely and beneficial effect since, from the use of them I gathered strength so rapidly."

Other chroniclers wrote of Ockett in similarly admiring terms. She was said to be large-framed women who carried herself with dignity and tended to be outgoing. And given the vulnerability of the surviving Pigwackets Abnaki, she often showed considerable courage in her willingness to stand up to the English. One story recounts how she was reprimanded by a minister's wife for picking blueberries on the Sabbath. Ockett stormed away, then weeks later confronted the women. "I was right in picking the blueberries on Sunday," she insisted. "[I]t was so pleasant and I was so happy that the Great Spirit had provided them for me."

During the American Revolution (1775–83), some Pigwackets Abnaki sided with the English. Others, including Ockett, supported the American colonists. She even warned an American colonel of an imminent attack, thus saving his life.

The end of the war brought even more whites to the Bethel area, where several American soldiers were given land grants in exchange for their service. The influx meant Ockett had to compete with more hunters to make a living. She also faced competition in her medical practice after 1799, when a non-Indian physician arrived in the town.

When Ockett grew too old to care for herself, the colonel she had saved during the Revolution stepped in to help. He took her into his home in Boston for a year, then at her request built a house for her near Bethel. In 1816, Ockett became very ill. An Abnaki chief took her to the town of Andover, where she had non-Indian friends. They financed her care until her death on August 2. Throughout the old Abnaki homeland, the English named geographical locations—from Molly Ockett Mountain to Mollywocket Brooke—in her honor.

Further Reading

Johnson, Troy R. *Distinguished Native American Spiritual Practitioners and Healers.* Westport, Conn.: Oryx Press, 2002.
McBride, Bunny. *Women of the Dawn.* Lincoln: University of Nebraska Press, 1999.

McBride, Bunny, and Harald E. L. Prins. "Walking the Medicine Line: Molly Ockett, a Pigwacket Doctor." In *Northeastern Indian Lives: 1632–1816,* edited by Robert S. Grumet. Amherst: University of Massachusetts Press, 1996.

Oden, Loretta Barrett

(1942–   )   *Potawatomi chef*

Chef Loretta Barrett Oden is on a mission to bring Native American cooking to the forefront of the American culinary world. She was born in 1942 on the reservation of the Citizen Potawatomi in Shawnee, Oklahoma. While she was growing up, Oden watched her mother and grandmother cook, often using ingredients they grew in their garden or gathered in the wilderness. She also became familiar with the wide variety of dishes cooked by other Oklahoma Indians. As she once recalled, "When I was a little girl we would go out and gather wild plums, my grandmother and my mother and I, and we would make wonderful jelly. But women from other tribes who lived near us would make something else from those same plums. The wild grapes that we would make into jelly would become grape dumplings for cooks of the Creek people."

Oden married at 15 and raised two sons. After they left home, she and her husband divorced. Faced with making a new life for herself at 48, Oden moved to southern California. Always curious about American Indian cuisine, she decided to devote herself to learning more about it. For three years, she traveled throughout North and South America, collecting recipes and studying the foods and dishes enjoyed by dozens of indigenous groups.

In 1993, her research led her to open the Corn Dance Café in the Hotel Santa Fe. The restaurant was the first in the United States to showcase the food of Native America using all organic ingredients, often grown or produced by Native Americans. Describing the café's fare, Oden said, "My food encompasses literally all the Americas. I take all of the ingredients that were here in such abundance and whomp up a creative native cuisine to appeal to today's palate. It's been referred to as haute cuisine, Indian style." The restaurant was an immediate success, as much because of its chef as for the food it served. Oden often visited the dining room, entertaining her patrons with stories about the origins of the dishes they were eating.

Soon Oden took her stories to a national forum. On Thanksgiving in 1994, she made her first television appearance on *Good Morning America.* She has since appeared on numerous television shows, including *Cooking Live* and the *Today Show,* and has regularly been heard on National Public Radio. Oden has also shared her knowledge of Native American cuisine in many publications, such as the *New York Times* and *National Geographic Traveler,* and during personal appearances. Oden frequently lectures at the prestigious Copia: The American Center for Wine, Food and the Arts.

Oden's goal is to educate non-Indians about the Indian origins of many popular foods—from gumbo to chocolate cake to Boston baked beans. She also hopes to revive American Indian cooking to help guide Indians toward a healthier diet. Oden often points out the role of "white man's food" in creating health problems, especially diabetes and obesity, within Indian groups. She is particularly critical of fry bread, a dish often mistakenly thought of as a traditional Indian food. (In fact, fry bread became popular among American Indians only during the reservation era, when they often had nothing to eat except for U.S. government rations of white flour and lard.) Oden hopes to replace this fat-filled dish with what she calls "unfry bread"—her "Little Big Pies" made from baked dough covered with nutritious toppings such as barbecued buffalo.

In 2001, Oden closed her Santa Fe restaurant and returned to Shawnee. She opened a new Corn Dance Café there, but it soon closed. She has since been busy with a number of projects, including consulting with several food companies. Recently, Oden has taken her promotion of American Indian cooking to the airwaves in *Seasoned with Spirit: A Native Chef's Journey with Loretta Barrett Oden.* For this 13-part PBS series, Oden traveled across the country to demonstrate to viewers the wonders and diversity of the foods she loves.

Further Reading

Hill, Judyth. "Native Restaurants: Celebrating the Delicious Diversity." *Native Peoples,* September/October 2001, pp. 38–42.

Severson, Kim. "Native Foods Nourish Again." *New York Times,* 23 November 2005. Available online. URL: http://www.nytimes.com/2005/11/23/dining/23nati.html?ex=1290402000&en=a7a582e3aefdcfd1&ei=5088&partner=rssnyt&emc=rss. Downloaded on February 2, 2006.

P

Parker, Cynthia Ann (Preloch)
(1827–1870)   *Comanche captive*

The life of Cynthia Ann Parker has long been the source of legends. Even during her lifetime, newspaper articles and fictionalized accounts often repeated the story of Parker's transformation from a pioneer girl to a Comanche woman.

The eldest child of the Parker clan, Cynthia was born in Illinois in 1827. Five years later, her family decided to move to Texas in search of farmland. Their Texas settlement, known as Fort Parker, was surrounded by a enormous wall to protect it from raids by local Indians. At the time, white settlers were arriving in Texas in ever-increasing numbers and encroaching on the hunting grounds of the Indians native to the area. As competition for prime land increased, so did the tensions between Indians and whites. Violent attacks—initiated by both groups—were common.

On the morning of May 19, 1836, a party of several hundred warriors from the Comanche, Caddo, and Kiowa tribes entered Fort Parker through a gate that had been left unlocked. The terrified settlers fled the fort, but before the attack was over, five members of the Parker family were dead, including nine-year-old Cynthia's father. Five others—Cynthia, her brother John, two women, and an infant boy—were taken captive. Indian warriors usually took captives after a successful raid. Traditionally, captives were adopted into a tribe to bolster its population if too many tribal members had been killed in warfare. But at the time of the Fort Parker attack, warriors more often took captives to extract a ransom from their relatives.

Within six years, all of the Parker captives, except for Cynthia, had been ransomed and returned home. Family members and other whites tried to negotiate for her release, but the Comanche, with whom she lived, refused all their offers. The tribal leaders told the Parkers that Cynthia had chosen to stay with her adoptive Indian parents, Chatua and Tabbi-nocca, who had given her the Comanche name Preloch. Cynthia's reluctance to leave her Indian family was confirmed by several reports of would-be rescuers. One army officer who tried to secure her freedom in 1840 insisted on a meeting with Cynthia, but she would not speak when he talked to her about returning to the Parker family. Another story held that after John's release, he searched out his sister and begged her to come home. By this account, she firmly explained that her home was with the Comanche. By this time, she had married Peco Nocoma, a respected warrior who had led the raid on Fort Parker. Together, they had three children—two sons, Pecos and Quanah, and a daughter, Topsannah.

In the 1850s, relations between Indians and Texans further deteriorated as the U.S. government attempted to move Indians from their territory and onto reservations. Resisters—including Nocoma—staged raids in retaliation, which were met by even bloodier attacks by the U.S. Army. After a spate of looting and killing instigated by Nocoma, the military discovered his camp on the Pease River in December 1860. Soldiers rushed the camp, killing every Indian they could. Most of their victims were women and children, because the warriors—the real target of the soldiers' wrath—were away on a hunting expedition.

Cynthia Ann Parker holds her infant daughter Topsannah, circa 1861.
(Joseph Taulman Collection, CN #00805, The Center for American History, The University of Texas at Austin)

Cynthia Parker's sons were able to flee. She, too, tried to escape on horseback with her baby girl. One account of the massacre holds that, when a soldier was about to shoot her, she held up the infant and shouted "Americanos" to dissuade him from murdering her child.

Parker and Topsannah were taken alive and sent to live with her uncle Isaac on his farm in Birdville, Texas. Newspaper articles and published stories about the "rescue" described the supposed horrors and degradation she had had to endure during her 25 years among the Comanche. But for Parker the true horror was being separated from her husband and sons and forced to live far from her tribe. Barely able to remember her childhood at Fort Parker, she was frightened of whites and found their ways peculiar and disturbing. Her unhappiness and loneliness in her new surroundings grew worse after she learned in 1863 that Pecos had died of smallpox. Several months later, she became even more despondent when Topsannah fell victim to a fatal case of influenza. Weakened by her attempt to starve herself in order to end her misery, Parker also died of influenza in 1870.

Her only surviving child, Quanah, became a leader among the Comanche, respected by Indians and whites alike for his skill as a diplomat. For many years, he searched for his mother but did not learn of her whereabouts until five years after her death. Not until 1911, when Quanah's body was buried next to hers, was Cynthia Parker finally reunited with her son.

Further Reading

Exley, Jo Ella Powell. *Frontier Blood: Saga of the Parker Family.* College Station: Texas A&M University Press, 2001.
Hacker, Margaret Schmidt. *Cynthia Ann Parker: The Life and the Legend.* El Paso: Texas Western Press, 1990.

Parrish, Essie (Essie Pinola)
(1902–1979)   *Pomo medicine woman, basketmaker*

For much of the 20th century, Essie Parrish was the beloved religious leader of the Kashaya Pomo.

On November 29, 1902, she was born Essie Pinola in Sonoma County, California, on Haupt's Ranch, where many Pomo worked as laborers. One of nine children in her family, Essie was reared by her maternal grandmother, Rosie Jarvis.

When she was six, Essie was recognized as a Dreamer—the last of four prophets and healers that would come to help the Kashaya Pomo. In her dreams, she received instructions about how to cure the sick and perform ceremonies. Her dreams also delivered prophecies of the future. For instance, she foresaw the invention of jet planes and the outbreak of World War II (1939–45).

On the small Kashaya Pomo Reservation, Parrish helped revitalize the tribe's Dream Dance religion. She was also well known for her healing powers. She treated her patients by administering herbal medicines, singing medicinal songs, and sucking disease from their bodies. As she explained, "I had something in my throat to suck pains out with. . . . That power is always near me. But other people can't see it. I alone can see it." Parrish was one of the last sucking doctors among the Indians of California.

On the reservation, Parrish raised 13 children—four with her first husband, Daniel Scott; nine with her second husband, Sidney Parrish. While working as a manager in an apple cannery, she also distinguished herself as an artist. Parrish was famed for her traditional Pomo baskets, which are now found in museum collections across the United States.

Throughout her life, Parrish helped scholars preserve Pomo culture. She appeared in more than 20 anthropological films, including *Chishkale*, which was named best documentary at the 1969 Cannes Film festival. In addition to working with noted anthropologists Alfred Kroeber and Samuel Barrett, she collaborated with linguist Robert Oswalt on a dictionary of the Kashaya Pomo language. She also contributed to Oswalt's *Kashaya Texts* (1962), a collection of Pomo legends and stories.

Dedicated to passing along the Kashaya's cultural heritage to a new generation, Parrish taught

Essie Parrish, photographed in 1960, pounds acorns into meal.
(Courtesy of the Phoebe Apperson Hearst Museum of Anthropology and the Regents of the University of California, Photographed by Josepha Haveman, Cat. no. 15-19 554)

in the reservation school. She also frequently lectured at other schools and universities, including the University of California at Berkeley.

When in her seventies, Parrish helped persuade the U.S. government to give the Indians of Sonoma County title to an old building once used by the Central Intelligence Agency near Forestville, California, along with 125 acres of land surrounding it. The area was renamed Ya-Ka-Ama, meaning "our land" in Kashaya. Ya-Ka-Ama has since become a job training and education center for California Indians.

After decades of service to her people, Parrish died on July 9, 1979, at the age of 76. She was buried in the cemetery on the Kashaya Pomo Reservation.

Further Reading

Johnson, Troy R. *Distinguished Native American Spiritual Practitioners and Healers.* Westport, Conn.: Oryx Press, 2002.

Sarris, Greg. "Parrish, Essie." In *Notable American Women: A Biographical Dictionary Completing the Twentieth Century,* edited by Susan Ware, 496–497. Cambridge, Mass.: Belknap Press, 2004.

Ya-Ka-Ama Indian Education and Development, Inc. Available online. URL: http://www.yakaama.org. Downloaded on April 4, 2006.

Pearson, Maria (Darlene Elvira Drappeaux, Running Moccasins)
(1932–2003) *Nakota Sioux activist*

For more than 30 years, Maria Pearson fought for more respectful treatment of Indian gravesites and remains. She was born Darlene Elvira Drappeaux on July 12, 1932, in Springfield, South Dakota. Her mother, a Nakota Sioux, gave her the Indian name "Running Moccasins." When she was confirmed by the Catholic Church, she received the Christian name "Margaret Mary," although she called herself "Maria."

Maria Drappeaux married an engineer named John Pearson. After spending seven years in Germany, the couple eventually settled in Iowa. There, they raised six children. Maria Pearson worked a variety of jobs and attended classes at Iowa Western Community College and Iowa State University. By the 1960s, Pearson was involved in Indian issues, especially advocating for improvements in Indian health care and education.

In 1971, John Pearson told his wife a disturbing story. An employee of Iowa's Department of Transportation, he saw a crew accidentally dig up an old cemetery near Greenwood, Iowa. The crew meticulously buried all the remains of white people. Just as carefully, they boxed up the bones of Indian people so they could be sent to the Office of the State Archaeologist. This was then a common practice. Considered objects of scientific interest, uncovered Indian bones were often sent to scholars or museums for further study.

Maria Pearson was horrified. She met with Governor Robert Ray to demand that the state government change its policies toward Indian remains. It was the beginning of a six-year battle that led to the passage of the Iowa Reburial Law of 1976—the first state law to protect Indian gravesites. Iowa also established the Indian Advisory Committee for the Office of the State Archaeology. For decades, Pearson served as the committee chair.

Pearson's campaign in Iowa brought attention to the repatriation movement, which called for museums to return bones and burial objects to the Indian tribes from which they were taken. A leading voice in the movement, Pearson asked in the *New York Times* in 1986, "If we allow . . . people to dig up my ancestors today, what is to stop them from doing it to you tomorrow?" Pearson's work on this issue was documented in the BBC documentary *Bones of Contention.*

Due in part to Pearson's efforts, President George H. W. Bush signed the Native American Graves Protection and Repatriation Act (NAGPRA) into law in 1990. It called for all Indian remains and related paraphernalia in museum collections to be returned to their tribes of origin. The act also set down guidelines for the treatment and study of newly uncovered bones.

Maria Pearson remained active in a wide array of Indian causes and served as the national president of the Governors' Interstate Indian Council from 1992 to 1994. She died on May 24, 2003, at the age of 70.

Further Reading/Resources
Fine-Dare, Kathleen S. *Grave Injustice: The American Indian Repatriation Movement and NAGPRA.* Lincoln: University of Nebraska Press, 2002.

Lewis, Peter H. "Indian Bones: Balancing Research Goals and Tribes' Rights." *New York Times,* 20 May 1986, sec. C, p. 3.

Peck, Danielle, and Alex Seabourne, producers. *Bones of Contention.* Princeton, N.J.: Films for the Humanities & Sciences. VHS, 49 min., 1995.

Pease, Janine (Janine Pease Pretty on Top, Janine Windy Boy)
(1949–) *Crow educator, activist*

Renowned educator Janine Pease was born in 1949 on the Colville Indian Reservation in Washington.

Both of her parents were teachers. They instilled in her at an early age a respect for learning and scholarship. From the example of her father, who was a Crow Indian, she also came to see education as a force that could better the lives of Indians without necessarily threatening their native cultures.

Janine Pease attended Central Washington University, where she earned dual bachelor's degrees in sociology and anthropology in 1970. She worked for a year as a counselor at the Navajo Community College before becoming the director of the Upward Bound program at Big Bend Community College in Moses Lake, Washington, in 1972. Three years later she decided to move to the Crow Indian Reservation in Montana, where she had spent several summers as a child. There she worked for the Crow tribe as a promoter of adult education.

Pease married in 1975 (temporarily taking her husband's last name Windy Boy) and had two children, Roses and Vernon. She gave up her job to care for her family but was left destitute after she and her husband divorced in 1979. A single mother with no income, she was forced to go on welfare, an experience that would later make her particularly sensitive to struggles of the poor. After two years on public assistance, Pease finally found a job at Eastern Montana College, where she helped Native American graduates find jobs.

In 1982, Pease, with the support of the Crow tribe, launched a new enterprise. Given only an abandoned house and $50,000, she took on the challenge of establishing a college for Crow students. Pease was named the school's president and chief executive officer but in its early years she took on any task that needed doing. In addition to teaching, she drove students to and from school and even cleaned classrooms and mopped floors when necessary. Within a decade, her hard work had helped to create Little Big Horn College, a fully accredited two-year college that enrolls nearly 300 students a year. The college also developed a program to train Crow scientists with Montana State University, from which Pease earned a doctorate in education in 1994.

Pease has also devoted her energy and expertise to a number of Indian rights issues. During the mid-1980s, she was the lead plaintiff in *Windy Boy* (Pease's married name) *v. Bighorn County,* in which she accused the county of discriminating against Indians in its voter registration policies. The landmark case forced the county to revise a redistricting plan that would have made Crow children ineligible to attend public school.

Pease has received many honors for her work in furthering educational opportunities for Native Americans. The National Indian Education Association named her their 1990 Educator of the Year, and President Bill Clinton appointed her to the National Advisory Committee of Indian Education in 1994. In the same year, she was awarded a MacArthur Fellowship, popularly known as a "genius grant." Pease has also served as a trustee of the National Museum of the American Indian in Washington, D.C., and of the Native American College Fund, a non-profit organization that offers scholarships to Indian youths.

In 2000, Pease left her post at Little Big Horn College and established a consulting firm specializing in program development at tribal colleges and universities. Since 2003, she has served as the vice president for American Indian Affairs at Rocky Mountain College in Billings, Montana. Working in this capacity, Pease plans to expand the institution's educational partnerships with tribal colleges throughout the state. Pease also serves on the Montana Board of Regents, which oversees the state's university system.

Further Reading

Kasee, Cynthia R. "Jeanine Pease-Windy Boy." In *Notable Native Americans,* edited by Sharon J. Malinowski, 322–323. Detroit: Gale Research, 1995.

Nelson, Douglas, and Jeremy Johnston. "Janine Pease Pretty-on-Top." *The New Warriors,* edited by R. David Edmunds, 281–298. Lincoln: University of Nebraska Press, 2001.

Peña, Tonita (Quah Ah)
(1893–1949)   *San Ildefonso Pueblo painter*

The first Native American woman to gain fame as a painter, Maria Antonia Peña (nicknamed

"Tonita") was born on May 10, 1893, at San Ildefonso Pueblo in what is now north-central New Mexico. According to Pueblo custom, when she was four years old she was given an Indian name—Quah Ah, which has been translated as "little bead" and "pink shell."

Although she was raised in the traditions of the Pueblo, as a child she was baptized and sent to the San Ildefonso Indian day school, which she attended until 1905. In that year, Tonita's mother and younger sister died from influenza. Unable to rear Tonita and her older sister and brother by himself, her father sent Tonita to live with her maternal aunt, Martina Montoya, in Cochiti Pueblo. The Pueblo at Cochiti had different customs and spoke a different language from those at

Tonita Peña was renowned in the Southwest for her paintings.
(Photo by T. Harmon Parkhurst, Courtesy Palace of the Governors [MNM/DCA], Neg. no. 46988)

San Ildefonso. (While all the Pueblo groups had similarities, they represented a number of different tribes, such as Tewa, Zuni, and Hopi.) To help her niece feel comfortable to her new setting, Montoya shared her techniques for making pottery with Tonita. Montoya was highly respected among the Pueblo for her skills. Famed San Ildefonso potter MARIA MARTINEZ once said that Montoya was the greatest Pueblo potter of all.

As a young teenager, Peña was sent to St. Catherine's Indian School in Santa Fe. There she was introduced to a different art form—watercolor painting. A teacher gave her a set of watercolors and thick paper, which Peña used to paint Pueblo pottery designs and scenes of Pueblo life. While still a student, she sold several of her works to her teacher for pocket money.

In 1908, 15-year-old Peña returned to Cochiti to marry Juan Rosario Chavez. The union was arranged by her aging aunt and uncle, who wanted to be sure Peña would be taken care of after their death. The Chavezes had two children, Richard and Helia, before Juan died in 1912. Peña briefly returned to St. Catherine's but once again left the school to marry Felipe Herrera in 1913. Seven years later, she gave birth to Hilario J. Herrera, who as an adult would become well known as an artist working under the name Joe H. Herrera. Two months after the boy was born, Tonita Herrera was left widowed when Felipe was killed in a mining accident. She then married her third and final husband, Epitacio Arquero, a Cochiti farmer who became a leader in tribal politics in the 1940s and 1950s. With Arquero, Tonita had five more children.

During her marriages to Herrera and Arquero, Peña returned to painting. She was encouraged by Edgar Lee Hewitt, a professor of archaeology at the University of New Mexico. Beginning in 1909, Hewett supervised the excavation of the ancient Indian site of Frijoles Canyon. He hired several San Ildefonso Pueblo to work on the dig and was fascinated by the drawings the Pueblo laborers made of the designs found on the old pottery shards they unearthed. Hewitt gave the men watercolors and commissioned them to paint pictures of Pueblo ceremonies and daily life. When the professor learned of Tonita Peña's interest in painting, he also became her patron.

A school of watercolorists, called the San Ildefonso Group, emerged with Hewitt's encouragement. This group of artists—which in addition to Peña, included her cousin Romando Vigil, Fred Kabotie, and Awa Tsireh—were among the first Indians to paint on paper and canvas. Perhaps because of Hewitt's influence, most of their works were painted in a common style and dealt with similar subject matter. They usually featured highly detailed, linear figures of Pueblo, frequently dressed in ritual garb, set against a stark white background. The only woman among the San Ildefonso Group, Peña concentrated on female figures. As well as being works of art, her paintings are also visual documents of the roles and duties of women in traditional Pueblo society.

During the 1920s, Peña found customers for her paintings among the tourists who visited the city square in the center of Santa Fe. Art lovers were soon clamoring to buy Peña watercolors and those of the other artists of the San Ildefonso Group. As Peña's reputation grew, her works were sold in galleries to noted collectors and museums. In the early 1930s, she was commissioned by the federal government to help paint a series of murals for the Santa Fe Indian School. Peña also joined the faculty of the school, where she taught Indian students how to mold and paint pottery.

Although she was well respected in the art world of the Southwest, Peña was sometimes treated with contempt among her own people. Traditionally, Pueblo women were expected to devote themselves to raising children and managing their family's household. Although she reared eight children and maintained a happy marriage with Arquero for more than 25 years, some Pueblo felt that Peña was shirking her domestic duties by working outside the home. That Peña was fairly well paid for her work probably also fueled their resentment. Still others took exception to her paintings of Pueblo ceremonies, which they claimed depicted rites that

should not be shared with non-Indians. On this charge, Arquero came to his wife's defense. He reminded his people that white tourists could witness Pueblo ceremonies while visiting their reservations, so Peña's paintings were hardly giving away any secrets.

By the time of Peña's death on May 1, 1949, many Native American artists, female and male, had adopted paints and canvas as their favorite medium. Among them was PABLITA VELARDE, who credited Peña's example with making her own career possible. She once said that she respected Peña for being a "good wife like a good woman" but also admired the "little bit of rebellion" in her mentor. Velarde explained, "She always wanted to show the men that not only a man can paint a good picture, and she did it."

Further Reading

Gray, Samuel L. *Tonita Peña: Quah Ah.* Albuquerque, N.Mex.: Avanyu Publishing, 1990.
Jantzer-White, Marilee. "Tonita Peña (Quah Ah), Pueblo Painter: Asserting Identity through Continuity and Change." *American Indian Quarterly,* June 1994, pp. 369–383.

Peterson, Helen
(1915–2000) *Cheyenne-Lakota Sioux activist*

A distinguished leader in the Pan-Indian Movement, Helen White Peterson was born on the Pine Ridge Indian Reservation in South Dakota on August, 3, 1915. Although of Cheyenne heritage, she was enrolled as a member of the Oglala band of the Lakota Sioux. When Helen was a young girl, her grandmother took a special interest in teaching her about the traditions and culture of the Sioux.

After graduating from a local public high school, Peterson attended Chadron State Teachers College in Nebraska before earning her bachelor's degree in education from Colorado State College. She took a job as secretary to the college's education department, but soon became involved in Indian rights organizations in Denver. She was eventually named the director of the Rocky Mountain Council of

Inter-American Affairs. Through her involvement in the council, she traveled to Cuzco, Peru, to serve as an adviser to the U.S. delegation at the 1949 Inter-American Indian Conference.

In 1948, Peterson founded the city of Denver's Mayor's Commission on Human Relations (later called the Denver Commission on Community Relations). In the same year she joined the National Congress of American Indians (NCAI). This national organization had been founded in 1944 by Indian leaders from more than 100 tribes. Its goals included advancing Indian rights, preserving Indian cultures, and maintaining the land bases of tribal groups. The formation of NCAI was part of a movement toward Pan-Indianism. Advocates of Pan-Indianism believed that Indians from different tribes were facing similar problems, such as discrimination, poverty, and unjust treatment from the U.S. government. Rather than fighting these destructive forces alone, Pan-Indian proponents believed that Indians of different tribes should unite and wage their battles together.

Peterson was named the executive director of the NCAI in 1953, a year that marked the appearance of a grave threat to Indian nations. Congress passed a resolution stating its intention to dissolve its financial and legal responsibilities established by treaties with many Indian groups. The government maintained that its relationship with Indians should be the same as its relationship with any other American citizens. But most Indians leaders opposed this policy, which was known as termination. They saw that, without government funds for education, health care, and housing, terminated tribes would likely become even more impoverished.

With Peterson as its leader, the NCAI helped to organize the American Indian Charter Conference in Chicago in 1961. Attracting some 500 representatives of 67 tribes, it was the largest multicultural gathering in decades. The members of the conference issued a manifesto—the Declaration of Indian Purpose—in which they demanded the government grant Indian leaders a greater involvement in the formation of its policies. The declaration also condemned termination as "the greatest threat to

Indian survival since the military campaigns of the 1800s." This attack persuaded U.S. officials to reexamine the policy, which was eventually abandoned. The Chicago conference also had a lasting effect on American Indian leadership. By demonstrating the influence Indians of different tribes could have by working together, it helped usher in an new era of Indian activism that culminated in the Indian rights movement of the late 1960s and early 1970s.

Peterson left her post with the NCAI in 1961 and returned to Denver. After continuing her work with the Denver Commission on Community Relations, she joined the staff of the Bureau of Indian Affairs (BIA)—the agency of the U.S. government charged with overseeing its official dealings with Indians. In 1970, she became the first female assistant to the commissioner of Indian affairs. Before retiring in 1985, Peterson also worked in the BIA office in Portland, Oregon. There, she established the Church of the Four Winds, an ecumenical ministry for urban Indians.

Throughout her career, Peterson lectured widely on Indian rights issues and received many honors and awards. She was named an "Outstanding American Indian Citizen" at the 1968 American Indian Exposition, given a Distinguished Service Award by Columbia University, and granted an honorary doctorate from Chadron State Teachers College. On July 10, 2000, Helen Peterson died in Vancouver, Washington, at the age of 84.

Further Reading

Zimmerman, Karen P. "Helen Peterson." In *Notable Native Americans,* edited by Sharon J. Malinowski, 328–329. Detroit: Gale Research, 1995.

Picotte, Susan La Flesche
See LA FLESCHE, SUSAN

Pictou, Anna Mae
See AQUASH, ANNA MAE

Piestewa, Lori (Kocha-Hon-Mana)
(1979–2003) *Hopi soldier*

The first Native American female U.S. soldier to die in combat, Lori Ann Piestewa was born on December 14, 1979, in Tuba City, an Arizona town on the Navajo Indian Reservation. Her father was a Hopi, and her mother was of Mexican heritage. As a baby, Piestewa was given the Hopi name Kocha-Hon-Mana, meaning White Bear Girl.

Outgoing and strongwilled, Piestewa was a natural athlete, playing on every sports team she could join. While attending Tuba City High School, she was named the commanding officer of its junior ROTC program. Piestewa wanted to go on to college but did not have money to pay tuition. Finding herself pregnant at 17, she married her boyfriend. The couple had two children, Brandon and Carla, before they divorced.

A single mother living with her parents, Piestewa decided to join the U.S. Army. Her family had a history with the military. Her father served in the Vietnam War, and her grandfather served in World War II. But Piestewa's main motivation for entering the army was to build a career and make a steady income for her children.

Leaving Brandon and Carla behind with her parents, Piestewa was stationed at Fort Bliss military base in Texas in October 2001. There, she tracked supplies and performed other clerical work. Her roommate, Jessica Lynch from West Virginia, quickly became a close friend. When they learned they were being deployed to Iraq, each made a promise to take care of the other's family if something happened to her.

Piestewa arrived in Iraq as a Private First Class with the 507th Maintenance Company, which was made up of repairmen, clerks, cooks, and other service personnel. On the third day of the Iraq War, she was driving a Humvee toward the rear of a large convoy headed for Baghdad. Traveling with slow supply trucks, her part of the convoy, made up of a few dozen vehicles, became separated from the main group.

On the early morning of March 23, 2003, the mini-convoy came upon Nasiriyah in southern Iraq. It was clear they had taken a wrong turn, leading them headlong into a heavily fortified city. Taken off guard, the Iraq army did not attack the U.S. vehicles as they drove through. But on the other side of the city, the officers with the mini-convoy made a disturbing discovery—the only way out of the area was backtrack on the same road, taking them into Nasiriyah a second time.

Now the Iraq troops were ready. Almost immediately, the vehicles were bombarded with machine-gun fire and rocket-propelled grenades. Still at the rear, Piestewa carefully guided her Humvee, managing to avoid hitting the piles of debris Iraqi soldiers had set in the road as blockades. According to her fellow troops, she remained calm even after two bullets came through a side window, narrowly missing her head.

In front of her, a U.S. truck jackknifed, causing her to swerve to avoid hitting it. At the same time, a grenade hit the Humvee. The vehicle crashed into the truck, killing three soldiers onboard. Piestewa and Lynch survived but were severely injured. Both were taken as prisoners of war.

For days, the Hopi and Navajo (Dineh) gathered for vigils to pray for Piestewa. On April 1, they were heartened by the news that Lynch had been found alive during a raid by Special Forces. But three days later, they learned that Piestewa had not been so lucky. Her body was discovered in a mass grave. After being taken prisoner, she was sent to hospital, where she died of her injuries. She was one of 11 soldiers killed during and after the Nasiriyah battle.

After her death, Piestewa was awarded the Purple Heart and the Prisoner of War Medal and promoted to the rank of Specialist. The state of Arizona honored her by renaming Squaw's Peak as Piestewa Peak. Arizona also now hosts the annual Lori Piestewa National Native American Games, a competition for Native American amateur athletes.

Once Lynch recovered from her injuries, she made good on her promise to Piestewa. She arranged for the television series "Extreme Make-over: Home Edition" to build a new house for Piestewa's family. She also established the Jessica

Lynch Foundation, which collects funds to send the children of veterans, including Piestewa's children, to college. Lynch was hailed in the press as a hero after the Nasiriyah attack, although she maintains she was only a survivor. In her words, "Lori is the real hero."

Further Reading

Davidson, Osha Gray. "A Wrong Turn in the Desert." *Rolling Stone,* 27 May 2004. Available online. URL: http://www.oshadavidson.com/Piestewa.htm. Downloaded on March 23, 2006.

Younge, Gary. "What about Private Lori?" *Guardian,* 10 April 2003. Available online. URL: http://www.guardian.co.uk/Iraq/Story/0,2763,933586,00.html. Downloaded on March 24, 2006.

Pitseolak (Pitseolak Ashoona)
(1904–1983) *Inuit printmaker*

Known for the strong personal statements of her drawings and prints, Pitseolak (meaning "sea pigeon" in Inuit) was a native of Nottingham Island in Hudson Bay in north-central Canada. Born in 1904, she was reared by her parents, Ottochie and Timangiak, in the traditional Inuit manner. With the seasons, her family traveled from camp to camp, moving to wherever the best hunting and fishing could be found. From her mother, as a girl she learned to construct kayaks and tents and sew clothing from the skins of caribous, seals, and walrus, which her father hunted using only a bow and arrow.

When Pitseolak was a child, few non-Indians lived among the Inuit of Hudson Bay. In her 1971 autobiography *Pitseolak: Pictures out of My Life,* she noted that her earliest memory was of a trip with her father to buy a wooden boat from white traders. During the expedition, she saw for the first time white people and the wooden houses in which they lived, an encounter with the unfamiliar that left the little girl frightened. Soon, however, whites became a common sight in her world. With them they brought many commercial trade goods that made life much easier in the Inuit's harsh Arctic environment. But they also introduced the Inuit to a trade-and-barter economy, which threatened their traditional ways, and to new diseases against which most Inuit had no natural immunities.

As a young woman, Pitseolak married a successful hunter named Ashoona. The couple had 17 children, several of whom died in childhood during epidemics. During one hunting trip, Ashoona himself fell victim to disease and died. Faced with raising her children alone, Pitseolak moved her family to the remote settlement of Cape Dorset on Baffin Island. Unable to find work, she and her children were plunged into poverty. As she recalled in her autobiography, "for a long time, we were very poor and often we were hungry."

The family finally found relief with the arrival of Canadian artist and writer James A. Houston in Cape Dorset in 1957. During the late 1940s, Houston began traveling among Inuit communities in northern Canada and learned firsthand about their centuries-old tradition of carving stone and bone into simple, elegant sculptures. Impressed by these works, he took examples to Montreal, where they were exhibited to great acclaim at the Canadian Handicraft Guild, an organization dedicated to promoting native Canadian arts and crafts.

Printmaker Pitseolak created scenes of Inuit life. *(Pitseolak Ashoona,* 1968, Photo by/Gift of Norman E. Hallendy, McMichael Canadian Art Collection Archives)

Hired first by the guild and later by the Canadian government, Houston spent much of the late 1950s and early 1960s in Cape Dorset, where he encouraged the Native artists there to make carvings for sale. Houston also introduced the Cape Dorset Inuit to new styles of art—such as drawing on paper and printmaking—that they quickly made their own.

After Houston settled at Cape Dorset, Pitseolak was able to make a modest living by selling him parkas she sewed and decorated with embroidery. The work was difficult, however, so when other Inuit artisans began selling small drawings to Houston, she decided to try her hand at this new art form. In 1959, she showed Houston her first effort—four small drawings of "little monsters" that she later described as "funny-looking." Houston paid her twenty dollars for the work, but suggested she try drawing pictures of the "old ways"—meaning scenes of traditional Inuit life and customs that were threatened by the growing presence of non-Indians in the region.

Sifting through her memories, Pitseolak began drawing pictures—often as many as four in a single morning—based on "the things we did long ago before there were many white men." Her subjects included such everyday events as a smiling fisherman carrying home his catch, a crowd of children playing a game, a woman bringing a gift of fresh meat to a neighbor, and a team of men working together to build an igloo.

Although Pitseolak's style is less exacting than that of other Inuit artists, the very roughness of her drawings lend them a charm and energy that quickly attracted a following among connoisseurs of native art. Prints made from her drawings by an Inuit artists' cooperative in Cape Dorset have been exhibited throughout the world, and several are in the permanent collection of the National Gallery of Canada. Owing to the popularity of her work, she was the subject of two documentaries—*The Way We Live Today* and *Spirits and Monsters*—and in 1974 received the Order of Canada, that country's highest honor for civilians.

Although drawing began only as a means of putting food on her family's table, Pitseolak almost immediately embraced her art as a way of recording the story of her own life and that of her people. At the conclusion of her autobiography, she explained her passion for her work: "To make prints is not easy. You must think first and this is hard to do. But I'm happy making prints. . . . I shall make them as long as I am well. If I can, I'll make them even after I am dead." Following a long period of illness through which she continued to draw, Pitseolak died on May 28, 1983, leaving behind a legacy of nearly 7,000 drawings and 200 prints.

Further Reading

Blodgett, Jean. *In Cape Dorset We Do It This Way: Three Decades of Inuit Printmaking.* Kleinburg, Ontario: McMichael Canadian Art Collection, 1991.

Pitseolak. *Pitseolak: Pictures out of My Life,* edited by Dorothy Eber. 2nd ed. Montreal: McGill-Queen's University Press, 2004.

Roch, Ernst, ed. *Arts of the Eskimo: Prints.* Barre, Mass.: Barre, 1975.

Pocahontas (Matoaba, Rebecca Rolfe)
(ca. 1596–1617)   *Powhatan peacemaker*

Perhaps the best known Native American in history, Pocahontas today remains something of a mystery. The recorded details of her life are few, and the truth of those that do exist is open to question. Further obscuring her image are the legends that have grown up around her. Nearly four centuries of myth-making about who she was and what she represented challenge efforts to bring the real Pocahontas fully into focus.

Born in about 1596, Pocahontas was the favorite daughter of Powhatan, a powerful Indian leader who led a confederation of some 30 tribes in the Chesapeake Bay area of what is now eastern Virginia. Her real name was Matoaba, which meant "playful." Pocahontas was a nickname that is most often translated as "frolicsome."

The only sources about Pocahontas's early years are the journals and other writings left by the English settlers of Jamestown. The first permanent English settlement in North America, Jamestown was founded in May 1607 in the middle of Powhatan's realm. The settlement was named after the English monarch, King James I, who licensed the Virginia Company to explore eastern North America and eventually exploit the continent's ample natural resources.

One of the leaders of Jamestown was Captain John Smith, whose writings include the first appearance of Pocahontas in the historical record. In December 1607, Smith was heading an exploratory expedition along the Chickahominy River. Suspicious of these newcomers in Powhatan's lands, a band of Indian warriors attacked the party, captured Smith, and led him to their chief. At Powhatan's village, Smith and two hundred warriors were treated to a great banquet. Powhatan then ordered his minions to place two large blocks of stone in front of him. At the chief's command, warriors forced Smith to kneel before the stones and lay his cheek on top of them. Seemingly intent on beating the Englishman to death, the warriors lifted their clubs over his head. According to Smith, his execution was then interrupted by Pocahontas, who was about 11 years old at the time. In his 1624 account of the event, he wrote (referring to himself in the third person): "Pocahontas the Kings dearest daughter, when no intreaty could prevaile, got his head in her armes, and laid her owne upon him to saue him from death." Smith concluded that, because of the girl's appeal on his behalf, Powhatan stopped the execution and allowed his prisoner to go free.

One of the most frequently told anecdotes in American history, the story of Smith's rescue by Pocahontas is probably more fiction than fact. Smith wrote several accounts of his capture by Powhatan. The earliest do not even mention Pocahontas—a peculiar omission if she in fact had saved his life. He first added Pocahontas to the tale nearly a decade after the incident—initially in

1616 in a letter to the English queen Anne and again in 1624 in his book *Generalle Historie of Virginia*. By this time, Pocahontas was a celebrity in England. Well known as a blowhard and a self-promoter, Smith may have made up or embellished the dramatic story of his first meeting with the famous Indian woman to add a little sparkle to his own reputation as an adventurer.

If the incident actually did occur, Smith may have misinterpreted the actions of Powhatan and Pocahontas. Some anthropologists have suggested that Smith's ordeal was an initiation ceremony through which the Powhatan Indians adopted outsiders into their tribes. According to this theory, Pocahontas's "rescue" was carefully staged by the Powhatans. By being saved symbolically by Powhatan's daughter, Smith became, in the Indians' eyes, Powhatan's son.

Even if Pocahontas was not Smith's "savior" as he claimed, she most likely did play a crucial role in helping Smith and the other Englishmen at Jamestown survive in their new surroundings. Most of the original settlers at Jamestown were gentlemen who hoped to make a quick profit from their adventure. Undisciplined and unaccustomed to menial labor, they failed to plant crops. Starvation and disease had claimed the lives of two-thirds of the 105 settlers by January 1608. That month the Powhatans began to deliver food to the foundering colony. According to Smith, these much-needed supplies were often delivered by Pocahontas, whom he praised for her "wit and spirit."

Other settlers confirmed that she was curious and vivacious by nature. William Strachey, the official historian of Jamestown, called her a "well featured but wanton [meaning frisky] young girle." He recorded watching her turn cartwheels in the nude through the middle of her village. (Although Strachey seemed somewhat shocked by her behavior, all Powhatan children probably wore little or no clothing in warm weather.)

In addition to bringing food to Jamestown, Pocahontas probably also acted as her father's official ambassador in some of his early dealings with the settlers. In May 1608, she traveled to Jamestown and successfully negotiated the release of seven Powhatan, whom the English had taken captive. Despite this, however, relations between the Indians and the English grew tense. With good reason, Powhatan feared that the settlers wanted to take over his land. In order to drive them out, he declared he would no longer trade with the settlers, who had grown dependent on food supplied by the Powhatans. According to Smith, Powhatan also plotted to kill him and some of his men. In his *Generalle Historie,* Smith claimed that Pocahontas warned the settlers of the attack and thus saved his life a second time: "Pocahontas [Powhatan's] dearest jewell and daughter, in that darke night came through the irksome woods, and told our Captaine . . . if we would live, shee wished us presently to be gone." The hostilities between the Powhatans and the English broke out into full-scale warfare in 1610. Pocahontas then stopped visiting Jamestown, and according to Strachey, she married a warrior named Kocoum.

Pocahontas did not encounter the English again until the spring of 1613. While visiting relatives at a village along the Potomac River, she was approached by an Englishman named Samuel Argall. John Smith had returned to England in 1609, and in his absence, Argall had assumed most of Smith's leadership duties. Offering Pocahontas various gifts, Argall lured her onto an English ship. There he took her hostage to use as a pawn in peace negotiations with her father.

According to English sources, the settlers agreed to return Pocahontas if Powhatan surrendered guns and swords that he had earlier obtained through trade with the English. Powhatan refused, and angered by her father's indifference to her well-being, Pocahontas refused to speak with Powhatan diplomats. Thomas Dale, who was charged with caring for the hostage, claimed that Pocahontas then decided to "dwell with the English men, who loved her." Dale's claim that Pocahontas chose to stay in Jamestown is questionable. Just as possible, the English, though disappointed in their failed attempt

This 1616 engraving is the only image made of Pocahontas during her lifetime (detail shown here).
(Virginia Historical Society, Richmond, Virginia)

to ransom her, still saw her as a convenient tool toward achieving their ends.

Pocahontas was taken to live in Jamestown, where she remained for a year. During that time, she was taught English and schooled in white customs. She was also instructed in Christianity. Claiming she had willfully converted to Anglicanism, Reverend Alexander Whitaker baptized her and gave the Christian name "Rebecca." The conversion and baptism of Pocahontas had great symbolic importance to the English. They morally justified their invasion of North America as an effort to save the souls of the "heathen" natives there. By converting the daughter of a powerful Indian chief, the residents of Jamestown could prove to themselves and to their king that they were making inroads in this mission.

Pocahontas's conversion was also necessary after her betrothal to John Rolfe, a devout settler who pioneered the farming of tobacco in Jamestown. Although Pocahontas and Rolfe may have had affection for one another, both probably entered the marriage in order to forge an alliance between their peoples. Tellingly, Rolfe asked first the governor of the Virginia colony and then Powhatan for permission to marry Pocahontas. The wedding, held on April 5, 1614, thus functioned almost as the signing of a treaty. If the marriage was purely diplomatic, it was certainly a success. Ushering in what is now know as the "Peace of Pocahontas," the wedding of Pocahontas and Rolfe ended years of skirmishes among the Powhatans and the English. The two groups would remain at peace for the rest of Pocahontas's life.

The Virginia Company recognized another possible benefit from the union of Rolfe and Pocahontas. After Pocahontas gave birth to a son, Thomas, in 1615, the corporation invited the family to tour England. Desperate to generate financial support for its efforts to colonize North America, the Virginia Company saw the Rolfes as an advertisement that could attract attention and much-needed funds to their enterprise.

Pocahontas and her family arrived in England in June 1616. She quickly caused a sensation among the British elite. As the Virginia Company had expected, people in highest social circles were curious to see an actual Indian, particularly one who had been billed as a "princess." Even King James granted an audience to the young woman. Pocahontas apparently impressed those lucky enough to meet her. Dubbed "la belle sauvage" ("the beautiful savage"), she was said by one witness to "carr[y] herself as the daughter of a King, and was accordingly respected . . . [by] persons of Honor."

During her stay in England, Pocahontas was visited by John Smith, whom she had not seen for nine years. He later wrote that "after a modest salutation, without a word she turned about, obscured her face, as not seeming well contented," then retired for several hours before she was ready to face him. Smith explained that she was in distress because she had believed he was dead. Some have interpreted her reaction as evidence that she was in love with Smith and regretted her marriage as soon as she saw that Smith was still alive. But considering that her acts of kindness toward Smith had been rewarded with her kidnapping, she possibly was overcome by fury at her former friend.

In spring 1617, Pocahontas, her husband, and her son set sail for home. After a few days, however, their ship docked at Gravesend, England because Pocahontas was in ill health. On March 21, Pocahontas died at the age of about 21. She had probably fallen victim to a European disease, then unknown in North America, to which she had not yet developed a natural immunity.

Leaving Thomas in the care of an uncle in England, John Rolfe returned to Virginia and informed Powhatan of his daughter's death. Powhatan soon also died, as did Rolfe in 1622. In the same year, Opechancanough, the new leader of the Powhatan confederacy, ended the Peace of Pocahontas with a devastating attack that left a quarter of the Virginia colonists dead. The English retaliated with the aim of exterminating the Powhatan people. The warfare continued for many years, but in the end, undermanned and underarmed, the Indians were defeated. If Pocahontas had lived to be an old woman, she would have seen her ancestral lands controlled by the leaders of a prosperous Virginia colony. Among them would have been her own son. In 1640, Thomas Rolfe came back to Virginia, where he added a fortune made by growing tobacco to his inherited wealth. Many prominent families in Virginia today trace their bloodline back to Thomas Rolfe and proudly proclaim Pocahontas as an ancestor.

Pocahontas also lived on in the imaginations of artists, writers, and other myth-makers. Particularly in the 19th century, as stories about her gained popularity, she came to be seen as the ancestor of all Americans. Just as George Washington was hailed as the "father of his country," Pocahontas was represented as America's mother.

This image of Pocahontas proved useful to Americans in power as the boundaries of the United States moved westward. It helped justify the further seizure of Indian lands that made the growth of the nation possible. Pocahontas's supposed role as a savior of the early colonists and a Christian convert eager to adopt a European language and customs made her a model Indian in the minds of many Americans. In contrast to Pocahontas's "good" Indian were the "bad" Indians who fought at all costs to retain their lands and culture. The image of Pocahontas thus served well as a propaganda tool for Americans who wanted to take control of Indian territory.

Like SACAGAWEA, the other prominent Indian woman icon, Pocahontas also became an object of fantasy. The only surviving image of Pocahontas made during her lifetime is a 1616 engraved portrait. Although she is dressed in dignified European garb, her face appears to have the dark skin and features of a Powhatan. Many 19th-century depictions of Pocahontas, however, give her Caucasian features and often even creamy white skin. Yet her attire tends to be a non-Indian conception of Indian clothing—a buckskin dress and a feathered headdress or headband. In many depictions, Pocahontas is shown solely as a sensual being, which reflected the stereotype of Indian women as sexually loose and uninhibited. Images of a barebreasted Pocahontas lying over the prostrate body of the captive John Smith were prevalent. Popular novels and plays of the 19th and 20th centuries, likewise, have depicted Pocahontas and Smith's relationship if not as sexual, then at least as romantic. As recently as 2005, the movie *The New World* promoted this view. In the film, Pocahontas once again is a shapely young woman in love with a dashing John Smith rather than the spirited and curious Powhatan girl of the historical record.

Further Reading

Allen, Paula Gunn. *Pocahontas: Medicine Woman, Spy, Entrepreneur, Diplomat.* San Francisco, Calif.: HarperSanFrancisco, 2003.

Barbour, Philip L. *Pocahontas and Her World.* Boston: Houghton Mifflin, 1970.

Price, David. *Love and Hate in Jamestown: John Smith, Pocahontas, and the Heart of a New Nation.* New York: Knopf, 2003.

Rountree, Helen C. *Pocahontas's People: The Powhatan Indians of Virginia through Four Centuries.* Norman: University of Oklahoma Press, 1990.

Smith, John. *Captain John Smith's History of Virginia.* Indianapolis, Ind.: Bobbs-Merrill, 1970.

Townsend, Camilla. *Pocahontas and the Powhatan Dilemma.* New York: Hill and Wang, 2004.

Pretty-Shield
(ca. 1858–ca. 1938)   *Crow autobiographer*

In 1932, a 74-year-old Crow woman named Pretty-Shield told her life story to Frank B. Linderman, a writer and adventurer who had spent much of his life among the Indians of the Plains. The result of their conversations was *Pretty-Shield* (1932), one of the few accounts of pre-reservation days left by an Indian woman.

Named by her grandfather after his most prized possession, Pretty-Shield was born in about 1858 in what is now southeastern Montana. At the time, white trappers and traders were only occasional visitors to Crow territory. As Pretty-Shield recalled, they were not always welcome. At age six, she had her first encounter with whites when three trappers asked the chief of her camp if they could live with the Indians. The chief refused, and the trappers were sent on their way.

When Pretty-Shield was a child, the Crows were a mobile people, traveling from camp to camp with the seasons, following the massive herds of wild buffalo that roamed through the Great Plains. Horses, which were brought to the Plains by whites in the 1700s, made this way of life possible. Pretty-Shield's grandmother had told her stories of the Crow's difficult existence before they had horses, and she considered herself lucky to have been born when the Crows were renowned horsemen and buffalo hunters. "Ahh, I came into a happy world," she told Linderman through a Crow interpreter. "There was always fat meat, glad singing, and much dancing in our villages. Our people's hearts were then as light as breath-feathers."

A fun-loving and witty woman, Pretty-Shield devoted much of her autobiography to recounting childhood games and diversions. She described playing with dolls and miniature tipis and enacting with her friends a play version of the Sun Dance, one of the most important Crow rituals. But she also depicts the Crow world as often dangerous. Noting that most Indians used to die from accidents or war, she explains how she nearly lost an eye when she accidentally fell on a digging stick she was using to uproot turnips and how she and her mother were almost captured by hostile Lakota. Although regarded as the source of supernatural powers, animals were also feared. Pretty-Shield recalled as a child watching a bear maul a woman

Pretty-Shield described the life of the Crow in her autobiography.
(Photo no. 7(VIII)425, K. Ross Toole Archives, University of Montana–Missoula)

to death. She herself was nearly killed in a buffalo stampede.

Wanting to satisfy Linderman's request for "a woman's story," Pretty-Shield also paid special attention to the role of women in Crow society in her autobiography. She explained that at 13, her father promised her to a young warrior named Goes-Ahead, who was already married to her older sister and would later become the husband of a younger sibling. Although she admitted that she did not love Goes-Ahead when they were married, she approved of the old Crow custom of arranged unions and claimed that "men and women were happier" with such marriages than those made for love.

Pretty-Shield also described the division of labor between the sexes in traditional Crow society. Men were responsible for hunting, warring, and caring for the horse herds. Women were charged with nearly every other task. As Pretty-Shield explained: "We women had our children to care for, meat to cook and to dry, robes to dress, skins to tan, clothes, lodges, and moccasins to make. Besides these things we not only pitched the lodges, but took them down and packed the horses and the travois, when we moved camp." In addition to this huge catalog of duties, women sometimes took on male roles as well. With great admiration, Pretty-Shield recounts the bravery of The-Other-Magpie, a Crow woman warrior who alongside U.S. soldiers fought the tribe's Sioux enemies at the 1877 Battle of Rosebud Creek.

In her autobiography, Pretty-Shield also took delight in challenging the historical assessments of several male leaders. She recalled a visit that Sitting Bull, the great Lakota Sioux chief and medicine man, paid to the Crows when she was about 30 years old. According to Pretty-Shield, Sitting Bull was berated by a Crow chief because the medicine man did not treat his followers well. She held that the Sioux were scared of Sitting Bull's supernatural powers, but they did not respect him as a leader. Pretty-Shield also blamed General George A. Custer for his soldiers' defeat at the hands of the Crows' Indian enemies in the Battle of Little Bighorn in 1876. Her husband Goes-Ahead fought with Custer's army but ran from the battlefield when it became apparent that they were outnumbered by the Sioux. Before the battle, Goes-Ahead had tried to warn Custer that they were outmanned, but according to Pretty-Shield, "too much drinking may have made that great soldier-chief foolish on that day when he died."

Despite the Crow military allegiance to the U. S. Army, the United States in the late 19th century forced the tribe onto a reservation composed of a fraction of its traditional homeland. Only when pressed by Linderman was Pretty-Shield willing to talk to him about life on the reservation. In one brief chapter at the end of her book, she describes the dual tragedy of the Crow confinement within reservation borders and the slaughter of the great buffalo herds by white hunters: "And then white men began to fence the plains so that we could not travel; and anyhow there was now little good in traveling, nothing to travel for. We began to stay in one place, and to grow lazy and sicker all the time." Traditionally dependent on the buffalo for their food, the Crow had to rely on meager government rations for survival. Weakened by malnutrition, many Crow fell victim to non-Indian diseases, such as smallpox. Almost as devastating as starvation and illness, they had to cope with the decimation of their culture. Women could no longer take pride in managing their families' movement from camp to camp; men could no longer earn respect as great hunters or warriors. In despair and disgust, some Crow turned to alcohol to relieve their pain. Pretty-Shield bitterly explained, "Our wise-ones became fools, and drank the white man's whiskey . . . Our old men used to be different; even our children were different when the buffalo were here."

Throughout her narrative, Pretty-Shield frequently paused to speculate on the future of the Crow. At the time she spoke with Linderman, she was raising the children of her two deceased daughters. She agreed to tell her story to the white man in part because her own grandchildren had little interest in the traditional ways of her tribe. Although a lively and confident woman even in her old age, Pretty-Shield admitted to Linderman a sense of desperation born of the great changes she had witnessed in her people. "I hope that I can save my grandchildren," she confided. "But times have changed so fast that they have left me behind. . . . Ours was a different world before the buffalo went away, and I belong to that other world."

Further Reading

Linderman, Frank B. *Pretty-Shield: Medicine Woman of the Crows.* 1932. Reprint, Lincoln: University of Nebraska Press, 1972.

Pretty Shield Foundation. Available online. URL: http://www.prettyshield.com. Downloaded on December 8, 2005.

Snell, Alma Hogan. *Grandmother's Grandchild.* Edited by Becky Matthews. Lincoln: University of Nebraska Press, 2000.

 **Princess Watahwaso**
See NICOLAR, LUCY

Qoyawayma, Polingaysi (Elizabeth Q. White)
(1892–1990)   *Hopi educator, autobiographer, potter*

Renowned Hopi educator Polingaysi Qoyawayma pioneered bicultural and bilingual education nearly fifty years before it became widespread in Indian schools. Born in 1892, she was raised in the Second Mesa village of Oraibi on the Hopi Indian Reservation in present-day northern Arizona. Her father Qoyawayma and mother Sevenka were cultural conservatives who brought up their children to revere and observe Hopi traditions. According to Hopi custom, Polingaysi (meaning "butterfly sitting among the flowers in the breeze") received her name during a ceremony held soon after her birth.

In her autobiography *No Turning Back* (1964), Qoyawayma describes her introduction into the difficult life of the Hopi. As a young girl, she spent most of her time playing, but she also watched her mother and other Hopi women laboring constantly to gather and prepare food and to keep a home for their family. She remembers, too, the bitter hunger of her people during the winter when the fall harvest of corn had not been plentiful and their nearly unendurable thirst when their spring dried up during periods of drought.

Although her father was a traditionalist, he worked for H. R. Voth, a Mennonite missionary who had come to Oraibi to convert the residents to Christianity. Polingaysi sometimes accompanied Qoyawayma to the religious services Voth held near the village. She enjoyed the church music and learned to sing several hymns, although she did not understand the words because she knew no English.

Soon after Voth's arrival, the missionary began building a school, which a progressive Hopi leader promised that the village's children would attend. Most traditionalists, however, refused to let their children go to the school. Many assumed that the big building was a jail and saw no reason that their children should be locked inside it all day long. Voth turned to the Hopi's neighbors and traditional enemies, the Navajo, for help. He and a crew of Navajo policemen began to go door-to-door to round up truants. Traditional Hopi parents were angered by their actions but feared any physical retaliation might bring the U.S. Army into the fray. Instead they adopted a policy of passive resistance. Whenever Voth went searching for students, parents hid their children. Polingaysi remembered nearly smothering under a sheepskin her mother once used to conceal her from the police.

In time most of Polingaysi's friends had been captured and sent to school. She began to feel lonely without her playmates and even envious when her sister, after being caught, came home in a soft cloth dress the school had given her as a uniform. Bored, curious, and weary of hiding, Polingaysi walked into the school one day and surrendered herself. When she returned home, her mother was furious at her for what she had done. According to Qoyawayma, she yelled, "You self-willed, naughty girl! You have taken a step in the wrong direction. A step away from your Hopi people. . . . You have brought this thing upon yourself, and there is no turning back."

Like most Indian schools of the day, Voth's school was committed to making its students adopt non-Indian ways and language. Toward this end, the children were forbidden to speak Hopi and beaten if they did not obey the instructions told to them in English, a language most had never even heard previously. Teachers resorted to verbal abuse as well. They insisted that all Hopi customs and beliefs were evil and humiliated students for looking or acting like Indians. Some of the children ignored the message, but others like Polingaysi took it to heart.

The influence of whites also divided the larger community. Tensions escalated between progressives, who welcomed the non-Indians, and traditionalists, who wanted the whites expelled from Oraibi. The situation came to a head in September 1906, when the progressives drove their traditional friends and neighbors from the village by force. To save his home and family, Polingaysi's father sided with the progressives, although he did not wholly support their stance. Soon after the incident, her family left Oraibi and relocated to a village that became known as New Oraibi, a move that Polingaysi Qoyawayma suggested was motivated by her parent's feelings of guilt. "Oraibi lost its heart" in Qoyawayma's eyes following the traditionalists' defeat.

As bitter as the confrontation at Oraibi had been, it still did not dull Polingaysi's enthusiasm for school. When she learned that Hopi students were being recruited for the Sherman Institute, an Indian boarding school in Riverside, California, she was eager to join them. Polingaysi was entranced by tales of the "land of oranges" and the "houses on wheels" (trains) that would take the students to their new school. She asked her parents' permission to attend Sherman, but they refused. When Polingaysi was discovered as a stowaway on the wagon that was transporting the students to the train, her parents hesitantly relented.

Although the adjustment to living away from Hopiland was difficult, Polingaysi enjoyed Sherman, particularly her music classes and the year-round availability of fresh fruits and vegetables. Other Hopi girls at Sherman obeyed the teachers but talked only about their dream of returning home, marrying, having children, and settling down into the life of a good Hopi woman. Polingaysi, however, sensed that she had become too "white" to feel comfortable at Oraibi. After graduating, she went back to her village but no longer seemed to fit in. Having internalized her teachers' message, she was contemptuous of Hopi ways, which in turn made the Hopi contemptuous of her.

Qoyawayma was relieved when her father arranged for her to live with a missionary family, the Freys, for whom she developed a sincere affection. Under their guidance, she was sent to Bethel College in Newton, Kansas. There she was trained to be a missionary with the understanding that one day she would minister to her people.

In summer 1914, Qoyawayma returned to Oraibi and unhappily attempted to convert the residents. Most were polite, but few were interested in her words. They had come to see her as a traitor to her people, as, in the words of one chief, "the little one who wanted to be a white man." In addition to her unenthusiastic reception by the Hopi, she was unsure about whether she wanted to be a missionary. Many white missionaries shared her teachers' belief that Hopi ways were primitive and should be eradicated. Although Qoyawayma had embraced many aspects of non-Indian culture, she still saw a great deal of worth in much of the Hopi way of life. In *No Turning Back,* she wrote that her goal was "to blend the best of the Hopi tradition with the best of the white culture, retaining the essence of good, whatever the source"—a philosophy that was held in suspicion by the missionaries and Hopi alike.

In 1924, Qoyawayma saw a way out of her difficult position when she was offered a job at the Indian school in the Hopi community of Hotevilla. Working first as a housekeeper and later as a teacher, she was determined that students have a better introduction to education than she and her classmates had had. Instead of forbidding her first graders from speaking Hopi, Qoyawayma began by teaching in the children's own language. Gradually, she would introduce them to English words, and within a few weeks they were able to put together complete English sentences on their own. She also built her lessons around things that were familiar to her young students. Instead of telling the story of Little Red Riding Hood, which was difficult for a Hopi child to follow, she repeated the stories they had learned from their elders. Only when her students felt comfortable in a classroom did she feel they were prepared to learn. Her motto became "reach them, then teach them."

Qoyawayma's unorthodox teaching methods again earned her the wrath of both her white friends and her Hopi neighbors. Her fellow teachers objected to her teaching in Hopi. The children's parents were angry that she was wasting time discussing Hopi stories and ways. In their eyes, school was only good for teaching white ways and English, a knowledge of which was growing more useful as the Hopi's contact with whites increased. She also was criticized by the Hopi for building a large house and buying a piano, indulgences that they found unseemly. That she had no husband or children inspired gossip as well. Qoyawayma surprised her neighbors by marrying Lloyd White, who was part Cherokee and part white, in 1931. But as the gossips predicted, the couple soon separated.

Despite the opposition Qoyawayma faced, she taught school among the Hopi and the Navajo for more than 30 years. Over time, she earned the respect of the officials in the Bureau of Indian

Affairs (BIA), the agency charged with overseeing Indian schools and other services provided to Native Americans by the federal government. One supervisor who visited her classroom to report on her performance told Qoyawayma that her style of teaching was the most effective he had ever seen. When she retired in 1954, the U.S. Department of the Interior, which encompasses the BIA, honored her long career with its Distinguished Service Award. By that time, she had also won the admiration of many Hopi, who came to believe that their children could benefit from a good education. Even after she had stopped teaching, parents still relied on Qoyawayma's counsel, especially her advice on how their children might pursue a college degree. Sensing a need, Qoyawayma founded the Hopi Student Scholarship Fund at Northern Arizona University in Flagstaff.

While in retirement, Qoyawayma also embarked on two new careers—pottery making and writing. Creating pots using the old Hopi methods, she gained a reputation as an excellent

Polingaysi Qoyawayma poses next to a bust of herself in 1974.
(NAU.PH.85.3.205.271, Fronske Collection, Image Courtesy of Cline Library, Northern Arizona University)

craftswoman. Her works are included in several prominent museum collections. She also began to write about how the Hopi world had changed during her lifetime. With the help of non-Indian author Vada F. Carlson, Qoyawayma wrote her autobiography and *Broken Pattern: Sunlight and Shadows of Hopi History* (1985). She also was the author of *The Sun Girl: A True Story about Dawamana* (1978), in which she retold an ancient Hopi tale.

In *No Turning Back,* Qoyawayma wrote that she had striven for "a good life, independent of both white people and her own Hopi people, but esteemed by both." By her death in 1990, few could dispute that she had achieved her goal.

Further Reading

Qoyawayma, Polingaysi, as told to Vada F. Carlson. *No Turning Back.* Albuquerque: University of New Mexico Press, 1964.
———, and Vada F. Carlson. *Broken Pattern: Sunlight and Shadows of Hopi History.* Happy Camp, Calif.: Naturegraph, 1985.

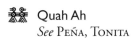 **Quah Ah**
See PEÑA, TONITA

R

Red-Horse, Valerie

(1959–) *Cherokee actress, filmmaker, businessperson*

With steely determination, Valerie Red-Horse has found success in two highly competitive fields— the entertainment world and the financial industry. An enrolled member of the Texas Band of Cherokees, she was born in California in 1959. Raised by her mother after her father abandoned them, Red-Horse grew up poor but still managed to win a full scholarship to Harvard University. She turned it down to go to University of California, Los Angeles, to follow her dream of becoming an actress.

Red-Horse graduated cum laude from UCLA's Theater Arts Department with a bachelor's degree in fine arts. She married her college sweetheart, former NFL football player Curt Mohl. The couple has three children.

After college, Red-Horse initially had trouble landing acting jobs. But years of auditioning finally began to pay off when she started appearing on television series such as *Santa Barbara, Murder She Wrote,* and *Babylon 5* under the stage name Valerie Redding. She also toured the country promoting a Pocahontas doll manufactured by the Mattel corporation, after she was selected as the model for it.

Although she was finding work, Red-Horse was frustrated by the course of her career. Her parts were usually small and often, she felt, demeaning to Indians. Red-Horse also bristled at the blatant racism of some producers and directors. In one instance, she recalled that "this director who I was auditioning for turned to me and said, 'You sound too educated to play a Native American woman,' and it really made me angry."

Red-Horse decided the only way she would be able to get the roles she wanted was to write them herself. She wrote a screenplay based on the life of the female Apache warrior Lozen. It was the first screenplay by an American Indian woman selected by the prestigious Sundance Institute's Writers Lab. She followed this success by contributing the story for a television drama (*My Indian Summer,* 1995), writing and starring in a live action short ("Looks onto the Night," 1996), and directing and writing a documentary (*True Whispers,* 2002).

But her greatest success as a filmmaker was *Naturally Native* (1999), which she produced, wrote, codirected, and starred in. Funded by the Mashantucket Pequot Tribal Nation, it was the first film financed by an American Indian tribe. *Naturally*

Native tells the story of three Native American sisters—Vickie (Red-Horse), Karen (Kimberly Norris Guerrero), and Tanya (IRENE BEDARD)—and their struggle to launch a line of cosmetics and hair care products made from traditional Indian recipes. The film touches on an array of issues in modern Indian life, from tribal gaming to alcoholism to Indian mascots.

Like her characters, Red-Horse founded a company that produced herbal hair care products—just one of several businesses she has established. With her husband, she has also developed an advertising specialty business. Even more ambitiously, she founded Native Nations Asset Management in 1999. Based on Wall Street, it was the first securities brokerage firm owned and operated by an American Indian. Able to bridge the Indian and non-Indians worlds, Red-Horse has worked with Indian tribes seeking advice on where to invest income from casinos and other profitable ventures. Recently, Red-Horse has headed the Tribal Finance Division of Coastline Capital Partners in Sausilito, California. In recognition of her entrepreneurial talents, Valerie Red-Horse was appointed to the National Small Business Advisory Council.

Further Reading

Dugan, Ianthe Jeanne. "Gold Rush: A Former Actress Links Worlds of Wall Street and the Reservation." *Wall Street Journal,* 6 September 2001, p. A1.

Naturally Native Cosmetics. Available online. URL: http://www.naturallynative.com/merch. Downloaded on June 10, 2006.

Yang, Sandy. "'Native' Aims to Entertain, Educate." Daily Bruin Online, University of California at Los Angeles. Available online. URL: http://www.dailybruin.ucla.edu/DB/issues/99/10.07/ae.native.html. Downloaded on June 1, 2006.

Roessel, Ruth
(1934–)   *Navajo educator, historian*

As a teacher and author, Ruth Roessel has instructed several generations of Navajo students about their tribal culture and history. Roessel was born in 1934 in the community of Rough Rock on the Navajo Indian Reservation in northern Arizona. She and her ten sisters and brothers were brought up by traditional parents, who educated their children in the Navajo (Dineh) ways and values by example. By the time Ruth was five, she had learned the fundamentals of Navajo weaving. At 11, she had taken full responsibility for the care of the family's herd of some 200 sheep. As a child Roessel also learned to build a corral, chop wood, and construct a hogan, the traditional Navajo dwelling. Through this hard work, Roessel later recalled, she "was learning to become a Navajo woman." She was also taught how to be a good Navajo by elders through their retelling of the ancient tribal tales of Changing Woman, Monster Slayer, and other mythic beings. According to Roessel, "I felt that my education really started when I began to hear and learn these Navajo stories."

Roessel began her formal schooling at the Lukachukai Day School in 1942. After five years, she left home to attend the Fort Wingate Boarding School in New Mexico. Like other Indian boarding schools at the time, Fort Wingate tried to make its students abandon their cultural heritage and adopt the language and customs of whites. Roessel has explained that after arriving there she felt as though she "had gone to a new country or at least to some place far, far away."

While coping with unfamiliar food and homesickness, Roessel received a vocational education in home economics. In her senior year, she was given an aptitude test that identified waitressing as the career for which she was best suited. But Roessel wanted to do more with her life. She applied to college but was rejected because her Fort Wingate education was deemed inadequate preparation for college-level classes. Roessel was outraged: She had been allowed no say in her course of study at Fort Wingate, which at the time was the only high school a Navajo girl was allowed to attend. Asking for help from influential friends, Roessel waged a successful campaign for admittance into Arizona State College (now Northern Arizona University) in Flagstaff. On a tribal scholarship, she earned both a bachelor's and master's degree in elementary education.

In addition to raising a family with her husband, Robert Roessel, Jr., Ruth Roessel has taught at many educational institutions on the Navajo reservation and served as the principal of the Round Rock Elementary School. She has also been an instructor at the Navajo Community College, which in 1968 became the first tribally controlled school to offer a two-year associate's degree. In the early 1970s, she was the director of the college's Navajo and American Indian Studies Program. Throughout her teaching career, Roessel has been an advocate for bilingual and bicultural education for Indian students. As she has explained, "I grew up with parents and family who were Navajo, who were proud of it and who taught me. . . . That is what we must do [for children] at home and at school if we wish to remain strong Navajos."

Roessel has also written several books that present Navajo history from a Navajo perspective. Two of her works are collections of personal accounts of tragic events in Navajo history. *Navajo Stories of the Long Walk Period* (1973) focuses on the U.S. Army's forced relocation of more than eight thousand Navajos to Bosque Redondo, New Mexico, in 1863. *Navajo Livestock Reduction: A National Disgrace* (1974) tells the story of the U.S. government's slaughter of Navajo sheep herds to prevent overgrazing during the 1930s. Roessel also has compiled *Stories of Traditional Navajo Life and Culture* (1976) and written *Women in Navajo Society* (1981), which combines historical essays and her own remembrances of growing up as a Navajo.

In 1995, Ruth Roessel became the subject of a children's book, *Songs from the Loom: A Navajo Girl Learns to Weave*. Written and featuring photographs by her son Monty, the book shows Roessel teaching her granddaughter Jaclyn the craft of weaving, thereby passing on this revered element of traditional Navajo culture to a new generation.

Further Reading

Roessel, Monty. *Songs from the Loom: A Navajo Girl Learns to Weave*. Minneapolis, Minn.: Lerner Publications, 1995.

Roessel, Ruth, ed. *Stories of Traditional Navajo Life and Culture*. Tsaile, Ariz.: Navajo Community College Press, 1976.
———. *Women in Navajo Society*. Rough Rock, Ariz.: Navajo Resource Center, 1981.

Rose, Wendy (Bronwen Elizabeth Edwards, Chiron Khanshandel)
(1948–) *Hopi-Miwok poet, educator, anthropologist, activist*

One of the best regarded Native American poets of her generation, Wendy Rose was born with the name Bronwen Elizabeth Edwards on May 7, 1948, in Oakland, California. There she was raised by her part-English, part-Miwok mother and a stepfather, who physically abused her. Her mother's family treated her little better. Ashamed of their Miwok heritage, both her light-skinned mother and grandmother were embarrassed by Bronwen, whose dark skin and features were more obviously Indian-like.

Bronwen felt more at ease with her father, a Hopi man who lived on his tribe's reservation in northern Arizona. Although the girl felt a kinship with the Hopi, she was told by her father that she could not become a member of the tribe. Because the Hopi trace ancestry through the mother's line, she could only be the daughter of a Hopi man, but never a Hopi herself. In an autobiographical essay from 1987, Rose described the misery of her childhood with the words, "Alone. Unwatched. Something wrong with me; everyone knows but me. They all leave me alone."

The lonely child grew up into a troubled adolescent. By her late teens, she had dropped out of high school, survived a brief and violent marriage, and started to experiment with drugs. During this difficult period, she also began to express herself through poetry. Several of her poems were collected in anthologies of the works of young Native American writers. Her poems appeared first under the pseudonym Chiron Khanshandel, then later under the name Wendy Rose.

205

Through the influence of a friend, who was an anthropologist, Rose stopped taking drugs and began studying anthropology at Cabrillo College, Contra Costa College, and the University of California at Berkeley. Berkeley awarded her a bachelor's degree in 1976 and a master's degree in 1978. While there, Rose met and married her second husband, Arthur Murata.

Although she has studied anthropology, Rose has been highly critical of the discipline, particularly of the condescending attitude of some non-Indian anthropologists toward their Indian subjects. In a 1995 interview, she recalled one of many incidents that had incurred her wrath as a student. During a lecture, one of her professors explained that her Hopi ancestors had been cannibals, an assertion she knew had no basis in truth. Moved by anger and "a warped sense of humor," she and another Indian student staged a quiet protest at the next class: "We sat in the front row—we each had a full dinner place setting with forks and knives in front of us, and we just sat there staring at him for the entire lecture."

During the 1970s, Rose became involved in the more public demonstrations of the American Indian Movement (AIM), a prominent Indian rights organization. Working as a mediator between AIM members and anthropologists, she voiced many Indians' objections to the excavation of Indian burial sites and display of the remains by museums. One of Rose's poems, "Protecting the Burial Grounds," was written while she and other protesters sat in front of a bulldozer to prevent the destruction of an Indian cemetery in San Jose, California.

As a student, Rose was inspired to take on another crusade—promoting the study of literature written by American Indians. Toward this end, she has taught American Indian literature and history at Berkeley and California State University at Fresno, and since 1984 has coordinated the American Indian Studies program at Fresno City College. She is also compiling a bibliography of works of Native American authors from the 16th century to the present.

Although a respected educator and scholar, Rose is best known for her work as a poet. She has published numerous collections, including *Lost Copper,* a nominee for the 1980 Pulitzer Prize in poetry. Her paintings have also appeared as illustrations in several of her books as well as those of other poets. Borrowing stylistic elements of Native American songs and chants, Rose's poetry has often explored her personal struggle for identity as an Indian of mixed ancestry. In her most recent works, she has expanded this theme, using her own sense of alienation as a metaphor for the anxieties felt by many in the modern world. As Rose has explained, "The way I grew up is symptomatic of something much larger than Indian-white relations. History and circumstance have made halfbreeds of all of us."

Further Reading

Bruchac, Joseph. "The Bones Are Alive: An Interview with Wendy Rose." In *Survival This Way: Interviews with American Indian Poets,* 87–104. Tucson: University of Arizona Press, 1987.

Coltelli, Laura. "Wendy Rose." In *Winged Words: American Indian Women Speak,* 121–133. Lincoln: University of Nebraska Press, 1990.

Rose, Wendy. *Bone Dance: New and Selected Poems, 1965–1993.* Tucson: University of Arizona Press, 1994.

———. *The Halfbreed Chronicles and Other Poems.* Los Angeles: West End Press, 1985.

———. *Itch Like Crazy.* Tucson: University of Arizona Press, 2002.

———. *Lost Copper.* Banning, Calif.: Malki Museum Press, 1980.

———. "You . . . Who Have Removed Us: At What Cost?" In *Messengers of the Wind: Native American Women Tell Their Life Stories,* edited by Jane Katz, 205–213. New York: Ballantine Books, 1995.

Ross, Mary G.
(1908–   ) *Cherokee mathematician, engineer*

The first-known American Indian female engineer, Mary G. Ross helped develop technologies for the defense industry and the early space program in the United States. She was born in Oklahoma on August 9, 1908. Her great-great-grandfather was

John Ross, who served as the Cherokee's principal chief from 1828 to 1866.

Graduating from high school at 16, Ross attended Northeastern State Teacher's College in Tahlequah, Oklahoma. There she indulged her fascination with science and mathematics. Ross later recalled, "I was the only female in my class. I sat on one side of the room and the guys on the other side of the room. I guess they didn't want to associate with me. But I could hold my own with them, and sometimes did better." After earning her degree in 1928, she spent nearly 10 years as a public school teacher, since at that time, in her words, "a woman who wanted a career either became a nurse or a teacher."

Craving a new challenge, Ross left teaching and moved to Washington, D.C., to work for the Bureau of Indian Affairs. After a year working as a statistician, she was hired as the girl's adviser at Santa Fe Indian School, a boarding school that served primarily Pueblo and Navajo (Dineh) students. The experience was eye-opening for her: "I went out to the Southwest and really began to learn about life at the reservation and what the culture was like. When I grew up, I went to public schools. I really didn't know much about my Indian heritage." During her summers off, Ross continued her education, earning a master's degree in mathematics from Colorado State Teachers College.

In 1942, Ross took a job at the Lockheed Aircraft Corporation in Burbank, California. It was unusual for the company to hire a female mathematician. But with the United States's entry into World War II, the aviation industry was growing fast. According to Ross, "If you could do the work, they needed you regardless of [your] shape."

For several years, Ross worked on developing fighter planes. Impressed by her work, the company then suggested she study engineering. Ross received on-the-job training while also taking night classes at the University of California at Los Angeles.

In 1953, Ross was one of 40 engineers assigned to Lockheed Missiles and Space Company (now Lockheed Martin). She was the only woman in this elite group and one of very few female engineers in the company. In fact, in 1958, Ross appeared on the game show *What's My Line?*, and none of the panelists were able to guess her profession.

While at Lockheed, Ross was responsible for helping develop ballistic missile systems for the U.S. military. She also worked on the Agena rocket, a precursor to the Apollo program, and set out criteria for future missions to Mars and Venus. Ross once explained that she considered herself "extremely fortunate to have been on the ground floor of space technology," particularly since "compared to the classified research, it was a lot more fun since you could talk about it."

After retiring in 1973, Ross cofounded the Los Angeles chapter of the Society of Women Engineers (SWE). She was eventually elected a life member of the society, which established a scholarship in her name. In 1992, the Silicon Valley Engineering Council inducted her into its Hall of Fame. More recently, she was honored at the 2001 Pan-American Exposition in Buffalo, New York, where a sculpture entitled "Mary G. Ross: Scientist, Engineer, Cherokee-American" celebrated her contributions to science.

Ross has also been honored by the American Indian Science and Engineering Society (AISES) and the Council of Energy Resource Tribes (CERT). Her experience with these organizations rekindled her interest in American Indian history and culture. They also helped inspire her to deliver lectures in high schools to encourage young people, especially Native Americans and young women, to consider careers in science. In lectures and interviews, Ross has always conveyed an infectious enthusiasm for her work. As she told a reporter in 1999, "I have been lucky to have had so much fun. It has been an adventure all the way."

Further Reading/Resources

"An Interview with Mary Ross: First Native American Woman Engineer." Society of Women Engineers. Available online. URL: http://swe-goldenwest.org/scvs/

www/history/MRoss.html. Downloaded on April 25, 2006.

"Mary G. Ross." Biographies of Women Mathematicians. Available online. http://www.agnesscott.edu/lriddle/women/maryross.htm. Downloaded on April 25, 2006.

Running Eagle (Brown Weasel Woman)
(ca. 1820–ca. 1850)   *Blackfoot warrior*

The famed woman warrior of Blackfoot legend, Running Eagle was born in the early 19th century in her tribe's homeland in what is now southern Alberta, Canada. The eldest of five children, she was given the name Brown Weasel Woman as a girl. Her father was a warrior of high standing among the Blackfoot. When his two sons reached their late boyhood, he instructed them in shooting a bow and arrow, hunting buffalo, riding horses, and battling the Blackfoots' many Indian enemies. Brown Weasel Woman asked her father if she could join her brothers' lessons even though these activities were traditionally performed only by older boys and men. Over her mother's objections, he taught her alongside her brothers, and soon she was able to kill a buffalo on her own.

On one hunting expedition, Brown Weasel Woman, her father, and the rest of their small party was set upon by a large group of enemy warriors. As they ran from their attackers, her father's horse was shot. When Brown Weasel Woman realized what had happened, she turned around, rode straight toward the enemy to where her father was stranded, and pulled him onto her own horse, which carried them both to safety. Among the Blackfoot, saving a fallen comrade was regarded as one of the most valiant acts of a warrior, so many of her tribespeople celebrated Brown Weasel Woman's courage. Some, however, feared that if she were allowed to continue to hunt and fight, other woman would join her and neglect their household duties.

In the midst of the debate, Brown Weasel Woman was forced to change her ways. Her mother fell ill, leaving her eldest daughter to care

for her younger children. Brown Weasel Woman ran the household well but apparently did not enjoy performing the work expected of a wife and mother.

When she was still a young woman, Brown Weasel Woman's father died in battle and soon after her mother succumbed to her illness. Left alone to rear her orphaned brothers and sisters, Brown Weasel Woman made an unconventional decision. She took a widow into her home to care for the children, and carrying at her side the rifle she inherited from her father, she began to live as a man.

Determined to be a warrior, she tagged along after a party of men planning to raid a Crow Indian camp in order to steal back horses the Crow had stolen from them. When the party's leader noticed Brown Weasel Woman bringing up the rear, he demanded that she go home. She refused. He then said that if she did not turn around, he would call off the raid. She replied that if he did, she would continue on and take on the Crow alone. The leader then relented and allowed her to come along.

The raid was successful, and the Blackfoot made off with many horses, including 11 that Brown Weasel Woman had caught single-handedly. While the Blackfoot raiders were resting on their return home, she kept watch over their horses. Situated on a butte high above the prairie, she saw two Indians from another tribe begin to make off with the Blackfoots' stolen goods. With no time to ask for help, she raced down to the two thieves, shot one, and continued shooting at the other as he rode away. Again she was heralded for her heroism, but disappointingly some of her people still disapproved of her behavior.

On the advice of several elders, she set out to convince the rest by going on a vision quest—a grueling ritual during which participants went to a remote area for four days and nights and waited for the spirits to present them with a vision to guide their destiny. When Brown Weasel Woman returned from the ritual, she announced that she had seen a vision that had given her great power. She was then allowed to join a second war party and invited to share her exploits at a medicine lodge ceremony, during which usually only men were permitted to speak. After hearing her tales, the Blackfoot's head chief gave her a new name: Running Eagle. In the past, the name had only been given to the greatest Blackfoot warriors, and it never before had been bestowed on a woman.

In the coming years, Running Eagle did justice to her honored name. She led many successful raids and war parties. Despite her triumphs as a warrior, several men asked to marry her. She always refused by explaining that she had had a vision of the Sun and therefore she could only belong to him. In the mid-1800s, Running Eagle fittingly died on the battlefield—the arena in which she thrived and made her people proud.

Further Reading

Buchanan, Kimberly Moore. *Apache Women Warriors.* El Paso: Texas Western Press, 1986.

Hungry Wolf, Beverly. *The Ways of My Grandmothers.* New York: William Morrow, 1980.

S

Sacagawea (Sacajawea, Bird Woman, Boinaiv)
(ca. 1788–1812 or 1884) *Shoshone interpreter*

For nearly 200 years, Sacagawea has been a mythic figure in American history. The only woman on the Lewis and Clark expedition of 1804–1806, she has inspired hundreds of biographies, novels, plays, paintings, statues, and monuments. Since 1999, when her image appeared on the U.S. dollar coin, she has even been a part of modern American life. The actual facts of her life, however, are scant. Aside from the occasional mention of Sacagawea in the diaries of the expedition's leaders, little is known for certain about this celebrated woman.

Sacagawea was probably born in the late 1780s in what is now central Idaho. A member of the Shoshone tribe, she was named Boinaiv, meaning "grass maiden" in her native language. When she was about 12 years old, the camp in which she was living was attacked by Hidatsa warriors. Boinaiv and another girl were taken captive and brought to a Hidatsa village in present-day North Dakota. There Boinaiv became known as Sacagawea—a Hidatsa word meaning "bird woman." (Some sources spell her name "Sacajawea," which means "boat launcher" in Shoshone.) The Hidatsa sold their captives to Toussaint Charbonneau, a French-Canadian trader. Charbonneau married both of the girls, but his relationship to Sacagawea remained more like that of a master to a slave than a husband to a wife.

At about the time of their marriage, President Thomas Jefferson negotiated the Louisiana Purchase with France. Through this deal, the United States gained control over the vast tract of land between the Mississippi River and the Rocky Mountains. This area had been inhabited by Indians for thousands of years, but few whites had ever ventured into the region. To learn more about this uncharted territory, Jefferson assembled a party of explorers. Led by Meriwether Lewis, the president's personal secretary, and William Clark, the former governor of Missouri, the expedition of about 45 men left St. Louis, Missouri, in May 1804. They planned to travel west until they reached the Pacific Ocean.

By late October, the party had made its way to the lands of the Hidatsa. Because traveling during the winter would be difficult, Lewis and Clark decided to establish a temporary settlement along the Knife River, where they could live until spring broke. Living in a nearby village, Charbonneau visited the explorers and offered his and Sacagawea's services as interpreters. Lewis and Clark hired the couple, and in April 1805, they joined the expedition as it once again set out for western lands. Strapped into a cradleboard on Sacagawea's back was her two-month-old baby, Jean-Baptiste, whom the explorers nicknamed "Pomp."

Following Jefferson's instructions, Lewis and Clark kept detailed journals throughout their journeys. In Lewis's diaries, Sacagawea was rarely mentioned. Clark, however, had great regard for the young Indian woman and noted on several occasions that she proved to be an asset to the expedition. He wrote that when food was scarce, she knew where to find and how to cook wild roots and berries. At times, the plant foods she gathered were the only thing that kept the party from starvation. Clark also recorded that, while traveling down the Yellowstone River in a canoe, Sacagawea's quick thinking saved valuable research notes, scientific tools, and medicines when the boat nearly capsized. Clark wrote, "The Indian woman, to whom I ascribe equal fortitude and resolution with any person on board at the time of the accident, caught and preserved most of the light articles which were washed overboard." According to Clark, Sacagawea's mere presence in the party at times protected the explorers from violent clashes with the Indians they met: "The wife of Shabono [sic] our interpreter we find reconciles all the Indians as to our friendly intentions a woman with a party of men is a token of peace."

Sacagawea probably made her greatest contribution to the expedition, however, when the explorers reached Shoshone territory in August. Lewis encountered a tribal chief named Cameahwait and called for Sacagawea to translate his words. Clark wrote, "She came into the tent, sat down, and was beginning to interpret, when in the person of Cameahwait she recognized her brother; she instantly jumped up and ran and embraced him, throwing over him her blanket and weeping profusely." Sacagawea learned from Cameahwait that most of her other relatives were dead. One of the only survivors was her deceased sister's son, Bazil, whom Sacagawea adopted.

Cameahwait had been wary of the white men. But discovering his long-lost sister among their ranks, he decided to help the explorers. He provided them the guides and horses they desperately needed to cross the Rocky Mountains. Without the advice and supplies of the Shoshone, the expedition may not have survived the arduous travel across the Continental Divide.

Generally, Lewis and Clark described Sacagawea as good-humored and uncomplaining. But when the expedition finally arrived on the Pacific coast in January 1805, Lewis recorded one instance in which Sacagawea became uncharacteristically demanding. Only some of the party members were to travel all the way to the ocean. When Sacagawea found out that she would be among those left behind, she confronted the expedition leaders: "The Indian woman was very importunate to be permitted to go . . . she observed that she had traveled a long way with us to see the great waters, and . . . thought it very bad that she could not be permitted to see [it]." Her passionate plea persuaded the expedition leaders, who allowed her to join the group that explored the shores of the Pacific.

The expedition headed back toward St. Louis. When it reached the Hidatsa homeland, Charbonneau announced that he and Sacagawea were going no further. Clark tried to convince them to continue on. He also asked if he could adopt Pomp, for whom Clark had developed a deep affection. Charbonneau first refused, but a year later the family resettled in St. Louis, where Clark sold them a tract of farmland. Charbonneau did not enjoy life as a farmer and soon returned to hunting and trading for his livelihood. In the meantime, Clark took over the care and education of Pomp.

The fate of Sacagawea after the Lewis and Clark expedition remains a subject of debate. Some historians believe that she stayed with Charbonneau, and together they eventually moved to Fort Manuel, a fur trading post in present-day South Dakota. This theory holds that she died there from disease in 1812 when she was only about 25 years old. One trader at the post recorded the death of the "wife of Charbonneau" in his journal. Other evidence comes from William Clark, who in a published report about the expedition members from the late 1820s listed Sacagawea among those who had died.

Another theory was advanced first by Grace Hebard, a professor at the University of Wyoming who wrote the biography *Sacajawea* (1933). Hebard claimed that Sacagawea left Charbonneau, lived among the Comanche Indians, and took a new husband, with whom she had five children. Eventually she moved to the Wind River Indian Reservation in what is now Wyoming, where she joined her sons Jean-Baptiste and Bazil. Hebard held that Sacagawea became an important leader on the reservation and died in 1884 as she was approaching 100 years of age. Hebard conducted hundreds of interviews with Shoshones at Wind River, who told her stories about a woman called Porivo who they thought was Sacagawea. Many Wind River residents still claim that they are her descendants. Critics of Hebard's theory, however, question whether Porivo and Sacagawea were in fact the same person.

Hebard has also been criticized for exaggerating Sacagawea's role on the Lewis and Clark Expedition. She was following the lead of other writers from the early 20th century who depicted Sacagawea as the party's primary guide, without whose advice and expertise the explorers would have been lost. According to Lewis and Clark, however, Sacagawea's role of guide was largely limited to pointing out a few landmarks in her homeland. Most of the writers who gave Sacagawea a more inflated role were advocates for women's rights. To promote their cause, they may have chosen to overstate Sacagawea's importance on the expedition in order to craft her into a glamorous feminist heroine.

Other popular fictions of the early 20th century promoted the myth that Sacagawea and William Clark were in love. As his diaries attest, Sacagawea clearly earned Clark's respect. But these romanticized depictions of their relationship have no basis in truth. Aside from making for a spicier story, the

Sacagawea is depicted in a statue outside the state capitol in Bismarck, North Dakota.
(State Historical Society of North Dakota)

suggestions of a romance between Sacagawea and Clark possibly pleased white audiences because they made them feel more comfortable about the non-Indian takeover of Indian lands. The information about the West uncovered by the Lewis and Clark expedition helped open the region to settlement by white Americans. These settlers built their new homes on Indian land that generally was stolen by white pioneers or by the U.S. government on their behalf. Fictions that portrayed Sacagawea as a fair maiden who loved whites and was happy to help them settle the West perhaps eased guilt felt by white consumers. Like similar myths about POCAHONTAS, these stories justified the past mistreatment of Indians by whites: Good, virtuous Indians like Sacagawea loved and protected whites, they suggested, while only bad Indians fought the conquest of their lands.

The many myths that surround Sacagawea show the enduring appeal that her story has for Americans. Throughout the country, statues and monuments to her have also helped make her a popular heroine in the public mind. Meriwether Lewis, however, paid her perhaps her most appropriate honor. In recognition of her contributions to the expedition, he named a "handsome river" in Montana after his trusted interpreter.

Further Reading

Clark, Ella E., and Margot Edmonds. *Sacagawea of the Lewis and Clark Expedition.* Berkeley: University of California Press, 1979.

Kessler, Donna J. *The Making of Sacagawea: A Euro-American Legend.* Tuscaloosa: University of Alabama Press, 1996.

Lewis, Meriwether. *The Journals of Lewis and Clark,* edited by Frank Bergon. New York: Penguin, 1989.

Ronda, James P. *Lewis and Clark Among the Indians.* Lincoln: University of Nebraska Press, 1984.

Sacred White Buffalo, Mother Mary Catherine (Ptesanwanyakapi, Mary Josephine Crowfeather)
(1867–1893)   *Lakota Sioux nun*

Renowned for her piety, Mother Mary Catherine Sacred White Buffalo was the mother superior of the Congregation of American Sisters, the first sisterhood for Lakota nuns. She was born in 1867 on the Standing Rock Reservation in present-day North Dakota. She was one of 11 children of Joseph Crowfeather, a leader of the Hunkpapa band of the Lakota Sioux. She was given the Indian name Ptesanwanyakapi, meaning "They See a White Buffalo Woman"—a reference to an incident that occurred when she was a baby. Holding the infant, Joseph Crowfeather was shot at by U.S. troops. Both he and the baby were unharmed. The Lakota attributed the miracle to an encounter with White Buffalo Woman, who, according to Sioux legends, gave the Lakota the sacred pipe.

At 14, Ptesanwanyakapi was baptized at St. Benedict's Mission in what is now South Dakota. She was given the Christian name Mary Josephine. Already interested in becoming a nun, she enrolled in the Benedictine Sisters' School in Fort Yates, North Dakota.

During her four years there, Crowfeather attracted the attention of Father Francis M. Craft, a missionary at the Standing Rock Indian Reservation. Catholic communities in the West faced a shortage of nuns. Craft saw a solution in encouraging Native women to join the sisterhood.

Craft was impressed by Crowfeather, particularly by the respect she received from her own people. He arranged for her and several other Lakota women to attend the Sisters of the Holy Childhood, a Benedictine academy in Minnesota. After three years, Crowfeather entered a nearby convent, taking her vows on Easter in 1890. She was sent to work as a cook at the Immaculate Conception Mission School on the Crow Creek Indian Reservation in South Dakota.

In late 1891, Craft established a new convent for Lakota nuns on the Fort Berthold Reservation

Sacred White Buffalo became a nun in the Congregation of American Sisters.
(Courtesy Marquette University Libraries, Bureau of Catholic Indian Missions Records)

in North Dakota. Crowfeather was named mother superior of the Congregation of American Sisters, also known as the Red Sisters. She was from then on known as Mother Mary Catherine Sacred White Buffalo. The nuns were charged with teaching English to Indians and with caring for the sick. They received special training to help them in their nursing.

Craft refused to allow the sisters to eat meat. Since meat made up most of the Lakota diet, the rule left several nuns hungry and ill. An even greater threat to their health was tuberculosis, a disease that was plaguing Indian communities at the time. Mother Mary Catherine Sacred White Buffalo died of tuberculosis on May 3, 1893, at the age of 26. The Congregation of American Sisters was short-lived as well. Only seven years later, because of death and disinterest, the sisterhood was disbanded.

Further Reading

Duratschek, Mary C. *Crusading along Sioux Trails: A History of the Catholic Indian Missions of South Dakota.* St. Meinrad, Ind.: The Grail Press, 1947.

Mathes, Valerie S. "American Indian Women and the Catholic Church." *North Dakota History* 47 (1980): 20–25.

Sainte-Marie, Buffy

(ca. 1942–   ) *Cree singer, songwriter, actress, activist, painter*

Internationally famous folksinger and Academy Award–winning songwriter, Buffy Sainte-Marie has used her success in the entertainment world to shine a spotlight on the fight for Indian rights. Particularly in the searing lyrics of her protest songs of the 1960s, her work has forced non-Indians to confront, many for the first time, the injustices faced by Native Americans in the past and present.

Beverly Sainte-Marie was born on February 20 in 1941 or 1942 on the Piapot Reserve in the Canadian province of Saskatchewan, the homeland of one branch of the Cree Indians. Following the sudden death of her parents, the infant was adopted by Albert and Winifred Sainte-Marie, who nicknamed the girl "Buffy" and reared her in their home in Wakefield, Massachusetts.

Shy and reserved as a child, Sainte-Marie spent much of her youth hiking through the woods and writing poetry. Having taught herself to play her family's secondhand piano, she began setting her poems to music when she was four. At 16, she discovered the guitar, which would become her preferred instrument. By trial and error, she developed a variety of unorthodox playing techniques. For instance, she invented 32 different ways of tuning the guitar, each of which allowed her to create a unique type of sound.

Despite the solace she found in her music, Sainte-Marie's teenage years were difficult. She felt uncomfortable at parties and was embarrassed by her appearance, particularly her olive skin and black hair. As Sainte-Marie explained in a 1975 interview in *Ms.* magazine, "I wanted above all to be blonde. I always wanted to be like the other girls in school. . . . What was wrong with me? I used to ask myself. Now I know I simply felt bored, but then I blamed myself."

In her mid-teens, Sainte-Marie escaped into a new hobby—researching her Indian heritage. Although her adoptive mother was half Micmac Indian, she had grown up knowing little about Indian history or about her own people. After reading every book about Indian culture she could find, she took a trip to the Piapot Reserve to learn more about the Cree firsthand. The warm welcome she received from her Cree relatives left a deep impression on the awkward adolescent, and she began to visit the reserve regularly. Sainte-Marie later stated that among the Cree she discovered a greater sense of security and community than she had ever known before.

In 1959, Sainte-Marie began studying at the University of Massachusetts. Initially she wanted to be a veterinarian, but she soon changed her major to Eastern philosophy and education with the intention of becoming a teacher. While in college, Sainte-Marie started singing her compositions for friends. With their encouragement, she performed at nearby coffeehouses for pocket money.

After graduating with honors, Sainte-Marie moved to Greenwich Village, a neighborhood in New York City known as the center of the folk music boom in the early 1960s. Some folksingers featured in nightclubs there concentrated on traditional American folk songs, but the most popular wrote their own material. Like Sainte-Marie's lyrics, theirs often dealt with social issues, particularly the struggles of the oppressed in American society. Despite their controversial material (or perhaps because of it), several veterans of the folk club circuit—most notably, Bob Dylan, Joan Baez, and Peter, Paul, and Mary—had crossed over into the mainstream to become some of the most successful recording artists of the period.

Appearing at an open-mike night at a small club, Sainte-Marie attracted the attention of Bob Dylan. In part through his influence, she was asked to make her debut at the renowned Gaslight Cafe on August 17, 1963. In the audience was Robert Sheldon, the music critic for the *New York Times*. In his article in the next day's paper, he declared that Sainte-Marie was "one of the most promising new talents on the folk scene." Other reviewers were equally enthusiastic, and Sainte-Marie quickly landed a contract with Vanguard Records, which recorded many of the most respected folk artists.

Sainte-Marie's first album, *It's My Way*, was released in 1964 to popular and critical acclaim. On its merits, *Billboard* magazine named her the "Best New Artist of the Year." With her new-found success, Sainte-Marie graduated from out-of-the-way clubs to huge concert houses, including Carnegie Hall and the New York Philharmonic. A dynamic performer, Sainte-Marie inspired a reporter from the *New York News* to write: "She sings in a clear, husky-timbered voice that can be sweet, low-down, bitter, compassionate, sprightly, sexy, or wryly humorous. She can purr or belt, warm you into a smile or near chill you with a trembling intensity." Concertgoers who thought of her primarily as a singer were awed by her skills as a musician, especially by her distinctive ways of playing the guitar and her unusual selection of instruments. Her shows often included a demonstration of the mouthbow, a Native American instrument introduced to Sainte-Marie by Cree folk artist Patrick Sky.

To Sainte-Marie, performing was a thrilling experience. She once explained that "on stage, the drums go up my feet, into my body, then kick me

Buffy Sainte-Marie has had a lengthy career as a musician, artist, and educator.
(Courtesy EMI Records Group)

right in the butt. . . . The bass just touches the surface of my skin, and the guitar reaches me between the muscle fiber and my skin." Still, she believed that songwriting was her greatest talent. She described the process of composing as always exciting and unpredictable, with the complete tune and lyrics often coming to her in a flash: "I could be riding a taxi, an airplane, or eating. I don't have to be sad or happy to write. It can't be forced. A song is there all of a sudden, when it wasn't there before." One of the most prolific popular songwriters of the 1960s, Sainte-Marie also had the impressive ability to work in a number of styles; she penned hits for country singers, hard rockers, and pop stars. Her greatest success as a songwriter came with the love ballad "Until It's Time for You to Go" (1965), which was covered by hundreds of performers, including Bob Dylan, Barbra Streisand, Sonny and Cher, and Sainte-Marie's childhood idol, Elvis Presley.

She also garnered recognition as the composer of "Universal Soldier," which became the unofficial anthem of the Vietnam War protest movement.

Sainte-Marie first performed "Universal Soldier" at coffeehouses in 1963, but because of the song's controversial message she was banned from singing it on radio and television. It only reached a mass audience when the rock artist Donovan's cover became a hit two years later.

By the public, Sainte-Marie was most closely associated with her songs that protested the United States's mistreatment of Native Americans, including "Native American Child," "Now That the Buffalo's Gone," and "My Country 'Tis of Thy People You're Dying." She also took an active role in Indian causes. In addition to touring reserves and reservations, where she gave lectures and performed benefit concerts, she also made large donations to charities that serviced Native Americans. Among these was the Nihewan Foundation, an organization she founded to provide law school scholarships to Indian students.

During the late 1960s, the popularity of folk music in the United States started to wane, but Sainte-Marie remained a top draw overseas. She toured extensively in Europe, Japan, and Australia, but following the birth of her son Dakota and the lackluster sales of several late albums, she decided to take a hiatus from recording in 1975 in order to explore working in television and film. From 1976 to 1981, Sainte-Marie was a cast member of the children's television series *Sesame Street.* She also scored two films, *Harold of Orange* (1986) and *Where the Spirit Lives* (1989), and narrated *Broken Rainbow* (1985), an Academy Award–winning documentary about the United States's treatment of the Navajo Indians. In 1982, she received her own Oscar as the cowriter of "Up Where We Belong," the love theme from the romantic drama *An Officer and a Gentleman.*

In the 1980s, after earning a Ph.D. in Fine Arts from the University of Massachusetts, Sainte-Marie set about educating herself in the latest advances in electronic and computer technology in order to create her own home recording studio. From her homemade tapes emerged a new album, *Coincidence and Likely Stories* (1992), which was recorded entirely at Sainte-Marie's house in Kauai, Hawaii.

Many of the songs on the album harken back to her earlier work. One song, "The Priests of the Golden Bull," is a savage attack on companies that mine uranium on Western reservation lands, destroying the environment and health of reservation residents in the process. In another track, "Starwalker," Sainte-Marie celebrates Native American culture and features sounds recorded at an Indian powwow on the Piapot Reserve. But despite her continuing interest in making her listeners aware of the struggles and triumphs of Native Americans, Sainte-Marie resists being viewed exclusively as a political artist. As she told *Los Angeles* magazine in 1992, "Regardless of what my career or my lyrics have been about, the record should be judged on only one thing: I either stand up to Mariah Carey and Bryan Adams or I've failed."

Sainte-Marie's interest in computers has also inspired her to begin a new career as a visual artist. Her paintings are created by scanning old photographs—often of 19th-century images of Indians—and using her computer to color and manipulate the pictures. In 1996, her digital art was featured in a one-woman exhibit at the Institute of American Indian Arts Museum in Santa Fe. In Sainte-Marie's eyes, her use of computer technology in her painting and music is a logical extension of her years of artistic experimentation. As she once explained, "Voice, mouthbow, guitar, computer . . . they're all just tools in the hands of artists." Her artwork has been exhibited throughout North America and featured in many publications, including *Art Focus, Ms.,* and *USA Today.*

Sainte-Marie continues to lecture and play concerts, including one to celebrate the 2004 opening of the National Museum of the American Indian in Washington, D.C. She also frequently teaches at institutions such as York University in Toronto, Saskatchewan Indian Federated College in Regina, and Evergreen State College in Washington. But since 1996, Sainte-Marie has devoted much of her time to the Cradleboard Teaching Project, a nonprofit organization she established to develop teaching materials from an American Indian perspective.

As part of this project, Sainte-Marie produced and directed the CD-ROM *Science: Through Native American Eyes* as well as online multimedia presentations about social studies and geography.

Further Reading

Braudy, Susan. "Buffy Sainte-Marie: 'Native North American Me.'" *Ms.* 4 (March 1975): 14–18.
Buffy-Sainte Marie Web site. URL: http://www.creative-native.com. Downloaded on November 7, 2005.
Cradleboard Teaching Project Web site. URL: http://www.cradleboard.org. Downloaded on November 8, 2005.
Sainte-Marie, Buffy. *The Buffy Sainte-Marie Songbook.* New York: Grosset and Dunlap, 1971.
Sonneborn, Liz. "Buffy Sainte-Marie." In *Performers.* New York: Facts On File, 1995.
Turbide, Diane. "Songs that Sear." *Maclean's* 105 (April 20, 1992): 53.

Sakiestewa, Ramona
(1949–)   *Hopi weaver*

Inspired by the mixture of cultures in the Southwest, Ramona Sakiestewa produces textiles that meld past weaving traditions with a modern sensibility. Sakiestewa was born in Albuquerque, New Mexico, in 1949 to a Hopi father and a German-Irish mother. She was reared in the city by her mother and stepfather, who filled their home with Native American art. Working at a trading post also helped to introduce Sakiestewa to the artistic roots of many different tribes in the region.

Sakiestewa was always fascinated with fabric. As a girl, she meticulously sewed doll clothes by hand. As a teenager, she began studying the weaving methods used by the Pueblo and Navajo in the 19th century. By reading anthropological literature, she taught herself to weave on a vertical loom.

To further her understanding of design and color, Sakiestewa traveled to New York City in the late 1960s to study at the School of Visual Arts. She then returned to the Southwest, where she took a job as an arts administrator at Santa Fe's Museum of New Mexico. In her spare time, she worked on her weaving and help to establish

ATLATL, a national organization for Native American artists and craftspeople.

In 1975, Sakiestewa received her first major commission. The National Park Service asked her to create a reproduction of a turkey feather blanket, the remnants of which had been excavated at the Bandelier National Monument in Los Alamos, New Mexico. The blanket had been made by the Anasazi, the ancient ancestors of the Pueblos. While working on the project, Sakiestewa studied the Anasazi in order to develop a method of producing yarn from plant fibers as they had thousands of years before. Such in-depth research is a hallmark of much of her work.

With the formation of her own company in 1982, Sakiestewa turned to weaving full time. Initially, she concentrated on designing floor rugs and upholstery fabric. But soon she specialized in fine-

Ramona Sakiestewa often draws inspiration for her weaving from Navajo and Pueblo designs.
(Photograph by Jack Parsons, Courtesy of the Wheelwright Museum of the American Indian)

art tapestries, which she often created in series. Within a decade, she and her assistants were producing some thirty tapestries a year. Her works are distinguished by bold color combinations that often come to her in dreams. Sakiestewa's patterns are abstracted from Navajo and Pueblo pottery designs or from shapes she sees in the southwestern landscape. She also looks to other cultures for ideas. Visits to Japan and to South America have inspired Sakiestewa tapestry series.

Among her best-known works are 13 tapestries based on drawings by architect Frank Lloyd Wright that were commissioned by the Taliesen Foundation in 1989. In the same year, her work was showcased in "Ramona Sakiestewa: Patterned Dreams," a major exhibit at the Wheelwright Museum of the American Indian in Santa Fe. Sakiestewa's tapestries are in the permanent collection of museums across the United States, including the Museum of New Mexico, Arizona's Heard Museum, and the National Museum of the American Indian (NMAI). The NMAI has further honored Sakiestewa by naming her its head interior designer.

Recently, Sakiestewa has begun to work on multimedia pieces in which she stitches cloth elements onto paper. She sees these experiments as an expansion on, rather than a departure from, her tapestries. "After all," she has explained, "fiber and paper are not that removed from each other."

Further Reading

Baizerman, Suzanne. *Ramona Sakiestewa, Patterned Dreams: Textiles of the Southwest.* Santa Fe, N.Mex.: Wheelwright Museum of the American Indian, 1989.

Indyke, Dottie. "Ramona Sakiestewa." *Southwest Art* 31 (May 31, 2002): 44–46.

Marshall, Ann. "Ramona Sakiestewa." *Native Peoples,* November/December 2002, pp. 67–68.

Sanapia

(1895–1984)   *Comanche medicine woman, autobiographer*

The last eagle doctor of the Comanche Indians, Sanapia was born in a tipi camp outside of Fort Sill, Oklahoma, in 1895. Her parents were part of a group of Yaqui Comanche who had come to Fort Sill to collect food rations from the U.S. government. The Comanche had been buffalo hunters of the Great Plains. But by the time of Sanapia's birth, the buffalo was largely extinct, and the Comanche had been forced to leave their homeland and relocate to reservations. Unable to hunt for their livelihood, the Comanche had become dependent on government rations for their survival.

As a girl, Sanapia left her home to attend the Cache Creek Mission School, a boarding school for Indian students. During summer vacation when Sanapia was 13, her mother asked her to train to become an eagle doctor, a traditional Comanche healer. Her mother and her maternal uncle were both eagle doctors and wanted to pass along their knowledge to the next generation.

At first, Sanapia was hesitant. The training of an eagle doctor was an arduous process that took several years. She would also have to agree to live a disciplined life when she began to practice. As an eagle doctor, she would be able to call up supernatural powers. If she did not behave properly or follow the special rules her mother would teach her, this power could do great ill to her patients.

But, as Sanapia knew, being an eagle doctor also had its rewards. With this knowledge, she could cure her people of "Indian sicknesses." Although the Comanche recognized that white physicians could successfully treat some maladies, they believed other illnesses were unique to Indians. These Indian sicknesses could only be remedied with traditional medicine. Being an eagle doctor would also bring Sanapia great status. Among the Comanche, women were considered to be inferior to men. The only exception was medicine women, who not only were thought to be men's equals but also were among the most revered members of the tribe.

Sanapia's father did not want her to become an eagle doctor. A Christian convert, he preached to the Comanche and urged them to adopt white people's values and ways, a position that earned him the contempt of many traditional Yaqui. In his mind, their world had changed forever, and the Comanche needed to recognize that they could prosper on the reservation only if they emulated whites. Sanapia's maternal grandmother—who, following Comanche tradition, had raised her—agreed with her father that the Comanche could not escape the influences of whites. But instead of forgetting the old ways in favor of the new, she urged Sanapia to do everything she could to preserve Comanche traditions. In the end, her grandmother's encouragement finally persuaded Sanapia to become an eagle doctor.

Her three-year training program involved several steps. During the first year, her mother taught her about herbal medicines. Sanapia learned where to collect the herbs, how to prepare medicines from them, and finally how to administer them to patients. After she had mastered these skills, she was educated in diagnosing illnesses and their proper treatment. The final and most important stage of her training was the transfer of supernatural powers to her from her teacher. Because an eagle doctor's powers were dangerous if used improperly, the transfer could begin only if Sanapia were deemed ready by four respected relatives—her mother, uncle, maternal grandmother, and paternal grandfather. Her uncle's approval was the most hard-won. Sanapia fell ill during an influenza epidemic, and her uncle, while treating her, explained that she would never recover unless she committed herself wholly to becoming a healer. Frightened for her life, Sanapia promised him that she would be a good woman and a good doctor. Her uncle gave her a new name—"Memory Woman"—so she could never forget her promise. He then announced that she was ready to receive powers from her mother.

The transfer of powers occurred through a series of rituals. Her mother explained that through these ceremonies she had placed an eagle feather in Sanapia's mouth and an eagle egg in her stomach. Sanapia would now take on certain traits of the eagle that she would need to be a doctor. The transfer concluded with a four-day-and-night rite, during which Sanapia was sent alone to an isolated spot. Her mother warned her that evil ghosts would appear and try to frighten her into giving up her profession. The stories so terrified Sanapia that, unknown to her mother, she sneaked back home every night to sleep. Sanapia later regretted her cowardice. Because she had not performed the ritual properly, she later believed that she was not as powerful as her mother and her uncle. For difficult cases, she often had to call upon their spirits for help.

Immediately after Sanapia had completed her training, her family gave her presents and held a great feast in her honor. But many years passed before she was permitted to use her education. Only after a medicine woman had gone through menopause was she allowed to treat patients. During the intervening years, Sanapia married three times and gave birth to three children, one daughter and two sons.

When Sanapia finally began to practice medicine, the primary Indian illness afflicting the Comanches was "ghost sickness." A person contracted the malady if he or she came in contact with evil ghosts and exhibited fear. The faces of victims of ghost sickness were usually contorted and their hands and arms were often paralyzed. Anthropologist David E. Jones, who interviewed Sanapia in the late 1960s, has speculated that the illness was caused by anxiety. Many Comanche afflicted with ghost sickness were unable to reconcile Indian traditions with the pressure to become part of white society. By turning themselves over to Sanapia's traditional treatments, Jones theorized, her patients were able to resolve their internal conflict and thus were cured of their physical problems.

While studying the Comanche, Jones asked Sanapia to teach him her curing rituals, and she was pleased to oblige. Well into her seventies, she was looking to pass on her wisdom, but none of her children was interested enough in old Indian ways to undergo the training process. To make sure that her knowledge was not completely lost, she adopted Jones as a son and instructed him about her medicines and treatments, which he documented in his book *Sanapia: Comanche Medicine Woman* (1972). Sanapia herself died in 1984 without having the chance to train a successor.

Further Reading

Jones, David E. *Sanapia: Comanche Medicine Woman.* New York: Holt, Rinehart & Winston, 1972.

Schoolcraft, Jane Johnson (Shau-gush-co-da-way-Quay)
(1800–1841)   *Ojibwa writer*

By recording Ojibwa stories, Jane Johnson Schoolcraft helped spark interest among non-Indians in the oral traditions of Indian peoples. She was born Jane Johnson on January 31, 1800, in Sault Ste. Marie on the northern border of Michigan Territory. Her father, John Johnson, ran a fur trading post near La Pointe, Wisconsin, where he met Jane's mother, Susan, who was also known by the Ojibwa name Shau-gush-co-da-way-Quay ("Woman of the Green Valley"). Jane's own Indian name, Bame-wa-wa-ge-zhik-a-quay, translated to "Woman of the Sound That Stars Make Rushing through the Sky."

During Jane's youth, Sault Ste. Marie was a small frontier settlement. With no school nearby, she and her seven siblings were educated at home. Her father taught them to read, write, and study the Bible. He also shared with them his love of history and literature, particularly poetry, and gave them access to the extensive family library. John Johnson took Jane on trips to Detroit and Montreal. To complete her education, he accompanied her to Dublin, Ireland, for an extended stay in 1809.

Susan Johnson was also involved in her children's education. She instructed them in the Ojibwa language and taught them about her people's history, especially the exploits of her father, Waub Ojeeb, an important and influential Ojibwa leader. Like Waub Ojeeb, Susan was a skilled storyteller. She told Jane and her brother and sisters the Ojibwa legends and stories that had been passed by word of mouth for centuries.

In 1822, noted writer and explorer Henry Rowe Schoolcraft arrived in Sault Ste. Marie. He had been hired by the U.S. government to serve as the Indian agent for the region. While boarding with the Johnson family, Schoolcraft got to know Jane, who helped him compile an Ojibwa dictionary. They married in 1823. The couple had two children, Jane and John, who survived childhood.

The Schoolcrafts became leaders in Michigan's cultural life. Henry helped found the Historical Society of Michigan, and together they ran a reading group. Growing out of their work, they began to publish a magazine, *Literary Voyager,* that was distributed as far away as New York City. Its 14 issues included prose and poetry, mostly dealing with the Ojibwa. There were biographies of contemporary Ojibwa, essays about the tribe's culture, and stories based on their oral traditions.

In addition to helping edit the journal, Jane Schoolcraft also wrote much of its content. Most notable were her versions of Ojibwa tales, including "Mishosha, or the Magician and his Daughter" and "The Forsaken Brother." Given the education she received from her mother and father, she was in a fairly unique position. Her background allowed her to fully understand old Indian stories and to adapt them to a Western literary tradition. Schoolcraft's work was among the first efforts to transcribe American Indian oral literature into English for a non-Indian readership.

Fascinated by Indian lore, Henry Schoolcraft went on to write more than 20 books and hundreds of articles. His *Algic Researches* (1839) was particularly influential in introducing non-Indians to Indian literature. It also provided the source material for Henry Wadsworth Longfellow's "Song of Hiawatha." (This famous poem was based on Ojibwa legends recounted by Schoolcraft, but Longfellow borrowed the name of a legendary Iroquois leader for his hero.) It is possible that Jane Schoolcraft may have played a role, perhaps as a researcher or editor, in her husband's influential works.

Long plagued by illness and pain, Schoolcraft moved to Dundas, Ontario, in 1841 to be cared for by her sister. There, she died suddenly on May 22. Although her work was little known during her lifetime, her stories and poetry have recently appeared in several anthologies, including *Native American Women's Writing 1800–1924* (2000) and *The First West: Writing from the American Frontier, 1776–1860* (2002). The Johnson and Schoolcraft family houses in Sault Ste. Marie are now National Historic Sites.

Further Reading

Kilcup, Karen L., ed. *Native American Women's Writing 1800–1924.* Malden, Mass.: Blackwell Publishers, 2000.

Parins, James W. "Schoolcraft, Jane Johnson." In *The Oxford Companion to Women's Writing in the United States,* edited by Cathy N. Davidson and Linda Wagner-Martin, 780. New York: Oxford University Press, 1997.

Ruoff, A. LaVonne Brown. "Early Native American Women Authors." In *Nineteenth-Century American Women Writers,* edited by Karen L. Kilcup, 81–111. Malden, Mass.: Blackwell, 1998.

Sekaquaptewa, Helen (Dowawisnima)
(1898–1990)   *Hopi autobiographer*

In her autobiography, *Me and Mine* (1969), Helen Sekaquaptewa used her personal history to record the changes in the Hopi Indian way of life following the introduction of non-Indian ways and values. Sekaquaptewa was born in 1898 in the Second Mesa village of Oraibi in the Hopi Indian Reservation in present-day northern Arizona. Following Hopi tradition, she was given a name—Dowawisnima ("trail marked by sand")—during a ceremony held at sunrise when she was 20 days old. Her people's old ways also guided her early education. Like all Hopi girls, she was taught how to grind corn, cook, and gather water from the desert village's only well—physically taxing chores that she would one day be expected to perform for her family.

While she was a young girl, Dowawisnima also learned about the tensions growing among the residents of Oraibi. Officials from the U.S. government had come to live among the Hopi and encourage them to adopt non-Indian customs. Some Hopi at Oraibi welcomed these newcomers. They became known as "friendlies" by the government. Other Hopi, like Dowawisnima's parents, wanted nothing to do with whites and resented the friendlies willingness to abandon traditional ways. They were called "hostiles."

In September 1906, the conflict between the friendlies and the hostiles came to a head. The friendlies forcibly drove their traditional neighbors out of the village and confiscated their property. Fearing that the hostiles would soon retaliate, government officials intervened. When the hostiles' leader refused to back down, the government arrested 75 hostile men and sentenced them to ninety days of hard labor. Officials also forced their children to attend government schools. The seven-year-old Dowawisnima and many of her friends were rounded up and herded into wagons, which took them to a boarding school at Keams Canyon.

Dowawisnima's first experiences at the school were terrifying. She was given little food and was cruelly taunted by girls from families of the friendlies faction. Renamed "Helen" by a teacher, she had trouble following her lessons because she knew no English. Although some teachers were sympathetic, others were not. For giving a wrong answer, Helen was struck on the ear by one instructor, a punishment that resulted in a permanent hearing loss. In time, Helen found solace in her schoolwork. A hardworking student, she learned quickly and soon developed a love of reading, which remained a favorite hobby for the rest of her life.

After four years at Keams Canyon, Helen finally was allowed to return to her family for the summer. She stayed for a year until school authorities insisted she return. Helen remained at Keams Canyon until her graduation in 1915. Against her parents' objections, she then decided to continue her education at the Phoenix Indian School instead of going home. Helen's many years away had made her feel uncomfortable around her traditional parents. They belittled white ways, which were now the only ways Helen knew.

In Phoenix, Helen fell in love with a classmate, Emory Sekaquaptewa, and the two were married in 1919. The couple soon started a family and settled in Hotevilla, the village in which Helen's relatives lived. Living in this conservative community proved difficult for the family. In *Me and Mine,* Helen Sekaquaptewa explained that their "lives were a combination of what we thought was the good of both cultures, the Hopi way and what we had learned at school. Whenever we departed from the traditions, our neighbors would scorn us." Frustrated as outcasts, she and Emory moved to an isolated ranch twelve miles southwest of Hotevilla. There they reared their eight children, as well as two adopted sons, free from the interference of other Hopis.

Although government schooling had disrupted her own youth, Helen Sekaquaptewa insisted that her own children receive a formal education. Despite the meager livelihood the ranch provided, she and Emory saved enough money to send their children to the best schools they could. Their education was so important to Helen that in 1954 she moved to Phoenix to keep house for five of her children who were attending school there.

While living in the city, she became a member of the Church of Latter-day Saints, also known as the Mormon church. Through her church activities, she came to know Louise Udall, a Mormon woman who delighted in Helen's stories of her Hopi upbringing. She began to write down the stories Sekaquaptewa dictated. The project continued over ten years and ended with the publication of *Me and Mine* in 1969.

Sekaquaptewa's autobiography documents many ancient Hopi customs as she learned and practiced them as a child. But at its center is the story of the author's struggles as an outsider. Not wholly welcome in either the Hopi or the white worlds, Sekaquaptewa was forced to invent her own, in which she adopted and discarded Hopi and white ways as she saw fit.

Although the book was often critical of their traditions, the success of *Me and Mine* earned Sekaquaptewa the respect of many Hopis. In the 1970s, she decided once again to live among her people, who welcomed her return. Sekaquaptewa remained a prominent elder in the village of Kikutsmovi until her death in 1990.

Further Reading

Bataille, Gretchen M., and Kathleen M. Sands. "Two Women in Transition." In *Native American Women: Telling Their Lives,* 83–112. Lincoln: University of Nebraska Press, 1984.
Sekaquaptewa, Helen. *Me and Mine,* edited by Louise Udall. Tucson: University of Arizona Press, 1969.

Shaw, Anna Moore (Chehia)
(1898–1975) *Pima (Akimel O'odham) autobiographer, civic leader*

At 52, Anna Moore Shaw decided to become a writer with a specific goal in mind—"to help make both Indians and whites aware of the proud heritage of the original Americans." Twenty-four years of work produced two books. In *Pima Legends* (1968), Shaw recounted the tales she had heard as a girl from tribal elders. In *A Pima Past* (1974), she recorded the story of her own life with a focus on her efforts to remember her Pima (Akimel O'odham) roots while living in non-Indian society.

Born in 1898 with the Indian name Chehia, Anna Moore was the youngest of five surviving children of Red Arrow and Haus Molly of the Gila River Indian Reservation. The reservation was at the heart of the Pima Indians' traditional territory in what is now south-central Arizona. In the mid-19th century, white settlers were drawn to the region by the fertile land found adjacent to area rivers. By 1870, Presbyterian missionaries had targeted the Gila River Pima as possible converts. More than a decade passed before the first Pima became a Christian, but many others soon followed suit. The last holdout among reservation leaders was Anna's father, who accordingly was nicknamed "the Unbeliever." Several years before Anna's birth, however, he too converted and even became one of the Pima's most zealous converts. Red Arrow also happily adopted other elements of white culture. He

Anna Moore Shaw shares Pima legends with children on the Salt River Indian Reservation.
(Arizona State Museum, University of Arizona)

cut his long hair, began wearing a shirt and pants, and took the English name Josiah Moore.

In Anna's early years, she lived as a traditional Pima girl. But her father became insistent that his children learn English and receive an non-Indian education. Anna was eager to comply. Left at home alone while her brothers and sisters attended boarding school, she begged her parents to send her away as well. After a year at a mission school in Tucson, Anna became a student at the Phoenix Indian School in 1908. She remained at the school for a decade. For three of her years there, she shared a room with Hopi writer Helen Sekaquaptewa, whose impressions of the school are recorded in her autobiography *Me and Mine* (1963).

The Phoenix Indian School was extremely strict. Students were taught to march in military formations and were expected to be up at five in the morning to begin their chores, such as scrubbing floors and working in the kitchen. If students' work was not deemed acceptable, teachers would beat them with a strap. If children spoke their native language instead of English, school officials would tape their mouths shut as punishment. Such harsh treatment angered or even traumatized many Indian boarding students. In her autobiography, Anna Moore Shaw, however, claimed that she "did not mind, for the matron, teachers, and other employees were good to us." Her lack of ill will toward her teachers, despite their cruelties is characteristic of the friendly and forgiving nature she displays throughout her book. But her familiarity with non-Indian ways and her parents' approval of white educational methods probably also made her adjustment to boarding school somewhat easier than that of most students.

At the Phoenix school, Anna Moore met Ross Shaw when she was 14. The teenagers fell in love and decided to get married. Their plans were interrupted when Shaw was sent as a National Guardsman to Mexico to battle revolutionaries led by Pancho Villa. Shaw was then shipped to Europe to fight in World War I as a U.S. soldier. When he finally returned to Phoenix, Moore was in the process of finishing her education at the Phoenix Union High School. She graduated in 1920 and became the first Indian woman to earn a high school diploma in Arizona.

The same year Moore and Shaw married. They hesitantly decided to settle in Phoenix instead of returning to the reservation. As Anna Moore Shaw later explained, in the city they could "bring in money from the white man's world," some of which they could send home to help out their struggling parents. Nevertheless, the Shaws "felt pangs of guilt and loss" about their choice: "True, we had been educated in the white man's ways, but we were still traditional Pimas with strong feelings of duty to our families and an intense love of the land."

Living in a multiracial neighborhood, Ross worked for the Santa Fe Railroad, while Anna reared their three children. Through frequent visits to the reservation on vacations and weekends, they stayed in close contact with their relatives. When their aging parents became infirm, the couple brought them to Phoenix to spend their last days with family.

For a week, Anna Shaw also helped care for Carlos Montezuma. The renowned Indian activist was a friend of Shaw's brother, who suggested the elderly Montezuma visit Shaw while he was traveling home to die. Shaw's conversations with Montezuma changed her life. In her autobiography, she quotes a speech of his that inspired her to challenge the racial prejudice she encountered among

whites in Phoenix: "To fight is to forget ourselves as Indians in the world. To think of one's self as different from the mass is unhealthy. . . . Make good, deliver the goods and convince the world by your character that the Indians are not as they have been misrepresented to be." From her encounter with Montezuma, Shaw determined that her best weapon against bigotry was assimilation. Putting this philosophy into action, the Shaws moved into a previously "restricted" white neighborhood. Some of their neighbors began to circulate a petition calling for their removal, but largely because of Anna Shaw's friendly overtures and sterling character, the movement petered out. Working on the theory that interaction between races breeds tolerance, Shaw also purposely joined civic groups, such as the Parent-Teacher's Association (PTA) and Church Women United, that had no people of color in their membership. Her hard work won her respect and position. Eventually she was selected to represent Church Women United at conferences in New York City and San Francisco.

After nearly 50 years in Phoenix, the Shaws retired to the Pima's Salt River Indian Reservation. To ease their transition back to a poor, rural community, they built a large house with many of the conveniences to which they had become accustomed in the city. Soon Shaw began to divert her energy into ensuring that similar comforts of white society were available to other Pima. She was particularly determined to better the lot of Pima elders. Shaw was appalled by the "dirt and squalor" of some of their homes and noted in *A Pima Past* that traditionally Pima youths would never allow their older relatives to live in such conditions. She lamented, "What have we Pimas done to ourselves in adopting the white man's ways? Our old people now had to face life all alone, without help, love, or comfort." To help improve the housing and day-to-day lives of the elders, she founded the Aid to the Elderly program in 1966.

Shaw also was concerned that Pima children were no longer learning about the traditional ways. She admitted in her autobiography that her own city-reared children had little interest in old Pima customs. In addition to writing *Pima Legends,* Shaw hoped to reverse this trend through workshops she organized at which elder women taught young Pima the traditional art of basketweaving and through classes she oversaw in which kindergartners learned the rudiments of the Pima language. She also spearheaded an effort to found a Pima museum on the reservation and edited the Pima newsletter *Awathn Awahon.*

Through her community work, Shaw hoped that Pima youths would no longer have to choose between "farming in wretched poverty on the reservation or working hard to get ahead at the city job in the white's man world" as she had. She continued her tireless efforts to improve reservation conditions up until her death in 1975 at 77. Revered by the Pima, Shaw was also honored by non-Indians with her posthumous induction into the Arizona Hall of Fame in 1981.

Further Reading

Bataille, Gretchen M., and Kathleen M. Sands. "Two Women in Transition." In *Native American Women: Telling Their Lives,* 83–112. Lincoln: University of Nebraska Press, 1984.

Shaw, Anna Moore. *A Pima Past.* Tucson: University of Arizona Press, 1974.

———. *Pima Legends.* Tucson: University of Arizona Press, 1968.

Shenandoah, Joanne
(1958–)   *Oneida singer, composer*

According to the Associated Press, Joanne Shenandoah is the "most critically acclaimed Native American singer of her time." Born in 1958, she grew up near Syracuse, New York, on lands traditionally occupied by the Oneida, one of six tribes of the Iroquois Confederacy. Her father, a tribal chief, was a jazz guitarist, and her mother was a music teacher. In addition to learning traditional Iroquois songs at social gatherings, she grew up listening to her parents' records by non-Indian artists, such as Hank Williams, Patsy Cline, and Billie Holiday. Her own passion for music earned her the Indian name Tekaiawahway, meaning "She Sings." Shenandoah has explained that as a child, "singing was as natural to me as breathing."

Attending a private school where she was the only Indian student, Shenandoah threw herself into her music classes. She learned how to play every instrument she could, including the cello, flute, clarinet, and piano. She also studied how to read and write music. But instead of pursuing a career in music, Shenandoah gravitated to the computer industry, where she thought she could more easily earn a living for herself and her daughter, Leah, whom she was raising alone. As she later recalled, "I was working very hard and was doing all the things I thought were important in life."

After 14 years, Shenandoah was a computer executive living in Washington, D.C. One day, looking out her office window, she watched a 200-year-old tree being cut down to make way for a new parking lot. In a moment, she started questioning the choices she had made: "[T]he realization hit me! I just couldn't continue in that lifestyle anymore knowing the Earth was being destroyed. I recognize myself as part of the Earth, and that did it for me." Then and there, she decided she would commit herself to making the most of her talent for singing.

Pursuing a singing career seemed a risky thing to do, especially since there were then few American Indian performers. But from the beginning, Shenandoah received great support from those there were, including Floyd Westerman, Charlie Hill, and Buffy Sainte-Marie. She also credits her work ethic for her early success: "I . . . saw the necessity of developing strong work habits, a common characteristic in every successful Native musician."

In 1989, Shenandoah's first album was released, and the next year, she became a full-time performer. Her music quickly found a following, especially after her work appeared on the soundtrack of the television series *Northern Exposure.* She was soon appearing and collaborating with other popular artists, including Rita Coolidge, Neil Young, and Robbie Robertson.

She has since produced more than a dozen CDs and has had songs on numerous compilations. Shenandoah, who sings in Iroquois, also writes many of her songs. Her work often blends elements of traditional Iroquois music and of contemporary genres, including pop, country, and techno. She has appeared live at many prominent events, such as Woodstock '94, Earth Day on the Mall, and three presidential inaugurations. Her work has also been featured in the PBS program *Songs of the Spirit* (2004), and she was the subject of the PBS documentary *Daughter of Mother Earth* (2003). Recently, Shenandoah has been exploring acting with a prominent role in the 2006 thriller *The Last Winter*.

Shenandoah is also an author. With her husband—journalist and activist Douglas M. George—she wrote *Skywoman: Legends of the Iroquois* (1998). They cofounded Round House Productions, a nonprofit foundation. According to Shenandoah, "The focus is education and the preservation of Oneida culture. We're building a recording studio and maintain one of the largest private collections of Iroquois music."

Throughout her career, Shenandoah has received a wide array of honors, including numerous Native American Music Awards. In 1994, she was nominated for a Pulitzer Prize in music for her composition *Ganondagon,* and in 2002, she was granted an honorary degree from Syracuse University. After helping to lobby for the award category, in 2001 and 2004 she was nominated for the Grammy Award for Best Native American Music Album for her albums *Peacemaker's Journey* and *Covenant.* In 2005, she contributed two songs to the category's Grammy winner *Sacred Ground.*

For Shenandoah, making music remains a mission. She views her gift as a meaningful way of sharing her people's wisdom with others. "Our music is healing, eternal, earth conscious," Shenandoah has explained. "Our songs celebrate our survival and have a deep spiritual essence which will resonate around the world which needs Native music, our music."

Further Reading/Resources

Joanne Shenandoah's Web site. http://www.joanneshenandoah.com. Downloaded on April 25, 2006.

Shenandoah, Joanne. "Native Music Read to Set the World on Fire." *Native Peoples,* March/April 2001, p. 12.

———. *Peace and Power: The Best of Joanne Shenandoah.* Boulder, Colo.: Silver Wave Records, 2002.

Shenandoah, Joanne, and Douglas M. George. *Skywoman: Legends of the Iroquois.* Santa Fe, N.Mex.: Clear Light Publishers, 1996.

Wright-McLeod, Brian. "Joanne Shenandoah." *Native Peoples,* May/June 2004, pp. 36–38.

Silko, Leslie Marmon
(1948–)   *Laguna Pueblo novelist, poet*

"Without question Leslie Silko is the most accomplished Indian writer of her generation," declared the *New York Times Book Review* on the publication of Silko's first novel *Ceremony* (1977). As her career has evolved, Silko has maintained her reputation as one of America's best contemporary novelists.

Leslie Marmon was born on March 5, 1948, in Albuquerque, New Mexico, but grew up on the nearby Laguna Pueblo Indian Reservation. Her father, Lee, was from a prominent reservation family of Laguna and white heritage. Her mother, Virginia, was of Plains Indian and Mexican descent. Reared largely by her great-grandmother and other elder female relatives, Marmon later recalled, "I grew up with women who were really strong, women with a great deal of power . . . within the family." Encouraged to take on traditionally masculine roles, she learned to ride horses and round up her father's cattle at an early age. From her grandmother and great aunt, she was also taught the Laguna Pueblo's ancient stories, which would help to shape her career as a writer.

As a teenager, Marmon commuted to a Catholic school in Albuquerque. Following graduation, she continued her education at University of New Mexico, where she studied English. During her sophomore year, she married John Silko and gave birth to a son, Robert. Busy with her newborn, she signed up for a creative writing class, wanting only an "easy A" that would "bring up [her] grade point average." As she expected, writing did come easy to her. Her upbringing among storytellers also gave her plenty of subject matter for her stories. Recalling the class years later, she explained, "This guy says, 'Write a story.' A lot of people were saying, 'I don't know what I'm going to write about.' And I thought, I don't know what I'm going to start writing about first." Silko also brought to writing a keen knowledge of American and European literature. An avid reader, she has named Flannery O'Connor, Henry James, Kate Chopin, and Isak Dinesen among her influences.

Before graduating with honors, Silko wrote a short story titled "The Man to Send Rainclouds" for a school assignment. Focusing on an encounter between a priest and a group of Pueblos at an Indian funeral, the story was published in the *New Mexico Quarterly*. It also earned her a grant from the National Endowment for the Arts in 1971. At the time, she was attending her third semester at law school at the University of New Mexico. The grant convinced her to abandon the idea of becoming a lawyer in order pursue a career as a writer.

During the early 1970s, Silko financed her writing through other grants and by teaching at the Navajo Community College in Tsaile, Arizona. She completed a book of poems, published as *Laguna Woman,* in 1974. In the same year, seven of Silko's stories appeared in *The Man to Send Rainclouds,* an anthology of the work of young Native American writers.

Taking a job with Alaska Legal Services, Silko moved to Ketchikan, Alaska, where she began writing her first novel, *Ceremony* (1977). The story focuses on Tayo, a Pueblo man who has trouble adjusting to reservation life after he returns from serving in World War II. While many of his fellow Indian soldiers use alcohol to cope, he turns to a Laguna medicine man, who restores Tayo's sense of well-being through the performance of a ceremony that combines traditional elements with modern innovations. The narrative is intertwined with Silko's retelling of traditional Pueblo stories.

Ceremony was published to more acclaim than any Native American novel since N. Scott Momaday's *A House Made of Dawn,* which won the Pulitzer Prize in 1968. Also centering on an Indian veteran's alienation, *Dawn* shared some thematic elements with *Ceremony.* Silko's work, however, concluded on a much more positive note, presenting old traditions as a means to help modern Indians rediscover their connection to their land and to their peoples' past.

After completing *Ceremony,* Silko joined the faculties of the University of New Mexico and later of the University of Arizona. Also struggling with a divorce and custody battle, Silko had trouble finding the time both to teach and to write. She documented her frustrations in a series of letters to James Wright, a poet who became Silko's friend after writing her of his admiration for *Ceremony.* Silko and Wright exchanged correspondence until 1980, when Wright died of cancer. His widow edited a collection of their letters, which was published as *The Delicacy and Strength of Lace* in 1986.

In the early 1980s, Silko's interest in film and photography emerged in several unique projects. With a grant from the National Endowment for the Humanities, she created four films of traditional Laguna stories. In *Storyteller* (1981), she gathered many of her previously written poems and stories in a volume that featured photographs from her own collection.

Silko was honored in 1981 with a fellowship from the John D. and Catherine T. MacArthur Foundation. Popularly known as a "genius grant," the MacArthur fellowship provided Silko with a total of $159,000 tax-free over the next five years. With this income, Silko was free to leave her teaching post and concentrate on her second novel. She originally intended to write a short work about drug-dealing and corruption on the Tucson, Arizona, police force. But as the story evolved, it grew longer and more complex. After nearly a decade of writing, Silko finally published *Almanac of the Dead* (1991), a controversial novel that condemns capitalism and the 500-year history of exploitation of Indians by Europeans and Americans. Since then, Silko has written *Yellow Woman and a Beauty of the Spirit: Essays on Native American Life Today* (1996) and *Gardens in the Dunes* (1998), her third novel.

Silko attributes her success and ambitiousness as a writer to growing up in a culture of storytellers. As she explained in a 1990 interview, "I learned the best thing you can have in life is to have someone tell you a story."

Further Reading

Arnold, Ellen L. *Conversations with Leslie Marmon Silko.* Jackson: University Press of Mississippi, 2000.

Barnes, Kim. "A Leslie Marmon Silko Interview." *Journal of Ethnic Studies* 13 (Winter 1986): 83–105.

Coltelli, Laura. "Leslie Marmon Silko." In *Winged Words: American Indian Writers Speak,* 135–153. Lincoln: University of Nebraska Press, 1990.

Fitz, Brewster E. *Silko: Writing Storyteller and Medicine Woman.* Norman: University of Oklahoma Press, 2004.

Seyersted, Per. *Leslie Marmon Silko.* Boise, Idaho: Boise State University, 1980.

Silko, Leslie Marmon. *Almanac of the Dead.* New York: Simon and Schuster, 1991.

———. *Ceremony.* New York: Viking Press, 1977.

———. *Gardens in the Dunes.* New York: Simon & Schuster, 1998.

———. *Sacred Water: Narratives and Pictures.* Tucson, Ariz.: Flood Plain Press, 1993.

———. *Storyteller.* New York: Seaver Books, 1981.

———. *Yellow Woman and a Beauty of the Spirit: Essays on Native American Life Today.* New York: Simon & Schuster, 1996.

Smith, Jaune Quick-to-See
(1940–) *Flathead-Cree-Shoshone painter*

Jaune Quick-to-See Smith once wrote, "My work comes right from a visceral place—deep, deep—as though my roots extend beyond the soles of my feet into sacred soils." This passion has made her one of the most successful contemporary Native American painters. Smith's work has been exhibited in more than thirty solo shows and can be found in museum collections around the world.

Jaune Smith was born in 1940 on the Flathead Indian Reservation in southwestern Montana. She traces her ancestry from several western Indian groups, including a Salish tribe called the "Flathead" by non-Indians, the Shoshone, and the Cree. Smith is also part French—an element of her heritage reflected in her first name, the French word for "yellow." In her twenties, she was given her middle name, Quick-to-See, by her grandmother, who admired Smith's powers of observation.

Jaune was raised by her father Alfred Smith. Following in the footsteps of many of the women in his family, including his grandmother, Smith made his living as a horse trader. His job kept him always on the move, journeying from reservation to reservation throughout the West to trade the animals he bred. Jaune often accompanied him on his travels. Sometimes, however, he had to leave her behind, frequently in a foster home. By her own count, she lived in more than 50 locations during her childhood.

Despite the constant upheaval in her life, Smith has fond memories of growing up. She enjoyed helping her father take care of his herd. The work was hard, but it gave Jaune a sense of pride in her abilities. Smith later recalled that she was "expected to do whatever a man could do and nobody ever said to [her] 'be a little lady.'" Alfred Smith also taught his daughter to love art. He collected prints of the cowboy scenes and Western landscapes of popular artist Charles M. Russell. Smith himself was an amateur artist, specializing in sketches of animals. When Jaune presented him with her own drawing of a horse, he was so pleased that he hung her work above his bed. By the time Jaune began school, she had decided to become an artist.

After graduating from high school, Smith was determined to continue her education but did not have enough money to attend a four-year college. Working part time, she paid her way through a two-year associate program at Olympia Junior College in Washington State. When she told her art instructor there that she planned to pursue a bachelor's degree in art, the teacher discouraged her. She told Smith that, as a woman, she could never have a career as a painter. The comment haunted her, but she still dreamed of art school. During the next 18 years, she raised a family of three children while working and taking classes. Finally, in 1976, she was awarded a degree in art education from Framingham State College in Massachusetts.

Smith wanted to go on to graduate school at the University of New Mexico, but the school of fine arts rejected her application for admission three times. Smith believes the department was then hesitant to admit any artist whose work displayed "a hint of Indian imagery." In many of her paintings from the 1970s, Smith incorporated simple human and animal figures reminiscent of images Plains Indian artists painted on hides in the 19th century. Only when *Art in America* magazine printed a glowing review of an exhibit of her work in New York City did the university relent. Smith was awarded a master's degree in fine arts in 1980.

While at the University of New Mexico, Smith learned about the history of early 20th-century art in the United States and in Europe. Most of the artists discussed in her classes were white men, but despite the differences between her background and theirs, she was inspired by many of their works. Among the artists who influenced her painting most were Pablo Picasso, Paul Klee, and Willem de Kooning. Their paintings displayed a familiarity with "primitive" art, particularly the sculpture of ancient Africans. Smith also looked to the art of early peoples—the rock paintings, cave paintings, and petroglyphs (carvings or engravings on rocks) left behind by Indians centuries ago.

Smith's paintings from the late 1970s and early 1980s included numerous landscapes featuring abstract forms representing humans, horses, and tipis. Most were painted in a muted palette of earth tones. Smith has explained that the warm grays and deep browns she favored emerged from her memories of the smoky air and leather tools and equipment in her father's bunkhouse.

Starting in the late 1980s, Smith's work changed direction. As she explained in a 1995 interview, "I began to throw caution to the winds and experi-

ment with more materials and mixed media. I also began to see that what I had to say was equally as important as the painting surface. Perhaps more so." In this period, Smith's work became more political. One theme that often appeared in her paintings was the destruction of the natural world. For example, in *Rain* (1990) she attached several stainless-steel spoons, with the bowls pointed down, to a canvas painted with oil and wax. According to Smith, the spoons represent acid rain—a form of air pollution produced by industrial emissions. The painting was inspired by a trip to the Akwesasne Reservation in New York State, where forests of maple trees are dying from acid rain created by nearby steel mills.

Smith has also used her art to protest the theft of Indian land and other abuses committed by non-Indians. In *Trade* (1992), a mixed-media piece, a row of tourist trinkets—such as a plastic tomahawk and a Cleveland Indians sports cap—are hung above a canoe. The work is a humorous commentary on the "trades" made in negotiations, during which the U.S. government took control of Indian land and offered cheap trade goods in return. Also making use of Smith's ironic streak was a controversial work she made in 1992 in response to celebrations of the 500-year anniversary of Christopher Columbus's arrival in the North America. *Paper Dolls for a Post-Columbian World with Ensembles Contributed by the U.S. Government* is a set of paper dolls Smith named Ken and Barbie Plenty Horse. Through their outfits, the artists tells the history of her people's relations with whites. The dolls' clothing includes a housekeeper's uniform (a comment on menial work poor Indians perform for whites at low wages) and a "smallpox suit" (a reference to smallpox-infested blankets given to Indians by government officials in the 19th century).

Throughout her career, Smith has received a wide array of honors. In 1998, she was granted an honorary doctorate from the Pennsylvania Academy of the Arts in Philadelphia. The following year, Smith was awarded an Eiteljorg Museum Fellowship for Native American Fine Art. More recently, the Fort Collins Museum of Contemporary Art paid tribute to Smith's body of work with the 2005 retrospective exhibit "Jaune Quick-to-See Smith: She Paints the Horse."

By her own admission "an obsessive worker," Smith often spends as many as eleven hours a day in her studio in Corrales, New Mexico. For several months a year, however, she travels throughout the country to teach classes and deliver lectures. She has also found time to establish two artists' cooperatives and to organize many exhibits to help young Indians sell their artwork. Among Smith's greatest successes as a curator was "Women of Sweetgrass, Cedar and Sage," a 1985 exhibit featuring the work of thirty female Indian artists ranging in age from their twenties to their seventies. Although Smith cites working in her studio and being with her family as "the two things [that] keep me healthy and balanced," her commitment to helping other Indian artists is strong. To Smith, "the idea of giving back" is "an innate responsibility placed on you when you are born a tribal person."

Further Reading

Abbott, Lawrence, ed. *I Stand in the Center of the Good: Interviews with Contemporary North American Artists.* Lincoln: University of Nebraska Press, 1994.

Hammond, Harmony, and Jaune Quick-to-See Smith. *Women of Sweetgrass, Cedar and Sage.* New York: Gallery of the American Indian Community House, 1985.

Hirschfelder, Arlene. "Jaune Quick-to-See Smith: Salish/Shoshone/Cree Painter." In *Artists and Craftspeople,* 109–116. New York: Facts On File, 1994.

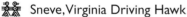 Sneve, Virginia Driving Hawk
(1933–   ) *Lakota Sioux novelist, autobiographer, educator*

Drawing on historical research and her personal experience, Lakota Sioux author Virginia Driving Hawk Sneve strives to present young readers with realistic stories about American Indian life. Born on February 21, 1933, she was raised on the Rosebud Indian Reservation in South Dakota. Virginia's childhood was happy, although her parents were financially strapped. They frequently needed to leave the reservation to find work. Virginia was then placed in the care of one of her grandmothers, both of whom she remembers as great storytellers.

As a girl, Virginia was eager to learn as much as she could. She discovered a 20-volume encyclopedia titled *The Book of Knowledge* and read each volume twice. After attending reservation and parochial schools, she headed to South Dakota State College, where she earned her bachelor's degree in English and history in 1954. Fifteen years later, she received a master's degree in education and guidance.

In 1954, she began teaching high school English. For the next 39 years, she was a teacher and a counselor in both Indian and non-Indian schools in South Dakota. At the same time, she raised three children with her husband, Vance Sneve. His Norwegian heritage prompted their children to refer to themselves jokingly as "Siouxwegians."

Virginia Driving Hawk Sneve began her writing career after her daughter Shirley read *Little House on the Prairie* (1935)—a children's book by Laura Ingalls Wilder based on her childhood memories of life in the 19th-century Midwest. Inspired by her daughter's enthusiasm, Sneve began reading Wilder's "Little House" series. She was appalled that the books had only one reference to Indians, which involved Laura encountering several "naked wild men" who emitted a "horrible bad smell." As Sneve later wrote, "I wondered what ideas my daughter was acquiring about Indians in the fiction she read."

Sneve took the experience as a challenge. She set out to write her own children's stories about Indians without stereotypical or negative language. Her first novel was *Jimmy Yellow Hawk* (1972). The manuscript won an award from the Interracial Council of Minority Books for Children. In this novel, Sneve recounts a Lakota teenager's struggle to reconcile old ways with the modern world. She has since written dozens of books, including *When Thunders Spoke* (1974), *The Trickster and the Troll* (1999), and *Bad River Boys: A Meeting of the Lakota*

Sioux with Lewis and Clark (2005). In addition, Sneve has penned the nonfiction "First American" series, in which each volume explores one American Indian tribe's history and culture.

Sneve has also written several books for adults, most notably *Completing the Circle* (1992). Combining extensive research with personal remembrance, it tells the life stories of the women on both sides of her family. For the book, Sneve won the North American Indian Prose Award.

Sneve has been awarded numerous other honors for her writing. In 1984, she was named Writer of the Year by the Western Heritage Hall of Fame. In 1997, she was given the South Dakota Living Indian Treasure Award. And in 2000, she traveled to Washington, D.C., to receive the prestigious National Humanities Medal. When awarding Sneve the medal, President Bill Clinton celebrated her achievements as "a gifted teacher and story teller": "Her stories have helped us to better define the American experience, to understand the Native Americans who were here before the rest of us had the good fortune to have our ancestors arrive."

Further Reading/Resources

"Sneve, Virginia Driving Hawk." Internet Public Library: Native American Authors. Available online. URL: http://www.ipl.org/div/natam/bin/browse.pl/A118. Downloaded on April 27, 2006.

Sneve, Virginia Driving Hawk. *Bad River Boys: A Meeting of the Lakota Sioux with Lewis and Clark.* New York: Holiday House, 2005.

———. *Completing the Circle.* Lincoln: University of Nebraska Press, 1995.

———. *When Thunders Spoke.* 1974. Reprint, Lincoln: University of Nebraska Press, 1994.

Spotted Elk, Molly (Mary Alice Nelson)
(1903–1977) *Penobscot actress, journalist*

In both the United States and Europe, Molly Spotted Elk was a famed stage performer during the 1920s and 1930s. She was born on November 17, 1903, on Indian Island, a community on the small Penobscot Indian reservation in Maine. She was christened Mary Alice Nelson by a local priest, but the Penobscot pronounced her first and middle names "Molly Dellis."

Molly's father, who once served as tribal chief, supported his family by hunting, fishing, and other traditional activities. Her mother contributed to their income by making baskets for sale to non-Indian tourists. As a girl, Molly helped her mother market her wares. She attracted customers by dancing. Although she knew authentic Penobscot dances, her movements were wild and exaggerated versions that were more pleasing to the non-Indian crowd. Molly loved dancing enough to scrub floors to pay for ballet lessons in Bangor.

Seeing her daughter's talent, Molly's mother encouraged her to go into show business. At the time, several Penobscot performers, including LUCY NICOLAR, had found success in vaudeville. At 15, Molly left home to travel on the vaudeville circuit throughout New England. Even with the relatively low wages earned by Indian entertainers, she was able to send her parents much needed cash. Still, she found the travel wearing and her unsophisticated audiences annoying.

While on tour in Philadelphia, Molly looked up Frank Speck, an anthropologist at the University of Pennsylvania who had spent time on the Penobscot reservation. With Speck's urging, Molly decided to give up show business to study journalism and anthropology at the university. She worked as Speck's assistant while also delivering lectures about Penobscot culture and legends, which she had been collecting since she was a child.

After a year, she was enticed into signing a contract with Miller Brothers' 101 Ranch Wild West Show. Earning a paycheck allowed her again to send money home and to save for college. However, she soon soured on the touring show, which featured reenactments of Indian massacres, and struck out on her own. By 1925, she was working in shows in New York City under the stage name Molly Spotted Elk. She had her greatest success headlining at upscale speakeasies. Scantily dressed and wearing a floor-length headdress, Spotted Elk greeted crowds with the tagline, "Hello, Suckers," before performing her provocative dances. After seeing her act, a film director invited Spotted Elk to star in *The Silent Enemy* (1930), a silent drama about the Ojibwa Indians. Although it failed at the box office, she landed small roles in several other movies, including *Ramona* (1936) and *Lost Horizon* (1937).

In 1931, Spotted Elk headed for France with the United States Indian Band to dance at the International Colonial Exposition. She started performing in Paris, where she was pleased to find crowds interested in realistic accounts of Indian culture. There, Spotted Elk also began to deliver lectures as she had while in college.

In Paris, Spotted Elk met Jean Archambaud, a French journalist. They fell in love and began collaborating on articles for newspapers and magazines. Although Archambaud was supportive of her work, Spotted Elk was wary of marriage, fearing it would get in the way of her career.

The couple struggled financially as their employment opportunities dried up during the Great Depression. At the same time, Spotted Elk discovered she was pregnant. She decided to return home for the birth of child. For four years, she lived on Indian Island with her daughter, Jean, before returning to France. She and Jean Archambaud were reunited in 1938 and married the following year. After World War II broke out, however, Spotted Elk and her daughter decided to return to the United States—a painful decision since her husband was unable to obtain a U.S. visa. Leaving him behind, she and her children escaped France, reached Portugal, and boarded a ship bound for America. After arriving safely in Indian Island, Spotted Elk received news that Jean Archambaud had died in a refugee camp.

For several years, Spotted Elk tried to earn a living working odd jobs in New York, while she left her daughter on the reservation with her family. But the stress of this struggle and her sorrow over her husband's death eventually led to an emotional collapse and a year's stint in a mental institution.

Spotted Elk spent the rest of her life on Indian Island, living in the house she bought her parents with her movie earnings. After her active and flamboyant youth, she lived a quiet life in her old age, spending her time making baskets and dolls. After a fatal fall, she died on February 21, 1977, at the age of 73.

Further Reading

McBride, Bunny. *Molly Spotted Elk: A Penobscot in Paris.* Norman: University of Oklahoma Press, 1995.

Spotted Elk, Molly. *Katahdin Wigwam's Tales of the Abnaki Tribes,* edited by Pauleena MacDougall. Orono: Maine Folklife Center, 2002.

⚇ Swentzell, Roxanne
(1962–) *Santa Clara Pueblo sculptor*

A self-described "sculptor of human emotions," Roxanne Swentzell is one of the most innovative Pueblo artists working in the ceramic arts. She was born on December 9, 1962, in Taos, New Mexico, but spent much of her childhood on the nearby Santa Clara Pueblo. Her mother, Rina Swentzell, later became a noted activist and architect. But like many Santa Clara Pueblo women, she was also a skilled potterymaker. By watching Rina, Roxanne learned how to gather and process clay and how to shape and fire pots.

Roxanne, though, was less interested in pottery than in the human shapes she could fashion from wet clay: "My mom potted so the clay was right there where I saw it all the time. I had a speech impediment so I had to communicate in other ways, and I started making figures that would depict what I meant. I hated going to school so I made a clay figure of a little girl crying to explain how I felt." Hundreds of figurines, depicting her moods and the people around her, followed. By the time she was in junior high school, she started making larger clay figures that were hollow on the inside.

Swentzell continued to struggle in school until she was invited to enroll in the Institute of American Indian Art in Santa Fe. She flourished there and had her first show in the school's museum. Visitors to the museum wanted to buy her pieces, but Swentzell's parents refused to let them, fearing their daughter would too get caught up in the commercial end of the art-making. Nevertheless, they soon relented. Since she was 17, Swentzell has been able to make a living from her work.

Swentzell's large figures are technical marvels, requiring patience and painstaking labor. She starts forming the figures with large clay coils, winding them to form the midsection and padding the clay out to create arms, legs, and heads. Swentzell uses the postures and expressions of her figures to signal an emotional state, as noted by *Native Peoples* magazine in 2003: "From deep reflection to confrontation, wisdom to surprise, pain to heartfelt joy, the range of emotions and experiences communicated through the clay people's faces, gestures and body language is like our own. This, along with the artist's superb technical skill with clay, may explain the enormous popularity of her work."

To help satisfy the great demand for her work, in 1997 Swentzell began having bronze casts made of some of her sculptures. One notable bronze piece is "Life in All Directions." Commissioned by the National Museum of the American Indian, it depicts two Pueblo rain dancers, outside a circle of four figures, each pointing toward one of the cardinal directions.

Despite her recent bronzes, Swentzell has expressed mixed feelings about working in metal. She once observed, "I see bronze as cold and hard, a material that can't crumble back into earth. I was reminded of that one day when the rain was pouring in on my sculpture through an open window. I found myself thinking how easy it would be for my figures to melt back into the earth. There's something pleasing and natural about the idea."

Further Reading

Fauntleroy, Gussie. *Roxanne Swentzell: Extra Ordinary People.* Santa Fe: New Mexico Magazine, 2002.

Peterson, Susan. *Pottery by American Indian Women: The Legacy of Generations.* New York: Abbeville Press, 1997.

"Roxanne Swentzell." *Native Peoples,* January/February 2003, p. 27.

T

Tafoya, Margaret (Maria Margarita Tafoya, Corn Blossom)

(1904–2001)   *Santa Clara Pueblo potter*

Margaret Tafoya was the matriarch of the most famous family of Pueblo potters. One of eight children, she was born Maria Margarita Tafoya in August 13, 1904, and raised on Santa Clara Pueblo in New Mexico. Her Pueblo name was Corn Blossom, but outside of Santa Clara, she was best known as Margaret—the Anglicized version of her middle name.

Her early life was typical for a Pueblo girl at the beginning of the 20th century. She was expected to work hard for her family—carrying water, doing housework, and working in the family fields. Just getting enough food to eat was sometimes difficult. One year during Margaret's youth, her family suffered greatly after a flood destroyed their crops.

Among the Santa Clara, pottery making was a common way for women to earn some extra income for their families. Margaret's mother, Sara Fina, was among the best potters in the pueblo. By watching her at work, Margaret received her first lessons in this traditional art. Sometimes, her mother would give Margaret and her sisters a piece of clay "to make animals or maybe bowls. . . .

Sometimes mother fix[ed] it for us, and that is the way we started, putting our hands in the clay and whether we [knew] it or not, through our playing with clay we learned pottery making."

As a child, Margaret attended elementary school at Santa Clara. She learned to speak English, although she always preferred her Native language. To continue her education, she went to a boarding school in Santa Fe. During her summer home after her first year, her mother decided to train her in pottery making. Sara Fina was a strict teacher who was not shy about criticizing Margaret's work. She wanted to teach her daughter not only artistic techniques but also the discipline and perfectionism that had made her successful.

In 1918, Margaret Tafoya was called home from school when a worldwide flu epidemic struck Santa Clara. Several of her relatives died, including one sister. Her mother told Tafoya her formal education was over. To help her family recover from the crisis, Tafoya would have to start earning money. In addition to making pottery, she also worked as a waitress, cook, and housekeeper outside of the pueblo. Homesick for Santa Clara, she returned to her family. In 1924, she married a distant relative, Alcario Tafoya. Together, they had 12 children, 10 of whom survived infancy. As soon as possible after each pregnancy, Margaret Tafoya returned to pottery making. Her husband sometimes helped her by painting and carving decorations into her pots.

From the beginning of her career, Tafoya's pottery was of the highest quality. She worked in both traditional black-on-black and red-on-red styles. Her pots were often polished to a high sheen and sometimes were adorned with a bear claw design—a symbol of good luck. She was best known for her large-size pots, some of which were as big as three feet tall. Making pots this large was an enormous technical achievement, one that very few Pueblo potters could match.

Especially early in her career, Tafoya liked to experiment with new shapes and designs. But she, like her mother, insisted on using traditional methods. For instance, she always dug her own clay and used a corncob, instead of sandpaper, to polish her work. Tafoya was also determined to preserve these methods by passing them along to her children and grandchildren. As one granddaughter, noted potter NANCY YOUNGBLOOD, recalled, "She always told us, 'if you kids don't carry this on, it's gonna be lost.'"

Tafoya was proud of the money she earned with her pottery. She once said, "I have dressed my children with clay." In fact, with one collector, she had a long-standing arrangement of trading her pots for handmade children's clothing. More often, she and Alcario would load her work into a horse-drawn wagon and take it to Taos or Santa Fe, where she would sell it to art dealers. Tafoya also exhibited her pots at festivals and fairs, such as the Santa Fe Indian Market. In the 1920s, she won her first prize there, a woolen blanket that she treasured for the rest of her life. By 1930, one record shows that she earned $20 for a single pot—then an extremely high purchase prize. At about this time, non-Indians started arriving in Santa Clara on bus tours and by car. These tourists were also eager to buy Tafoya's wares.

In the 1950s, Tafoya became a regular fixture at the Royal Gorge resort in Colorado. Each summer for 10 years, she was hired to exhibit her pottery for visitors. In addition to earning money, the trips were a vacation for her family. Tafoya also enjoyed attending festivals where Indian art was shown. For her, they were mostly social occasions, where she could meet other artists and satisfy her curiosity about their work. Tafoya once said, "It's really nice to go and see your friends and see what kind of things they have—the art they know. They will be different the next year. If you keep coming every year, you see many different things."

The market for Indian art exploded in the 1960s and 1970s. Dealers began visiting pueblos, seeking out artists, and promising to buy anything they made. Yet the art world was slow to recognize Tafoya's talents. By the late 1970s, however, she gained a reputation as one of the greatest Indian potters. In 1978 and 1979, she won back-to-back best-in-show awards at the Santa Fe Indian Market. In 1983, she had her first major show at the Wheelwright Museum in Santa Fe. The next year, she was named folk artist of the year by the National Endowment of the Arts. Among the many other honors she was given were a Lifetime Achievement Award from the Southwest Association of Indian Affairs and a Master Artist Award from the Heard Museum in Phoenix, Arizona.

After an extraordinary career, Margaret Tafoya died on February 25, 2001, at the age of 96. She left behind a legacy of work, that is displayed in collections and museums around the world. But just as important to Tafoya, she kept knowledge of traditional Santa Clara pottery making alive. There are now at least 75 pottery makers in the Tafoya family.

Tafoya once said, "You have to have a good heart when you sit down to make this pottery. . . . You have to live a good life, because the clay knows." Her devotion to her family and to her art continue to stand as a testament to her long, well-lived life.

Further Reading

Blair, Mary Ellen, and Laurence Blair. *Margaret Tafoya: A Tewa Potter's Heritage and Legacy.* Santa Fe, N.Mex.: Schiffer Publishing, 1986.

Dillingham, Rick. *Fourteen Families in Pueblo Pottery.* Albuquerque: University of New Mexico Press, 1994.

Fauntleroy, Gussie. "Great Women Potters of the Past." *Native Peoples,* September/October 2001, pp. 26–27.

Tallchief, Maria
(1925–) *Osage ballerina*

"Onstage, she looks as regal and exotic as a Russian princess; offstage, she is as American as wampum and apple pie," raved *Time* magazine about prima ballerina Maria Tallchief at the height of her fame. One of the most high-profile Indian women of the twentieth century, Tallchief was also the first American dancer in the history of ballet to achieve international fame.

Elizabeth Marie Tallchief (known as Betty Marie to her family) was born on January 24, 1925, in Fairfax, Oklahoma, a small town located on the Osage Indian reservation. About 20 years earlier, oil had been discovered on the Osage lands. Royalties received for leasing their oil-rich tracts to drilling companies made many Osage very wealthy very fast.

Although far from the wealthiest person on the reservation, Tallchief's father Alexander was affluent enough to finance a life of leisure for his family. His wife, Ruth, a white woman of Dutch, Scottish, and Irish descent, however, made sure that her children were always busy. A strict mother, she demanded that Betty Marie and her little sister Marjorie be well educated in the arts and high culture as befitting proper young ladies of the upper class. As toddlers, the girls began a rigorous regimen of lessons in music and dance. Both showed early promise, but driven by her desire to please her stern mother, Betty Marie was determined to stand out. By four, she was already dancing ballet in toe shoes and playing the piano.

Wanting her talented daughters to receive the very best instruction, Ruth insisted that the family move to Beverly Hills, California. There they began to perform before paying audiences. During some performances, the two Osage girls wore buckskin skirts and headdresses for an "Indian" dance. The dance, invented by one of their white teachers, bore no relation to the traditional dances of the Osage. Although they had seen ceremonial dancing on the reservation when they were very young, Betty Marie and Marjorie had never participated in these events.

In her teens, Betty Marie enrolled in the dancing school of Bronislava Nijinska, a famous Russian ballerina and choreographer. Betty Marie had been considering a career as a concert pianist, but awed by the glamorous life of her teacher, she decided to devote herself to ballet instead. In 1942, after graduating from Beverly Hills High School, she moved to New York City and landed her first job in the Canadian touring troupe of the Ballet Russe de Monte Carlo, then the world's best-known ballet company. Singled out as a talented young ballerina, she was soon invited to join the

Maria Tallchief dances in *Firebird,* circa 1950. (Jerome Robbins Dance Collection, The New York Public Library for the Performing Arts, Astor, Lenox and Tilden Foundations)

Ballet Russe's permanent company. Her new employers asked to her take a stage name. They suggested "Tallchieva," which they thought might give their audience the impression that she was from Russia, the home of many of the world's greatest ballerinas. Citing family pride, she refused, but did agree to change her first name to the elegant-sounding "Maria."

In May 1943, she was given the chance to dance her first solo in *Chopin Concerto,* a ballet that had been choreographed by her old teacher Nijinska. An instant sensation, Tallchief was promoted by the Ballet Russe as the "beautiful dancing Osage." The publicity was intended to make Tallchief seem exotic, but to her it seemed silly and slightly embarrassing.

In 1944, Tallchief became the protégé of the Ballet Russe's new ballet master George Balanchine. A brilliant Russian-born choreographer, Balanchine would dictate the course of Tallchief's career. Well-known for recognizing and nurturing young talent, he immediately spotted her potential. In her profound sense of discipline and determination to be the best, he also saw a soul mate. Tallchief quickly became Balanchine's favorite ballerina and won lead parts in many of his works, including *Danses Concertantes* (1944), *La Sonnambula* ("Night Shadow," 1946), and *Le Baiser de la Fée* ("The Kiss of the Fairy," 1947).

Few who had seen Tallchief dance were surprised that Balanchine was enamored of her as a performer. But even their friends were stunned when the two were married on August 16, 1946. More than 20 years younger than her new husband, Tallchief herself was caught off guard by Balanchine's proposal. She later recalled, "When we were married, it was almost really like I was the material he wanted to use. . . . By this time he knew he wanted to start [a] company, and I think he knew that here was the beginning of a company."

In spring 1947, Tallchief and Balanchine journeyed to France. She had been invited to join the prestigious Paris Opera for a season as a guest artist. Her appearance in the company was a historic event: She was the first American ballerina to perform on its stage in 108 years. The European newspapers covering the event were fascinated by her Indian heritage, despite Tallchief's efforts to play down her personal life to the press. Some reporters even made up stories about her youth as an "Indian princess." Rumors also started to circulate that Tallchief was not really a Native American or in fact an American at all. Based on their prejudice that only a European could dance as well as Tallchief, some reviewers speculated that she was actually of French and Russian descent, but had been given an Indian name by the company as a ruse to make her seem like an American.

After returning from Paris, Tallchief joined the new company Balanchine had founded, the Ballet Society (later renamed the New York City Ballet). The Ballet Society was known for its innovative productions, and Tallchief felt lucky to be a part of it. As she explained in a 1987 interview, "I was in the right place and I knew it. I worked hard as I could to be able to dance the way I knew George wanted me to dance."

In the company's early years, Balanchine adapted his choreography to take full advantage of all of Tallchief's strengths as a dancer—her speed of movement, physicality, stamina, and perfect technique. She danced to great acclaim in *The Four Temperaments* (1946), *Symphonie Concertante* (1947), and *Orpheus* (1948). But only after performing the title role in *Firebird* (1949), Balanchine's version of a classic Russian ballet, did she become an international star. Tailored to showcase the steps at which she excelled, *Firebird* was hailed as a masterpiece, but reviewers at the ballet's premiere reserved their highest accolades for her performance. One critic praised her "almost frightening technical range." Another said her firebird "was truly an amazing figure—she preened, she shimmered, she gloried in speed and airy freedom." The audience shared their enthusiasm. At the end of the ballet, she received a standing ovation as her fans mixed shouts of "bravo" with a new cheer: "Tall-chief, Tall-chief, Tall-chief."

Reviewers and audiences continued to lavish praise on Tallchief through the New York City Ballet's next few seasons. But the pressure to top each celebrated performance with an even better one weighed heavily on the young dancer. Balanchine's constant demands and challenges were another source of tension. Unable to endure the stress both at work and at home, Tallchief decided she preferred Balanchine as a mentor to Balanchine as a husband. The two separated in 1950, and their marriage was annulled the next year. Their working relationship, however, continued. In fact, the years following Tallchief's personal split with Balanchine were among her most successful. During this period, she danced many of her greatest parts in ballets choreographed by Balanchine: *Swan Lake* (1951), *Serenade* (1952), *Scotch Symphony* (1952), and *The Nutcracker* (1954).

In 1953, Tallchief's success was celebrated by the Osage Tribal Council, the governing body of the Osage Nation. The council members bestowed on her a title that recognized her importance to the Osage community and the world beyond: Princess Wa-Txthe-thonba, meaning "the Woman of Two Standards." The Oklahoma State Senate further honored her by declaring June 29, 1953, Maria Tallchief Day.

The next year, Tallchief's career hit still another landmark when she appeared on the cover of the October 11, 1954, issue of *Newsweek* magazine. The cover story focused on her new salary of $2,000 a week, which the Ballet Russe had used to lure her away from Balanchine's New York City Ballet. The Ballet Russe desperately needed her star power to boost audience interest in an upcoming tour of Europe, where Tallchief was known as the only living dancer who could rival in technical mastery the greatest European and Russian ballerinas. As *Newsweek* breathlessly exclaimed, the Ballet Russe's offer had made Tallchief the highest-paid ballerina in the world.

Tallchief's tenure with the Ballet Russe was brief. Disappointed with the company creatively, she left after a season and returned to Balanchine and the New York City Ballet. Tallchief remained there for ten years, but her finest years as a dancer were over. As Balanchine turned his attention to younger bal-

lerinas, she lost her prominence in the company. Her frustration that she no longer received the best roles was made worse by her exhaustion. She had to commute to New York from Chicago, where she lived with Henry "Buzz" Paschen, Jr., a construction company executive whom she married in 1956, and their daughter Elisa. This hectic schedule came to an end in 1965, when Tallchief announced her decision to quit the company in order to spend more time with her family.

Nine years later, Tallchief was lured out of retirement by the Lyric Opera of Chicago, which asked her to train its singers to enter and exit the stage gracefully. Soon Tallchief's Ballet School of the Lyric Opera developed its own corps of dancers and began touring. Balanchine, with whom she had remained close, told Tallchief she should start her own company. The result of his encouragement was the Chicago City Ballet, which Tallchief founded in 1980. Her company was affiliated with Balanchine's School of the American Ballet and concentrated on performing his major works.

Although the underfunded Chicago City Ballet was disbanded in 1989, Tallchief is still a major influence in the world of dance. She also remains a powerful symbol as a Native American who has achieved the highest level of success in the arts. For more than 50 years, her grace and discipline has provided a highly visible challenge to the stereotype of the savage, uncivilized Indian. For her contributions to American culture, Tallchief was awarded a Kennedy Center Honor in 1996.

Further Reading/Resources

Belle, Anne, producer. *Dancing for Mr. B: Six Balanchine Ballerinas.* Los Angeles: Direct Cinema, Ltd. VHS, 94 min., 1989.

Livingston, Lili Cockerille. *American Indian Ballerinas.* Norman: University of Oklahoma Press, 1997.

Maynard, Olga. *Bird of Fire: The Story of Maria Tallchief.* New York: Dodd, Mead, & Company, 1961.

Rautbord, Sugar. "Maria Tallchief." *Interview* 17 (March 1987): 60–63.

Sonneborn, Liz. "Maria Tallchief: Osage Ballerina." In *Performers,* 53–65. New York: Facts On File, 1995.

Tallchief, Maria, with Larry Kaplan. *Maria Tallchief: America's Prima Ballerina.* New York: Henry Holt, 1997.

✿ TallMountain, Mary (Mary Randle)
*(1918–1994)   Koyukon Athabascan poet,
short story writer*

"This ability [to write] hadn't been given solely for my pleasure . . . I had an obligation to myself and my peers to use it constructively to rebuild, perhaps, some part of the world I live in," wrote Mary TallMountain about the moment she realized how best to employ her poetic gifts. In eight collections of poems and short stories, TallMountain vividly recreated the world of Nulato. She lived in this small Alaskan village for only six years but it occupied her imagination for a lifetime.

When TallMountain was a child, few non-Indians had ever ventured to her remote home village, which was located about 200 miles west of present-day Fairbanks, Alaska. Although Nulato had housed a few Russian fur traders and Catholic missionaries, most of the residents were Koyukon Athabascan Indians. Mary's mother was of Athabascan and Russian descent; her father, a soldier stationed in Alaska Territory, was of Scottish and Irish ancestry. They fell in love, had Mary and her brother, Billy, and lived together happily for 10 years. They were not allowed to marry, however, because both the U.S. Army and the Catholic church disapproved of mixed-race unions.

TallMountain remembered her childhood as idyllic. Her mother, known as Mary Joe, taught her the old Athabascan customs. "As a child I watched Mary Joe beading by kerosene lamplight, and the brilliant gleam of beads still stirs in my brain the echo of soft-woman talk," she recalled. TallMountain also enjoyed spending time with Billy. "We were as free and happy as storybook children," she once wrote. "Around us always was the infinitely various land. We never imagined such joy would end."

An epidemic of tuberculosis destroyed this happy period for TallMountain. When her beloved mother fell ill, she was treated by a non-Indian physician with the surname Randle. Convinced Mary Joe would soon die, he and his wife offered to adopt her two children and take them away from the infected village. Mary Joe agreed, but the village elders objected to the adoption of Athabascan children by whites. As a compromise, they allowed Mary to leave with the Randles but insisted that Billy should stay with his natural mother.

With her adoptive parents, Mary moved to Oregon. Her mother died, but she continued to write to Billy until he, too, at 17 fell victim to tuberculosis. In her new home, Mary was despondent over her separation from her family. Adding to her despair were the children she encountered in Oregon, who ridiculed her because she was an Indian. Mary was relieved when the Randles relocated to Unalaska, an island off the Alaskan coast, where, TallMountain later wrote, "the beautiful country lured me into a deep sense of the earth, its touch, smell, its spirit." Her adoptive mother, Agnes, also gave her comfort. Agnes Randle taught Mary to appreciate poetry. Together they would recite poems by English masters such as Percy Shelley, John Keats, and Mary's favorite, William Wordsworth. Agnes also encouraged Mary to write her thoughts and stories in a daily journal, a habit she kept throughout her life. One of her stories, a tale about polar bears she had seen in the Seattle zoo, was published in *Child Life* magazine when she was only 10.

At 14, Mary moved with the Randles to California. Soon after she graduated from high school, Doctor Randle died of a heart attack. Still grieving her loss, Agnes was diagnosed with Parkinson's disease and chose to kill herself rather than battle her illness. During this troubled period, Mary married twice, but both relationships were as unhappy as they were brief.

In 1945, Mary Randle left for Reno, Nevada, where she trained to become a legal secretary. She soon moved to San Francisco. There a friend introduced her to Catholicism. She became a student of the faith and discovered that she had been baptized a Catholic as an infant. Although fascinated by her

Mary TallMountain (right) poses with student Cheryl Ann Payne at the University of Alaska, Fairbanks, in 1990. (Mary TallMountain Collection, Alaska and Polar Region Archives, Rasmuson Library, University of Alaska, Fairbanks)

new religion, she began to look to alcohol for relief from the despair of her parents' deaths and her own failed marriages. Overwhelmed by alcoholism and depression, she forced herself to confront her future. Through her self-reflection, she became determined "to make a substantially useful life" and immediately stopped drinking cold turkey. As she set about rebuilding her life, she was faced with a new setback—a diagnosis of cancer. Treatment put the disease in remission, but Randle also credited the "strong survival instinct from my staunch mother and grandmother" with helping her to overcome her illness.

In the early 1960s, Randle began to concentrate on her writing. Tentatively she started to submit her writing for publication using the surname Tall-Mountain, which she had invented during a camping trip. Several of her stories and a collection of her poems were published by the Friars Press. In 1969, she also began to write a regular column for *Way,* a Catholic magazine.

Looking for some guidance in her new career, TallMountain enrolled at San Francisco State College. There she became the student and friend of PAULA GUNN ALLEN, a professor in the Indian Studies Department. TallMountain credits Allen with helping her to hone her talents. Under Allen's direction, she crafted eloquent poems that expressed her sense of personal loss from the many tragedies she had experienced in her life. Allen once compared TallMountain to the trickster hero Coyote, who appears in many Native American myths: "Like that quintessential old survivor, she knows that if you're going to face death, and if you're going to engage the sacred, you'd better have your sense of humor intact."

In 1976, TallMountain decided to return to Nulato, her memories of which figured prominently in much of her work. Although outside influences had changed the village since she had last seen it 50 years before, she still felt a connection to the arctic environment. "My roots are here. I feel them deep in my memories, in the hidden spaces of my blood," she later wrote of her visit home. The trip also breathed new life into her search for her father, whom she had tried to locate for years. At last she discovered him in Phoenix and lived with him there for two years. Before his death in 1978, he shared with her stories of Nulato from her childhood and passed along a deathbed message from her mother. Mary Joe had wanted her daughter to know that she loved her and had sent her away only because she wanted to save her life. The message helped TallMountain overcome the feelings of abandonment that she had struggled with ever since she left Nulato.

In San Francisco, she returned to her writing with a new sense of peace and resolve. During this period, she produced the poems in her second collection, *There Is No Word for Goodbye* (1982). The title poem earned her national attention when in 1982 it received a Pushcart Prize, an award for excellent work published by a small press. Throughout the 1980s and early 1990s, the prolific TallMountain wrote enough poems and stories to fill six more volumes. Her works also frequently appeared in anthologies of Native American literature. TallMountain perhaps reached her widest audience, however, when she was interviewed by Bill Moyers for *The Power of the Word*, a television series produced for the Public Broadcasting Service.

On September 2, 1994, Mary TallMountain died in San Francisco. A memorial service was held at the Tenderloin Reflection and Education Center, which now honors her memory with the annual TallMountain Awards for achievement in creative writing and community service. She asked, however, that her ashes be returned to Alaska. Although she had not lived there for more than sixty years, she still considered it "my talisman, my strength, my spirit's home."

Further Reading

Bruchac, Joseph. "We Are the Inbetweens: An Interview with Mary TallMountain." *Studies in American Indian Literature* 1 (Summer 1989): 13–21.

TallMountain, Mary. *A Quick Brush of Wings.* San Francisco, Calif.: Freedom Voices Publications, 1991.

———. *There Is No Word for Goodbye.* Marvin, S.Dak.: Blue Cloud Quarterly Press, 1981.

———. "You Can Go Home Again." In *I Tell You Now: Autobiographical Essays by Native American Writers,* edited by Brian Swann and Arnold Krupat, 2–13. Lincoln: University of Nebraska Press, 1987.

Welford, Gabrielle. "Reflections on the Writing of Mary TallMountain: Facing Mirrors." *Studies in American Indian Literatures* 9 (Summer 1997): 61–68.

Tantaquidgeon, Gladys

(1899–2001)   *Mohegan historian, anthropologist, curator, medicine woman*

By preserving the Mohegan's cultural heritage, museum founder Gladys Tantaquidgeon was instrumental in obtaining federal recognition for her tribe. On June 15, 1899, Tantaquidgeon was born in Uncasville, Connecticut, the third of seven children of John and Harriet Fielding Tantaquidgeon. Her surname meant "Going along Fast." Like most Mohegan, Gladys could trace her ancestry to Uncas, a famous Mohegan chief of the Revolutionary War era.

When Gladys was young, the Mohegan were made up of a handful of families living in Uncasville. The tribe had no reservation, but they were linked by the presence of the Mohegan Congressional Church, which was built for Mohegan converts in 1831.

The Mohegan were also united by the knowledge of tribal matriarchs. Three elder women, whom Gladys later referred to as grandmothers, decided to share what they knew with her. As she later recalled, "It was customary that the women would observe some of the girls. They would discuss their choice, saying, 'Perhaps it might be well to take this one to learn certain skills.'" When Gladys was five, these grandmothers took her into the woods to gather herbs. They taught her about traditional Mohegan spiritual beliefs and instructed her in how to use herbs to cure the sick.

When she was a teenager, another mentor helped her receive a very different education. He was anthropologist Frank G. Speck, who met Tantaquidgeon while he was studying the Mohegan. Impressed by her, he arranged for her to attend the University of Pennsylvania in 1919. For eight years, Tantaquidgeon studied anthropology at this institution. She then returned home and began a formal study of the herbalism of the Mohegan and other New England tribes. Her research resulted in several books and articles. The most famous was *A Study of Delaware Indian Medicine Practice and Folk Beliefs* (1942).

In 1931, with the help of her father and her brother Harold, Tantaquidgeon founded the Tantaquidgeon Indian Museum. In this one-room structure, they displayed an array of Mohegan artifacts, including an 18th-century beaded belt, portraits of Mohegan leaders, and dozens of traditional baskets.

Tantaquidgeon left home in 1934, when Commissioner of Indian Affairs John Collier asked her to be a social worker among the Yankton Sioux of South Dakota. Four years later, she joined the staff of the recently formed Indian Arts and Crafts Board. This organization, funded by the federal government, was dedicated to helping Indian artisans market their wares. Tantaquidgeon's work with the board helped revive the crafting of ceremonial paraphernalia among some western tribes. Tantaquidgeon returned to Connecticut in 1947. Thereafter, she devoted most of her time to her museum. For decades, she welcomed school groups and other visitors, using the objects in the museum to introduce them to Mohegan history and culture. She believed that by sharing her knowledge she could teach non-Indians to respect the Mohegan people. Tantaquidgeon subscribed to her brother's contention that "you can't hate someone that you know a lot about."

In the 1990s, Tantaquidgeon's work reaped incredible rewards for the Mohegan. The tribal leadership was applying to the U.S. government for official recognition as an Indian tribe. The application required that the Mohegan show they had long been and continued to live as a united tribe. Tantaquidgeon's museum helped establish the Mohegan's tribal history. But even more important were the piles of more recent records that she had been saving over the decades. In Tupperware containers kept under her bed, Tantaquidgeon had stashed away countless letters and postcards, documenting the births, marriages, and deaths of tribal members. This documentation proved crucial in the Mohegan's receipt of recognition in 1994. According to Bureau of Indian Affairs historian Virginia De Marre, "we needed those pieces of paper. They left no questions whatsoever [of the Mohegan's tribal identity]."

Once officially recognized, the Mohegan were able to establish the Mohegan Sun—one of the most successful casinos in the country. Outside the casino now stands a statue of Gladys Tantaquidgeon. She visited the resort once and commented that it was "too green"—a color traditionally considered unlucky by the Mohegan. The green walls were promptly repainted out of respect for Tantaquidgeon.

Tantaquidgeon retired from her museum in 1998, though her grandniece, tribal historian Melissa Tantaquidgeon Zobel, noted that she "still [gave] us direction." Although the Mohegan Sun brought a great deal of income into the tribe, the Mohegan decided to keep the museum in its humble quarters. As Zobel explained, "If we transformed [the museum] into something extravagant, we'd lose the message."

Throughout her long career, Tantaquidgeon received many honors, including honorary doctorates from the University of Connecticut in 1987 and from Yale University in 1994. She was also given the Harriet Tubman Award from the National Organization for Women and awarded admittance into the Connecticut Women's Hall of Fame. In 2000, tribal historian Melissa Jayne Fawcett honored the first hundred years of Tantaquidgeon's life with the biography *Medicine Trail: The Life and Lessons of Gladys Tantaquidgeon.*

On November 1, 2005, Gladys Tantaquidgeon died at her home at the age of 106. Eight years earlier, her niece Jayne Fawcett summed up Tantaquidgeon's great service to her people: "She instilled in us a sense of who we were. We wouldn't have survived the century without her."

Further Reading

Fawcett, Melissa Jayne. *Medicine Trail: The Life and Lessons of Gladys Tantaquidgeon.* Tucson: University of Arizona Press, 2000.

"Gladys Tantaquidgeon, Mohegans' Medicine Woman, Is Dead at 106." *New York Times,* 2 November 2005. Available online. URL: http://www.nytimes.com/2005/11/02/nyregion/02tantaquidgeon.html.

Martin, Douglas. "Tribe's Past and Future Are the Legacy of Its Anthropologist Matriarch at 98." *New York Times,* 4 June 1997, sec. B, p. 1.

Tapahonso, Luci
(1953–) *Navajo (Dineh, Diné) poet, short story writer*

With both critics and readers, Luci Tapahonso is among the most acclaimed young Native American poets. Tapahonso was born in 1953 in Shiprock, New Mexico, on the Navajo Indian Reservation. The sixth of 11 children, she grew up in a large family that, like many reservation Navajo (Dineh), earned its livelihood by farming. According to Tapahonso, her household was "semitraditional." Although she learned Navajo ways and values as a young girl, she was also familiar with the culture of non-Indians. Characteristic of this

upbringing, her first language was Navajo, but as she grew older her parents taught her to speak English fluently so that she could communicate with people living outside of the reservation.

After graduating from Shiprock High School in 1971, Tapahonso decided to become a investigative reporter. With this goal in mind, she participated in a training program for aspiring journalists sponsored by the National Indian Youth Council. In 1976, she also enrolled in the journalism department of the University of New Mexico. There, while taking an English class with Native American novelist LESLIE MARMON SILKO, Tapahonso began to consider a new career. While in high school, she had started writing poetry but had been too shy to share her work with others. Feeling comfortable with Silko, she showed her teacher these and more recent poems she had written. Silko was excited by Tapahonso's talent and urged her to submit them for publication. Tapahonso approached several publications, and to her surprise they were eager to print her work. From then on, Tapahonso has explained, "things just fell into place"; her early success made it easy for her to devote herself to her poetry.

Tapahonso earned a bachelor's degree in English in 1981, then started classes toward an advanced degree in creative writing. Before receiving her master's in 1983, she published two books of poetry. *One More Shiprock Night* (1981) was illustrated by Tapahonso's husband, Earl Ortiz, an Acoma Pueblo artist. *Seasonal Woman* (1982) featured works by the prominent Native American painter R. C. Gorman. After several years of lecturing at the University of New Mexico, Tapahonso joined the faculty as an assistant professor in 1987. That year, her next volume of poetry, *A Breeze Swept Through* (with art by JAUNE QUICK-TO-SEE SMITH), appeared. In 1990, Tapahonso moved to the University of Kansas where she is currently an associate professor. Tapahonso combined short stories and poems in two subsequent books, *Saanii Dahataal, The Women Are Singing* (1993) and *Blue Horses Rush In* (1997). She has since become a professor of American Indian Studies and English at the University of Arizona.

In writing her poetry, Tapahonso draws on her knowledge of both the Navajo and the English language. The words usually come to her in Navajo; she then translates them into English before writing them down for others to read. She developed the technique because she has little command of written Navajo. But this method of composition also reflects her emotional response to her two languages. "I learned Navajo first, and then learned English at home as a matter of necessity," she explained in 1990 interview. "I have always connected English with matters outside my home, and I connect Navajo with the language of my home, and food, and sounds, and descriptions, and people telling me about various things."

Much of Tapahonso's work deals with her memories of reservation life and with the stories and remembrances other Navajo have shared with her. Many of her poems, often with a gentle humor, tell of the everyday experiences of her friends and relatives. For example, one of her best-known poems, "Hills Brothers Coffee," recounts the simple pleasure of sharing a cup of coffee with her uncle. Her two daughters—Lori Tazbah and Misty Dawn—also make frequent appearances in her poems.

In the contemporary Navajo world of Tapahonso's work, traditional Navajo ways and non-Indian influences blend easily. References to Spam and Diet Pepsi are as likely to be sprinkled through her poems as mentions of Navajo dishes. In her own life, she has also achieved a balance between the traditional and nontraditional. Although her career has required her to spent much of her adult life living among non-Indians, her Indian identity and bond to the reservation remain strong. In 1981, she wrote of the connection to the Navajo homeland that continually inspires her work: "I know that I cannot divide myself or separate myself from that place—my home, my land, and my people. And that realization is my security and my mainstay in my life away from there."

Besides her stories and poems, Tapahonso has also published several children's books, including *Navajo's ABC: A Diné Alphabet Book* (1995) and *Songs of Shiprock Fair* (1999). In 1996, she was fea-

Luci Tapahonso is best known for her poetry.
(Courtesy University of Arizona Press, Photo by Monty Roessel)

tured on Rhino Records' *In Their Own Voices: A Century of American Poetry.*

Further Reading

Crawford, John, and Annie O. Eysturoy. "Luci Tapahonso." In *This Is about Vision: Interviews with Southwestern Writers,* edited by William Balassi, John Crawford, and Annie O. Eysturoy, 194–202. Albuquerque: University of New Mexico Press, 1990.

Bruchac, Joseph. "For What It Is: An Interview with Luci Tapahonso." In *Survival This Way: Interviews with American Indian Poets,* 271–285. Tucson: University of Arizona Press, 1987.

Tapahonso, Luci. *Blue Horses Rush In.* Tucson: University of Arizona Press, 1997.

———. *A Breeze Swept Through.* Albuquerque, N.Mex.: West End Press, 1987.

———. *Navajo's ABC: A Diné Alphabet Book.* New York: Simon & Schuster Books for Young Readers, 1995.

———. *One More Shiprock Night.* San Antonio, Tex.: Tejas Art, 1981.

———. *Seasonal Woman.* Santa Fe, N.Mex.: Tooth of Time, 1982.

———. *Saanii Dahataal: The Women Are Singing.* Tucson: University of Arizona Press, 1993.

Te Ata (Mary Francis Thompson, Te Ata Fisher)

(1895–1995) *Chickasaw storyteller*

World renowned as a storyteller and performer, Te Ata was born Mary Frances Thompson on December 3, 1895. She was raised in Tishomingo in present-day Oklahoma. When she was seven, her elderly aunt gave her the name Te Ata, which in Chickasaw meant "bearer of the dawn."

Te Ata's father was half-Chickasaw and once served as the treasurer for the Chickasaw Nation. He refused to teach his children the Chickasaw language, seeing it as unnecessary for getting ahead in non-Indian society. He did, however, share with them the old stories of the Chickasaw's oral traditions. Te Ata memorized the tales and acted them out for the family. Her fascination with Indian oral history was encouraged by her high school teacher MURIEL H. WRIGHT. A distinguished Chickasaw historian, Wright urged her to collect Indian stories to add to her repertoire.

In 1915, Te Ata enrolled in the Oklahoma College for Women (now the University of Science and Arts of Oklahoma), where she studied theater. After graduating, she continued her studies at the Carnegie Institute of Technology. She also began performing on the Chautauqua Circuit, which featured lecturers and entertainment meant to edify the audience. Her performances took her all around the country. At each stop, she sought out people would could tell her new Indian stories she could adapt for her act.

Te Ata moved to New York City in 1922. She performed in Shakespeare plays and Greek tragedies, including a production of Euripides's *The Trojan Women* on Broadway. But soon she concentrated on developing a one-woman show, in which she sang Indian songs and told Indian stories. Wearing a deerskin dress, she often performed in character—playing everyone from a dying tribal elder to a young warrior. Te Ata strove to make her act not only entertaining but also educational. She hoped to give her non-Indian audiences a better understanding and appreciation for Indian cultures.

Te Ata's act garnered great acclaim. One of her biggest fans was Eleanor Roosevelt, who repeatedly invited her to New York's governor's mansion. After Roosevelt's husband had won the presidency, she asked Te Ata to perform at the White House in 1933 and at a picnic held for the English king and queen in 1939. Roosevelt had a lake in upstate New York named in Te Ata's honor.

Te Ata was photographed in the 1930s during a visit with Menominee elder John V. Satterlee.
(Neg. no. 284212, photo by Clyde Fisher, courtesy the Library, American Museum of Natural History)

While in New York, Te Ata also became friends with Clyde Fisher. Fisher was a scientist at the American Museum of Natural History and the founder of its Hayden Planetarium. Te Ata and Fisher were married from 1933 until his death in 1949.

After decades in New York City, Te Ata returned to Oklahoma in 1966. There, she continued to perform until about 1980. She received many honors during her long career, including admittance to the Oklahoma Hall of Fame in 1958. In 1987, she was the first Oklahoman to be named a "State Treasure." A few weeks shy of her 100th birthday, Te Ata died in Oklahoma City on October 26, 1995.

Further Reading

Green, Richard. *Te Ata: Chickasaw Storyteller, American Treasure.* Norman: University of Oklahoma Press, 2002.

Tekahionwake

See JOHNSON, EMILY PAULINE

Tekakwitha, Kateri (Catherine Tekakwitha, Lily of the Mohawks)
(1656–1680)   *Mohawk nun*

Kateri Tekakwitha, also known as the Lily of the Mohawks, is revered by Catholics throughout the world. The Catholic church declared Tekakwitha venerable in 1943 and blessed in 1980—the first two of three steps toward sainthood. If she is canonized as a Catholic saint, she will be the first Native American to be granted this distinction.

Tekakwitha was born in 1656 in a Mohawk village near present-day Auriesville, New York. Her mother, an Algonquin Indian, had converted to Christianity. She was taken captive by Mohawk warriors who invaded her homeland and brought her to live among their tribe. She was made a full member of the Mohawk and married Tekakwitha's father, a noted warrior and village leader.

In 1660, when Tekakwitha was four, a smallpox epidemic swept through her village. The Mohawk there died in great numbers. Among the victims were Tekakwitha's little brother and both of her parents. She escaped with her life, but lost much of her eyesight because of the disease. Smallpox also ravaged her appearance, leaving her face severely scarred with pockmarks.

The orphaned Tekakwitha was taken in by the husband of her mother's sister, who was an important Mohawk chief. He was known for his hatred of Christians, particularly the French Catholic priests of the Jesuit order who had come to North America intent on converting Indians to their religion. The government of France supported the priests' efforts because it hoped to win the friendship and allegiance of Native Americans in what is now the northeastern United States and Canada. By trading with the Indians, Frenchmen obtained animal furs, primarily beaver pelts, which they could resell in Europe at an enormous profit. To keep the fur trade active, the French government was eager to establish close ties with Indian tribes and encouraged the Jesuits to convert as many Indians as possible. The Jesuits had had great success in converting the Huron Indians, the Mohawk's greatest enemies and competitors in the fur trade. As friends of their enemies, the priests along with their Christian teachings were held in contempt by many Mohawk. In the decade before Tekakwitha's birth, they had tortured and executed several Jesuits, including three in her home village.

For many years, the Mohawk warriors routinely attacked French settlements and the villages of their Indian allies. To end the raids once and for all, the French government waged a great counterattack in 1666. Their troops were so successful that the Mohawk agreed to suspend the fighting. In the peace that was negotiated, tribal leaders hesitantly agreed to allow three Jesuit priests to live among them.

The priests arrived in Tekakwitha's village in 1667. For three days, they were housed by her uncle, and the 11-year-old girl seemed impressed by their gentle manner. She soon became fascinated with the Jesuits' Christian teachings and to the disgust of her uncle declared in 1676 that she wanted to receive their formal instruction with the aim of becoming a Catholic convert. The priests found her an unusually enthusiastic student. After several months, she was deemed ready to enter the church. On Easter Sunday, she was baptized in the chapel the Jesuits had built in her village. She was given the baptismal name "Catherine," which when spoken by the Mohawk became "Kateri."

With her conversion, Tekakwitha became an object of ridicule among her Mohawk neighbors. She was mocked and jeered, and on Sundays, when she refused to work the fields with the other women, she was pelted with stones. She was accused of practicing sorcery and scorned for refusing to take a husband. From the priests, Tekakwitha learned about Catholic nuns and their vow of chastity. Against the objections of her family and of the Jesuits, she declared that she too would never marry. Her insistence deeply offended the Mohawk, who were angered by her unwillingness to start her own family and take on the work and responsibility befitting a proper Mohawk woman.

Amidst mumbled death threats, Tekakwitha escaped from her village with the help of three Christian Mohawk. One night when her uncle was away she traveled with them by canoe to a new Mohawk settlement named Kahnawake. At Kahnawake the consumption or trade of alcohol was prohibited. The village had been founded by Mohawk who were alarmed by the ill effects on the tribe caused by liquor given to them by European traders. The discipline of the residents in turn made the village an attractive home and haven for a large number of recently converted Mohawk like Tekakwitha.

At Kahnawake's Christian mission, Tekakwitha resumed her study of Catholicism with increased fervor. Although the priests there encouraged her to marry, she continually insisted that she wished to remain chaste as a nun would. With two other Mohawk converts, she also asked to be permitted to start her own convent. Although impressed by their all-encompassing embrace of Catholicism, the Jesuits felt their conversions were too recent to take this step. The priests refused their request but agreed in 1679 to allow Tekakwitha to take the vow of chastity.

The Jesuits also were simultaneously heartened and disturbed by the passion with which Tekakwitha practiced her new religion. To express her love of Christ, she embraced a life of complete self-sacrifice. She ate very rarely, and the little food she allowed herself she mixed with ashes. Tekakwitha often prayed outside in the dead of winter, in few clothes and surrounded by snow, to show her devotion. She was also known to sleep on a bed of thorns and to whip herself as a demonstration of her religious ardor.

Kateri Tekakwitha appears in this 18th-century engraving.
(General Research Division, The New York Public Library, Astor, Lenox and Tilden Foundations)

Although regarded by all as an exemplary Christian, Tekakwitha alarmed the mission priests with the extremity of her behavior. Some historians have speculated that her actions may have been rooted in the Mohawk culture in which she was raised. Among the Mohawk, who often inflicted great physical pain on their war captives, the ability to endure torture without emotion was greatly respected. Tekakwitha had heard of and perhaps visited nuns in Montreal, who were known to flog themselves. Perhaps as a Mohawk, Tekakwitha saw special worth in this form of self-torture. To her it may have functioned both as evidence of devoutness as a Catholic and also as proof of personal honor as a Mohawk.

The physical trials to which Tekakwitha subjected herself may also have reminded her of actions the Mohawk sometimes took to encourage themselves to dream. Dreaming was very important in the Mohawk's worldview. The Mohawk believed that the proper interpretation of dreams was necessary to ensure a person's physical and mental well-being. Not dreaming was considered unhealthy, so if someone did not have dreams while sleeping, they were made to hallucinate, often through fasting or self-mutilation. Tekakwitha may have emulated the similar self-inflicted sacrifices of the Montreal nuns because they reminded her of her own native religion.

Even Tekakwitha's insistence in remaining chaste may have emerged from her Mohawk upbringing. Traditionally, Mohawk women could decide to remain virgins throughout their lives. Such women were permitted to live together in a cloistered setting, much as Catholic nuns do. The Mohawk, however, had put an end to this practice after several cloistered women became drunk from alcohol given to them by non-Indian men. The women's behavior was so embarrassing to Mohawk leaders that the virgin enclaves were disbanded. Perhaps the memory of this incident, still fresh in the minds of many Mohawk, contributed to their shunning of Tekakwitha after she announced her determination to remain a virgin.

The physical abuse Tekakwitha inflicted on herself at the Kahnawake mission quickly took its toll. On April 17, 1680, during Holy Week, she died at the age of 24. Later accounts held that on her deathbed the pockmarks on her face disappeared, and she became radiantly beautiful.

Soon after Tekakwitha's death, several Jesuits wrote about her life as a model Christian convert. As her legend spread, her grave received more and more visitors. Many attributed visions or cures to her intercession with God on their behalf.

The Catholic clergy continued to document her life and miracles. In 1884, the Jesuits drafted a petition to the Third Plenary Council of the Bishops of the United States that called for her consideration for sainthood. Their request was formally presented to the Vatican in Rome, the headquarters of the Roman Catholic Church, in 1932. Having been named both venerable and blessed, her canonization remains under consideration. Several organizations are devoted to promoting the declaration of her sainthood; they claim more than 10,000 members in the United States alone. Tekakwitha has also become an important symbol to Native American Catholics. The growing Kateri Tekakwitha Movement today advances a unique form of Catholicism practiced by many American Indians.

Further Reading

Blanchard, David. ". . . To the Other Side of the Sky: Catholicism at Kahnawake, 1667–1700." *Anthropologica* 24 (1982): 77–102.

Grassmann, Thomas. "Tekakwitha, Catherine." In *Notable American Women: 1607–1950,* edited by Edward T. James, 436–7. Cambridge, Mass.: Belknap Press, 1971.

Greer, Allan. *Mohawk Saint: Catherine Tekakwitha and the Jesuits.* New York: Oxford University Press, 2005.

Mathes, Valerie Sherer. "American Indian Women and the Catholic Church." *North Dakota History* 47 (Fall 1980): 20–25.

Peterson, Jacqueline, and Mary Druke. "American Indian Women and Religion." In *Women and Religion in America, vol. 2,* edited by Rosemary Radford Ruether and Rosemary Skinner Keller, 1–41. San Francisco, Calif.: Harper & Row, 1983.

Teters, Charlene

(1952–   )   *Spokane activist, installation artist, educator*

Through her art and activism, Charlene Teters protests the demeaning of Indian peoples and cultures. Born on April 25, 1952, she grew up in Spokane, Washington, but later relocated to the nearby reservation of the Colville Confederate Tribes. There she raised her two children, George and Kristal, while working as an illustrator, a tutor, and an adviser to the National Park Service.

At 32, Teters moved to Santa Fe, New Mexico, to attend the Institute of American Indian Arts. She concentrated on painting, creating traditional images of Indian women and children. After two years, she continued her studies at the College of Santa Fe, earning a bachelor's degree in 1988. The next year, she was recruited to study for a master's degree at the University of Illinois, Urbana.

Attending a university football game with her children, Teters was horrified by the team mascot, Chief Illiniwek, a non-Indian dressed in Plains Indian regalia who did a mock war dance for the crowd. "My kids just sank in their seats," Teters later said. "I saw my daughter trying to become invisible." Teters responded with a one-woman protest. On game days, she stood outside the sports arena, holding up a sign reading "Indians are not mascots. We are human beings." She continued to draw attention to the issue by founding the National Coalition on Racism in Sports and Media. Her role in sparking the movement to put an end to Indian mascots was highlighted in the documentary *In Whose Honor* (1997), which aired on the PBS series *Point of View.* On October 10, 1997, Teters also appeared on *ABC World News Tonight,* where she was honored as the "Person of the Week."

Teters's political activism changed her art. She abandoned painting and began making installations. In pieces such as *What We Know about Indians* (1991) and *It Was Only an Indian* (1994), she has used her art to comment on mainstream America's dehumanization of Indians. As she once explained, "I think there's no such thing as apoliti-

cal work. Because you're either reinforcing the status quo or you're not." In 2002, Teters became the first artist-in-residence at the American Museum of Natural History. The museum commissioned from her an installation dealing with the Indian mascots for its "Baseball as America" exhibit.

In addition to making art, Teters began teaching at the Institute of American Indian Arts in 1997 and joined the faculty of California State Polytechnic University in 2006. Teters has won numerous awards for her work, including an honorary doctorate from Mitchell College in 2000 and the Allan Houser Memorial Award in 2002.

Further Reading/Resources

Charlene Teters Web site. URL: http://www.charleneteters.com. Downloaded on May 12, 2006.

Rosenstein, Jay, producer. In *Whose Honor?* Harriman, N.Y.: New Day Films. DVD, 47 min., 1997.

Thanadelthur

(ca. 1695–1717)   *Chipewyan peacemaker, interpreter*

In the early days of the Canadian fur trade, Thanadelthur forged a peace between her people, the Chipewyan, and their traditional enemies, the powerful Cree. She was probably born at the end of the 17th century but nothing is known about her life until 1713. In that year, she was captured by a band of Cree warriors and taken to live in their village as a slave. After more than a year, she and another Chipewyan captive managed to escape. Surviving by hunting small animals as they traveled, they tried to return home but had to turn back when winter set in. Her companion died of starvation and exhaustion, but Thanadelthur pressed on. At last she was able to save herself by following tracks left by English traders on a hunting expedition. They took her to York, a post operated by the Hudson's Bay Company, an English fur-trading operation. The Hudson's Bay employees took in the young Chipewyan woman, who was near death after her harrowing escape.

As she was recovering, the governor of the post, James Knight, eagerly extended his friendship to her. Knight was impressed by Thanadelthur's courage and strength, but he had an ulterior motive for welcoming her to York. Knight wanted to establish a new post to the north in Chipewyan territory, from which his men could trade European goods to Chipewyan hunters in exchange for animal furs. The company could then sell the furs in Europe for an enormous profit. At York, the Englishman had already begun to trade in this way with the Cree. Because the English were Cree allies, the Chipewyan did not trust them. Knight concluded that the only way the English could be trading partners of both the Cree and the Chipewyan would be to establish a truce between the two warring tribes. Thanadelthur was central to his plan. Because she could speak both Indian languages, she could act as an interpreter in the negotiations.

Knight asked Thanadelthur to join a peace delegation of 150 Englishmen and Cree. He entrusted her with a supply of trade goods to present to her people as a sign of the English traders' good intentions. The delegation set off for Chipewyan territory in June 1715. Disease and bad weather forced most of the men to return to York, but Thanadelthur and a band of about a dozen Cree continued on until they stumbled upon the corpses of nine Chipewyans, who they presumed had been massacred by other Cree. Thanadelthur's companions refused to go any further. They feared that a retaliation party of Chipewyan would mistake them for the killers and take their revenge. Thanadelthur, however, would not let them abandon the mission. She told them to set up camp and journeyed into Chipewyan territory alone. In a few days, she returned with a delegation of more than 100 Chipewyan, ready to negotiate. The representatives of both tribes were afraid of one another. Their discussions continued only because Thanadelthur insisted to each group that the other wanted peace as much as they did. Anyone who was hesitant to negotiate received a severe dressing-down. An English eyewitness wrote, "She made them all Stand in fear of her she Scolded at Some and pushing of others . . . and forced them

to ye peace." In the end, the mission was a success. Thanadelthur triumphantly returned to York in May 1716 with a party of ten Chipewyan, which probably included her brother.

Continuing to live at the post, Thanadelthur became Knight's trusted adviser. To cement the new Chipewyan-English alliance, he asked her to take another trip into Chipewyan territory in the spring. She eagerly agreed and even promised that she would leave the Chipewyan man she had recently married if he refused to accompany her. Despite her determination, disease prevented her from carrying out her plans. She and several of the other Chipewyan at York fell deathly ill during the long, harsh winter. On February 5, 1717, the day of Thanadelthur's death, Knight's journal entry paid an emotional tribute to his friend and counselor: "I am almost ready to break my heart. . . . She was one of a Very high Spirit and of the Firmest Resolution that ever I see any Body in my Days."

Further Reading

McCormack, Patricia A. "The Many Faces of Thanadelthur: Documents, Stories, and Images." In *Reading beyond Words: Contexts for Native History*, 329–364. Orchard Park, N.Y.: Broadview Press, 2003.

Van Kirk, Sylvia. *Many Tender Ties: Women in Fur Trade Society in Western Canada, 1670–1870*. Norman: University of Oklahoma Press, 1980.

Thorpe, Grace
(1921–   )   *Sauk-Fox activist*

Grace Thorpe has been an effective activist for Indian causes for nearly four decades. Born in 1921 in Yale, Oklahoma, she was the youngest of the three daughters of Jim and Iva Thorpe. Her famous father was a football star and an Olympic champion who won gold medals in both the pentathlon and decathlon in 1912.

After attending her father's alma mater—the Indian boarding school in Carlisle, Pennsylvania—Thorpe joined the Women's Army Corps (WACs). During World War II, she was stationed in New Guinea and Japan, where she served on the staff of General Douglas MacArthur. While in the military,

Thorpe met and married Fred Seeley. The couple had one daughter and one son before divorcing. In 1950, Thorpe returned to the United States and settled in the town of Pearl River, New York.

With the emergence of the Indian rights movement in the mid-1960s, Thorpe became involved in a variety of issues regarding Native Americans. In 1966 she helped to obtain land for the Deganawidah-Quetzalcoatl University, a school in California for Indian and Chicano students. She also worked as a conference coordinator of the National Congress of American Indians (NCAI), the largest multitribal organization in the United States.

Radicalized by her experiences, Thorpe was on the front line of several Indian protests of the late 1960s. She was particularly affected by the occupation of the island of Alcatraz by the members of the American Indian Movement (AIM) in 1969. The protest made Thorpe determined to devote herself to furthering Indian rights. She later explained, "Alcatraz was the catalyst . . . It made me put my furniture into storage and spend my life savings." During the occupation, Thorpe acted as the protesters' public relations representative. She arranged for visits to the island by Jane Fonda, Candice Bergen, and other celebrities sympathetic to Indian causes and thus helped put a media spotlight on the protesters' demands. Thorpe also participated in the attempted takeover of a military base at Fort Lawson, Washington, by the Nisqually Indians and in the battle between the Pit River Indians of California and the powerful Pacific Gas and Electric Company for control of the tribe's homeland.

Recognizing Thorpe's skill as an organizer, the U.S. Senate Subcommittee on Indian Affairs hired her as a legislative assistant in 1974. Thorpe later served for two years on the House of Representative's American Indian Policy Review Board. During the 1970s, she also found the time to return to school. She received a paralegal certificate from the Antioch School of Law in 1974 and a bachelor's degree in history from the University of Tennessee at Knoxville in 1980.

In the same year, Thorpe returned to Yale, Oklahoma, and became active in the Sauk and Fox tribal government. She has served as a tribal court judge and member of the tribe's health council. Her interest in health issues recently has made her an opponent of nuclear waste disposal companies, who with the support of the federal government have targeted Indian reservations as potential dumping sites. To battle the nuclear industry and inform Indians about the dangers of nuclear waste, she founded the National Environmental Coalition of Native Americans (NECONA) in 1993. In recognition of her work, she was named an honoree at Oklahoma's Native American Heritage Celebration Day in 2003.

On a personal front, Thorpe has also staged a battle to restore her father's Olympic gold medals. Jim Thorpe had been stripped of the medals in 1913, when it was reported that prior to the Olympic games he had played a season of semipro baseball. Although technically he had violated of the Olympic committee's rules, many felt that the Olympic hero was treated unfairly because he was an Indian. To right what they believed were past wrongs, Grace Thorpe and her sister Charlotte helped found the Jim Thorpe Foundation. Largely due to the organization's efforts, the International Olympic Committee reversed its decision against Jim Thorpe and in 1983, 30 years after his death, presented duplicate gold medals to his family.

Further Reading

Morrison, Scott. "Grace F. Thorpe." In *Notable Native Americans,* edited by Sharon J. Malinowski, 433–434. Detroit: Gale Research, 1995.

National Environmental Coalition of Native Americans. Available online. URL: http://oraibi.alphacdc.com/necona. Downloaded on February 14, 2006.

Thorpe, Grace F. "The Jim Thorpe Family." *Chronicles of Oklahoma* 59 (Summer 1981): 91.

Tibbles, Susette La Flesche
See La Flesche, Susette

Tse-Sah-Wee-Ah
See Hardin, Helen

Tse Tsan
See Velarde, Pablita

V

 Velarde, Pablita (Tse Tsan)

(1918– 2006) *Santa Clara Pueblo painter*

A pioneer in the field of Native American painting, Pablita Velarde created images of Pueblo life that have been admired internationally for their beauty and power. But throughout her long career, Velarde painted with another purpose in mind. As she once explained in an interview, she saw her work as visual learning tools about the Pueblo people: "I think if I leave enough paintings it will be an education of everybody about very true things that happened in the pueblo."

Pablita Velarde was born on September 19, 1918, as the Sun rose over Santa Clara, a Pueblo Indian village approximately 30 miles south of Santa Fe, New Mexico. Four days later, her grandmother Qualupita gave the infant her Indian name during a traditional naming ceremony. A medicine woman trained in using herbal medicines and in performing rituals, Qualupita held the baby to the north, south, east, and west, then to the sky and to the ground. She then declared that her granddaughter's name was Tse Tsan ("golden dawn" in the Tewa Pueblo language).

When Tse Tsan was three, her mother, Marianita Velarde, died of tuberculosis. Soon after, the girl fell ill with an eye infection that left her blind. Her father, Herman, treated her with traditional medicines, and two years later, her vision returned. Seeing the world again was a thrilling experience for the five-year-old Tse Tsan. She started to look at objects, people, and the landscape with a new determination to memorize the slightest detail about them. As she later recalled, after she regained her sight, "I wanted to see everything."

The next year, Herman Velarde sent Tse Tsan and her two older sisters to St. Catherine's, a boarding school for Indian students in Santa Fe. The nuns who ran the school gave Tse Tsan a new name—"Pablita," the Spanish version of "Pauline." From the nuns, Pablita learned English and academic subjects taught in non-Indian schools. But during the summers, when she returned to Santa Clara, her relatives gave her an education befitting a traditional Pueblo girl. Qualupita shared with Pablita her knowledge of curing and showed her how to use clay to make pots and adobe bricks, the building blocks of Pueblo houses. Herman instructed her about Pueblo customs and history by telling her stories that had been passed down by word of mouth for centuries. Wandering around the cliffs and caves near Santa Clara provided Pablita with an additional history lesson. There she saw the huge cliff-dwellings built by her Pueblo ancestors and studied the petroglyphs—pictures scratched onto rock faces—that they left behind.

At 14, Pablita Velarde left St. Catherine's to start the eighth grade across town at the Santa Fe Indian School. Her first year there, a new teacher, Dorothy Dunn, came to the school and established the Studio, which she was determined to make a center for art training for Native Americans. Dunn concentrated on teaching her students to create pictures using charcoal and paint on paper and canvas. Indian artists had only recently begun to use these non-Indian materials. At the time, among the few who had developed an expertise in drawing and painting were a group of artists at the San Ildefonso Pueblo, who had begun painting scenes of Indian life with watercolors in the 1910s. The only woman among them was TONITA PEÑA. By her people, she was considered to be a rebel because traditionally only Pueblo men were painters. Female artists were responsible for carefully molding the Indians' beautiful pottery, but male artists were given the honor of painting them with geometric designs.

Inspired by the San Ildefonso watercolorists, Dunn encouraged her students at Santa Fe to use their art to record the traditional customs of their peoples. She told them not to draw from life, but instead to tap their childhood memories for subject matter. In the 1930s, non-Indian influences were rapidly changing Indian communities in the Southwest. In the minds of many whites at the time, the students' somewhat romanticized childhood impressions provided a more "authentic" view of Indian life than a visit to a reservation or Indian village could.

Dunn also advocated the same painting style that had developed at San Ildefonso. With the encouragement of white teachers and patrons, the San Ildefonso artists painted flat, unshaded figures against an almost bare background. The figures themselves, however, were highly detailed, with their clothing, hair, and other features intricately rendered. As Velarde started studying with Dunn, she took to this style immediately. Because of her keen attention to her surroundings following her

bout with blindness, she was able to remember and represent everyday scenes from her youth with the utmost care. Also at Dunn's urging, she incorporated the ancient designs and petroglyphs she had seen on rocks near her pueblo.

Velarde quickly emerged as one of Dunn's best students. Yet, as the only female pupil taking all of the classes Dunn offered, her first year at the school was difficult. Because painting was traditionally a male activity, the boys taunted her, telling her that she should give up art class and go to work in the school kitchen. Velarde endured their abuse, and her courage inspired other girls to take courses with Dunn. Velarde's own confidence was boosted when Tonita Peña paid a visit to the Santa Fe school. The example of Peña, who had fearlessly flouted tradition to become an artist, moved Velarde to ignore the opinions of others and make the most of her talent.

Following her first year at the Studio, several of Velarde's works were displayed in a student show at the Museum of New Mexico. Her paintings attracted the attention of Olive Rush, a Santa Fe artist who invited Velarde and two other students to help her paint a series of murals on the theme "A Century of Progress" for the 1933 Chicago World's Fair. Rush was so impressed by Velarde's work that the next year she asked the student to assist her on murals commissioned by the Works Progress Administration (WPA), a federal government program that hired artists to create public artwork during the depression of the 1930s.

In 1936, Velarde graduated from the Santa Fe school, thus becoming the first member of her family to earn a high school diploma. She then returned to Santa Clara, where she took a job as an assistant teacher at an Indian day school. She also worked as a nanny for Edward Thompson Seton, the founder of the Boy Scouts of America. This post gave her a precious opportunity to travel, when she agreed to accompany Seton and his family on a four-month lecture tour of the eastern United States.

When Velarde returned to Santa Clara, Rush asked her to contribute a mural to a series to be exhibited outside of the Maisel Trading Post in Albuquerque, New Mexico. Like many of Velarde's works, the mural depicted Pueblo women. In this image, a row of the women appear in richly patterned calico dresses standing behind a display of traditional pottery.

In 1938, she received an even more exciting commission from the National Park Service. This federal government agency hired her to paint a series of murals at the Bandelier National Monument Museum, which was built at the site of ancient cliff dwellings like those in which she had played as a girl. The series took nearly two years to complete and included paintings depicting a wealth of traditional Pueblo activities, which Velarde researched extensively through historical research and interviews with Santa Clara elders. The scenes portrayed Pueblo ceremonies and rituals; artistic endeavors such as basket making and beadwork; and daily work such as house building, farming, and gathering wild plants. The incredible detail of these paintings make them of value not only as art but also as documents about the Pueblo way of life.

As the United States prepared to enter World War II (1939–45), the National Park Service, in the face of budget cuts, was forced to lay off Velarde. She then moved to Albuquerque where she worked as a telephone operator and met Herbert Hardin, a white man whom she married in 1942. The couple soon had a family. In 1943, Velarde gave birth to a daughter, HELEN HARDIN. The next year, a son, Herbert Hardin II (known as "Herby"), followed.

The war years were difficult for Velarde. With her husband in the armed services, she had to care for her two young children largely on her own. To make ends meet, she sold handmade jewelry and dolls as well as her paintings. Despite her financial difficulties, she made a point of taking Helen to Santa Clara after her birth so that her baby could be given a name in the traditional Pueblo manner by her great-grandmother Qualupita.

After the war, the family settled in Albuquerque. There Hardin took a job with the police department,

Pablita Velarde poses next to a painting in this photograph from the mid-1950s.
(Courtesy Palace of the Governors, Neg. no. 16927)

and Velarde again began to work for the National Park Service. She also started exhibiting her paintings in local shows and competitions. At the time, art lovers and tourists in the Southwest were developing an enthusiasm for "Traditional Indian Painting," as the style shared by the Santa Fe Studio artists and the San Ildefonso watercolorists was called. In 1948, Velarde won her first major prize in a competition sponsored by the Philbrook Art Center in Tulsa, Oklahoma. Many more honors followed, and she quickly became a favorite of Indian art collectors. Journalists wrote articles about her work, and several times television producers asked her to appear on their shows to talk about Pueblo culture.

Although Velarde was excited by the attention, her new celebrity made her husband uncomfortable.

Tensions between them grew until they were divorced in 1959. Velarde then returned to Santa Clara, where she sought out her father for comfort and companionship. The two had fallen out of touch after he had remarried in the mid-1930s, but after the emotional strain of the end of her marriage, Velarde was eager to renew the ties between them.

When she visited her father, she often asked him again to share the old Pueblo stories with her. Fearing that the tales would be forgotten as traditional elders such as her father died, Velarde began to write them down and translate them into English. The project inspired her to create a new series of paintings to illustrate the ancient myths. One of these works, *Old Father, the Story Teller,* is now one of her most famous paintings. It depicts her father telling a group of children the story of how the Pueblo people were created and how all creatures came to earth from a lower world. As the storyteller describes the creatures, they appear to come to life above him against the dark blue background of the night sky. In 1960, the stories Velarde transcribed and her illustrations of them were collected in a book titled after this painting.

In the late 20th century, Velarde was acknowledged both throughout the United States and abroad as a major Native American artist. In recognition of her achievements, she received many honors. The most notable include the 1954 Palmes Académiques from the French government, the 1977 New Mexico Governor's Award, and the 1990 award from the Women's Caucus of Art.

On January 10, 2006, Pablita Velarde died in Albuquerque, New Mexico, at the age of 87. In commemorating her death, Stuart Ashman of the state's Department of Cultural Affairs said, "Her work is a defining element in the aesthetic of the Southwest."

Perhaps just as important was the example her career provided to younger Indian women. Her trailblazing in a previously male domain paved the way for many female artists, including her daughter Helen, who became one of the most distinguished Indian painters of the next generation.

Further Reading

Gridley, Marion E. "Pablita Velarde, Artist of the Pueblo." In *American Indian Women,* 94–104. New York: Hawthorn Books, 1974.

Hirschfelder, Arlene. "Pablita Velarde: Santa Clara Potter." In *Artists and Craftspeople,* 53–60. New York: Facts On File, 1994.

Nelson, Mary Carroll. "Pablita Velarde." *American Indian Art* 3 (1978): 50–57, 90.

Ruch, Marcella J. *Pablita Velarde: Painting Her People.* Santa Fe: New Mexico Magazine, 2001.

Velarde, Pablita. *Old Father, the Story Teller.* 1960. Reprint, Santa Fe, N.Mex.: Clear Light Publishers, 1989.

W

Waheenee (Buffalo Bird Woman)
(ca. 1839–1932) *Hidatsa autobiographer*

From 1906 to 1918, Waheenee, an elderly Hidatsa woman, had countless conversations with a white man named Gilbert L. Wilson, an anthropologist who came to study her people. The relationship between Waheenee and Wilson grew close enough that she asked him to become her adopted son. An even more lasting result of their friendship was two books, based on remembrances Waheenee shared with her son Edward Goodbird, who then translated her Hidatsa words into English for Wilson to transcribe. *Waheenee* (1921) is the story of her youth, during which the Hidatsas still practiced most of their centuries-old customs. *Agriculture of the Hidatsa Indians* (1917), her description of how Hidatsa women farmed their lands, is possibly the most detailed account of traditional Native American farming methods ever recorded.

Waheenee was born in about 1839 in one of three Hidatsa villages located near the mouth of the Knife River in present-day North Dakota. The Lewis and Clark Expedition had encountered the Hidatsa in 1804, and soon after, other non-Indians, including the artist Karl Bodmer, had visited the tribe. Through this early contact with whites,

the Hidatsa were infected with smallpox, a non-Indian disease to which they had developed no natural immunities. Two years before Waheenee's birth, a terrible epidemic struck the Hidatsa and their close relatives and neighbors the Mandan. Smallpox killed more than half of the Hidatsa, while the disease decimated nearly the entire Mandan population.

After this disaster, the Hidatsa and Mandan banded together. Nevertheless, their numbers were so reduced that they were still vulnerable to their Indian enemies, particularly the Dakota Sioux. To escape the Dakota, the Hidatsa leaders decided in 1845 to relocate their people to Like-a-Fishhook Point, located upstream along the Missouri River about 30 miles from their traditional villages. One of Waheenee's first memories was traveling to this new tribal home.

Waheenee was the daughter of a Hidatsa leader named Small Ankle and his wife Weahtee. Following tribal custom, Small Ankle was also married to Weahtee's three sisters. Waheenee therefore grew up in a female-dominated household, in which she regarded her three aunts as mothers. As a baby, Waheenee was given a name meaning "Good Way." But when she proved sickly, her father, understandably concerned about her contracting a deadly illness, insisted that she take on a new name that might protect her. As a result, she was renamed Waheenee (meaning "buffalo bird" or "cowbird") because birds were believed to have great power. Waheenee grew into a healthy child and later in her autobiography concluded that the name had "brought [her] good luck from the gods."

Unfortunately, her good fortune did not extend to all of the Hidatsa. When she was six, they experienced another great smallpox outbreak. Her mother, her brother, and one of her aunts were among the victims. After her mother's death, Waheenee was left in the care of her grandmother Turtle. As an adult, Waheenee remembered Turtle as a tough old woman whose harsh pronouncements scared many of her friends. Turtle was also a traditionalist who refused to use the manufactured goods that many Hidatsa were then acquiring from non-Indian traders at Fort Berthold, a trading post established near Like-a-Fishhook in 1845. Although iron hoes from the traders were durable and effective farm tools, Turtle was unwilling to give up the hoe she made from the shoulder blade of a buffalo in the traditional Hidatsa manner. She told Waheenee, "I am an Indian. I use the ways my father used."

Waheenee (left) slices prairie turnips in a photograph by anthropologist Gilbert Wilson, circa 1910.
(Neg. no. 286314 [photo by Gilbert Wilson], courtesy the Library, American Museum of Natural History)

In her autobiography, Waheenee describes a childhood filled with playing games, caring for the tribe's dog pack, and listening to old Hidatsa stories told by her father. Only when she reached the age of twelve was she expected to give up her playtime and set about learning the tasks and responsibilities of a Hidatsa woman. Waheenee enjoyed women's work, particularly tanning hides and sewing them into clothing. She was proud of her sewing and embroidery and noted that one of her aunts rewarded her tanning talents by giving her a belt, a prized possession of Hidatsa women. Waheenee also learned to weave mats and baskets, to build earth lodges, and perhaps most important to plant and maintain the tribe's fields. Like the men of tribes of the central Plains, Hidatsa males hunted buffalo as well as smaller game. But the corn, beans, and squash grown by the women of the tribe were the staples of their food supply. For this reason, the labor of Hidatsa women was at the center of the tribe's traditional economy.

At 18, Waheenee's family arranged for her to take on another women's role, that of wife. She and her half-sister married Magpie, a man from a neighboring family, and according to custom he moved into their earth lodge. Thirteen years later, Magpie died of tuberculosis. After mourning for a year, Waheenee was told by her relatives that she needed to remarry. As she recalled, "My family wished me to marry again, for, while an Indian woman could raise corn for herself and her family, she could not hunt to get meat or skins." Waheenee took Son of a Star as her new husband. In 1869, she had her only child, a son they named Goodbird.

Waheenee's adulthood coincided with a period of great change for the Hidatsa. From 1850 to 1870, many Americans settled in the region surrounding Like-a-Fishhook and Fort Berthold. To acquire land for these whites, the U.S. government pressured the Hidatsa to give up their territory. In 1870 a treaty established the Fort Berthold Indian Reservation and confined the Hidatsa within its borders. In 1885, the government dissolved the reservation it created only 15 years earlier in order to end the tribal practice of owning land in common. Instead each Hidatsa household was allotted 160 acres of land as private property. In addition to forcing the Hidatsa to adopt this non-Indian method of landownership, the United States also compelled the Indians to take on the customs of non-Indian society. As part of this assimilation campaign, Waheenee's son was sent to mission schools where he was taught to speak English and schooled in the tenets of Christianity.

When anthropologist Gilbert Wilson came to study the Hidatsa in 1906, the influence of whites had drastically transformed the Indian society in which Waheenee had grown up. Wanting to leave a written record of the Hidatsa past, he asked her to tell him about the old ways. He was particularly interested in the Hidatsa's farming methods, which became the subject of the dissertation he wrote to earn his doctorate. Wilson encouraged Waheenee to tell him not only about how she farmed but also about what this labor meant to her. As a consequence, she shared with him all aspects of her lifelong work as an agriculturist. His book records the Hidatsa's ecologically sound farming techniques, Waheenee's favorite recipes, the ceremonies she performed and songs she sang to make her crops grow, and a description of the social ties among women that resulted from their working together in the fields.

To transcribe Waheenee's stories, Wilson enlisted the translation skills of her son, who had been given the Christian name Edward. The anthropologist also took down Edward's autobiography, which was published under the title *Goodbird the Indian* (1914). During the course of his research, Wilson developed a relationship with Waheenee's younger half-brother Wolf Chief as well. Wilson discovered that Wolf Chief and Goodbird had in most ways assimilated into white society, whereas Waheenee remained a steadfast traditionalist. In large part, the men had no choice but to take a new path. Traditionally, Hidatsa males were hunters and warriors. With the destruction of the great buffalo herds and the confinement of their enemies to reservations, they could no longer perform their traditional roles. Women, however, had more options.

They could adopt white ways, or like Waheenee, choose to live as Hidatsa women, whose skills as farmers were still valued.

Waheenee made some concessions to changing times. She moved out of her earth lodge into her son's log house. But until her death in 1932 she preferred to live as Hidatsa women had for many centuries. As she stated in her autobiography's final chapter, "For me, I cannot forget our old ways."

Further Reading

Gilman, Carolyn, and Mary Jane Schneider. *The Way to Independence.* St. Paul: Minnesota Historical Society Press, 1987.

Goodbird, Edward. *Goodbird the Indian: His Story, Told by Himself to Gilbert L. Wilson.* New York: Fleming H. Revell, 1914.

Wilson, Gilbert L. *Buffalo Bird Woman's Garden: Agriculture of the Hidatsa Indians.* 1917. Reprint, St. Paul: Minnesota Historical Society Press, 1987.

———. *Waheenee: An Indian Girl's Story Told by Herself to Gilbert L. Wilson.* 1921. Reprint, St. Paul: Minnesota Historical Society Press, 1987.

WalkingStick, Kay
(1935–)   *Cherokee painter*

One of the most distinguished Native American painters working today, Kay WalkingStick was born in 1935 in Syracuse, New York, far from the Oklahoma homeland of her Cherokee ancestors. Months before her birth, her mother had left Oklahoma and Kay's alcoholic father to build a new life for her family in the East. As a result, WalkingStick grew up in white society with little knowledge of Cherokee culture. As she has explained, "My view of myself as an Indian was based on an idea alone"— an idea that she later used her art to explore.

WalkingStick graduated from Beaver College in Glenside, Pennsylvania, with a bachelor's degree in fine arts in 1959. For the next 10 years, she raised her family while painting and working as an art teacher. Her work during this period was, by her own description, "realistic" and "hard-edged." Sensing that she had taken her representational

style as far as she could, she started moving toward abstraction in the early 1970s. At the same time, WalkingStick's Indian identity became a focus of her life and work. "I was going through a period in which I was trying to discern just how Indian I really am," she stated in a 1994 interview. After delving into a study of Native American history and art, WalkingStick turned to her painting for answers. In her words, "Creativity is an investigation for me. So this was a way to investigate my Indianness."

This period of self-analysis produced WalkingStick's "Chief Joseph" series. These 36 abstract paintings expressed her emotions toward the story of the 19th-century Nez Perce chief, who unsuccessfully resisted the U.S. government's efforts to force his people to live within reservation borders. WalkingStick created the works by covering canvases with layers of a paint-and-wax mixture and then cutting designs into the layers with a razor blade. With this series, she began applying the paint with her hands, a technique that grew out of her research into her Indian roots: "I felt a lot of the energy of . . . tribal work came through the fact that the artists made these pieces with their hands rather than with tools."

During this period, WalkingStick also created *Messages to Papa* (1974), a tipi-like sculpture in the middle of which she hung a letter to her father and a copy of the Lord's Prayer written in the Cherokee language. The piece was an attempt to come to terms with her ambivalent feelings toward her father. WalkingStick used the image of a tipi, though it is not a traditional Cherokee dwelling, because it symbolizes Indianness to many non-Indians. "I was making this tepee for my father . . from a white view, my white view, the white side of myself," she has explained.

In the mid-1980s, WalkingStick began to paint the diptychs (two-paneled canvases) for which she is now best known. As WalkingStick once explained, "[T]he diptych is an especially powerful metaphor to express the beauty and power of uniting the disparate and this makes it particularly attractive to those of us who are biracial."

On most of these works, one side is abstract and the other is representational. She has also concentrated increasingly on landscapes as a subject. Among these works are paintings of ancient southwestern Indian sites, including Canyon de Chelly and Mesa Verde.

Following the death of her husband in 1989, WalkingStick began work on a series of diptych drawings and paintings that often featured waterfalls, which she has described as "a metaphor for the onrush of time and the unstoppable, ultimate destiny of our lives." Some of her most recent works have also included self-portraits and human forms.

For many years, WalkingStick taught art at Cornell University, but in 2004, she left this post to work full time at her New York City studio. WalkingStick has shown her work in many solo and group exhibitions. In 2003, the Eiteljorg Fellowship for Native American Fine Art named her the year's Distinguished Artist. Kay WalkingStick received another great honor in 1995 when she became the first Native American artist to have her work appear in H. W. Janson's *History of Art,* the standard textbook for art history students in American colleges and universities.

Further Reading

Abbott, Lawrence. "Kay WalkingStick." In *I Stand in the Center of the Good: Interviews with Contemporary North American Artists,* 269–283. Lincoln: University of Nebraska Press, 1994.

Archuleta, Margaret. "Kay WalkingStick (Cherokee)." In *Path Breakers,* 13–30. Indianapolis, Ind.: Eiteljorg Museum of American Indians and West, 2004.

Kay WalkingStick Web site. URL: http://www.kaywalking-stick.com. Downloaded on January 8, 2006.

WalkingStick, Kay. "Democracy, Inc.: Kay WalkingStick on Indian Law." *Artforum* 30 (November 1991): 20–21.

———. "Native American Art in the Postmodern Era." *Art Journal* 51 (Fall 1992): 15–17.

Ward, Nancy (Nanye'hi)

(ca. 1738–ca. 1822)   *Cherokee tribal leader*

As a teenager, Nancy Ward was given the title *Ghighau* ("Beloved Woman")—the highest honor the Cherokee people could bestow on a woman—in recognition of her bravery on the battlefield. Throughout her life, the Cherokee relied on Ward's courage to help them in the greatest battle they would ever face—the fight to retain their southeastern homeland and live there in peace.

Born in the Cherokee village of Chota near present-day Knoxville, Tennessee, Ward was given the Indian name Nanye'hi ("One Who Goes About"). She was reared by her mother, Tame Deer, and her father, Fivekiller, who was probably half Delaware Indian. Her mother's brother, Attakullakulla, was the chief in charge of all civic affairs.

When Nanye'hi was in her early teens, she married a young warrior named Kingfisher. The couple had two children—Fivekiller and Catharine. That they called their boy by an Indian name and their girl by an English name reflects the ways in which the Cherokee world was changing. Many European settlers were moving into Cherokee territory—a large expanse in portions of what are now Kentucky, Tennessee, Virginia, North Carolina, South Carolina, Alabama, and Georgia. Some Cherokee, such as Nanye'hi's uncle Attakullakulla, believed that the tribe should learn to live peacefully with these foreigners and even take on some of their ways. Others felt that, unless the Cherokee struck out with force against the intruders, more and more would follow.

In 1755, Kingfisher went into battle against the Cherokee's old Indian enemies, the Creek. By his side was Nanye'hi, who shouted words of encouragement to him while she handed him bullets for his gun. She first chewed ridges into each bullet so that any wound they made would be tearing and bloody. During the fray, Kingfisher was shot. Nanye'hi reached over his dying body, grabbed his weapon, and continued the fight. She also sang a Cherokee war song to inspire fierceness in her fellow warriors.

The Cherokee won the conflict—the Battle of Taliwa—and, with the victory, gained control over areas in present-day Alabama and Georgia previously occupied by the Creek. The tribe credited Nanye'hi for their triumph and chose her to be their Beloved Woman. The tribute carried with it weighty responsibilities and duties. As a Beloved Woman, Nanye'hi could go to meetings of the Cherokee Council. This council was usually only attended by men, although women had great influence and power in Cherokee society. Nanye'hi also became the head of the Women's Council and was in charge of preparing Black Drink, a power-giving tea that warriors drank before going into battle.

Several years after Kingfisher's death, Nanye'hi married an Irish trader, Brian Ward, who lived in Cherokee territory. They had a daughter, Elizabeth, before separating. In traditional Cherokee marriages, couples could declare themselves divorced whenever circumstances recommended that they part. Ward had a European wife, who had resettled in present-day South Carolina and with whom he wanted to be reunited. Nanye'hi—who became known as Nancy Ward to white settlers after her marriage—apparently remained on good terms with her second husband. Several historical documents indicate that she and Elizabeth periodically paid visits to Ward's white family.

Perhaps through her affection for her second husband, Nancy Ward developed a regard for the settlers among her people. She resisted the Cherokee faction that advocated attacking whites, particularly after the outbreak of the American Revolution (1776–83). Some Cherokee were drawn into this conflict between British soldiers and the rebellious American settlers. The Cherokee had been allies of the British, who urged the tribe to join the war effort on their side. Of course, many warriors needed little encouragement. They were eager to go into battle against the American farmers who were taking over their lands.

In July 1776, Ward heard that her cousin, Dangerous Canoe, was planning to lead an attack against several white settlements. She secretly sent a message warning the settlers of the impending raid. Most were able to escape before the warriors arrived, but in the ensuing fight, one white woman, known in surviving documents only as Mrs. William Bean, was taken captive. Traditionally, the Cherokee killed their war captives. Bean was to be burned alive, but as she was being tied to the stake, Ward intervened. One of the special powers she had as a Beloved Woman was to reverse a captive's death sentence. On Ward's demand, Bean was set free and came to live with Ward while she recovered from wounds sustained in the raid. While living with Ward, Bean passed along her knowledge of weaving cloth and raising dairy cows. With hunting lands becoming scarce, both of these skills were of great use to the Cherokee. In the past, the tribe had primarily worn clothing made of buckskin, but as hunting grew difficult they needed cloth garments. The lack of available game animals also had made meat scarce. Dairy products such as milk and cheese could take its place in the Cherokee food supply. Because of her kindness to Bean, Ward was able to bolster the Cherokee economy by passing along the valuable skills her white friend had shared with her.

A less fortunate result of the Cherokee raid was a counterattack leveled by the Americans. Now seeing the Cherokee as enemies equal to the British, American soldiers attacked many of the tribe's major villages. Ward's home village, Chota, however, was spared, perhaps because of the Americans' appreciation of Ward's help.

In 1780, Ward heard of another Cherokee attack planned on American civilians. Again she sent a message of warning, and again the Americans launched a devastating counterattack after the Indians' raid. As a letter sent to Thomas Jefferson, then governor of the colony of Virginia, recorded, "the famous Indian Woman Nancy Ward came to Camp, . . . gave us various intelligence, and made an overture on behalf of some of the Cheifs [sic] for Peace." This peace council proved frustrating to Ward. Representing the Cherokee, she met with an American official, John Sevier. Rather than greeting her with words of gratitude for twice warning the Americans of Indian raids, he was appalled that a woman had been sent to discuss the peace. She was, in turn, irritated that the whites had no women negotiators. She demanded that Sevier discuss the peace terms with the female settlers: "Let your women hear our words."

In 1783, the war came to an end with an American victory. Two years later, Ward was one of the tribal representatives who helped negotiate the tribe's first treaty with the new United States. At the conclusion of the negotiations in the settlement of Hopewell in South Carolina, she was asked to deliver a speech, in which she stated her happiness that peace had come at last: "Your having determined on peace is most pleasant to me for I have seen much trouble during the late war. . . . The talk I have given is from the young warriors I have raised in my town, as well as myself. They rejoice that we have peace, and we hope the chain of friendship will never be broken." This "chain of friendship" had come at a high price. As punishment for their support of the British in the war, the Cherokee were forced to give a huge amount of their territory to the U.S. government in the Treaty of Hopewell.

In the years that followed, the United States took more and more land from Cherokee. Eventually, Ward began to feel less warmly toward the Americans and to question whether ceding portions of the tribe's homeland was too high a price to pay for peace. She became especially embittered as the United States intimated that it wanted the Cherokee to leave the Southeast altogether. American settlers were eyeing the tribe's lush eastern lands, so the U.S. government was considering relocating the Cherokee to lands to the west. Ward vigorously protested any removal plans in a message she sent to tribal representatives at an 1817 treaty negotiation: "Our beloved children and head men of the Cherokee nation we address you warriors in council we have raised all of you on the land which we now have, which God gave us to inhabit and raise provisions. . . . Your mothers and sisters ask and beg of you not to part with any more our lands."

Despite Ward's pleas, the new Cherokee leaders continued to give over land, including, in an 1819 treaty, her village of Chota. Forced to leave her home, Ward moved to eastern Tennessee, where she opened a successful inn. There, well into her eighties, Nancy Ward died in about 1822. Rela-

tives at her deathbed said that a white light emerged from her body and floated back to Chota to spend eternity.

Perhaps, fortunately, Ward did not live to see the removal of the Cherokee, now known as the Trail of Tears. In 1838, most of the Cherokee finally were forced to leave their homeland in the East for unknown lands to the west. During the painful journey, many thousands of Cherokee died, but despite the magnitude of this tragedy, the tribe survived and, in time, once again thrived. Today Cherokee continue to revere Ward. Since 1994, they have gathered for Nancy Ward Cherokee Heritage Day, an annual event held to commemorate the Beloved Woman, who, in a period of great turmoil, provided their people with sound and sane counsel.

Further Reading

Felton, Harold W. *Nancy Ward, Cherokee.* New York: Dodd, Mead & Company, 1975.

Gridley, Marion E. "Nancy Ward: Beloved Woman of the Cherokees." In *American Indian Women,* 39–46. New York: Hawthorn Books, 1974.

McClary, Ben Harris. "Ward, Nancy." In *Notable American Women: 1607–1950,* edited by Edward T. James, 541–43. Cambridge, Mass.: Belknap Press, 1971.

Wauneka, Annie Dodge
(1910–1997)   *Navajo activist, tribal leader*

The first woman to serve on the Navajo Tribal Council, Annie Dodge Wauneka dedicated her life to helping her people overcome the health problems that plagued them in the 20th century. She was born on April 10, 1910, in the present-day town of Old Sawmill, Arizona, in a traditional Navajo (Dineh) hogan that belonged to her mother, K'eehabah. K'eehabah was the third wife of Henry Chee Dodge, then the wealthiest man of the tribe. Following traditional custom, Dodge married several related women. His first two wives were distant cousins of K'eehabah.

When Annie was only a year old, Dodge took her from her mother and moved the baby into his large house near Window Rock, the capital of the Navajo Nation. There he managed a successful ranch that had made him rich. In the lush surroundings of her youth, Annie was shielded from the daily reality of most Navajo, who were exceedingly poor. Dodge, however, insisted that she learn the value of hard work by rising at dawn to care for a herd of sheep, an important responsibility traditionally assigned to Navajo children.

As a boy, Henry Chee Dodge had suffered through one of the worst tragedies in Navajo history. In the 1860s, the tribe was forced by the U.S. Army to leave their homeland so that the government could mine for gold and other minerals on their lands. A large number of tribespeople died during the 300-mile migration—known as the Long Walk—to their new reservation in what is now eastern New Mexico. There, disease and starvation killed many more. The Navajo lived under these devastating conditions for four years before they were permitted to return home. During this time, Dodge learned to speak English and provided older Navajo with the invaluable service of translating their words for the soldiers on the reservation. His fluency in English later served him well in business. In raising Annie, he stressed to her the importance of learning the language of whites well and precisely.

In order to prepare her for dealing with non-Indians, Dodge also wanted Annie to have the best education possible. When she was eight, he sent her to a government-run school on the reservation. That year, an epidemic of influenza spread across much of the globe. When it reached the reservation, it took the lives of thousands of Navajo, including many of the students at the school. Annie suffered only a mild case, which left her resistant to the disease. After recovering, she set about caring for her classmates, feeding those too ill to feed themselves and wiping their feverish faces with cloths soaked in cool water.

An excellent student, Annie moved to New Mexico to receive further schooling at the Albuquerque Indian School. There she struck up a friendship with George Wauneka, a fellow student.

After graduating, she announced to her father that she was going to marry George. Although her announcement violated the Navajo custom of arranged marriages, her family liked her fiancé and did not object to her plans. The Waunekas' marriage also proved to be nontraditional. George stayed home caring for their six children and large flock of sheep, while Annie traveled around the reservation as her father's aide. While she was in Albuquerque, Henry Chee Dodge had been elected chairman of the Navajo Tribal Council, the governing body of the tribe. Although his term ended in 1928, he continued for many years to serve the Navajo by making speeches and offering help to families in need.

Touring the reservation with her father, Annie Wauneka saw firsthand the way most Navajo lived. Many were poor and hungry. Their homes had no electricity or indoor plumbing—luxuries Wauneka had taken for granted when she was growing up. Most alarming to Wauneka was their ill health. Germs spread quickly in Navajo hogans, which had dirt floors, little ventilation, and only one room so that healthy people had constant, close contact with the ill.

Wauneka's concern for the ailing earned her the respect of her people. Although traditionally only men served as political leaders among the Navajo, in 1951 she was elected to the tribal council, the first woman so honored. She quickly established a reputation as a dynamic force on the council, which earned her four more terms in office.

During her first term, Wauneka was named the head of the council's Health Committee. In this role, she took on the mission of ridding the reservation of tuberculosis. For three months, Wauneka studied the cause of tuberculosis and the treatment of the disease by white medical doctors at the laboratories of the U.S. Public Health Service. She then told her people about their medical techniques. All the while, Wauneka was careful not to offend the Navajo's traditional healers, who were revered by the tribe. Their attempts to treat the disease with plant medicines and curing ceremonies had not halted its spread. Wauneka insisted that these traditional cures had not worked because tuberculosis was so powerful. It could be quelled on the reservation, she explained, only if Navajo and white doctors worked together.

Even after Wauneka convinced the Navajo healers of the wisdom of her plan, many Navajo patients resisted treatment by whites. They thought that white medicine was witchcraft. To calm their fears, Wauneka visited the afflicted in their homes and carefully explained the procedures white doctors used, often making up new Navajo words for unfamiliar English medical terms. Largely through

Annie Wauneka receives the Medal of Freedom from President Lyndon B. Johnson in 1963.
(LBJ Library, Photo by Cecil Stoughton)

her efforts, 20,000 Navajo were convinced to have X-rays to see if they were infected. The lives of nearly 2,000 Navajo with the disease were saved by the hospital visits Wauneka advocated.

To spread her message further, Wauneka became the host of a weekly radio show. Speaking in Navajo, she told her audience how to prevent and treat a variety of health problems. In a 1982 interview, she explained the wide focus of her program: "I talked about everything under the sun about health that pertains to my People. I went with the cycle of the weather, like in the winter I'd be talking about pneumonia: how to take care of yourself, how you must be dressed; and then when the spring came, I'd talk about flies and diarrhea." Wauneka also made two films about health and sanitation that were shown in Navajo schools and wrote a dictionary of her Navajo translations of non-Indian medical terms.

Despite her busy schedule, Wauneka decided to continue her education by attending the University of Arizona, from which she earned a bachelor's degree in public health. Her alma mater later awarded her an honorary doctorate in recognition of her tireless efforts to improve the health and well-being of her people. This honor was only one of the many Wauneka received during her long career. Most notably, she served on the advisory boards of the U.S. Surgeon General and U.S. Public Health Service. In 1963, she also became the first Native American to receive the Presidential Medal of Freedom, which President Lyndon B. Johnson awarded her during a ceremony held at the White House. Immensely proud of this honor, Wauneka took to wearing the medal on her blouse, earning her the playful nickname "Badge Woman" from her tribespeople.

Wauneka continued to provide advice to the tribal council and much-needed information to her people until her death on November 10, 1997, at the age of 87. Calling her "one of the great Navajo leaders," Navajo president Albert A. Hale summed up the enormous influence she and her work had had on the tribe in her obituary in the *Navajo Hopi Observer:* "Her efforts in education,

health and the quest for justice and equality with our neighbors profoundly improved the lives of every one of us."

Further Reading

Gridley, Marion E. "Annie Dodge Wauneka: A Modern Crusader." In *American Indian Women,* 119–130. New York: Hawthorn Books, 1974.
Nelson, Mary Carol. *Annie Wauneka.* Minneapolis, Minn.: Dillon Press, 1972.
Niethammer, Carolyn J. *I'll Go and Do More: Annie Dodge Wauneka, Navajo Leader and Activist.* Lincoln: University of Nebraska Press, 2001.
Sherrow, Victoria. "Annie Dodge Wauneka: Navajo Health Crusader." In *Political Leaders and Peacemakers,* 98–108. New York: Facts On File, 1994.

Wa Wa Chaw (Bonita Wa Wa Calachaw Nuñez)
(1888–1972) *mission activist, painter*

In *Spirit Woman* (1980), a collection of diary entries published after her death, Bonita Wa Wa Calachaw Nuñez tells the strange story of how she became an activist for Indian rights. Born in southern California on Christmas Day in 1888, she was named Wa Wa Chaw by her mother, a member of the Luiseño tribe of the Mission Indians. Soon after the delivery, the infant's family was visited by Mary Duggan, a wealthy New Yorker who was traveling through the region. Alarmed by the family's poverty, Duggan decided to take charge of the child. Wa Wa Chaw never knew for certain how Duggan came to be her caretaker. In her later life, she claimed alternately that she was bought or stolen by her adoptive mother.

Duggan took the baby to her New York apartment, which she shared with her brother Cornelius, a prominent physician. After some initial hesitation, Cornelius agreed to rear the Indian infant as their own daughter. The Duggans saw that Wa Wa Chaw lived in elegant surroundings and had the finest private teachers that money could buy. From her tutors, the girl learned to love books and reading.

Her new father and mother also had their own plans for her education. Cornelius Duggan taught Wa Wa Chaw about the latest scientific theories and involved her in his own experiments. To his delight, she proved to be a talented scientific illustrator and spent much of her time intricately sketching the doctor's specimens. Mary Duggan as well encouraged the girl to take an interest in her avocation—fighting for the rights of American Indians. In the late 19th century, many rich and educated easterners, such as Duggan, were determined to better the lot of impoverished and landless Native Americans. These reformers were often called "friends of the Indians."

By Wa Wa Chaw's own account, she was well loved by the Duggans. Yet her mother sometimes treated the girl more as a public testament to her good works than as a daughter. For example, Wa Wa Chaw later remembered with some bitterness that her mother would not allow her to wear cloth dresses like her playmates. To show her respect for Wa Wa Chaw's Indian heritage, Duggan instead dressed the girl in buckskin clothing. Wa Wa Chaw felt embarrassed by the costume, which was not the native dress of her California tribe. Nevertheless, wearing this outfit, Wa Wa Chaw often accompanied Duggan to meetings with her fellow reformers. At one get-together sponsored by the famous feminist Carrie Chapman Catt, the girl made her debut as a public speaker. One of the attendees handed the 10-year-old a speech denouncing the U.S. government's treatment of Indians and asked her to read it before the group. The obedient girl did as she was told and unwittingly began her career as an activist.

Although the wealthy and famous often paid visits to the Duggan house, Wa Wa Chaw had such a sheltered childhood that she was frightened to leave home as she grew older. The Duggans encouraged her to marry a suitor—a handsome Puerto Rican labor organizer named Manual Nuñez—but even after the wedding she chose to live with her parents rather than with her husband. Owing to Wa Wa Chaw's disinterest in being a wife and the death of her only child in infancy, the marriage disintegrated.

Wa Wa Chaw proved more adventurous as she began to accompany Mary Duggan on her travels. With Duggan, she visited many western Indian reservations and was appalled by the living conditions of the residents. Through this experience, she later wrote, she developed "a strange feeling of resentment": "Land and Water everywhere, but none for *My People,* who once roamed the whole Country. It was not Justice." She also began to feel uncomfortable about her mother's attitudes toward Indians; for Duggan, Indians were a cause more than living, breathing human beings. As Wa Wa Chaw explained in her diary, "My family showered Me with so much affection. I was unable to see the World I was Living in. . . . Mother was fighting not for Me, but for the *Indian Race* of the *U.S.A.*"

During her tours of the West, Wa Wa Chaw's growing activism was nurtured through her acquaintance with Carlos Montezuma. A Yavapai Indian, Montezuma founded the magazine *Wassaja* in 1916. Devoted to publicizing the battle for Indian rights, *Wassaja* was particularly critical of the Bureau of Indian Affairs (BIA), the agency of the U.S. government that implemented policies concerning Indians. Wa Wa Chaw shared Montezuma's belief that the BIA was to blame for many of the problems reservation Indians faced. Inspired by his ideas, she also took up the cause of Indian soldiers in World War I (1914–18). Many Indian men who wanted to serve in the American military were not permitted to enlist because they were not considered U.S. citizens. In part because of the protests of activists such as Wa Wa Chaw during the war, all Indians were granted citizenship in 1924.

Wa Wa Chaw continued to speak out on a variety of Indian issues, but also found time for a second career. While still in her teens, she had begun to paint on canvas. As an adult, she supported herself by selling these paintings on New York City streets to tourists and other passersby. Most of her works are portraits of Indians featuring thick black lines surrounding patches of warm browns, reds, and yellows. She painted countless works for sale or as gifts for friends before her death on May 12, 1972, at the age of 84.

Further Reading

Steiner, Stan, ed. *Spirit Woman: The Diaries and Paintings of Bonita Wa Wa Calachaw Nuñez.* New York: Harper and Row, 1980.

✹ Weetamoo

(ca. 1635–1676)   *Wampanoag tribal leader*

As leader of the Pocasset village of the Wampanoag Indians, Weetamoo played an influential role during one of the first wars between Indians and whites in North America. Few details of her early life have been recorded. She was probably born in about 1635 near the mouth of the Taunton River in present-day Rhode Island.

Some 15 years earlier, English settlers arrived on what is now the coast of New England and established the colony of Plymouth. Massasoit, the sachem (leader) of the Wampanoag, welcomed the newcomers. As the leader of the approximately 30 villages of the Wampanoag Confederacy, he set the tone of these Indians' initial relations with the colonists. Committed to maintaining peace, Massasoit negotiated the first treaty between Indians and whites. His followers were the Indian guests at the original Thanksgiving.

In the following decades, the friendship between the Wampanoag and the English deteriorated. The Indians resented the colonists' efforts to take over their land, and the resulting tensions often erupted in violence. Massasoit's sons—Wamsutta and Metacom—tried to tell him of the treachery of the English, but he refused to listen.

With Massasoit's death in 1660, Wamsutta became the new Wampanoag sachem. He took Weetamoo as his wife. As the daughter of the sachem of Pocasset—one of the Wampanoag villages—Weetamoo was no stranger to the demands and pleasures of leadership. Both the bride and groom probably saw the marriage as advantageous to their political careers.

In his father's tradition, Wamsutta attempted to keep peace with the colonists. But by the time he came to power, the English were belligerent and arrogant in their dealings with their former friends. In 1662, the colony's leaders summoned Wamsutta to Plymouth to pledge his loyalty to them. Always terrified that various tribes would band together and attack them, the English had come to believe (incorrectly) that Wamsutta was plotting against the colony. The demand irritated the sachem, and he refused to come. A military contingent then came to him and escorted him to the English leaders. During the meeting, Wamsutta was clearly ill, and on the way home, he died, probably with Weetamoo by his side. Although Wamsutta most likely died of disease, Weetamoo and his brother Metacom became convinced that the sachem had been poisoned by the English. Wamsutta's widow swore to avenge his death.

Weetamoo returned to Pocasset. When her father died, she became the new village sachem, with an army of at least 300 warriors at her command. She also took a new husband named Quequequananachet.

Metacom—known as King Philip to the colonists—succeeded Wamsutta as the great sachem. During his years in power, hostilities between the Indians and the colonists grew to a fever pitch. By late 1675, he felt that he had no choice but to launch a full-scale attack against Plymouth. He began to approach leaders of individual Wampanoag villages and of nearby tribes for support. Weetamoo was one of the first to commit her soldiers to his campaign. At about the same time, she left Quequequananachet because he became friendly with the English. She then took a new husband, Quinnapin, the nephew of the sachem of the Narraganset tribe. She probably saw in the marriage a chance to increase her power base and to help persuade the Narraganset to join Metacom's war effort.

Very soon Weetamoo's new alliance with this tribe proved useful. One of the first battles in King Philip's War—the name the English gave to Metacom's series of attacks—occurred at Pocasset Swamp near her village. Weetamoo escaped the colonial troops and fled to Narraganset territory. The English followed her and demanded that the Narraganset sachem turn her over to them. He refused, thereby becoming an instant enemy of the English and an ally of Metacom. Weetamoo had fulfilled her hope of bringing the Narraganset into the war.

In February 1676, Metacom's warriors attacked Lancaster, Massachusetts. Following customary war practices, they took several captives, including a settler named Mary Rowlandson. Quinnapin bought the white woman from her captors and made her a servant of him and his wife. Rowlandson lived with Weetamoo for 11 weeks before Quinnapin ransomed her to her family. She later wrote a book about her captivity, which was enormously popular among the English settlers. It was the best-selling nonreligious book in the colonies throughout both the 17th and 18th centuries.

In her memoir, Rowlandson offers the only surviving detailed descriptions of Weetamoo. She wrote of the sachem's regal demeanor, her confident manner, and her elaborate dress: "A severe and proud Dame she was, bestowing every Day in dressing herself near as much Time as any of the Gentry of the Land: Powdering her Hair and painting her Face, going with her Necklaces, with Jewels in her Ears, and Bracelets upon her hands."

By summer 1676, the tide of the war had turned in the colonists' favor, and the Indians were preparing for defeat. Weetamoo was living in a temporary camp, when on August 6 English troops found her and surrounded the location. She attempted to escape by canoe on the Taunton River, but English musketmen filled the boat with holes. The canoe sank, and despite a frantic effort to swim to shore, Weetamoo drowned. The colonists retrieved her body, decapitated it, and placed her severed head atop a high post for display. Within a month, Metacom was also killed, and his corpse was likewise defiled.

With Metacom's death, King Philip's War came to an end. The conflict had decimated the Wampanoag and Narraganset populations and left their villages and fields in ruins. For Weetamoo, a defiant leader who met force with force, perhaps death was a kinder end than the fate of the few survivors—

facing life as a conquered people in the lands they once ruled.

Further Reading

Gridley, Marion E. "Wetamoo: Squaw Sachem of Pocasset." In *American Indian Women,* 13–21. New York: Hawthorn Books, 1974.
Roman, Joseph. *King Philip: Wampanoag Rebel.* New York: Chelsea House, 1992.

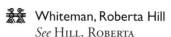 **Whiteman, Roberta Hill**
See HILL, ROBERTA

Winema (Nan-ook-too-wa, Kaitchkona Winema, Tobey Riddle)
(1836–1932) *Modoc peacemaker, interpreter*

The courageous peacemaker of the Modoc War of 1872–73, Winema was born in 1836 in the Modoc Indian homeland in northern California. The baby was given the name Nan-ook-too-wa (meaning, "strange child") because her reddish-brown hair made her stand out among the black-haired Modoc. As a young girl, she earned a new name by fearlessly navigating a canoe full of children through the rapids of the Klamath River. She became known as Kaitchkona Winema (often shortened to "Winema")—or "strong-hearted woman" in the Modoc language. Again and again, throughout her life, she would live up to this honor.

When Winema was a child, white miners were flocking to Modoc lands. They were soon followed by many more white settlers, who wanted to make the area their home. Her father Se-cot often took Winema to local trading posts to trade with whites for manufactured goods that were novel to the Modoc. During these trips, Winema became familiar with white customs and began to learn the English language.

At 15, Winema was deemed ready for marriage. A mate named Uleta was chosen for her, but she refused him. The headstrong Winema decided she wanted to marry Frank Riddle, a white miner from

Kentucky who had frequently visited the Modoc's camps. Riddle had a fiancé back home, but he, too, chose to risk the censorship of his family to marry Winema. The couple moved to Riddle's ranch, and Winema became known to her white neighbors as Tobey.

Winema's marriage to a white man earned her the ill will of many members of her tribe. The Modoc were increasingly coming into conflict with the white newcomers, so they saw her act as a betrayal of her people. However, her husband did his best to earn the Modoc's acceptance. He often joined Modoc hunting and fishing parties and presented Winema's family with gifts after the wedding, as Modoc grooms were expected to do. In time, the Modoc came to forgive Winema and to respect her white husband.

In the 1860s, the Modoc's conflicts with whites and with rival tribes were growing increasingly violent. Tribal members often came to the Riddles asking for help in settling these disputes. Winema was one of the few Modoc fluent in both her own language and in English. But she proved more than just an able interpreter. Winema also had a knack for negotiating nonviolent resolutions to potentially volatile disagreements. Officials of the U.S. government recognized her diplomatic skills and requested her help in establishing the terms of the Treaty of 1864, which brought at least a temporary peace between the Americans and the Modoc.

A wave of violence again broke out in 1869. A band of Modoc led by Winema's cousin Kintpuash (known to whites as Captain Jack) came into conflict with white settlers near the Lost River, where the Modoc had hunted and fished for some 9,000 years. The federal government, represented by Captain Alfred Meachem, called a peace conference at which the Riddles were asked to serve as interpreters. The conference produced a treaty stating that the Modoc would relocate to the Klamath Indian Reservation in Oregon.

The plan was a disaster from the start. The Klamath Indians were the Modoc's traditional enemies and had little desire to share their land with them. Their leaders refused to let the Modoc hunt and fish

on the reservation. After several months, a disgusted Kintpuash took his band back to the Lost River in violation of the treaty. Years passed without any serious incidents between Kintpuash's Modoc and their white neighbors there. Nevertheless, in 1872, the U.S. Army decided that the renegade Modoc had to return to their designated reservation.

As soon as Winema heard that soldiers were coming to fight the Lost River Modoc, she rushed to warn her cousin. She rode her horse for 75 miles before she arrived in Kintpuash's camp. Winema told her cousin what she knew, but he refused to listen to her. He told her that because of her marriage and past cooperation with whites she was dead to

The U.S. government honored Winema for her efforts to make peace between the Modoc and Americans.

(Oregon Historical Society, Neg. no. OrHi 12715)

the Modoc. Then he delivered his worst insult: To him, she was nothing but a white woman.

The soldiers soon arrived, and the battle began. After many Indians were killed, the Modoc retreated to lava beds on the shore of Lake Tule. The lava beds were an ideal, natural stronghold. The Modoc knew their way through the beds' caves and could easily hide there from their white pursuers. Underground rivers provided the Modoc with an ample supply of fresh water. Entire families holed up in the caves, ready to wait out the soldiers for as long as necessary.

In the meantime, Winema ran messages back and forth from the Modoc to the army officials. A peace conference was finally arranged. Before the appointed meeting, a Modoc told her that Kintpuash was planning to assassinate the government officials. She warned Captain Meachem and his superior, General Edward Canby, but the general refused to call off the conference.

The tension was thick as the two sides came together to negotiate. Three times Kintpuash repeated that his band must remain in the Lost River area. Three times Canby said they could not. Both Winema and Meachem urged Canby to compromise, but he stood firm. Just as Winema feared he might, Kintpuash then drew a revolver and shot and killed the general. Another Modoc fired a fatal shot at an American soldier. A third assassin emptied his gun into Meachem. Winema threw her body over Meachem to end the gunfire. When another Modoc ran toward Meachem's fallen body with a knife, she screamed that more U.S. troops were coming, a lie that scattered Kintpuash's warriors just as she had hoped.

Winema wrapped Meachem in a blanket and rushed off to get help. For two weeks, she stayed with the captain and nursed him back to health. Largely due to her care, he survived the seven bullet wounds he suffered.

Kintpuash was soon captured by the army and, with five other Modoc warriors, he was hanged. Before his execution, he asked Meachem, who had always been sympathetic to the tribe, to tell his story. The Modoc War had been reported through-

out the nation, and in most accounts, Kintpuash was painted as a villain. Respecting Kintpuash's dying wish, Meachem provided a more balanced view in his book *Wi-Ne-Ma (The Woman-Chief) and Her People* (1876).

The hero of Meachem's story was, of course, Winema. His book and other press accounts of the war made her a national celebrity. The U.S. government invited her to Washington, D.C., where she was honored with a parade and a meeting with President Ulysses S. Grant. A popular dramatist, James Redpath, wrote a play about her exploits, in which she was asked to play herself. From 1874 to 1881, she, Frank Riddle, their son Jefferson, and several other Modoc traveled throughout the country presenting the drama.

After the successful tour, Winema went home and lived out the rest of her life on the reservation. In 1890, in appreciation of her peacemaking efforts, the U.S. government granted her a monthly pension of $25, a considerable sum at the time. She distributed most of the money to other Modoc who were in need. The United States later also honored her in the naming of the Winema National Forest.

In 1932, Winema died on the reservation and was buried in the Modoc cemetery. Her gravestone reads "Winema—Strong Heart," a fitting epitaph for a woman who was known for her bravery and goodheartedness by Modoc and whites alike.

Further Reading

Gridley, Marion E. "Winema: The Peacemaker." In *American Indian Women,* 61–65. New York: Hawthorn Books, 1974.

Sherrow, Victoria. "Winema: Brave Mediator in the Modoc War." In *Political Leaders and Peacemakers,* 88–97. New York: Facts On File, 1994.

Winnemucca, Sarah (Thocmetony; Sarah Winnemucca Hopkins)
(ca. 1844–1891)   *Northern Paiute activist, autobiographer, interpreter*

One of the most famous Indian women of the 19th century, Sarah Winnemucca was a renowned advocate of peace and justice. Through her work as an interpreter and army scout, she sought to end the conflicts between Indians and whites on the western frontier. With the lecture tours that made her name, she also brought attention to the abuses her tribe, the Northern Paiute, had long suffered at the hands of the U.S. government.

Born in about 1844 near Humboldt Lake in what is now northwest Nevada, she was given the Indian name Thocmetony, meaning "Shell Flower." The fourth of nine children, Thocmetony was born into one of the most prominent families of the Northern Paiute. Her father and maternal grandfather—later known as Old Winnemucca and Truckee among whites—were both respected leaders among her people.

At the time of Thocmetony's birth, the Paiute controlled lands in what are now western Nevada, southeastern Oregon, and northeastern California. Unlike most Indian tribes to the east and to the west, they had not yet encountered whites. Their desert homeland was not attractive to outsiders. Only through the experience of living in the region for many centuries had the Paiutes learned how to thrive in this harsh environment. They survived by gathering wild roots and seeds and hunting wild animals. To ensure a steady water supply, they built their settlements along the few lakes and rivers in the region.

In 1844, Truckee came upon a band of explorers, the first whites to travel through the Paiute homeland. He became friendly with the band's leader, John C. Frémont, and offered to guide the men to their destination in California. When Truckee returned home, he told the Paiute about his white friends and encouraged his tribespeople to welcome non-Indians into their lands. Other tribespeople, however, were growing suspicious of these newcomers. By the late 1840s, non-Indians were beginning to flock to the area in large numbers. Rumors spread among the Paiute about these strange people. One told of the Donner Party, a group of settlers who, trapped in the California mountains during a 1847 blizzard, survived by eating their dead. This story convinced many Paiute—including Thocmetony—that all whites were cannibals. She was filled with terror by her father's warnings that white people hunted and ate Indian children.

When Thocmetony was six, her grandfather Truckee decided to return to California with a large party of his Paiute followers. At his encouragement, his daughter and grandchildren, including Thocmetony, came along. At the beginning of their travels, Thocmetony would only ride on horseback behind her brother, covering herself with a blanket to hide from hostile whites. However, when she came down with poison oak and was nursed back to health by a white woman, her fear of non-Indians began to fade. As she encountered more whites, she came to feel comfortable with them and their ways. In time, Thocmetony even learned to speak their languages. As a young teen, she became fluent in English and Spanish as well as several Indian dialects. During this time, Thocmetony took the English name Sarah and became a Christian, although throughout her life she would continue to hold many of the Paiute's traditional religious beliefs.

Sarah Winnemucca's early dealings with non-Indians were not always pleasant, however. To fulfill a promise made to Truckee on his deathbed in 1859, her parents sent their children to non-Indian schools. Sarah and her sister Elma traveled to San Jose, California, to attend a convent school, but they were told to leave after only three weeks. The parents of their white classmates had objected to their children learning lessons alongside Indian "savages."

Returning home, Winnemucca found that relations between the Paiute and the white settlers in their lands had deteriorated. As Indians and whites began to compete for control of the well-watered lands along the rivers and lakes in the region, conflicts between the two groups often erupted in violence. The Paiute were heartened when the U.S. government established an Indian reservation for them on Pyramid Lake. But to their frustration, the government officials hired to oversee the reservation—known as agents—generally were at best incompetent and at worst corrupt. They often kept or sold food and supplies that the government had provided for the Paiute, and they rarely even tried to keep white settlers out of the reservation as they were supposed to do.

Crowded out of their lands, many Paiute faced starvation. In an attempt to make money to feed his people, Old Winnemucca, with the help of Sarah and Elma, developed a stage show and lined up bookings in nearby Virginia City, a booming mining town, and in San Francisco, California. The show included a series of *tableaux vivants* (French for "living pictures")—a stage entertainment in which actors in costume stood frozen in a scene as it was described by a narrator. The Winnemuccas' program featured scenes of Indian life with titles such as "The Indian Camp," "The War Dance," and "Scalping the Prisoner." As her father described the scenes in Paiute, Sarah translated his words to the crowd. Stage shows starring Indian players were popular among western settlers—especially those that sensationalized native life and depicted Indians as exotic, as the Winnemuccas' show did. Nevertheless, their foray on the stage was unsuccessful and brought in scant funds for the needy Paiute.

As the tribe's situation grew more desperate, the Paiute began to congregate around Fort McDermit, an army post where food rations were distributed to the Indians. Sarah Winnemucca came to respect many of the army officers there, whom she considered far more responsible and reasonable than the reservation agents. In turn, they were impressed by Winnemucca and appointed her as their interpreter, a position she held from 1868 to 1871. During this time, she met and married an officer, Edward C. Barlett. Due to his alcoholism and erratic behavior, the couple soon separated and were eventually divorced.

The fortunes of Old Winnemucca's followers improved in 1875, when they relocated to the Malheur Reservation in southeastern Oregon. The agent there, Sam Parrish, had a sincere regard for the Indians' welfare and earned their trust. Although Sarah had grown weary of dealing with reservation affairs, she agreed to serve as Parrish's interpreter because of her high regard for him.

Unfortunately, Parrish soon left his post, and his replacement, William Rinehart, had more in common with the greedy, inept agents Winnemucca had known in the past. The two almost immediately became enemies, and Rinehart eventually banished her from Malheur. At about this time, Winnemucca also suffered a personal disappointment. In 1876, she married Joseph Salwalter, but after spending two years together in Oregon, the two separated.

Other Paiute were becoming dissatisfied with their treatment at Malheur. Many chose to leave and join the Bannock Indians, who had a reservation in present-day Idaho. The Bannock were so angry at their treatment at the hands of whites that they were preparing to go to battle.

In June 1878, the Bannock War broke out. Although some Paiute decided to fight alongside the Bannock, Sarah Winnemucca chose to volunteer her services to the U.S. Army. During the conflict, she became the official interpreter for General Oliver O. Howard. She also served as a scout and guide for his soldiers.

At the start of the war, Winnemucca learned that a camp of Paiute—including her father, brother, and sister-in-law—were being held against their will by the Bannock. According to her autobiography, she raced on horseback into Bannock territory, found her relatives, and led them and the other captive Paiute to freedom. She described the escape over hundreds of miles of the roughest terrain in the West as "the hardest work I ever did for the army."

When the war ended with the Bannock's defeat, Winnemucca expected that the Paiute who did not join the fighting would be allowed to return to Malheur. To her shock and disgust, the federal government declared that all Paiute involved in the war—regardless of whether they were the enemies or friends of the army—were to be punished. They were ordered to relocate to the Yakima Indian Reservation in eastern Washington State. Even worse, they were to travel to Yakima in the dead of winter. Winnemucca's denouncement of the decision was loud and angry: "I have never seen a president in my life and I want to know whether he is made of wood or rock, for I cannot for once think that he can be a human being. No human being would do such a thing as that—send people across a fearful mountain in mid-winter." Winnemucca communicated her outrage to army officials, who sent a letter to President Rutherford B. Hayes on her behalf.

The Paiute suffered horribly during their journey to Yakima, but their arrival provided little comfort. Their housing and food on the reservation was sorely

Sarah Winnemucca poses in her "Indian Princess" costume, circa 1879.
(Nevada Historical Society)

inadequate, and during spring 1879, many Paiute died because of the wretched conditions. Winnemucca vowed to travel to Washington, D.C., to meet with the president herself. She wanted to confront him directly with the injustices the government had committed against her tribe.

To fund her trip, Winnemucca returned to the stage. She organized a lecture tour in San Francisco, during which she delivered speeches about the Paiute and their troubles. Despite the seriousness of her mission, she did not hesitate to add some showy touches to her program to help draw an audience. Billed as an "Indian princess," she appeared on stage dressed in an elaborate costume, including a fringed and embroidered buckskin dress and a feathered headdress. The tour was a great success and earned Winnemucca extravagant praise from a *San Francisco Chronicle* reviewer, who wrote, "The lecture was unlike anything ever before heard in the civilized world—eloquent, pathetic, tragical at times; at others her quaint anecdotes, sarcasms, and wonderful mimicry surprised the audience again and again into bursts of laughter and rounds of applause."

In January 1880, Winnemucca at last made her way to Washington. She met briefly with President Hayes and spoke at length with the Secretary of the Interior, Carl Schurz. Schurz promised her that the Paiute would be permitted to return to Malheur. After Winnemucca's return to the West, however, the agent at Yakima refused to let the Paiute leave his reservation. He feared that if the Indians traveled back to Malheur, conflicts would break out between white settlers and the Indians en route. During the next year, the U.S. government opened Malheur to white settlement, thereby ending any possibility of the area serving as a reservation for the Paiute.

At General Howard's request, Winnemucca briefly took a job teaching at an Indian school at Vancouver Barracks in Washington. She saved her earnings to fund a new lecture tour of the major cities along the east coast. Before setting out, she married her third husband, Lieutenant Lewis H. Hopkins, in San Francisco.

When Winnemucca arrived in the East in 1883, she found that many prominent and wealthy reformers had taken an interest in Indian affairs. Two sisters from a highly respected New England family—Mary Peabody Mann and Elizabeth Palmer Peabody—became feverish supporters of Winnemucca and the Paiute cause. They introduced her to their famous friends—including essayist Ralph Waldo Emerson and poet John Greenleaf Whittier—and organized her lecture tour. For the next year, she gave speeches throughout Massachusetts, Rhode Island, Connecticut, New York, Pennsylvania, and Maryland. To help fund the tour, she also wrote *Life among the Piutes* (1883), copies of which she signed and sold to her audiences. The book was part autobiography, part tribal history, and part political tract. It concluded with a petition outlining Paiute demands that readers could sign and send to Congress. The volume also holds the distinction of being the first published book written in English by a Native American woman.

When Winnemucca's tour ended, she moved to Lovelock, Nevada, where her brother Natchez had a ranch. At the urging of Mary Peabody Mann, she opened a school for Indian children. At government-run schools at the time, Indian students were taught to despise native cultures and to adopt white ways and customs. In Winnemucca's classroom, however, children were taught about their own history and heritage and lessons were conducted in both English and their native languages.

After four years of teaching, Winnemucca retired and moved in with her sister Elma in Montana. In her final years, her health deteriorated rapidly. On October 16, 1891, at the age of about 48, she died, probably of tuberculosis, the disease that killed her third husband five years before. Winnemucca was buried with Indian rites, and her obituary appeared on the front page of the *New York Times*. In the end, her campaign on behalf of the Paiute was in many ways a failure: The tribe never received the land base she sought for them. But she did succeed in shining a spotlight on their plight, as well as the plight of all Indians. In cele-

bration of her remarkable life, a statue of Sarah Winnemucca was installed in the National Statuary Hall in Washington, D.C., in 2005. She is the only American Indian woman so honored.

Further Reading

Canfield, Gae Whitney. *Sarah Winnemucca of the Northern Paiutes.* Norman: University of Oklahoma Press, 1983.
Hopkins, Sarah Winnemucca. *Life among the Piutes.* 1883. Reprint, Reno: University of Nevada Press, 1994.
Scordato, Ellen. *Sarah Winnemucca.* New York: Chelsea House, 1992.
Zanjani, Sally. *Sarah Winnemucca.* Lincoln: University of Nebraska Press, 2001.

Woman Chief
(ca. 1806–ca. 1854)   *Crow warrior*

The great female warrior of the Crow, Woman Chief was born into the Gros Ventre (Atsiha) tribe of the central Plains in the early years of the 19th century. When she was 10, she was captured by Crow, the traditional enemies of her people. She was taken back to her captors' camp and, following Crow custom, was adopted into their tribe.

At an early age, Woman Chief displayed an inclination toward activities that were considered masculine by the Crow. Her adoptive father encouraged her, perhaps because his own sons had been killed by Blackfoot warriors. Raising her as a boy, Woman Chief's father taught her to use a bow and arrow, shoot a gun, and hunt on horseback and on foot. Tall and strong, she grew up to be a great markswoman and proficient buffalo killer.

Woman Chief earned her name during a Blackfoot raid on her band while they were camped outside a trading post and fort operated by non-Indians. The Blackfoot attacked the camp and killed several people before the Crow were able to run to the fort for safety. Locked outside the fort walls, the Blackfoot warriors stood just beyond rifle distance and demanded to talk to a representative of the Crow. None of the Crow dared to venture out except Woman Chief. She mounted her horse and rode out of the fort alone. As she approached the Blackfoot, five warriors moved forward to meet her. Instead of trying to negotiate with the young woman, one of the men opened fire. He missed his target, but Woman Chief did not. She shot the man with her gun and wounded two others with her bow and arrow before the uninjured retreated. Angry that their comrades had been hurt and disgraced, the entire party of Blackfoot then rushed toward her. Her excellent horsewomanship allowed her to get safely inside the fort before they could reach her. The Crow and whites inside cheered her victory, and word soon spread through the Crow Nation of Woman Chief's bravery.

About a year later, Woman Chief assembled a party of warriors whom she led in a series of raids against the Crow's enemies. In one excursion into Blackfoot territory, she and her men made off with some 70 horses. The success of their raids made Woman Chief rich. She soon had enough material wealth to care for a family of four women, whom she took into her household as male Crow leaders took wives. Her talents as a warrior and raider also brought her further prestige and power. She was so revered by the tribal elders that she served as the only female member of their council of chiefs.

In 1851, the Crow and several other major Plains tribes entered into the Treaty of Fort Laramie with the U.S. government. The treaty marked boundaries between the Indian groups' territories and called for the end of intertribal warfare. By its terms, the Crow were no longer enemies of the Blackfoot and the Gros Ventre. These groups invited the Crow to come into their lands, but the Crow were still fearful of their old enemies. Again the only one who dared was Woman Chief. With four Crow warriors at her side, she rode into the Gros Ventre homeland in 1854. She wanted to visit her Gros Ventre relatives, whom she had not seen for nearly 40 years. She also hoped that, because she spoke both Gros Ventre and Crow, she would able to cement the tenuous peace between her people and her adoptive tribe.

En route to Gros Ventre territory, Woman Chief came on a large group of Gros Ventre, who were returning home after an excursion to a trading post.

Initially they were friendly, but when they discovered that she was the great warrior of their longtime enemies, they shot her and her companions. Because of her unconventional life and extraordinary valor, Woman Chief remains a mythic figure in the history of the 19th-century American West.

Further Reading

Capps, Benjamin. *Woman Chief.* Garden City, N.J.: Doubleday, 1979.

Denig, Edwin Thompson. "Biography of Woman Chief." In *Five Indian Tribes of the Upper Missouri,* edited by John C. Ewers, 195–200. Norman: University of Oklahoma Press, 1961.

Woody, Elizabeth

(1959–) *Warm Springs–Wasco–Navajo poet, visual artist, photographer*

A leading force in literary circles in the Northwest, poet Elizabeth Woody was born in 1959 in Ganado, Arizona. She spent most of her youth until age 13, however, in Madras, Oregon, a town 14 miles from the Warm Springs Indian Reservation. Established by the Treaty of 1855 with the U.S. government, the reservation houses many small Northwest tribes who were forced out of their homelands along the Columbia River Plateau. Traditionally, these tribes' cultures centered around the cycle of traditional food systems based on four sacred foods—salmon, deer, edible roots, and berries. The relocation of these Indians to Warm Springs, located more than 100 miles from the Columbia, was heart wrenching. In the introduction to her poetry collection *Seven Hands, Seven Hearts* (1994), Woody protests that the move took her ancestors away from "the pathways of the salmon that my mother's people cherished, celebrated, harvested, dried, and incorporated into their lifeways for over fourteen thousand years."

From her relatives at Warm Springs, Woody learned to treasure her Indian heritage. She later recalled that her grandmother "made sure that I understood her reverence for the land and the traditional beliefs by taking me as a child to the places where the people gathered for worship—places still filled with symbolism and ceremony." Woody, however, was not educated in one of the most important elements of her ancestors' culture—their language. Still, she was deeply affected by the rhythms of the Indian languages spoken around her when she was young. According to Woody, these sounds had a great impact on her as a poet: "Even though I've had to become proficient in a language and speaking style entirely different from that of my . . . ancestors, I believe the language I use in my poetry comes from the deep well of these ancient American languages."

Woody began to write poetry when accepted as one of the inaugural 12 Oregon High School Writers, and she studied with Sandra McPherson and James Welch in 1978. She also studied with Henry Carlile, Primus St. John, and Tom Doulis at Portland State University and with Philip Foss, Jr., at Santa Fe's Institute of American Indian Arts. She received her bachelor's degree from Evergreen State College in Olympia, Washington, studying with Gail Tremblay and Joe Feddersen, who became her collaborator. Woody became well known in the Northwest for her poems, short stories, and essays, which have been widely published in journals and anthologies. In 1988, she furthered her influence by cofounding the Northwest Native American Writers Association. Woody is also a board member of Soapstone, Inc., which oversees a retreat for women writers near the Oregon coast.

In 1990, Woody gained national recognition with the publication of her first poetry collection, *Hand Into Stone.* Featuring illustrations by painter Jaune Quick-to-See Smith, *Hand into Stone* won the American Book Award from the Before Columbus Foundation. Woody has since produced two more volumes of poetry, *Luminaries of the Humble* (1994) and *Seven Hands, Seven Hearts* (1994), which includes the poems from *Hand into Stone* as well as more recent work. The following year, she received the William Stafford Memorial Award for Poetry from the Pacific Northwest Bookseller's Association. In 1997, Woody was given a J. T. Stewart Award and Fellowship from Hedgebrook,

a women's writers retreat on Whidby Island in Washington.

Through her politically charged writing, Woody addresses many of the issues most crucial to contemporary Northwest Indians. Her work has attacked the "eradication of Indian languages through colonization" and soundly criticized the U.S. government's policies concerning environmental resources and nuclear energy. She has also been a highly vocal advocate for Northwest Indian treaty rights, particularly the tribes' right to use their ancestral fishing sites along the Columbia.

A noted visual artist as well as a writer, Woody's art has been shown in galleries throughout the

Elizabeth Woody stands before boulders marked with petroglyphs.
(Courtesy Elizabeth Woody; Joe Cantrell, photographer)

Northwest and in exhibits in San Francisco, Minneapolis, New York City, and Washington, D.C., and New Zealand. Her primary passion is drawing, but she is also a painter and multimedia artist who has collaborated extensively with Okanogan artist Joe Feddersen. Woody's photographs have also been reproduced in several books, including *Faces of a Reservation: A Portrait of the Warm Springs Indian Reservation* (1987), *We the Human Beings: 27 Contemporary Native American Artists* (1992), and *Old Shirts and New Skins* (1993).

Further Reading

Woody, Elizabeth. *Hand into Stone.* New York: Contact II Publications, 1988.
———. *Luminaries of the Humble.* Tucson: University of Arizona Press, 1994.
———. *Seven Hands, Seven Hearts.* Portland, Oreg.: Eighth Mountain Press, 1994.

Wright, Muriel H.
(1889–1973)   *Choctaw historian*

Muriel H. Wright, an eminent historian of the Indians of Oklahoma, was born on March 31, 1889, in the Choctaw Nation in Indian Territory. Her father, Eliphabet, was a physician whose family had included some of the Choctaw's finest leaders. Muriel's mother, Ida, was a teacher of English and Scottish descent. Her ancestors had been among the first European settlers to arrive in North America.

The Choctaw traditionally had lived in a large territory in present-day Alabama and Tennessee. Like other large southeastern tribes, such as the Cherokee and the Chickasaw, they were compelled to move west in the 1830s by the U.S. government, which wanted to open up their homeland to settlement by whites. The Choctaw's journey to their new lands in Indian Territory (now Oklahoma) was grueling: Thousands of people died along the way. Despite this catastrophe, within several decades the tribe had built a prosperous Choctaw Nation in the west. One of its architects

was Muriel's grandfather, Allen Wright, who served as the chief of the Choctaw Nation from 1866 to 1870.

Among the Choctaw's greatest achievements was their school system, which included some of the best educational facilities in the region. Like most Choctaw families, the Wrights wanted their children to have the best schooling possible. They sent Muriel to local schools, and her mother also tutored her at home. Following a family tradition, she was sent to the East for college in 1906. She later recalled that her arrival at Wheaton College in Norton, Massachusetts, "caused a flurry." Her teachers and fellow students had never met an Indian before and were wary of her. In time, however, her success in both academics and sports won her many friends.

After two years, Wright left Wheaton to move to Washington, D.C., with her family. Her father was elected to represent the Choctaw in their increasing dealings with the U.S. government. In 1907, the tribe's lands had become part of the new state of Oklahoma.

Soon, Wright returned to Oklahoma to aid in creating its school system. The excellent Choctaw schools were closed when the tribal territory was absorbed into Oklahoma, and the new state's government desperately needed help to replace them. After receiving a teaching degree from East Central State Normal School in 1911, Wright began a distinguished career as a high school teacher, coach, and principal.

In the 1920s, she started to devote more of her time to another passion—historical research and writing. She wrote numerous articles before publishing her first major work, the four-volume *Oklahoma: A History of the State and Its People* (1929). In 1943, her further studies of Oklahoma history earned her the job of editing *The Chronicles of Oklahoma*, the journal of the Oklahoma Historical Society. During the 30 years she held this post, she succeeded in making *Chronicles* one of the most respected scholarly journals in the United States.

Throughout her career, Wright focused much of her time and energy on researching the Choctaw and their Indian neighbors in Oklahoma. Most non-Indian historians at the time did not think Indian people merited study. Wright, however, did not want their achievements or their crucial role in the history of the state to be forgotten. Adding to her many articles on the subject, she published her most influential work, *A Guide to the Indian Tribes of Oklahoma,* in 1951.

Wright also served the Choctaw in a variety of posts in their tribal government. She was particularly effective as the secretary and cofounder of the Choctaw Advisory Council. This organization sought compensation from the U.S. government for the southeastern lands it had taken from the tribe in the early 19th century. In part because of the council's labor, the Choctaw won a $20 million settlement from the United States. Muriel Wright received many awards for her work, including an honorary doctorate from the University of Oklahoma in 1964 in recognition of her research into the history of the state's Indian population. Another of her greatest honors came two years before her death from a stroke on February 27, 1975. Citing her efforts in the "preservation of American heritage," the North American Indian Women's Association named her the "outstanding Indian woman of the twentieth century."

Further Reading

Arrington, Ruth. "Muriel Hazel Wright." In *Notable American Women: The Modern Period,* edited by Barbara Sicheman and Carol Hurd Green, 751–52. Cambridge, Mass.: Belknap Press, 1980.

Muriel H. Wright, who worked in the offices of *The Chronicles of Oklahoma,* is pictured here in 1965.
(Courtesy of the Oklahoma Historical Society, Neg. no. 12679)

Fischer, LeRoy H. "Muriel H. Wright, Historian of Oklahoma." *Chronicles of Oklahoma* 52 (Spring 1974): 3–29.
Loughlin, Patricia. *Hidden Treasures of the American West: Muriel H. Wright, Angie Debo, and Alice Marriott.* Albuquerque: University of New Mexico Press, 2005.
Wright, Muriel H. *A Guide to the Indian Tribes of Oklahoma.* 1951. Reprint, Norman: University of Oklahoma Press, 1987.

X-Y

Xehaciwinga

See MOUNTAIN WOLF WOMAN

Yellow Robe, Rosebud
(1907–1992)   *Lakota Sioux educator*

Through her storytelling performances at Long Island's Indian Village, Rosebud Yellow Robe taught several generations of New Yorkers about Indian lore and culture. She was born on February 26, 1907, in Rapid City, South Dakota. Her father, Chauncey, was from a prominent Sioux family. Rosebud's paternal grandmother was the niece of Sitting Bull, perhaps the Sioux's most distinguished chief of the 19th century.

The oldest of three daughters, Yellow Robe was taught by her father to value education. After graduating from a Rapid City public school, she became one of the first Native American students at the University of South Dakota. While attending college, Yellow Robe presented President Calvin Coolidge with a Sioux war bonnet during a ceremony held while he was visiting Sioux territory. Described as a "beautiful Indian maiden" by the press, Yellow Robe particularly caught the attention of a newspaper reporter named A. E. Sey-

mour. He and Yellow Robe courted, married, and settled in New York City.

In the 1930s and 1940s, Yellow Robe frequently worked in radio, both as a writer and a performer. One of her colleagues, Orson Welles, may have borrowed her name for the script of his classic film *Citizen Kane* (1941), in which the title character's dying word is "Rosebud." In the 1950s, Yellow Robe experimented with the new medium of television. She appeared as a regular on an NBC children's show and was featured on *Bob Montgomery Presents.*

Perhaps Yellow Robe's most influential work was her teaching at the Indian Village Project at Jones Beach in Long Island, New York. Through this educational program, Yellow Robe introduced thousands of schoolchildren to Indian history and culture. She often shared with them the traditional Sioux stories that her father had told her when she was a girl. In the 1970s, she wrote down these tales in a popular collection titled *Tonweya and the Eagles* (1979). In recognition of her ability "to pass her scholarly knowledge on to mixed audiences of young and old," she was given an honorary doctorate in 1989 from the University of South Dakota.

On October 5, 1992, Rosebud Yellow Robe died of cancer. Two years later, her career as an educator was once again honored with the performance

Rosebud Yellow Robe poses in front of a portrait of her in the W. H. Over Museum in Vermillion, South Dakota, circa 1984.
(W. H. Over Museum)

of "Rosebud's Song" at New York City's Madison Square Garden. Presented by the National Dance Institute, the event featured a dance performed to the music of folk singer Judy Collins and a chorus of 1,000 children from around the world. The dance program noted that the performance was dedicated to Rosebud Yellow Robe for "devot[ing] her life to children and to preserving and passing on Native American stories and culture."

Further Reading

Weinberg, Marjorie. *The Real Rosebud: The Triumph of a Lakota Woman.* Lincoln: University of Nebraska Press, 2004.
Yellow Robe, Rosebud. *Tonweya and the Eagles and Other Lakota Indian Tales.* New York: Dial Press, 1979.

Zimmerman, Karen P. "Rosebud Yellow Rose." In *Notable Native Americans,* edited by Sharon J. Malinowski, 328–329. Detroit: Gale Research, 1995.

⚌ Yellowtail, Susie Walking Bear
(1903–1981)   *Crow nurse*

Throughout her life, Susie Walking Bear Yellowtail was an advocate for better health care for Indians across the United States. She was born in a one-room cabin on January 27, 1903, in Pryor, a community on Montana's Crow Indian Reservation. Her father was killed in an accident before her birth, and her mother died when she was 10.

Once orphaned, Susie Walking Bear was sent to a Baptist boarding school in Muskogee, Oklahoma. A promising student, she moved to Massachusetts, where she attended the Greenfield Nursing School. When Walking Bear graduated in 1927, she became the first Native American registered nurse.

After working briefly at the Boston City hospital, Walking Bear returned to the Crow reservation in 1928. The next year, she married Tom Yellowtail, who became a noted religious leader. With the encouragement of Tom's relatives, Susie Yellowtail began relearning Crow ways. With her hair in braids and sporting a long calico dress, she adopted the dress of Crow traditionalists. She and Tom were also at the forefront of a movement to resurrect old Crow customs, including a revival of the Crow Sun Dance. In the 1950s, the couple was invited by the State Department to join a goodwill tour that took Indian cultural leaders to Europe and the Middle East. Susie and Tom Yellowtail also raised two daughters and one son, as well as several adopted children.

Despite her family obligations, Susie Yellowtail continued to work as a nurse. After coming back to the reservation, she joined the staff of the hospital at Crow Agency. She was appalled by what she saw there. The doctors were largely unqualified. They also routinely sterilized Crow women, without their consent or knowledge. Yellowtail began speaking out about this and other practices that were endangering the health of the Crow and other Indians.

Working for the U.S. Public Health Service, Yellowtail traveled to reservations across the country, documenting health care problems and recommending solutions. She became well known to public health care officials for her outspokenness and wit. For her work, she was awarded the Presidential Award for Outstanding Health Care in 1962.

By the 1970s, Yellowtail had become a national figure. She was appointed to the President's Council on Indian Education and Nutrition and to the Council on Indian Health, Education and Welfare during the Nixon administration. In addition to calling for improvements in Indian health care, she also fought for better educational opportunities. As she once explained, "The Indians' needs are many, but most urgent is the need for better education."

Susie Yellowtail died in 1981 at the age of 74. Posthumously, she was admitted to the Montana Hall of Fame in 1987 and to the American Nursing Association Hall of Fame in 2002.

Further Reading

Cohen, Betsy. "The 100 Most Influential Montanans of the Century: Susan Walking Bear Yellowtail." Available online. URL: http://www.missoulian.com/specials/100montanans/mont100.html. Downloaded on April 15, 2006.

Yellowtail, Thomas, as told to Michael Oren Fitzgerald. *Yellowtail, Crow Medicine Man and Sun Dance Chief: An Autobiography*. Norman: University of Oklahoma Press, 1991.

Weatherly, Marina Brown. "Susie Walking Bear Yellowtail: A Life Story." *North Dakota Quarterly* 67 (Fall/Summer 2000): 229–241.

Youngblood, Mary
(ca. 1960–) *Aleut-Seminole flutist*

Grammy winner Mary Youngblood is the first woman to record music played on the Native American flute. Born in California in about 1960, she spent her first seven months in a hospital. Her birth parents, an Aleut woman and a Seminole man, had decided to give her up for adoption. Mary was finally taken home by a non-Indian couple. Growing up in their household, she became comfortable among both Indians and non-Indian. As she explained, "I learned to walk in both worlds."

Even at a young age, music was her passion. She starting learning to play the piano at six, the violin at eight, and the classical flute and guitar at 10. She played in every forum she could—from a marching band to a concert hall to a rock-and-roll band.

As an adult, Mary Youngblood struggled to explore music while also raising four children. In 1993, she was working at a gallery across the street from a store selling new age paraphernalia. The man in charge showed Youngblood a Native American flute, an instrument traditionally only played by men: "I thought [it] was so beautiful. I picked it up and started playing it and people in the store clapped when I was done; I didn't even know what I was doing." Although she was new to the instrument, her 20 years of playing classical flute allowed her to master it quickly. About a month later, she started playing the Native flute professionally.

Youngblood first gained attention for the Public Broadcasting Service's special "American Indian Circles of Wisdom," for which she supplied all the music. She also contributed to the soundtrack of the film *Naturally Native* (1998) and the television program *Healing the Waters* (1998).

In 1997, Youngblood released her first CD, *Offerings,* to rave reviews. A collection of solo flute pieces, she recorded it in an underground chamber in California's Moaning Cavern. In her next recording, *Heart of the World* (1999), Youngblood collaborated with Oneida singer JOANNE SHENANDOAH. Youngblood's own vocals accompanied her flute music on her third CD, the highly acclaimed *Beneath the Raven Moon* (2003). On *Beneath,* each song featured a different flute from Youngblood's collection of more than 250. Youngblood has since recorded *Dance with the Wind* (2006) and *Feed the Fire* (2005), which features tracks with the flute playing of Youngblood's idol, Jethro Tull flutist Ian Anderson.

For her CDs, Youngblood has won numerous Native American Music Awards. She has been named Flutist of the Year (1999 and 2000), won Best New Age Recording (2001 and 2002), and has been given the Best Female Artist award (2002). Youngblood had also twice won the Grammy Award for Best Native American Music Album—in 2003, for *Beneath the Raven Moon,* and in 2007, for *Dance with the Wind.*

In Youngblood's eyes, when she plays the Native American flute she is "simply a vessel between the Creator and this sacred instrument." Seeing her talent as a sacred gift, she approaches her work with a sense of humility: "I just hope and pray that I always use this gift the Creator has given me, in a good and honorable way."

Further Reading/Resources

Ingersoll, Karl. "Humble Beginnings Remain with Grammy Winner." *Indian Country Today,* March 5, 2003.

"Mary Youngblood." Silver Wave Records Web site. URL: http://www.silverwave.com/youngblood.shtml. Downloaded on April 2, 2006.

Youngblood, Mary. *Beneath the Raven Moon.* Boulder, Colo.: Silver Wave Records, 2003.

———. *Feed the Fire.* Boulder, Colo.: Silver Wave Records, 2005.

Youngblood, Nancy (Nancy Youngblood Lubo)

(1955–) *Santa Clara Pueblo potter*

One of the most successful American Indian potters, Nancy Youngblood was born in 1955 in Fort Lewis, Washington. With her father in the army, her family frequently moved, living throughout the United States and Europe. When Nancy was 12, her father was sent to Vietnam, and her mother, Mela, returned with her children to the Santa Clara Pueblo in New Mexico. Mela was a member of the Tafoya family, who were internationally famous as pottery makers.

Once at Santa Clara, Nancy Youngblood decided she, too, wanted to make pottery. She studied her mother and aunts as they worked. But

the greatest influence on her was her grandmother, Margaret Tafoya, who was often called the matriarch of American Indian pottery. She provided Youngblood with invaluable critiques of her work: "A lot of times, my grandmother would take one look at the piece and know exactly what had happened. . . . She could tell just by looking at the piece what had gone wrong." Through rigorous trial and error, Youngblood honed her skills. In 1972, she entered her first piece in a competition at the Gallup Inter-Tribal Indian Ceremonial. Youngblood took home the second-place prize in the juvenile category.

At her father's insistence, Youngblood attended college at the San Francisco Art Institute. But she soon realized she wanted to be an artist rather than a student of art. She returned to Santa Clara and struggled to make a living from her work, selling miniature pots for about $20 each.

In 1979, Youngblood married medical student Paul Cutler. (They were divorced in 1990. Youngblood's second marriage to George Lubo lasted from 1993 to 2002.) Youngblood and Cutler moved to Kansas. With her husband working long hours, Youngblood devoted all her time and energy to pottery making, often working 80 hours a week. From time to time, she traveled back to the pueblo so she could fire her work in the traditional way. She continued to work largely on miniatures, partly because small pieces were easier to transport on a plane.

As Youngblood became more confident in her talents, she became more ambitious, yet she was still nervous about attempting larger works. Her brother Nathan, himself a noted potter, encouraged her: "Nathan took me aside and told me that the only thing that was limiting me was my mind. 'Don't say you can't do it. You can,' he said. It was a big inspiration."

Youngblood became particularly drawn to the melon jar style, in which a roughly melon-shaped vessel is decorated with deep cuts to create a series of ridges. Sometimes the ridges on her pottery are vertical; sometimes they take a swirling shape. Some of Youngblood's most dramatic pots are decorated with deep S-swirls. This design requires a great deal of technical skill since the swirls have to be carved out of a pot before it has been hardened by firing. Also, it is tremendously difficult to give the ridges the high polish Youngblood prefers. Larger pots have as many as 64 ridges, each requiring hours of careful polishing.

Youngblood also insists on firing all her pottery herself outdoors. Following Pueblo tradition, she always offers a special prayer during the firing process: "We the human potters don't know whether or not the pottery will turn out, but it's your will, Clay Mother, that will direct it."

Youngblood has had great success. Her work brings high prices from collectors and is found in many major museums. She has won more than 250 prizes, including the coveted best-in-show award at the 1989 Santa Fe Indian Fair. Early in her career, Youngblood worried that the accolades she received were due to her distinguished lineage, but now she celebrates her part in the Tafoya legacy. As she has explained, "Being a Tafoya brings with it a tremendous responsibility. People's expectations of us are incredible. It's also the greatest privilege, because we will carry on the tradition."

Further Reading

Cohen, Lee M., ed. *Art of Clay: Timeless Pottery of the Southwest.* Santa Fe, N.Mex.: Clear Light Publishers, 1993.

Peterson, Susan. *Pottery by American Indian Women: The Legacy of Generations.* New York: Abbeville Press, 1997.

Robinson, Andrea. "Nancy Youngblood Lubo." *Indian Artist,* Fall 1998, pp. 58–60.

Z

Zepeda, Ofelia
(1954–) *Tohono O'odham linguist, educator, poet*

The foremost scholar of Tohono O'odham, Ofelia Zepeda is a leader in the movement to preserve Indian languages. She was born on March 24, 1954, in the small rural community of Stanfield, Arizona, located near the reservations of the Tohono O'odham and Pima Indians. Members of the Tohono O'odham tribe (also known as the Papago), her parents had grown up in Mexico. Ofelia and her six brothers and sisters usually spent summers visiting with their Mexican relatives and participating in tribal ceremonies.

Zepeda started school knowing only the Tohono O'odham language. Nevertheless, she quickly mastered English and became the first member of her family to graduate from high school. Encouraged by her teachers, she decided to continue her education. She was further inspired by the Indian rights movement of the early 1970s. Because the movement's activists were fighting to improve educational opportunities for young Indians, she felt a responsibility to take advantage of her hard-won right to attend college. Zepeda also did not want to work as a farm laborer as most Tohono O'odham

did to make their living. Studying and teaching was an appealing option to the hard work of picking the cotton and harvesting the crops grown on nearby farms.

After beginning her college education at Central Arizona State, Zepeda transferred to the University of Arizona in Tucson, where she studied sociology. While in school, she became involved in a program to record the oral traditions of the Tohono O'odham. Zepeda interviewed elders and translated their stories but was frustrated that she could not write them down in Tohono O'odham, which traditionally was not a written language. She shared her problem with Kenneth Hale, a linguistics professor from the Massachusetts Institute of Technology who was visiting her university. She and Hale analyzed the linguistic structure of Tohono O'odham, and with the help of a Tohono O'odham elder, Albert Alvarez, Hale developed a system for writing in the Indian language.

Through her work with Hale, Zepeda decided to change her major to linguistics. As an undergraduate she began teaching her tribal language at the university and at the Papago Reservation Teacher Training Program. She was so enthusiastic about her work and research that by taking classes through the summer she received a bachelor's, master's, and doctorate degree in the space of four years. In 1983, the year before she was awarded her Ph.D., she published *A Papago Grammar*. Originally conceived as a textbook for her classes, this well-regarded work now serves as a model for the compilation of Indian language dictionaries.

When Zepeda completed her education, she joined the faculty of the University of Arizona, where she has taught classes in Tohono O'odham, oral traditions, and bilingual curriculum development. In 1986, she was named the director of the institution's American Indian Studies Program. She is also active in the American Indian Language Development Institute. This organization grew out of concerns of linguists and Native American parents that Indian languages were becoming extinct because children were no longer learning them at home. The institute is dedicated to developing classes and training teachers so that Indian languages can be taught in schools. Zepeda's pioneer work in preserving Indian languages earned her a MacArthur Fellowship in 1999.

In addition to her distinguished academic career, Zepeda is a noted poet. Her work has appeared in numerous anthologies and in two bilingual collections, *Ocean Power: Poems from the Desert* (1995) and *Jewed 'I-Hoi/Earth Movements* (2005). The latter is accompanied by a CD with Zepeda reading her work in English and in Tohono O'odham. Zepeda began writing poetry in graduate school and cites the Tohono O'odham's oral traditions as the primary influence on her work. She has edited *When It Rains* (1982), an anthology of Papago and Pima poetry, and *Home Places* (1995), a collection of poems, fiction, and essays by Native American writers. Zepeda is also the coauthor of *Home: Native People in the Southwest* (2005), a companion book to an exhibit at the Heard Museum in Phoenix, Arizona.

Further Reading

Di Filippo, JoAnn. "Ofelia Zepeda." In *Notable Native Americans,* edited by Sharon J. Malinowski, 476–477. Detroit: Gale Research, 1995.

Zepeda, Ofelia. *Jewed 'I-Hoi/Earth Movements.* Tucson, Ariz.: Kore Press, 2005.

————. *Ocean Power: Poems from the Desert.* Tucson: University of Arizona Press, 1995.

————. *A Papago Grammar.* Tucson: University of Arizona Press, 1983.

Zintkala Nuni (Lost Bird)

(1890–1920)   *Lakota Sioux survivor of the Wounded Knee massacre*

The tragedy of Zintkala Nuni began several months after her birth in 1890 while her band of Lakota Sioux was traveling to the Pine Ridge Indian Reservation in South Dakota. After decades of war with the U.S. Army, the defeated Sioux had been confined to reservations but the government and its soldiers remained suspicious of the tribe's warriors and warrior spirit. They were particularly alarmed by the Sioux's enthusiasm for the Ghost Dance, an Indian religion that had recently swept through the Plains. The Ghost Dance taught that one day the buffalo herds of the Plains would return, the Indians' dead relatives would come back to life, and, most disturbing to the army, all whites would die.

On December 29, 1890, Zintkala Nuni's band was met on their way to Pine Ridge by five hundred soldiers of the Seventh Cavalry, the army division that was decimated by the Sioux at the Battle of Little Bighorn in 1876. The Indians surrendered to the troops, but while the soldiers were roughly disarming a confused, deaf Sioux man, a shot was fired. The panicked soldiers began to slaughter the unarmed Sioux. The official death toll of the horrible massacre was 146, but it is likely that more than three hundred Indian men, women, and children were murdered.

Four days later, crews came to Wounded Knee, the site of the killings, to bury the snow-covered corpses in mass graves. At the same time, a search party for survivors led by Dakota Sioux author and physician Charles Eastman arrived. Eastman's men wandered through a wide area around Wounded Knee in search of Sioux who had fled the massacre only to be chased down for miles by soldiers intent on killing them. During the men's search, they heard a faint, shrill wail. The crying led them to the body of a young woman, frozen to the ground in her own blood. The corpse was wrapped around an infant girl, who wore a tiny buckskin cap decorated with red, white, and blue beads in the shape of an American flag. Though the baby was severely frostbitten and dehydrated, miraculously she was still alive.

Leonard W. Colby, a brigadier general in the U.S. Army, became intrigued by the story of the infant survivor. He brought food to her family, who were starving in the wake of the catastrophe. Colby asked the baby's grandmother to give him the child. Claiming to be a Seneca Indian, he told her he would make sure the baby was well fed and well cared for. In desperation, the woman handed her granddaughter to Colby. While doing so, she cried out "Zintkala Nuni," meaning "lost bird," because she knew the child would forever be lost to her people.

Colby took Zintkala Nuni to his home in Nebraska. Although his wife, Clara, had not been consulted about the adoption, she accepted the baby as her own child. Leonard's motivation for taking Zintkala Nuni may have been to please Clara, who had no children of her own. But just as likely, Colby, who was prone to be dishonest and cruel, may have valued the girl primarily as a living trophy of the army's "victory" at Wounded Knee.

Zintkala Nuni's life with the Colbys was troubled. In addition to the discrimination she faced as an Indian growing up in non-Indian society, she had to endure the constant bickering of her adoptive parents. Clara Colby finally divorced her philandering husband, who may have sexually abused Zintkala Nuni when she was an adolescent. Leonard Colby definitely exploited his daughter by using her to convince Indian tribes to hire him as a legal adviser in their disputes against the government. Although Zintkala Nuni and her mother enjoyed a comparatively loving relationship, Clara Colby also used the girl to advance her reputation as a reformer and newspaper editor. For instance, to attract readers she wrote a regular column about her Indian daughter's adjustment to "civilized" society called "Zintkala's Corner."

As a teenager, Zintkala Nuni's unhappiness led to erratic behavior. In an attempt to control her, Clara sent her daughter to several prisonlike Indian boarding schools, from which Zintkala Nuni invariably escaped by running away or being expelled. Zintkala Nuni believed her separation from her people was the basis of her frustration. She traveled to Pine Ridge in search of her roots but discovered that, because of her upbringing, the Lakotas did not consider her a Sioux.

Uneasy in both Indian and non-Indian society, Zintkala Nuni spent several years working in Wild West shows and Hollywood films. After a disastrous first marriage, during which her husband gave her syphilis, she married two more times and gave birth to three boys, only one of whom survived infancy. Living with her third husband in Hanford, California, Zintkala Nuni fell victim to influenza during the worldwide epidemic of 1919. She died in 1920 on Valentine's Day at the age of 29.

Some 60 years later, historian Renée Sansom Flood discovered Zintkala Nuni's grave in Hanford while researching the woman's biography. With the help of Marie Not Help Him of the Wounded Knee Survivor's Association, Flood had the body exhumed and transported to South Dakota, where Zintkala Nuni's remains were reburied next to the mass grave that holds her mother's bones. Marie Not Help Him has also honored Zintkala Nuni by founding the Lost Bird Society. This organization is dedicated to providing support and information to Indians who have been adopted by non-Indian parents.

Further Reading

Flood, Renée Sansom. *Lost Bird of Wounded Knee: Spirit of the Lakota.* New York: Scribner, 1995.

Zitkala-Ša

See BONNIN, GERTRUDE SIMMONS

RECOMMENDED SOURCES ON AMERICAN INDIAN WOMEN STUDIES

Books

Ackerman, Lillian A. *A Necessary Balance: Gender and Power among Indians of the Columbia Plateau.* Norman: University of Oklahoma Press, 2003.

Albers, Patricia, and Beatrice A. Medicine, eds. *The Hidden Half: Studies of Plains Indian Women.* Lanham, Md.: University Press of America, 1983.

Allen, Paula Gunn. *The Sacred Hoop: Recovering the Feminine in American Indian Traditions.* Boston: Beacon Press, 1986.

———. *Spider Woman's Granddaughters: Traditional Tales and Contemporary Writing by Native American Women.* Boston: Beacon Press, 1989.

Anderson, Owanah, ed. *Ohoyo One Thousand: A Resource Guide of American Indian/Alaska Native Women.* Wichita Falls, Tex.: Ohoyo Resource Center, 1982.

Bataille, Gretchen M., and Laurie Lisa, eds. *Native American Women: A Biographical Dictionary.* 2nd ed. New York: Routledge, 2001.

Bataille, Gretchen M., and Kathleen Mullen Sands. *American Indian Women: A Guide to Research.* New York: Garland Publishing, 1993.

———. *American Indian Women: Telling Their Lives.* Lincoln: University of Nebraska Press, 1984.

Bloom, Harold, ed. *Native American Women Writers.* Philadelphia: Chelsea House, 1998.

Boyer, Ruth McDonald, and Narcissus Duffy Gayton. *Apache Mothers and Daughters.* Norman: University of Oklahoma Press, 1992.

Brant, Beth, ed. *A Gathering of Spirit: A Collection by North American Indian Women.* Ithaca, N.Y.: Firebrand Books, 1988.

Broder, Patricia Janis. *Earth Songs, Moon Dreams: Paintings by American Indian Women.* New York: St. Martin's Press, 1999.

Bruhns, Karen Olsen. *Women in Ancient America.* Norman: University of Oklahoma Press, 1999.

Buchanan, Kimberley M. *Apache Women Warriors.* El Paso: Texas Western Press, 1986.

Buffalohead, Priscilla K. "Farmers, Warriors, Traders: A Fresh Look at Ojibway Women." *Minnesota Society,* Summer 1983.

Devens, Carol. *Countering Colonization: Native American Women and Great Lakes Missions 1630–1900.* Berkeley: University of California Press, 1992.

Erdrich, Heid L., and Laura Tohe, eds. *Sister Nations: Native American Women Writers on Community.* St. Paul: Minnesota Historical Society Press, 2002.

Farley, R., ed. *Women of the Native Struggle: Testimony of Native American Women.* New York: Orion Books, 1993.

Fitzgerald, Judith, and Michael Oren Fitzgerald, eds. *The Spirit of Indian Women.* Bloomington, Ind.: World Wisdom, 2005.

Foreman, Carolyn Thomas. *Indian Woman Chiefs.* Washington, D.C.: Zenger Publishing, 1934.

Green, Rayna. *Native American Women: A Contextual Bibliography.* Bloomington: Indiana University Press, 1984.

———. "The Pocahontas Perplex: The Image of Indian Women in American Culture." *Massachusetts Review,* Autumn 1975.

———. *That's What I Said: Contemporary Fiction and Poetry by Native American Women.* Bloomington: Indiana University Press, 1984.

———. *Women in American Indian Society.* New York: Chelsea House, 1992.

Gridley, Marion. *American Indian Women.* New York: Hawthorne Books, 1974.

Hammond, Harmony, and Jaune Quick-to-See Smith. *Women of Sweetgrass, Cedar and Sage.* New York: Gallery of the American Indian Community House, 1985.

Harjo, Joy, and Gloria Bird, eds. *Reinventing the Enemy's Language: Contemporary Native Women's Writing of North America.* New York: W. W. Norton, 1997.

Heard Museum. *Watchful Eyes: Native American Women Artists.* Phoenix, Ariz.: Heard Museum, 1994.

Hungry Wolf, Beverly. *The Ways of My Grandmothers.* New York: William Morrow, 1980.

Katz, Jane, ed. *I Am the Fire of Time: The Voices of Native American Women.* New York: E. P. Dutton, 1977.

———. *Messengers of the Wind: Native American Women Tell Their Life Stories.* New York: Ballantine Books, 1995.

Kilcup, Karen L., ed. *Native American Women's Writing, 1800–1924: An Anthology.* Malden, Mass.: Blackwell Publishers, 2000.

Klein, Laura F., and Lillian A. Ackerman, eds. *Women and Power in Native North America.* Norman: University of Oklahoma Press, 1995.

Mathes, Valerie Sherer. "Native American Women in Medicine and the Military." *Journal of the West,* April 1982.

———. "A New Look at the Role of Women in Indian Society." *American Indian Quarterly* 2 (1979).

Medicine, Beatrice. *Native American Women: A Perspective.* Austin, Tex.: National Educational Laboratory, 1978.

Mihesuah, Devon A. *Indigenous American Women: Decolonization, Empowerment, Activism.* Lincoln: University of Nebraska Press, 2003.

Miller, Christine, and Patricia Chuchryk, eds. *Women of the First Nations: Power, Wisdom, and Strength.* Winnipeg: University of Manitoba Press, 1996.

Niethammer, Carolyn. *Daughters of the Earth: The Lives and Legends of American Indian Women.* Reprint, New York: Simon & Schuster, 1995.

Penman, Sarah, ed. *Honor the Grandmothers: Dakota and Lakota Women Tell Their Stories.* St. Paul: Minnesota Historical Society Press, 2000.

Perdue, Theda, ed. *Sifters: Native American Women's Lives.* New York: Oxford University Press, 2001.

———. *Cherokee Women: Gender and Culture Change, 1700–1835.* Lincoln: University of Nebraska Press, 1998.

Perrcault, Jeanne, and Sylvia Vance, eds. *Writing the Circle: Canadian Indian Women Writing.* Edmonton, Alta.: New West Publishers, 1990.

Pesantubbee, Michelene E. *Choctaw Women in a Chaotic World: The Clash of Cultures in the Colonial Southeast.* Albuquerque: University of New Mexico Press, 2005.

Peters, Virginia Bergman. *Women of the Earth Lodges: Tribal Life on the Plains.* North Haven, Conn.: Archon Books, 1995.

Randle, Martha Champion. "Iroquois Women, Then and Now." *Smithsonian Institution Bureau of American Ethnology Bulletin* 196. Washington, D.C.: United States Government Printing Office, 1951.

Reyer, Carolyn. *Cante Ohitika Win: Images of Lakota Women from the Pine Ridge Reservation, South Dakota.* Vermillion: University of South Dakota Press, 1991.

Roessel, Ruth. *Women in Navajo Society.* Rough Rock, Ariz.: Navajo Resource Center, 1981.

Schwarz, Maureen Trudelle. *Blood and Voice: Navajo Women Ceremonial Practitioners.* Tucson: University of Arizona Press, 2003.

Schweitzer, Marjorie M., ed. *American Indian Grandmothers: Traditions and Transitions.* Albuquerque: University of New Mexico Press, 1999.

Silman, Janet. *Enough and Enough: Aboriginal Women Speak Out.* Toronto: The Women's Press, 1987.

Simonsen, Jane E. *Making Home Work: Domesticity and Native American Assimilation in the Ameri-*

can West, 1860–1919. Chapel Hill: University of North Carolina Press, 2006.

Sleeper-Smith, Susan. *Indian Women and French Men: Rethinking Cultural Encounter in the Western Great Lakes.* Amherst: University of Massachusetts Press, 2001.

Stockel, H. Henrietta. *Women of the Apache Nation.* Reno: University of Nevada Press, 1991.

Tsosie, Rebecca. "Changing Women: The Cross-Currents of American Indian Feminine Identity." *American Indian Culture and Research Journal* 12 (1988).

Van Kirk, Sylvia. *Many Tender Ties: Women in Fur Trade Society in Western Canada, 1670–1870.* Norman: University of Oklahoma Press, 1980.

Vannote, Vance. *Women of White Earth.* Minneapolis: University of Minnesota Press, 1999.

Wall, Steve. *Wisdom's Daughters: Conversations with Women Elders of Native America.* New York: HarperCollins, 1993.

Web Sites

American Women's History, A Research Guide: American Indian Women. URL: http://www.mtsu.edu/~kmiddlet/history/women/wh-indn.html.

Indian Country Today. URL: http://www.indiancountry.com.

Indianz News Service. URL: http://www.indianz.com.

National Museum of the American Indian. URL: http://www.nmai.si.edu.

Native American Women, Labriola National Indian Data Center, Arizona State University. URL: http://www.asu.edu/lib/archives/naw.htm.

Storytellers: Native American Authors Online. URL: http://www.hanksville.org/storytellers.

U.S. Census Bureau: American Indian and Alaska Natives Populations. URL: http://www.census.gov/population/www/socdemo/race/indian.html.

Voices from the Gaps: Women Artists and Writers of Color. URL: http://voices.cla.umn.edu.

Western History/Genealogy Department, Denver Public Library: Native American Women Gallery. URL: http://photoswest.org/exhib/gallery4/leadin.htm.

Women Artists of the American West: Pottery by American Indian Women. URL: http://www.cla.purdue.edu/WAAW/Peterson.

ENTRIES BY AREA OF ACTIVITY

Activist

Anderson, Owanah
Aquash, Anna Mae
Bennett, Ramona
Bonnin, Gertrude Simmons
Brave Bird, Mary
Bronson, Ruth Muskrat
Campbell, Maria
Chrystos
Cobell, Elouise
Dann, Carrie and Mary
Deer, Ada
Erdrich, Louise
Harjo, Suzan Shown
Harris, LaDonna
Jemison, Alice Mae
Kellogg, Minnie
LaDuke, Winona
La Flesche, Susette
Lovelace Nicholas, Sandra
Mankiller, Wilma
Maracle, Lee
Mourning Dove
Nicolar, Lucy
Pearson, Maria
Peterson, Helen
Pease, Janine
Rose, Wendy
Sainte-Marie, Buffy

Teters, Charlene
Thorpe, Grace
Wa Wa Chaw
Wauneka, Annie Dodge
Winnemucca, Sarah

Actress

Bedard, Irene
Cardinal, Tantoo
Johnson, Emily Pauline
Red-Horse, Valerie
Sainte-Marie, Buffy
Spotted Elk, Molly

Anthropologist

Deloria, Ella
Medicine, Beatrice
Rose, Wendy
Tantaquidgeon, Gladys

Athlete

Big Crow, SuAnne
Lang, Naomi

Autobiographer

Brave Bird, Mary
Campbell, Maria
Chona, Maria
Cuero, Delfina

Maracle, Lee
Mountain Wolf Woman
Pretty-Shield
Qoyawayma, Polingaysi
Sanapia
Sekaquaptewa, Helen
Shaw, Anna Moore
Sneve, Virginia Driving
    Hawk
Waheenee
Winnemucca, Sarah

Ballerina

Tallchief, Maria

Basketmaker

Allen, Elsie
Dick, Lena Frank
Keyser, Louisa
Lubo, Ramona
McKay, Mabel
Nicolar, Lucy
Parrish, Essie

Businesswoman

Cobell, Elouise
La Flesche, Rosalie
Nicolar, Lucy
Red-Horse, Valerie

Captive

Parker, Cynthia Ann

Chef

Oden, Loretta Barrett

Civic Leader

La Flesche, Marguerite
Lawson, Roberta Campbell
Shaw, Anna Moore

Curator

Harjo, Suzan Shown
Tantaquidgeon, Gladys

Educator

Allen, Elsie
Allen, Paula Gunn
Aquash, Anna Mae
Armstrong, Jeannette
Bennett, Ramona
Bronson, Ruth Muskrat
Brown, Catharine
Callahan, Sophia Alice
Cook-Lynn, Elizabeth
DeCora, Angel
Deer, Ada
Deloria, Ella
Glancy, Diane
Harjo, Joy
Heth, Charlotte
Hill, Roberta
Hogan, Linda
La Flesche, Marguerite
Loloma, Otellie
Pease, Janine
Qoyawayma, Polingaysi
Roessel, Ruth
Rose, Wendy
Sneve, Virginia Driving Hawk
Teters, Charlene
Yellow Robe, Rosebud
Zepeda, Ofelia

Engineer

Ross, Mary G.

Environmental Scientist

House, Donna

Essayist

Bonnin, Gertrude Simmons
Brant, Beth
Cook-Lynn, Elizabeth
Glancy, Diane
Hale, Janet Campbell
Hogan, Linda
Johnson, Emily Pauline
LaDuke, Winona

Ethnobiologist

House, Donna

Ethnomusicologist

Heth, Charlotte

Exploration Survivor

Blackjack, Ada

Filmmaker

Naranjo-Morse, Nora
Niro, Shelley
Obomsawin, Alanis
Red-Horse, Valerie

Flutist

Youngblood, Mary

Guide

Dorion, Marie

Historian

Roessel, Ruth
Tantaquidgeon, Gladys
Wright, Muriel H.

Illustrator

DeCora, Angel

Installation Artist

Niro, Shelley
Teters, Charlene

Interpreter

Dorion, Marie
Musgrove, Mary
Natawista
Sacagawea
Thanadelthur
Winema
Winnemucca, Sarah

Journalist

Harjo, Suzan Shown
Kauffman, Hattie
Spotted Elk, Molly

Last Survivor of Tribe

Juana Maria

Lawyer

Locklear, Arlinda

Linguist

Deloria, Ella
Zepeda, Ofelia

Massacre Survivor

Zintkala Nuni

Mathematician

Ross, Mary G.

Medicine Woman

Chona, Maria
Coocoochee
McKay, Mabel
Modesto, Ruby

Ockett, Molly
Parrish, Essie
Sanapia
Tantaquidgeon, Gladys

News Anchor

Kauffman, Hattie

Novelist

Allen, Paula Gunn
Armstrong, Jeannette
Callahan, Sophia Alice
Cook-Lynn, Elizabeth
Deloria, Ella
Erdrich, Louise
Glancy, Diane
Hale, Janet Campbell
Hogan, Linda
LaDuke, Winona
Maracle, Lee
Mourning Dove
Silko, Leslie Marmon
Sneve, Virginia Driving
    Hawk

Nun

Sacred White Buffalo,
    Mother Mary Catherine
Tekakwitha, Kateri

Nurse

Yellowtail, Susie Walking
    Bear

Outlaw

Lowry, Rhoda Strong

Painter

Hardin, Helen
Lomahaftewa, Linda
Niro, Shelley
Peña, Tonita
Sainte-Marie, Buffy
Smith, Jaune Quick-to-See

Velarde, Pablita
Wa Wa Chaw
WalkingStick, Kay

Peacemaker

Chipeta
Francis, Milly
Natawista
Pocahontas
Thanadelthur
Winema

Photographer

Niro, Shelley
Woody, Elizabeth

Physician

Alvord, Lori Arviso
La Flesche, Susan

Playwright

Glancy, Diane

Poet

Allen, Paula Gunn
Brant, Beth
Burns, Diane M.
Chrystos
Cook-Lynn, Elizabeth
Glancy, Diane
Hale, Janet Campbell
Harjo, Joy
Harjo, Suzan Shown
Hogan, Linda
Johnson, Emily Pauline
Maracle, Lee
Naranjo-Morse, Nora
Rose, Wendy
Silko, Leslie Marmon
TallMountain, Mary
Tapahonso, Luci
Hill, Roberta
Woody, Elizabeth
Zepeda, Ofelia

Politician

Lovelace Nicholas, Sandra

Potter

Cordero, Helen
Folwell, Jody
Lewis, Lucy M.
Loloma, Otellie
Martinez, Maria
Medicine Flower, Grace
Nampeyo
Naranjo-Morse, Nora
Qoyawayma, Polingaysi
Tafoya, Margaret
Youngblood, Nancy

Printmaker

Kenojuak
Lomahaftewa, Linda
Naranjo-Morse, Nora
Pitseolak

Public Servant

Deer, Ada
Harris, LaDonna

Quillworker

Blue Legs, Alice New Holy

Sculptor

Loloma, Otellie Pasivaya
Niro, Shelley
Swentzell, Roxanne

Short Story Writer

Bonnin, Gertrude Simmons
Brant, Beth
Cook-Lynn, Elizabeth
DeCora, Angel
Erdrich, Louise
Glancy, Diane
Hogan, Linda
Johnson, Emily Pauline

Maracle, Lee
TallMountain, Mary
Tapahonso, Luci

Singer

Coolidge, Rita
Harjo, Joy
Nicolar, Lucy
Obomsawin, Alanis
Sainte-Marie, Buffy
Shenandoah, Joanne

Soldier

Piestewa, Lori

Songwriter

Sainte-Marie, Buffy
Shenandoah, Joanne

Storyteller

Te Ata

Trader

Musgrove, Mary
Natawista

Tribal Leader

Awashonks
Bennett, Ramona
Brant, Molly
Cockacoeske
Deer, Ada
Fire Thunder, Cecelia
Jumper, Betty Mae Tiger
Mankiller, Wilma
Ward, Nancy

Wauneka, Annie Dodge
Weetamoo

Warrior

Lozen
Running Eagle
Woman Chief

Weaver

Sakiestewa, Ramona

ENTRIES BY TRIBE

Abnaki

Obomaswin, Alanis
Ockett, Molly

Aleut

Youngblood, Mary

Apache

Lozen

Blackfoot

Cobell, Elouise
Running Eagle

Blood

Natawista

Cahuilla

Lubo, Ramona
Modesto, Ruby

Chemehuevi

Burns, Diane M.

Cherokee

Bronson, Ruth Muskrat
Brown, Catherine
Coolidge, Rita
Glancy, Diane

Harjo, Suzan Shown
Heth, Charlotte
Jemison, Alice Mae
Mankiller, Wilma
Red-Horse, Valerie
Ross, Mary G.
WalkingStick, Kay
Ward, Nancy

Chickasaw

Hogan, Linda

Chipewyan

Thanadelthur

Chippewa. *See also* Ojibwa

Burns, Diane M.
Erdrich, Louise

Choctaw

Anderson, Owanah
Lomahaftewa, Linda
Wright, Muriel H.

Chumash

Juana Maria

Coeur d'Alene

Hale, Janet Campbell

Colville

Mourning Dove

Comanche

Harris, LaDonna
Parker, Cynthia Ann
Sanapia

Cree

Bedard, Irene
Sainte-Marie, Buffy
Smith, Jaune Quick-to-See

Creek

Callahan, Sophia Alice
Francis, Milly
Harjo, Joy
Harjo, Suzan Shown
Musgrove, Mary

Crow

Pease, Janine
Pretty-Shield
Woman Chief
Yellowtail, Susie Walking Bear

Dakota. *See* Sioux

Delaware (Lenni Lenape)

Lawson, Roberta Campbell

299

Diegueño
Cuero, Delfina

Flathead
Jaune Quick-to-See Smith

Hidatsa
Waheenee

Hopi. *See also* Pueblo
Loloma, Otellie Pasivaya
Lomahaftewa, Linda
Nampeyo
Piestewa, Lori
Qoyawayma, Polingaysi
Rose, Wendy
Sakiestewa, Ramona
Sekaquaptewa, Helen

Inuit
Bedard, Irene
Blackjack, Ada
Kenojuak
Pitseolak

Iowa
Dorion, Marie

Iroquois. *See* Mohawk, Oneida, and Seneca

Koyukon Athabascan
TallMountain, Mary

Karuk
Lang, Naomi

Lakota. *See* Sioux

Lumbee
Locklear, Arlinda
Lowry, Rhoda Strong

Luiseño
Wa Wa Chaw

Maliseet
Lovelace Nicholas, Sandra

Menominee
Chrystos
Deer, Ada

Métis
Campbell, Maria
Cardinal, Tantoo
Maracle, Lee

Micmac
Aquash, Anna Mae

Miwok
Rose, Wendy

Modoc
Winema

Mohawk
Brant, Beth
Brant, Molly
Coocoochee
Johnson, Emily Pauline
Niro, Shelley
Tekakwitha, Kateri

Mohegan
Tantaquidgeon, Gladys

Muskogee. *See* Creek

Nakota. *See* Sioux

Navajo (Dineh)
Alvord, Lori Arviso
House, Donna
Roessel, Ruth

Tapahonso, Luci
Wauneka, Annie Dodge
Woody, Elizabeth

Nez Perce
Kauffman, Hattie

Northern Paiute (Numu)
Winnemucca, Sarah

Okanagan
Armstrong, Jeannette
Mourning Dove

Ojibwa. *See also* Chippewa
LaDuke, Winona
Schoolcraft, Jane Johnson

Oneida
Hill, Roberta
Kellogg, Minnie
Shenandoah, Joanne

Omaha
La Flesche, Marguerite
La Flesche, Rosalie
La Flesche, Susan
La Flesche, Susettte

Osage
Tallchief, Maria

Paiute. *See* Northern Paiute

Pamunkey
Cockacoeske

Penobscot
Nicolar, Lucy
Spotted Elk, Molly

Pima
Shaw, Anna Moore

Pomo

Allen, Elsie
McKay, Mabel
Parrish, Essie

Potawatomi

Oden, Loretta Barrett

Powhatan

Pocahontas

Pueblo. *See* also Hopi

Acoma Pueblo

Lewis, Lucy M.

Cochiti Pueblo

Cordero, Helen

Laguna Pueblo

Allen, Paula Gunn
Silko, Leslie Marmon

San Ildefonso Pueblo

Martinez, Maria
Peña, Tonita

Santa Clara Pueblo

Folwell, Jody
Hardin, Helen
Medicine Flower, Grace
Naranjo-Morse, Nora
Swentzell, Roxanne
Tafoya, Margaret
Velarde, Pablita
Youngblood, Nancy

Puyallup

Bennett, Ramona

Sauk and Fox

Thorpe, Grace

Seminole

Jumper, Betty Mae Tiger
Youngblood, Mary

Seneca

Jemison, Alice Mae

Shoshone

Dann, Carrie and Mary
Sacagawea
Smith, Jaune Quick-to-See

Sioux

Dakota Sioux

Cook-Lynn, Elizabeth

Lakota Sioux

Big Crow, SuAnn
Blue Legs, Alice New Holy
Brave Bird, Mary
Fire Thunder, Cecelia
Medicine, Beatrice
Peterson, Helen
Sacred White Buffalo,
    Mother Mary Catherine
Sneve, Virginia Driving Hawk
Yellow Robe, Rosebud
Zintkala Nuni

Nakota Sioux

Bonnin, Gertrude Simmons
Deloria, Ella
Pearson, Maria

Spokane

Teters, Chalene

Tohono O'odham

Chona, Maria
Zepeda, Ofelia

Ute

Chipeta

Wampanoag

Awashonks
Weetamoo

Warm Springs

Woody, Elizabeth

Wasco

Woody, Elizabeth

Washoe

Dick, Lena Frank
Keyser, Louisa

Winnebago (Ho-Chunk)

DeCora, Angel
Mountain Wolf Woman

Wintun

McKay, Mabel

ENTRIES BY YEAR OF BIRTH

1910–1919

Cordero, Helen
Modesto, Ruby
Peterson, Helen
TallMountain, Mary
Velarde, Pablita
Wauneka, Annie Dodge

1920–1929

Anderson, Owanah
Blue Legs, Alice New Holy
Dann, Mary
Jumper, Betty Mae Tiger
Kenojuak
Loloma, Otellie Pasivaya
Medicine, Beatrice
Tallchief, Maria
Thorpe, Grace

1930–1939

Allen, Paula Gunn
Bennett, Ramona
Cook-Lynn, Elizabeth
Dann, Carrie
Deer, Ada
Harris, LaDonna
Heth, Charlotte
Medicine Flower, Grace
Obomsawin, Alanis
Pearson, Maria

Roessel, Ruth
Sneve, Virginia Driving
  Hawk
WalkingStick, Kay

1940–1949

Aquash, Anna Mae
Armstrong, Jeannette
Brant, Beth
Campbell, Maria
Chrystos
Cobell, Elouise
Coolidge, Rita
Fire Thunder, Cecelia
Folwell, Jody
Glancy, Diane
Hale, Janet Campbell
Hardin, Helen
Harjo, Suzan Shown
Hill, Roberta
Hogan, Linda
Lomahaftewa, Linda
Lovelace Nicholas, Sandra
Mankiller, Wilma
Oden, Loretta Barrett
Pease, Janine
Rose, Wendy
Sainte-Marie, Buffy
Sakiestewa, Ramona
Silko, Leslie Marmon
Smith, Jaune Quick-to-See

1950–1959

Alvord, Lori Arviso
Brave Bird, Mary
Burns, Diane M.
Cardinal, Tantoo
Erdrich, Louise
Harjo, Joy
House, Donna
Kauffman, Hattie
LaDuke, Winona
Locklear, Arlinda
Maracle, Lee
Naranjo-Morse, Nora
Niro, Shelley
Red-Horse, Valerie
Shenandoah, Joanne
Tapahonso, Luci
Teters, Charlene
Woody, Elizabeth
Youngblood, Nancy
Zepeda, Ofelia

1960–1969

Bedard, Irene
Swentzell, Roxanne
Youngblood, Mary

1970–1979

Big Crow, SuAnn
Lang, Naomi
Piestewa, Lori

INDEX

✦✦✦✦✦

Boldface numbers indicate entries.
Italic numbers indicate illustrations.

315